The American Ballot Box in the Mid-Nineteenth Century

During the middle of the nineteenth century, Americans voted in saloons in the most derelict sections of great cities, in hamlets swarming with Union soldiers, or in wooden cabins so isolated that even neighbors had difficulty finding them. Their votes have come down to us as election returns reporting tens of millions of officially sanctioned democratic acts. Neatly arrayed in columns by office, candidate, and party, these returns are routinely interpreted as reflections of the preferences of individual voters and thus seem to document unambiguously the existence of a robust democratic ethos. By carefully examining political activity in and around the polling place, this book suggests some important caveats that must attend this conclusion. These caveats, in turn, help to bridge the interpretive chasm now separating ethno-cultural descriptions of popular politics from political economic analyses of state and national policy making.

Professor Richard Franklin Bensel has taught in the Department of Government at Cornell University since 1993. Before that, he served on the Graduate Faculty of Political and Social Science in the New School for Social Research. He is the author of three previous books: *Sectionalism and American Political Development, 1880–1980* (1984; awarded the Mark H. Ingraham Prize in 1984); *Yankee Leviathan: The Origins of Central State Authority in America, 1859–1877* (1990); and *The Political Economy of American Industrialization, 1877–1900* (2000; selected by *Choice* as one of the "Outstanding Academic Titles of 2001" in economics and awarded the 2002 J. David Greenstone Prize by the Politics and History section of the American Political Science Association). He is a member of the American Historical Association, the American Political Science Association, the Economic History Association, the Organization of American History, the Social Science History Association, and the American Association for the Advancement of Science.

D1086026

The American Ballot Box in the Mid-Nineteenth Century

RICHARD FRANKLIN BENSEL ,1949-
Cornell University

CAMBRIDGE
UNIVERSITY PRESS

PUBLISHED BY THE PRESS SYNDICATE OF THE UNIVERSITY OF CAMBRIDGE
The Pitt Building, Trumpington Street, Cambridge, United Kingdom

CAMBRIDGE UNIVERSITY PRESS
The Edinburgh Building, Cambridge CB2 2RU, UK
40 West 20th Street, New York, NY 10011-4211, USA
477 Williamstown Road, Port Melbourne, VIC 3207, Australia
Ruiz de Alarcón 13, 28014 Madrid, Spain
Dock House, The Waterfront, Cape Town 8001, South Africa

http://www.cambridge.org

First published 2004

Printed in the United States of America

Typeface Sabon 10/12 pt.   *System* LATEX 2$_\varepsilon$ [TB]

A catalog record for this book is available from the British Library.

Library of Congress Cataloging in Publication Data

Bensel, Richard Franklin, 1949–
The American ballot box in the mid-nineteenth century / Richard Franklin Bensel.
p.   cm.
Includes bibliographical references and index.
ISBN 0-521-83101-6 – ISBN 0-521-53786-X (pbk.)
1. Voting – United States – History – 19th century.   2. Elections – United States –
History – 19th century.   3. United States – Politics and government –
19th century.   I. Title.
JK1967.B46   2004
324.973'07 – dc22   2003066277

ISBN 0 521 83101 6 hardback
ISBN 0 521 53786 X paperback

Contents

Preface

During the middle decades of the nineteenth century, the United States struggled through a long and bloody Civil War, settled much of the western prairie, and embarked upon a transition from an agrarian to an industrial society. During these two decades, Americans went to the polls, whether located in hamlets swarming with Union soldiers, wooden cabins so isolated that even neighbors had difficulty finding them, or saloons in the most densely populated sections of great cities. Their votes have come down to us as election returns reporting tens of millions of officially sanctioned and tabulated democratic acts. Neatly collated and arrayed in columns by office, candidate, and party, these returns are routinely interpreted as reflections of the preferences of the individuals composing the communities in which they were made out. Seen this way, we might conclude that the returns constitute unambiguous evidence of the existence of a robust democratic ethos. One of the purposes of this book is to suggest some important caveats that must attend this conclusion.

Most of the literature on mid-nineteenth-century politics has assumed that the electorate responded to the policy positions set down in party platforms. From this perspective, voters critically compared candidates and platform planks before choosing the alternative closest to their own personal tastes and policy positions.[1] Rational choice theorists, usually operating under strong assumptions characteristic of methodological individualism, are particularly prone to such interpretations. Party organizations wrote platforms and chose candidates precisely because they believed these platforms and candidates would attract voters.[2] In this rational and instrumental world, men first

[1] For example, William Gienapp stresses the "critical influence of state and local issues on mass voting patterns" in *The Origins of the Republican Party, 1852–1856* (New York: Oxford University Press, 1987), pp. 7–9.

[2] Barry Weingast provides a particularly apt example in his "Political Stability and Civil War: Institutions, Commitment, and American Democracy," in Robert H. Bates

reviewed the offerings presented by the various parties, chose one of the parties to support, decided whether or not to participate in the election, and then voted or failed to vote, as the case might be.

Many voters undoubtedly behaved in just this fashion and thus composed an individually autonomous, rationally calculating citizenry as they made up their minds and cast their ballots. However, other men operated on less familiar models. Such men are not quite aberrations, but they are clearly secondary figures in most political accounts of the period. The largest group is the teeming mass of party loyalists who made parties into more or less sacred cultural icons.[3] Such loyalists seldom compared party platforms or weighed the relative merits of candidates before casting their ballots. Other men fell out of their roles as autonomous, rationally calculating citizens when they accepted small bribes or favors in return for their vote. Although such exceptions are duly noted, the primary model, with its strong emphasis on the formation of individual preferences as the animating force behind electoral politics, still dominates most interpretations of American party competition.

While we know a great deal about the ways in which party organizations and candidates viewed the mass electorate in the nineteenth century, we know very little about how or why ordinary men participated in elections. Put another way, we know much more about the kind of strategies parties used in campaigns and the types of inducements they offered at the polls than we do about why ordinary men responded to these strategies and inducements.[4] As in all things, men varied in their familiarity with the policy positions of candidates and party organizations. At one end of this distribution, many voters had only the dimmest understanding of what might have been at stake in an election. A few literally did not understand what they did when they voted. The focus of this book is on these ordinary men, many of whom

---

et al., *Analytic Narratives* (Princeton, N.J.: Princeton University Press, 1998), pp. 148–93.

[3] Many scholars have viewed, as did contemporary observers, party identity and allegiance as a birthright inheritance for native-born Americans and a baptism into ethnic solidarity for immigrants. For exhaustive reviews of the literature on nineteenth-century parties and the organizing role they played at all levels of American politics, see Ronald P. Formisano, "The 'Party Period' Revisited"; Mark Voss-Hubbard, "The 'Third Party Tradition' Reconsidered: Third Parties and American Public Life, 1830–1900"; and Michael F. Holt, "The Primacy of Party Asserted," *Journal of American History* 86 (1999): 93–120, 121–50, 151–7.

[4] In their thick description of elections in the nineteenth century, Glenn Altschuler and Stuart Blumin provide numerous accounts of election practices, particularly enticements offered voters by party agents. However, almost all of their examples describe incidents from the point of view of these agents or other party elites (such as newspaper editors or party leaders). Ordinary voters rarely describe their own reasons for accepting such enticements or explain why they bothered to attend the polls in the first place. *Rude Republic: Americans and Their Politics in the Nineteenth Century* (Princeton, N.J.: Princeton University Press, 2000), esp. pp. 68, 70–82.

rarely formed policy-related preferences, seldom studied party platforms, and could not recall the names of the candidates for whom they voted.

We are particularly interested in these ordinary men for several reasons. First, their experiences reveal the multitude of ways in which men were incorporated into American democracy.[5] As seen below, public policy considerations had little, if any, relation to the social networks and understandings that shaped the behavior of many men at the polls. For many men, for example, the act of voting was a social transaction in which they handed in a party ticket in return for a shot of whisky, a pair of boots, or a small amount of money. While these transactions could be seen as simple bribery, the practices associated with these exchanges were, in fact, much more complex. As part of the social and political culture surrounding the polls, they were frequently embedded in long-term personal relationships between party agents and the men who voted; these relationships and their associated practices had become expectations in which, for instance, men came to think of themselves as Democrats because they were given things by men who worked for the Democratic party. Put another way, the men who were given things had become Democrats precisely because they had come to expect to be given things by Democratic agents at the polls. Such men were not so much bribed as rewarded for their votes.[6]

Other men came to the polls with friends and relatives who pressured, cajoled, or otherwise persuaded them to vote a particular ticket. Brothers, for example, sometimes "voted" their imbecilic siblings, in the process negotiating the necessary rituals for them (e.g., giving their names and residences to the judge of election). In other cases, fathers and brothers threatened "trouble in the family" if their sons and siblings voted wrong. In yet other instances, men belonging to ethnic and religious communities threatened their fellow countrymen and co-religionists with social ostracism if they transgressed party lines. Some employers, particularly landlords and farmers, watched how their tenants and employees voted, exploiting the asymmetries in their economic relationship. In army camps during the Civil War, soldiers often cast their tickets into cigar boxes and tin cups set down in front of the company commander's tent. In many of those camps, to vote for the Democratic party was considered a treasonous slur on the valor of fallen comrades. In

[5] "Incorporation into a democracy" is defined here as the creation of links between a citizen and the act of voting such that a citizen comes to have some reason to vote. Such reasons can include moral obligation (e.g., sense of civic duty), petty bribery, party loyalty, or preferences with respect to public policies or candidates. What matters is that a citizen voluntarily participates in the rituals associated with voting.

[6] Aside from the supposition that party allegiance was formed through interaction with party agents (and thus after at least the first gift of money or liquor), this interpretation is roughly compatible with that offered in Howard W. Allen and Kay Warren Allen, "Vote Fraud and Data Validity," in Jerome M. Clubb, William H. Flanigan, and Nancy H. Zingale, eds., *Analyzing Electoral History: A Guide to the Study of American Voting Behavior* (Beverly Hills, Calif.: Sage, 1981), pp. 156–7, 166.

all these circumstances, men sometimes discovered subterfuges in which opposition party agents helped disguise, in one way or another, the ticket they
cast at the polls. Those subterfuges themselves constituted social practices
helping to shape the public space outside the voting window.

At many polling places, men were physically prevented from voting for a
particular party. In some cities, for example, gangs ruled the polling place
and violently attacked those who attempted to vote for the opposition. And
during the Civil War, Union soldiers and state militia patrolled many civilian
polling places with bayonets afixed to their rifles. Throughout the border
states, many a "southern sympathizer" was violently evicted from polling
places by soldiers whose ostensible duty was merely to keep the peace. In
the frontier West, violence and intimidation similarly shaped elections. The
isolation of polling places and the absence of thickly settled communities
encouraged opportunistic subversion of the democratic process as men attempted to influence the siting of county seats on land they already owned
and the granting of government contracts by elected territorial officials. In
all these cases, the "formation of individual preferences" was a convenient
fiction shrouding organized collusion and intimidation.

There is a second reason we should be particularly interested in these ordinary men, men for whom the act of voting was not a simple transformation
of a personal issue preference into an instrumental vote on government policy. Many men, in fact, had only a rudimentary sense of the grand policy
issues at stake in national and state elections. If those issues had been the
only reason they went to the polls, turnout would have been much, much
lower than it was.

Instead, the polling place was usually congested with milling throngs of
men waiting for their turn to vote or, having voted, simply enjoying the
public spectacle.[7] In the latter group were usually men who had placed wagers on the outcome at that precinct. Monitoring what they saw before
them, they had an immediate, material interest in the way the election was
conducted. However, many men appear to have gone to the polls simply
because they were exciting, richly endowed with ethno-cultural themes of
identity, manhood, and mutual recognition of community standing.[8] Because

[7]   Many of these men were "floaters" who waited for one or the other of the parties
      to offer them something in return for their vote. Mark W. Summers, *The Plundering
      Generation: Corruption and the Crisis of the Union, 1849–1861* (New York: Oxford
      University Press, 1987), p. 57.

[8]   On the polling place as the setting for social activities associated with election day,
      see William E. Gienapp, "'Politics Seem to Enter into Everything': Political Culture in
      the North, 1840–1860," in William Gienapp, Thomas B. Alexander, Michael F. Holt,
      Stephen E. Maizlish, and Joel H. Silbey, *Essays on American Antebellum Politics, 1840–
      1860* (College Station: Texas A&M University Press, 1982), pp. 46–7. Many men, in
      fact, tarried at the polling place before and after they voted, both creating the public
      spectacle that made the polling place exciting and demonstrating the attraction that
      spectacle held for ordinary voters.

these themes were publicly contested in ways that dramatically reinforced the ethno-cultural alignments of men and parties, the physical arrangement of the polling place provided more than the material setting in which men negotiated their transactions and intimidated their neighbors.[9] That same setting also gave rise to practices that strengthened the ethno-cultural flavor of the American party system.[10]

Even though the polling place was populated by men who conceived of their political identities in ethno-cultural terms, it was also the site in which the great political economic issues of the day, such as secession, slavery, and civil war, were decided. From that perspective, there is an obvious disjunction between, on the one hand, the way in which men conceived of themselves as they voted and, on the other, the great policy consequences of their votes. Only close study of the social practices and organization of the polling place can allow us to bridge this chasm.[11]

[9] The emergence of ethno-cultural characteristics as important constitutive elements in party competition occurred some decades after the parties themselves had formed. As Richard P. McCormick has described, the party system was initially founded by ambitious political leaders who exploited the passions of an electorate that tended to focus on the presidential contest (in particular, Andrew Jackson and his competitors) as an aligning template for organizational development. This template at first only incidentally incorporated ethno-cultural characteristics into party identity and tactics. *Second American Party System: Party Formation in the Jacksonian Era* (Chapel Hill: University of North Carolina Press, 1966), esp. pp. 329–56. Although the suggestion cannot be elaborated on here, ethno-cultural themes in party competition in and around the polling place probably emerged and were certainly reinforced by the growing anonymity of the electorate in subsequent decades as a consequence of suffrage expansion, urbanization, and population growth. These developments would have made the stereotyping of prospective voters – men who were personally unknown to party agents – almost a necessity as party challengers attempted to prevent or at least to limit illegal participation by the opposition.

[10] In what Ronald Formisano described as "their first party contest," Michigan Democrats and Whigs fought over whether or not aliens would be allowed to vote if they had taken out their first papers (indicating that they intended to become naturalized citizens but were not yet naturalized). He notes that this issue was also salient in Illinois, Iowa, and Wisconsin. In all these cases, both the suffrage itself (as a public dispute between the parties) and enforcement of the eligibility requirement (as a practice in and around the polling place) would have provided an initial tilt to the parties, either toward (in the case of the Democrats) or against (for the Whigs) foreign-born ethnic minorities and, by association, Catholics. Once set in motion, party agents would have accelerated this tilt by aiding or obstructing men as they negotiated the procedural hurdles associated with their approach to the voting window. *The Birth of Mass Political Parties, Michigan, 1827–1861* (Princeton, N.J.: Princeton University Press, 1971), pp. 81–97. On the ethno-cultural origins of the American party system more generally, see pp. 3, 56–80, 102–18, 128–38. For the theoretical foundations of the ethno-cultural interpretation of nineteenth-century American politics, see pp. 9–12.

[11] Ever since the emergence of the ethno-cultural interpretation of nineteenth-century voting some four decades ago, the literature on nineteenth-century American politics has been almost schizophrenic. On the one hand, policy conflict has been viewed as the primary force driving party competition at both the federal and state levels as

Despite the importance of voting to the emergence and development of American democracy, actual voting acts and the physical and social settings in which they took place have been little studied. One explanation for this inattention is that scholars have often taken them for granted. From this perspective, voting is and was so routinized as to constitute nothing more than a banal background for competition between parties and ideologies. However, any notion that the nineteenth-century polling place had the often tomb-like quiet and well-behaved placidity of modern precincts must be immediately dismissed.

Although some people were killed at the polls, most violence took the form of pushing and shoving that did not cause serious injury. But violent threats and physical obstruction, including the covert display of weapons, were apparently very common, so common that a routine rebuttal for charges of election excesses was that voting had always been conducted under such conditions. In rural areas, violence and intimidation extended far beyond the immediate vicinity of the polling place and the hours when the polls were actually open. Because rural voters were thickly embedded in their

legislative divisions over slavery, secession, the tariff, and the banking system shaped and reshaped alignments in the party system. On the other hand, popular participation in elections has been viewed as driven by ethnic and cultural loyalties, the latter having little to do with policy contention after the voting is completed. For examples of the literature from the policy perspective, see Stephen Skowronek, *Building a New American State: The Expansion of Administrative Capacities, 1877–1920* (New York: Cambridge University Press, 1982); Daniel P. Carpenter, *The Forging of Bureaucratic Autonomy: Reputations, Networks, and Policy Innovation in Executive Agencies, 1862–1928* (Princeton, N.J.: Princeton University Press, 2001); Elizabeth Sanders, *Roots of Reform: Farmers, Workers, and the American State, 1877–1917* (Chicago: University of Chicago Press, 1999); Gretchen Ritter, *Goldbugs and Greenbacks: The Antimonopoly Tradition and the Politics of Finance in America, 1865–1896* (New York: Cambridge University Press, 1997); and Richard Franklin Bensel, *Yankee Leviathan: The Origins of Central State Authority in America, 1859–1877* (New York: Cambridge University Press, 1990) and *The Political Economy of American Industrialization, 1877–1900* (New York: Cambridge University Press, 2000). For an exhaustive review of the ethno-cultural literature, see Ronald P. Formisano, "The Invention of the Ethnocultural Interpretation," *American Historical Review* 99 (1994): 453–77. Formisano suggests, first, that "ethno-cultural" scholarship has strongly, almost exclusively focused on electoral politics, to the exclusion of policy decisions and implementation and, second, that the lowest common denominator underlying ethnocultural scholarship may have been a rejection of economic explanations of political behavior. Even so, most ethno-cultural historians have conceded at least some role for economic interest in nineteenth-century political behavior. See, e.g., Lee Benson, *The Concept of Jacksonian Democracy: New York as a Test Case* (New York: Atheneum, 1966), pp. 88–9, 140–50, 156–64, 290–1, 300. On the ethno-cultural foundation of antebellum politics, see Joel H. Silbey, *The Partisan Imperative: The Dynamics of American Politics before the Civil War* (New York: Oxford University Press, 1985), pp. xv–xix, and, more generally, Paul Kleppner, *The Third Electoral System, 1853–1892: Parties, Voters, and Political Cultures* (Chapel Hill: University of North Carolina Press, 1979).

communities, they inevitably carried their social and political histories to the polls with them. Their neighbors, serving as party observers or election judges, knew their names and political leanings and were thus able to dispense with stereotyped physical appearance and ethnic accents that, in the larger cities, served as proxies for partisan affiliation. Retribution could also be delayed for days or even weeks after an election because the voter, whose ballot had been monitored at the polls, could be located even after he had returned home. This also meant that retribution could be credibly threatened well before the election was held. Thus, unlike cities where the politicization of the community was largely restricted to the immediate proximity of the polling place on election day, rural areas could be effectively politicized for much longer periods and over much greater distances.

Because party agents in large cities were unacquainted with most of the men who approached the polls, partisans often relied on ethnic identities in order to separate supporters and opponents. This reliance in effect transformed national policy issues into contests between ethnic and religious communities. For example, in late antebellum St. Louis the sociology of voting transformed an issue-centered political competition between "free soil" and proslavery partisans into a social confrontation between "Germans" and "Irishmen" in and around the polls. In the broadest, most abstract perspective, what injected popular passion into the election was federal policy toward human bondage, but at the polling place, this translated into the social identification of "Germans" (universally considered to heavily favor "free soil" territorial policies) and "Irishmen" (just as heavily "proslavery").[12] Since partisans on both sides relied on the ascriptive characteristics of potential voters, these characteristics became the local basis of what was a much larger and more abstract ideological contest.

It is likely that these differences between city and country influenced the underlying political allegiances of voters as well. In St. Louis, for example, abuse at the polls by "Irish" Democrats probably turned more than one proslavery German away from the Democrats and toward "free soil" nativists. This tendency would have reinforced the ethnic coloration of the major parties in areas where anonymity was fairly high. In rural areas where anonymity was low, the tendency would have been toward political uniformity, turning communities into one-party bailiwicks.

---

[12] While Germans in St. Louis (and Missouri generally) overwhelmingly favored "free soil" policies, this was not the case in other American communities. Germans in Iowa, Michigan, and Pittsburgh, for example, probably inclined toward the Democratic party. In Illinois and Minnesota, on the other hand, they were probably at least as Republican as the remainder of the electorate. Frederick C. Luebke, ed., *Ethnic Voters and the Election of Lincoln* (Lincoln: University of Nebraska Press, 1971), pp. 108–9, 123–4, 173–4, 180, 209; Michael Fitzgibbon Holt, *Forging a Majority: The Formation of the Republican Party in Pittsburgh, 1848–1860* (New Haven, Conn.: Yale University Press, 1969), pp. 4, 356–7, 359–60, 367–8.

The significance of the way in which American men voted transcends the history in which they lived. Students of comparative politics, for example, sometimes discern at least a distant parallel between the United States during the nineteenth century and contemporary nations currently undergoing transformation from agrarian to industrial societies. The social and political stresses associated with industrialization appear to have a certain commonality, among them the emergence of working-class claims on wealth, the intensification of ethnic competition, and the subordination of the public weal to economic development. Furthermore, violent conflict in and around the polls, corruption, and a general politicization of society also seem to characterize contemporary industrializing nations attempting to combine democracy and development. There is at least a limited sense in which the earlier American performance can serve as a benchmark for these contemporary nations, allowing us to form expectations about what can be reasonably expected and about the long-term consequences of various election pathologies where they do emerge. We can also see that formal election procedures are not ever sociologically or politically neutral; certain groups and interests are favored and others disarmed by the rules themselves. The policy stakes are perhaps higher during industrialization than at most periods in a nation's history, adding to the concatenation of passion, interest, and identity congregating in and around the polling place.

When I first conceived of this project, I thought it would be possible to reconstruct a generic "act of voting" that could serve as a modal description of what I anticipated would be comparatively minor variations in particular times and places. Put another way, I believed that I could construct an "ideal type" of the voting process that, although it changed over time, would still anchor a general analysis of voting in America in the middle of the nineteenth century. This would have been a basically democratic model against which fraud, intimidation, and corruption could have been identified as pathologies. I still believe that such a model has utility, but much of its utility lies in the fact that it was so seldom approximated. In fact, our modern conceptions of democracy are largely anachronistic intrusions when transplanted into the nineteenth century.

Many citizens so strongly believed in the principles that drew them into the political process that any and all means of achieving victory were justified. Ballot stuffing and intimidation were thus interpreted as means of adjusting the franchise in such a way that the only legitimate (and thus democratic) outcome would occur. For example, in different times and places, the participation of immigrants, Catholics, and southern whites in elections were all seen as perversions of the franchise, perversions that could be corrected only by making certain that their votes would not constitute a majority of those cast at the polls. But these views were never hegemonic; encouraged by their leaders and sponsors, immigrants, Catholics, and southern whites still voted.

Their stubborn participation, despite the hostility of a large portion of public opinion, compelled the resort to fraud and intimidation. If these groups had peacefully acquiesced in their disfranchisement, these extraordinary methods of adjusting the outcome of elections would not have been necessary. And this set up what may have been the most fundamental contradiction in nineteenth-century American democracy, a contradiction arising out of the incompatibility of two basic principles of the period's politics. One of these was that the influence of social groups over the outcome of elections should somehow be weighted by their comparative characteristics, such as relative loyalty to the national government, ethnic identification with American nationality, or approximation to the Anglo-Saxon racial stereotype. The other principle was that the election process should accurately count and report all votes properly cast at the polls.

Attempts to resolve this contradiction produced a vague, ever-shifting boundary between what were considered legitimate and illegitimate means of shaping the outcome. Social and economic intimidation, for example, was publicly deplored but otherwise tolerated when carried out by private citizens.[13] However, when exercised by public authorities, particularly federal troops, this same intimidation made the American public much more uncomfortable.[14] Complicating matters even further, many of the most powerful private citizens donned public robes on election day, serving as election judges and clerks. Conversations between these men-as-judges and their

[13] Most accounts of urban elections describe polling places as increasingly violent and chaotic after the end of the 1830s. See, for example, Harriet E. Amos, *Cotton City: Urban Development in Antebellum Mobile* (Tuscaloosa: University of Alabama Press, 1985), p. 117. As the nineteenth century wore on, election violence and intimidation continued to rise, peaking in the North and border states in the 1850s and 1860s and in the South during and just after Reconstruction. In some ways the northern and border state pattern reflected a transition from a more personalistic and communal society in the opening decades of the century to a more highly regulated and institutionalized society at the end. The creation of effective registration laws and procedures, for example, placed responsibility for the determination of voter eligibility in the hands of government bureaucracies, thus removing one of the major sources of polling place contention. These laws and procedures required, as a precondition, the systematic identification of residence (e.g., numbers on houses) and clearly legible records (e.g., widespread adoption of the typewriter). Both developments came fairly late in the century. In the South, violence began to decline only once most blacks and poor whites were removed from the electorate, thus reducing much of the racial and class tension that previously divided the region.

[14] The leading authority on election law, for example, utterly condemned military intervention. "There can, however, be no doubt but that the law looks with great disfavor upon anything like an interference by the military with the freedom of an election. An armed force in the neighborhood of the polls is almost of necessity a menace to the voters, and an interference with their freedom and independence...." George W. McCrary, *A Treatise on the American Law of Elections* (Keokuk, Iowa: R. B. Ogden, 1875), p. 315. Also see pp. 319–20.

neighbors-as-voters were often a mixture of quasi-official rulings and threats of private retribution, the latter extending well beyond proceedings in the immediate vicinity of the polling place on election day.

This study begins in 1850 because, as Richard P. McCormick noted, the transition from the second to the third American party system occurred at about that time.[15] I originally intended to continue the analysis into the 1870s or beyond but later chose to stop in 1868 for several reasons. The most important was that I uncovered much more geographical and temporal variation in election practices than I had expected. To fully present the evidence that I had unearthed, I had to contract the scope of the study. The second reason was that southern elections during Reconstruction were, even given this variation, just very different from southern elections before the war or northern elections at any time. Practices in and around the southern polling place constituted a kind of social and political war between white Democrats and black Republicans in which the polling place was merely one site of conflict. For these reasons, only northern contests were analyzed during the postwar period and the study ends in 1868 when southern states began to reenter the Union.

I began telling stories of mid-nineteenth-century elections to friends and colleagues well before the first page of this book was written. In fact, one of my guidelines in reducing these narratives to a formal text was their reactions to tales of polling place debauchery and intrigue. Some of the most important conversations arose in connection with a presentation to the Institution for Social and Policy Studies at Yale. Later, both Karen Orren and Stephen Skowronek, in their editorial roles, pushed me to combine these individual anecdotes into a generalized account.[16] As one of the reviewers for *Studies in American Political Development*, Walter Dean Burnham pressed me in the same direction. All three are among the most important reasons I am happy to call American political development my home. Fabrice Lehouq generously offered to read the entire manuscript and then, even more generously, gave me advice on how to place the work in a more comparative frame. Although I have not been able to follow up on his suggestions in this book,

[15] McCormick, *Second American Party System*, pp. 13–14. More importantly, 1850 generally marked a change in many parts of the United States between what might be called "neighborhood" and "mass society" polling places, a transition that took place even earlier along the northeastern seaboard. Richard P. McCormick, *The History of Voting in New Jersey: A Study of the Development of Election Machinery, 1664–1911* (New Brunswick, N.J.: Rutgers University Press, 1953), pp. 122–3. However, even in the late 1860s much of the nation still voted in rural or small town communities in which most adult males were known to those attending the polls.

[16] The result was "The American Ballot Box: Law, Identity, and the Polling Place in the Mid-Nineteenth Century," *Studies in American Political Development* 17 (Spring 2003): 1–27. Although some of the text is reprinted in the present volume, most of this article contains narrative accounts that are not duplicated here.

I do believe that cross-national comparison of polling place organization and behavior would be a wonderfully colorful and theoretically rich project.

While Kathleen O'Neill, Greg Huber, and John Lapinski also pressed me on one point or another, my sternest critic was undoubtedly Michael Fitzgibbon Holt, which was exactly why I wanted him to read the earliest complete draft. I am certain that I have not entirely met the very high standards he set for me (and meets himself), but he nonetheless saved me from many errors and unsustainable conclusions. At Cambridge, Lew Bateman was a consistently supportive and helpful editor, even as he tried to restrain my verbosity. I hope he succeeded. And, for the second time in as many books, Stephanie Sakson has exquisitely refined my text. There are still a lot of things I do not understand about the English language. Through it all, Elizabeth and Seth listened to the stories I unearthed from the bowels of Olin Library. If these accounts now become part of the tapestry of American political development, they will deserve much of the credit. Particularly for "D-e-l-n-o-w."

1

Introduction

Broad economic interests clashed in national politics throughout the middle decades of the nineteenth century. These conflicts were mediated by local and national political institutions, particularly the party system and the federal allocation of power between the national and state governments. In terms of platform declarations and policy implementation, both the party system and government institutions more or less spoke the same language, executing a fairly transparent translation of economic interests into public policy. However, the logic and language of the great struggles dominating national politics were often garbled when transmitted into the electoral settings of the polling place. These settings were constructed out of material very different from that out of which the parties made policy in the state and national capitals. And they marshaled the attention and understandings of ordinary citizens whose concerns often were both different in quality and much more limited in scope. Many of the policy logics and disputes rending state legislatures and the federal Congress were simply beyond the event horizon of the individual voter.

Many elements entered into the construction of the local settings in which individual voters determined the fates of national parties. One of the most important was the sheer physicality of electoral practice, the arrangements through which citizen preferences were recognized and registered as official votes. Another was the social environment of the voter that determined how he aligned himself with others and thus distinguished between friend and foe. A third was the intermittent intrusion of national policy conflicts into the daily lives of citizens. For example, for many northerners, taxes and the draft were the most important ways that the Civil War materialized in their daily lives. Similarly, the tariff and the gold standard, along with the political reconstruction of the South, were at least imagined to be significant factors in the way the life chances of individual citizens played out after Appomattox. However, passions and interests at the polls were often related to one another in unusual ways; the typical voter placed himself within the political galaxy of American politics by combining his usually dim perception of national policy decisions with his often more pragmatic understanding of the orientations of local branches of the major parties as social and cultural institutions.[1]

Some of the men who approached the polls in the middle of the nineteenth century were, of course, informed citizens who understood the relationship between government policies, the local and national political economy, and the great party organizations that competed in elections. They needed little encouragement to participate in politics; in fact, they often provided the material resources, in the form of money and social prestige, that fed party competition. Other men, those belonging to the larger middle classes of the nation, also comprehended the links between policy making and the processes of democracy. They, too, voluntarily turned out in large numbers. For these men, politics was about interests and parties; party platforms were primarily written to win their approval and support. Widely trumpeted by party newspapers published in the largest and smallest of American cities and towns, these platforms were material commitments connecting the interests of the politically aware and economically well-heeled to one or the other of the party organizations.[2]

Completing that connection were still other men, such as ward heelers, patronage employees, and saloon keepers, who comprised the bone and tissue of American parties. Because their interests were bound up even more closely and narrowly with the fate of their party, they subordinated personal opinion to the party cause. But they too were well aware of party policy commitments, particularly with respect to the ways in which platform planks could influence the working of an election. These party agents were very pleased when men spontaneously voted the party ticket in large numbers.

The task of these agents was to make certain that men came to the polls and voted for their candidates. And, in the middle of the nineteenth century, many

---

[1]   On the primacy of "perceptions growing out of beliefs, experiences, and memories rooted in their home communities," even for the orientation of individual voters toward national issues, see Joel H. Silbey, *The Partisan Imperative: The Dynamics of American Politics before the Civil War* (New York: Oxford University Press, 1985), pp. xiv–xv.

[2]   In Michael F. Holt's words, the antebellum "Whig and Democratic parties advocated specific policies in order to gain office. They attempted to enact those policies once elected. And they expended enormous effort to educate voters about what officeholders had done. Voters knew what the parties stood for in terms of both specific legislation and general goals. They could judge the expected results of those programs because of recent experience with both. And they responded in rational ways to the contrasting programs and party images presented to them." *The Rise and Fall of the American Whig Party: Jacksonian Politics and the Onset of the Civil War* (New York: Oxford University Press, 1999), p. 83. While very well phrased, this description of the relationships among party organizations, public policy, and individual voting behavior applied only to a portion of the American electorate.

adult men simply could not comprehend the broad relationships among party, policy, and their personal stakes in the national political economy. Illiterate, impoverished, and often culturally isolated from that part of American society that we might term the "public sphere," many men came to the polls with little or no idea of how politics might significantly shape their lives. That they came to the polls at all often reflected the organizational activity of the party organization and, when studied in detail, the utilization of personal networks maintained by individual party agents. In some cases, these agents simply translated the policy commitments of their party into a popular vernacular with which the lumpen proletariat of democracy could resonate. As party agents repeatedly stressed, they were almost entirely indifferent as to which message was sent or received, as long as men went to the polls and voted the party ticket.

Party agents seized on any device or tactic that might strengthen their ticket at the polls. When dealing with the lumpen proletariat of American democracy, these devices and tactics often included deception, petty bribery, and symbolic manipulation. But, most important, party agents relied on the ethnic and religious identities of these voters, both in distinguishing whom to encourage or discourage as voters and in translating party commitments into the common dialect of the masses.[3]

Party agents who worked the polling place were responding to the material interests of those who funded and otherwise supported their activities. At the same time, and somewhat paradoxically, these same party agents also exploited and thus enhanced the intense ethno-cultural competition and hostility that characterized much of American society. Only by recognizing the "swinging door" roles of these party agents, as both conductors and transformers of material economic interest in and around the ballot box, can we understand the simultaneous existence of both a robust ethno-cultural politics in the street and an equally vigorous preoccupation with economic interests in national and state legislative chambers. Because these party agents

---

[3] What could be considered a typical "policy-related" discussion between a party agent and a voter was reported by Francis Rowley as he described how Rinaldo Craig came to vote for the Republican candidate in the 1866 congressional election in Mount Vernon, Ohio: "He [Craig] said that he didn't care much who was elected, but that he would vote for Columbus Delano. Said if they would pay him a small sum he would vote for Morgan, provided his mother and step-father didn't find it out. I told him I wasn't buying votes myself. I thought that it was his duty to vote for Morgan, and that if he wanted to vote that way I thought he could vote without his mother finding it out. He said he was afraid that his mother would find it out. I told him to do just as he pleased; that it was his privilege.... I don't know as I assigned any reason, particularly [in urging Craig to vote for Morgan]. I told him I thought by voting for Delano he was placing a negro on an equality with a white man." Ser. Rec. (hereafter S.R.) no. 1313: Contested Congressional Election in the Thirteenth District of Ohio: Mis. Doc. (hereafter M.D.) no. 38, Pt. 2, p. 207. Columbus Delano vs. George W. Morgan, election held on October 9, 1866.

dominated the American polling place, this book focuses almost exclusively on the very last stage of a political campaign: the act of voting on the day of election. This act must be retrieved from the historical record by examining the various temporal and social environments within which people went to the polls and then by reconstructing the ways in which they voted.

ELECTION CASES

The most detailed reports of the motivations and behavior of ordinary voters appear in hearings conducted in connection with contested congressional elections.[4] Under the Constitution, both chambers of Congress are empowered to judge the qualifications of their members, including whether they were duly elected by their constituencies. Under that power, the House of Representatives heard hundreds of appeals by losing congressional candidates during the nineteenth century. In these appeals, the losing candidate would claim that misconduct of the election had cost him his seat and urged that the House overturn the result, seating him in place of the winner certified by his state. In most of these cases, the House conducted hearings in the congressional district from which the appeal was made. The losing candidate presented witnesses who testified that abuses had occurred; the winner attempted to rebut this testimony with his own witnesses. In all these hearings, the witnesses were sworn. In many of them, a local judge would preside over the proceedings. While there is abundant evidence of fraud and violence in the transcripts, equally relevant descriptions of routine or normal election practices frequently appear as well.[5]

Much of this description cannot be independently confirmed. A few accounts offered by witnesses are probably false, fabrications made of whole cloth intended to support the claims of the seated member or the challenging contender. Other witnesses probably exaggerated the events they recounted, particularly the significance or frequency of abuses in the conduct of elections. But most of the testimony appears to be the honest renderings of common men and, sometimes, women who, from all appearances, were not

4   These hearings were printed in the permanent Serial Record of the U.S. Congress as Miscellaneous Documents collected in the annual volumes of Reports to the House of Representatives. These are cited in this book by volume (e.g., "S.R. no. 1269" refers to volume 1269 of the Serial Record set), followed by the title of the contest (e.g., "Contested Congressional Election in the Eighth District of New York"), the number of the document (e.g., "M.D. no. 7"), and the contestants and the date of the election (e.g., "William E. Dodge vs. James Brooks, election held on November 8, 1864").

5   For a review of the literature and evidence on election fraud in the nineteenth century, see Howard W. Allen and Kay Warren Allen, "Vote Fraud and Data Validity," in Jerome M. Clubb, William H. Flanigan, and Nancy H. Zingale, eds., *Analyzing Electoral History: A Guide to the Study of American Voting Behavior* (Beverly Hills, Calif. Sage: 1981), pp. 154–83.

equipped to understand the consequences of their testimony; even if they had been willing to twist the truth in favor of one of the contestants, these witnesses would not have known how to do so.

Many witnesses in fact corroborated, directly or indirectly, accounts given by witnesses for the opposition. In other instances, their simple narratives of how they came to be at the polls and what happened once they arrived bore only tangentially, if at all, on allegations of irregular or fraudulent election procedures. For some witnesses, merely reporting their experiences in a way that made sense to themselves, let alone their audience, was a struggle. Others were more aware of the political significance of the practices normally associated with the polling place; their narratives were probably accurate aside from the one possible violation to which their testimony pointed. In almost all cases, these ordinary men and women appear to have been more concerned with how they themselves appeared to the audience attending the hearing than with whether or not their testimony helped or harmed the contestant who had summoned them.

Aside from the testimony itself, there are several possible sources of bias in the hearings. One of these arises out of an imbalance in geographical and temporal coverage. Where elections were not contested, hearings were not held, and, thus, we have no testimony. Between 1850 and 1868, hearings were conducted in forty-eight contested elections (see Table 1.1). When printed as formal reports to the House, these hearings and the evidence associated with them occupy a little over 16,000 pages. In terms of temporal distribution, the evidence is fairly well balanced. The antebellum period, for example, is represented in fourteen contests containing just under 6,000 pages (29 and 37 percent, respectively). The Civil War years from 1861 to 1865 produced seventeen contests and 4,000 pages of testimony (35 and 25 percent). In the postwar period from 1866 to 1868, there were also seventeen contests, but the testimony, taking up over 6,000 pages, was more extensive (35 and 38 percent). Because the number of hearings and the pages of testimony gradually increased over the period, the evidence is slightly tilted toward the later years, particularly after the war ended.

In terms of spatial distribution, thirteen states and territories are represented in the hearings. Missouri led the list with twelve contests and over 3,500 pages of testimony (25 and 22 percent of the total, respectively). Pennsylvania and Kentucky were also overrepresented with Maryland, Ohio, and New York somewhat farther back. New England was seriously underrepresented and no contested elections at all emerged from the Deep South. While these might be serious problems, the balance between the nation's great sections was still fairly representative. Twenty-one of the contests and a little over 8,000 pages of testimony record behavior at polling places in the slave states (44 and 51 percent, respectively); the corresponding totals for the free states are, of course, the inverse (56 and 49 percent). In terms of urban-rural composition, hearings were held for elections in Baltimore, Boston,

Table 1.1. *Temporal and Spatial Distribution of Contested Election Hearings*

Year	Temporal distribution	
	Number of election contests	Total number of pages in hearings
1851	1	291
1855	1	271
1856	1	175
1857	3	1,261
1858	3	1,487
1859	4	2,405
1860	1	95
1862	8	1,576
1863	2	388
1864	7	2,097
1866	5	2,519
1867	3	365
1868	9	3,391
Summary by period		
Antebellum	14	5,985
Civil War	17	4,061
Reconstruction	17	6,275
Grand total	48	16,321
Spatial distribution (by state or territory)		
Dakota	1	176
Indiana	2	481
Kentucky	5	2,798
Maryland	4	1,930
Massachusetts	1	80
Michigan	2	122
Missouri	12	3,642
Nebraska	2	251
New Mexico	2	497
New York	3	1,396
Ohio	4	1,920
Pennsylvania	9	3,007
Utah	1	21
Summary by section		
Slave	21	8,370
Free	27	7,951
Grand total	48	16,321

Cincinnati, New York, Philadelphia, and St. Louis, as well as rural districts for almost all the states and territories on the list.

Another possible source of bias is that these hearings were, in fact, held when elections were contested. Peaceful, routinely conducted elections have occasioned little comment throughout American history. In this respect, they are like many mundane, familiar aspects of social life; they become important, and thus recorded for posterity, only when they are spectacularly violated in one way or another. Then, and only then, is normal practice set down as a foil against which abuse is demonstrated. The fact that an election was contested usually meant that the challenger (and his allies) felt that he could present enough evidence of fraudulent practices either to overturn the official result or, at least, to embarrass the opposition. However, this selection bias pertains only to the challenger's side in the hearings because the victor usually strove to present voting practices and the conduct of election officials as more or less normal. In some cases, the victor would impeach the results in precincts that the challenger had carried; in such instances, the contestants would trade positions on whether or not the election was routinely conducted.

For the most part, however, we are not interested in the merits of the contest. What is important is how witnesses described what a normal election should look like, the physical and sociological setting in which the polling place was located, and the actual texture of transactions between voters, party agents, and election officials. There is thus little reason to take sides in these contests (e.g., judging whether or not the challenger presented a strong case). But we can and should reject testimony that was effectively refuted by other witnesses. However, because witnesses were under oath, they appear to be quite reliable, at least in the sense that their testimony was not often convincingly challenged by the opposition.

In sum, the evidence that can be drawn from the hearings is neither perfectly distributed spatially or temporally nor entirely free from bias. These flaws, however, are strongly countered by what they do contain: extensive, detailed accounts of the personal experiences of ordinary voters in and around the mid-nineteenth-century polling place. As evidence for a social history of democracy, the testimony contained in these hearings is simply unmatched in the vast archives of American political development.[6]

---

[6] Although the hearings also contain hundreds of pages of additional evidence such as the names recorded in poll books and official notices associated with the appearances of witnesses, most of the testimony is narrowly focused on the experiences of ordinary voters as they approached the voting window or loitered in the immediate vicinity of the polling place. Aside from isolated anecdotes in personal memoirs or the rare entry in diaries, there is just no other source of such information in the historical record. For a few of the rare descriptions to appear outside the contested election hearings, see Kate Kelly, *Election Day: An American Holiday, an American History* (New York: Facts on File, 1991), chaps. 7–9, and Robert J. Dinkin, *Election Day: A Documentary History* (Westport, Conn.: Greenwood Press, 2002), sec. IV.

THE PRACTICE OF NINETEENTH-CENTURY
AMERICAN DEMOCRACY

This examination allows the construction of a theoretical framework resting on the actual *practice* of elections, especially the procedures and routines of voting.[7] Analysis of this practice begins by focusing on three aspects of the polling place. The first is the *physical setting*: the kind of building in which the voting is done, the type of neighborhood in which the polling place is located, and where the ballot boxes are situated with respect to election officials and voters. A second, equally important aspect of the polling place is the *sociological composition* of the community in which the voters reside: the ethnic and racial identities of the residents, the type of economy from which they draw their livelihoods, and whether or not the average voter can read or write. Here we should also include the conditions under which the election is conducted; the most important of these conditions involve social violence in the form of guerrilla raids, civil war, urban riots, racial and ethnic persecution, and military rule. Violence in and around the polls was not rare in the nineteenth century, and this dimension cannot be ignored in setting out our framework.

The third and last element that must find a place in our analytical frame-work is the *laws* regulating elections.[8] These include the statutes determining voter eligibility, empowering election judges and clerks, and shaping the way in which voters indicate their choices of candidates. Such laws structured the act of voting by formally defining the boundary between legitimate and illegitimate practice at the polls. For various reasons, however, these laws compelled election officials to exercise broad discretion in the determination of voter eligibility and other aspects of the election process.[9] The exercise

---

[7] By examining the material practice of voting, this book attempts to fill a void in both American political historiography and general democratic theory. In David Grimsted's words, "Interest in what and whom parties represented, or in why particular groups voted as they did, has absorbed historical attention, and almost no consideration has been given to the mechanics of the process." *American Mobbing, 1828–1861: Toward Civil War* (New York: Oxford University Press, 1998), p. 183.

[8] For an exhaustive survey of electoral laws in this and other periods of American history, see Alexander Keyssar, *The Right to Vote: The Contested History of Democracy in the United States* (New York: Basic Books, 2000).

[9] Election officials usually had at least some knowledge of the laws under which voting was to be conducted but tended to skirt formality whenever that seemed to conflict with community custom. At many polling places, however, books or pamphlets containing election laws were available, and those dissenting from the decisions of officials could and did make use of them. Even in these cases, appeal to the letter of the law was not always effective. For an example, drawn from the voting near Fort Randall in the Dakota Territory in 1862, see S.R. no. 1199: Contested Delegate Election from the Territory of Dakota: M.D. no. 27, pp. 64–5. J. B. S. Todd vs. William Jayne, election held on September 1, 1862. In addition, some judges of election were illiterate and thus

of this discretion, embedded in the social understandings of the community in which the voting took place and influenced by the partisan interests of the officials themselves, often determined whether and how individual men participated in elections.

THE PHYSICAL SETTING OF THE POLLING PLACE

Almost all polling places in the United States are now located in government buildings, often schools. In the nineteenth century, there were far fewer government buildings than there are today, and for that reason, most elections were held in privately owned structures. The one almost universal exception was the county courthouse, in which was located the polling place for what was usually the largest town in the county. But in the country, where most of the people in the United States lived, voting was conducted in barns, private homes, country stores, and churches – almost anything that could separate voters from the election officials and the ballot boxes they tended. On the frontier, where buildings were even harder to find, votes were sometimes cast in sodhouse saloons, sutler stores near army forts, the front porches of adobe houses, and temporary lean-tos thrown together at desolate desert crossroads. In the larger cities, fire stations, warehouses, and livery stables were commonly used. One of the most common venues was liquor establishments.[10] In some saloons, cloth sheets would be raised around the area in which voting was done so that patrons could drink while the election was held. Such an arrangement made an election noisy and, sometimes, violent.

Most of the polling places in large cities such as St. Louis were public buildings such as stores, factories, engine houses, city halls, or court houses. While private homes were sometimes used, larger structures were preferred (see Table 1.2). These polling places also had more formal names and

incapable of reading the laws under which they were to conduct the voting. In these instances, traditional custom must have exercised a particularly strong influence on the proceedings. See, for example, S.R. no. 1200: Contested Congressional Election in the Third District of Missouri: M.D. no. 43, pp. 21, 23, 88. James Lindsay vs. John G. Scott, election held on August 3, 1863. At one Philadelphia precinct, the Republican inspector admitted that he could neither write nor read "writing" but claimed he could read printed tickets. He signed his testimony with his mark. S.R. no. 1431: Contested Congressional Election in the Fifth District of Pennsylvania: M.D. no. 7, p. 89. Caleb N. Taylor vs. John R. Reading, election held on October 13, 1868.

10 Saloons were the most important gathering places for immigrants in the mid-nineteenth century and thus were primary centers for their political mobilization as voters. For this reason, many immigrant political officeholders owned drinking establishments, and, at least in New York, almost nine of every ten polling places in immigrant neighborhoods were saloons. Tyler Anbinder, *Nativism and Slavery: The Northern Know Nothings and the Politics of the 1850s* (New York: Oxford University Press, 1992), p. 145.

Table 1.2. *Precinct Locations in St. Louis City and County,*
August 1859 Election

1. St. George's Market-house
2. Coal scales, at the intersection of Gravois Road and Arsenal Street
3. Phoenix engine-house
4. J. Haupt's house, corner of Park and Second Carondelet avenues
5. Convent Market-house
6. House opposite Snyder's soap factory
7. Central House
8. Politz's House
9. School-house at Bridgton
10. William Berry's, in Manchester
11. City Hall, in the city of Carondelet
12. Mehl's store
13. Drienhoefer's
14. Washington engine-house
15. Gambel Market-house
16. Powell Sink's
17. White's house at Crere Coeur Lake
18. Court-house, Fifth Ward, city of Saint Louis
19. Barthold's house
20. Market Street House
21. Brown's Store
22. State tobacco warehouse
23. House opposite the Olive Street House
24. Virginia Hotel
25. School-house
26. Whitehill's lumber yard
27. Beehler's meat-house
28. Wiles' stable
29. Biddle Market
30. Mound engine-house
31. Mills's house
32. James Horton's house, Gravois mines
33. The Abbey, on Saint Charles road
34. George Sappington's
35. The Harlem House
36. John Stephens's, Normanby post office

Source: S.R. no. 1062: Contested Congressional Election in First District of Missouri: M.D. no. 8, p. 17. Frank P. Blair, Jr., vs. J. R. Barrett, election held in August 1858.

were probably widely recognized landmarks. In rural areas such as Indiana County, Pennsylvania, most of these kinds of buildings were far less common. In these districts, private residences, schoolhouses, and, in villages and small towns, perhaps a town hall were pressed into service (see Table 1.3). The use of informal names to designate residences and generic labels (e.g., "the schoolhouse") suggests more tightly organized communities in which neighbors shared a much deeper understanding of the local landscape than did city dwellers.

Regardless of the type of building used, the vast majority of polling places were set up along a common pattern. The most important feature was the voting window through which tickets were received.[11] The voting window separated voters from election officials who occupied what was, in most cases, a large room. Voters remained in the street, courtyard, or empty lot adjoining the building. The voting window was usually about five feet or so above the ground, high enough to restrict access to the election officials but not so high as to make it impossible for shorter voters to hand in their tickets. Men presented themselves at this window, handing their ticket to the election judges. The judges deposited the ticket in a ballot box that was out of reach but usually in sight of the voter. Beneath the window there was almost always a small platform, approximately a foot high and maybe a yard wide. To address the voting window and thus attract the attention of election officials, the voter had to ascend this platform. While this physical arrangement protected election officials from the jostling of partisans outside the building, it also exposed voters to the crowd around the polls.[12] The platform became the prime site of contestation as the dominant party attempted to take possession, refusing access to all but those who seemed certain to vote their way.

From a contemporary perspective, the layout of the nineteenth-century polling place may seem rather odd. The major purpose of this arrangement was to separate the public from the election officials. Although policemen sometimes monitored the polling place, arresting those who were particularly violent, the public space outside the voting window was usually

[11] By the middle of the nineteenth century, almost all states required voters to use paper tickets to indicate their choices. Keyssar, *Right to Vote*, p. 28.

[12] For descriptions of such arrangements, see, for example, S.R. no. 962: Contested Congressional Election in the Third District of Maryland: M.D. no. 68, pp. 117, 243, 268. William Pinkney Whyte vs. J. Morrison Harris, election held on November 4, 1857; S.R. no. 1060: Contested Congressional Election in the Fourth District of Maryland: M.D. no. 4, pp. 104, 108. William G. Harrison vs. H. Winter Davis, election held on November 2, 1859; and S.R. no. 1199: Contested Congressional Election in the Fifth District of Pennsylvania: M.D. no. 17, pp. 39, 59. Charles W. Carrigan vs. M. Russell Thayer, election held on October 14, 1862. In one Philadelphia precinct, a small panel was cut out of the door to a room in order to create this "window." Voters then stood outside, in the entryway, and handed their tickets through the opening (p. 66).

Table 1.3. *Precinct Locations in Indiana County, Pennsylvania,*
November 1868 Election

Center Township: "the new school-house, near the cross-roads, on the farm of John Barclay"
Washington Township: "the public school-house near Job McCreight's"
Rayne Township: "the house of Isaac Kinter"
Blacklick Township: "the house of David Ferguson"
Young Township: "school-house No. 5, near Hugh Blakeley's"
Conemaugh Township: "the house of the late Adam Thompson"
Saltzburg Borough: "the school-house"
Armstrong Township: "the school-house near David Anthony's"
South Mahoning Township: "the house late of James Hays, in the village of Plumville"
West Mahoning: "the house of Hezekiah Crissman"
Smicksburg Borough: "the school-house"
North Mahoning: "the house of Samuel S. Beck"
East Mahoning: "the house of Widow Ayers"
Green Township: "the house of Lewis B. Shaw"
Cherrytree Borough: "the school-house"
Cherryhill: "the house of Isaac Empfield, in Greenville"
Indiana Borough: "the building lately occupied by George Stadtmiller, on the corner of Clymer and Water streets"
White Township: "the building lately occupied by George Stadtmiller, on the corner of Clymer and Water streets" (same as above)
Shelocta Borough: "the house of Conrad Bley"
West Wheatfield: "the grist mill of Jacob Gamble"
East Wheatfield: "the town hall in Armagh Borough"
Jacksonville Borough: "the school-house"
Canoe Township: "the house of Simon Henry"
Montgomery Township: "the house formerly occupied by Samuel Spicher"
Pine Township: "the public school-house in Strongstown"
Buffington Township: "the old house on the farm of James McKee"
Banks Township: "the school-house in Smithport"
Burrell Township: "school-house No. 9"
Brush Valley: "the school-house in Mechanicsburg"
Mechanicsburg: "the school-house"
Taylorsville: "the shop of Jacob Boughter"
Blairsville: "the town hall"
Grant Township: "the house of Samuel Hawk"
Armagh Borough: "the town hall"

Source: S.R. no. 1431: Contested Congressional Election in the Twenty-first District of Pennsylvania: M.D. (no number, bound between nos. 24 and 25), p. 163. John Covode vs. Henry D. Foster, election held on October 13, 1868.

anarchic.[13] Almost anything was permitted in this public space in terms of speech, electioneering, and, all too often, physical intimidation. Under the law and almost inevitably in practice, election officials had no authority to maintain order outside the voting window. This, in many instances, was for their own protection because the kinds of physical and verbal abuse meted out to potential voters could also be aimed at them.[14] Inside the polling place, the ballot boxes were usually situated on tables at least several feet away from the voting window. The officials, called "judges of election," would receive tickets from voters who presented themselves at the voting window and deposit them in the boxes. At the same time, "clerks of election" would record the names of the voters, as relayed to them by the judges. The clerks usually sat at the same tables that supported the ballot boxes, but the election judges normally stood up.[15]

Because the floor of the building (if it had a floor) was usually higher than the platform outside the window, the election judges looked down on those who presented themselves as voters. This was clearly an advantage in the more boisterous precincts where voters or other bystanders might attempt to grab an official's arm or punch him in the face. In any case, the height of the window, which was still about three feet or so from the perspective of those inside the room, and the constant moving back and forth between the window and the ballot boxes made standing more or less a necessity for election judges.

To summarize, the voting window, set in the outside wall of a building, separated election officials from voters. Inside the polling place, the election process was usually quiet and orderly, with officials and ballot boxes efficiently arranged within an enclosed room. The public space outside the window, on the other hand, was chaotic with only minimal attempts at law enforcement. Although most elections in the United States during the nineteenth century were peaceful, a very sizable minority were conducted in situations where physical and verbal intimidation shaped the public space outside the voting window. In those cases, election judges usually attempted

[13] The police often tolerated more abusive behavior from members of their own party than they would accept from the opposition. But there were limits to even that tolerance. See, for example, S.R. no. 1060: M.D. no. 4 (1859): p. 94.

[14] Even so, election judges could be so intimidated by the crowd outside that they would accept fraudulent votes. For an instance from a Philadelphia precinct, see S.R. no. 1402: Contested Congressional Election in the Third District of Pennsylvania: M.D. no. 3, pp. 72–6, 185–6. Leonard Myers vs. John Moffett, election held on October 13, 1868.

[15] The number and names of election officials, of course, varied from state to state. Pennsylvania may have had the greatest number: a judge of election (from the party holding a majority in the precinct), two inspectors, two inspector clerks, two return inspectors, and two return clerks. The latter were equally divided between the two major parties. S.R. no. 1199: M.D. no. 17 (1862): pp. 66–7.

to preserve public order inside the building up to but not beyond the voting window itself.

PARTY TICKETS

Much of the arrangement of the polling place was dictated by just one aspect of elections: the laws and practices regulating "party tickets." A party ticket listed the candidates offered by one of the political parties in that community. Most tickets were printed on white paper of a quality very similar to newspaper. In fact, many of them were printed in newspapers; voters would clip them out and turn them in to election judges as their votes. Most tickets would list all the candidates offered by a party in that election district in what was sometimes a very long strip. However, some states required separate tickets for every office up for election. In those states, voters would present what were called "bundles" of tickets that the election judges would then distribute among the various ballot boxes. Either way, it was the responsibility of the parties, as private organizations, to provide these tickets to their supporters.[16]

This meant that the parties had both to print and to distribute tickets to the public. This responsibility, in turn, compelled parties to station their own partisans at each precinct in order to distribute tickets.[17] These partisans usually mingled with the crowd that gathered outside the voting window and gave out tickets to voters on request.[18] In some cases, where the voting

[16]   Once their tickets had been printed, most party organizations depended on individuals to take them to the polls. See, for example, S.R. no. 1431: Contested Congressional Election in the Twenty-first District of Pennsylvania: M.D. (no number, bound between nos. 24 and 25), p. 36. John Covode vs. Henry D. Foster, election held on October 13, 1868.

[17]   The San Francisco *Daily Alta California* in 1855 described the duty of a party agent as "to yell at the pitch of his lungs the ticket he espoused and the utter folly of the opponent's 'paper.'" In an 1860 election, "every other man" attending the polling place was said to be "holding in his hands big bundles of tickets." Philip J. Ethington, *The Public City: The Political Construction of Urban Life in San Francisco, 1850–1900* (New York: Cambridge University Press, 1994), p. 74.

[18]   Then, as now, voters made their decisions with varying degrees of commitment and information. The modal pattern for the latter half of the nineteenth century might have been best illustrated by one barely literate naturalized immigrant in 1862 Pennsylvania who offered the following description of how he voted: "very often, if I get my ticket from that man [a Democratic partisan at the polls], I look it over very little, knowing what his politics are.... I mostly get the ticket, put it in; sometimes turn away from the polls; more times stop about the porch a bit, but never bother any more about it...I cannot say exactly whether I read the ticket or not; mostly I get the ticket from a man, knowing his politics, and knowing that he feels as I feel myself. Sometimes I do not look much at the ticket." S.R. no. 1199: M.D. no. 17 (1862): p. 71. In this instance, the voter's reliance on the distributor was reinforced by the fact that he could have read the names on the ticket with only great difficulty, if at all. For a general discussion

seemed peaceful and the election judges were cooperative, the tickets were left in piles on the window ledge; the voters could then select the appropriate ticket at the same time that they presented themselves to the officials.[19]

MAJOR CONSEQUENCES OF THE TICKET SYSTEM

The ticket system profoundly influenced nineteenth-century American politics in several ways. First, although a ticket could be drawn up on a plain piece of paper by the voter himself, almost all tickets were manufactured by the parties. Acting more or less as sovereign private clubs, parties alone determined who would appear on their tickets through procedures entirely unregulated by law. Second, although the ticket system strengthened the hand of major party organizations, it also enabled political insurgents. When the major party organizations met in nineteenth-century conventions, the delegates struggled over issues such as slavery in which compromise was difficult and sometimes impossible. When a party convention failed to find common ground on which all their members could stand, the losers often bolted. The bolting faction would then either fuse with the opposition or field its own independent ticket. If the bolters fused, they would construct a single ticket with candidates drawn from both the bolters and the opposition party. If they fielded their own ticket, the bolters would simply draw up a list of candidates and print tickets to distribute at the polls. Unlike contemporary politics where a new party would have to circulate petitions, pay filing fees, and meet deadlines months before an election takes place, a party faction could become an effective contender at the polls even if it bolted only hours before the voting started.

Thus the ticket system, on the one hand, allowed the major parties, as private clubs, to be as undemocratic in their internal procedures as they wished; on the other, the system punished party organizations if they were unresponsive to their members by making it easy to bolt the party's ticket. In some respects, these features made nineteenth-century American politics far more issue-oriented and responsive to popular sentiment than our contemporary

of voter ignorance of tickets, see Glenn C. Altschuler and Stuart M. Blumin, *Rude Republic: Americans and Their Politics in the Nineteenth Century* (Princeton, N.J.: Princeton University Press, 2000), pp. 77–9, 177, 179.

[19] See, for example, S.R. no. 1062: Contested Congressional Election in the First District of Missouri: M.D. no. 8, p. 739. Frank P. Blair, Jr., vs. J. R. Barrett, election held in August 1858. In one of the precincts in New York City during the 1864 election, each party placed a box of tickets on the street outside the polling place. Voters would select the ticket they wished to vote before proceeding to the polls. S.R. no. 1269: Contested Congressional Election in the Eighth District of New York: M.D. no. 7, Pt. 1, pp. 21, 27. William E. Dodge vs. James Brooks, election held on November 8, 1864.

system, with its government-regulated primaries and strong restrictions on candidacy in general elections.[20]

The third influence on nineteenth-century politics arose out of the way in which the ticket system shaped the polling place. For example, tickets were recognized by the government only once they had crossed through the voting window into the hands of an election judge. Until then, they were meaningless scraps of paper. This distinction clearly demarcated the boundary between the formal process within the room holding the election officials and the anarchic conditions in the street or public square outside the voting window.

Finally, the ticket system demanded that political parties develop extensive, highly structured organizations. As already noted, it was the party's responsibility to see that tickets were available at every polling place. This required that the tickets be printed in advance. Since the tickets usually listed all the offices contested in an election, the office with the smallest geographical constituency dictated the printing. For example, if the only office contested was the presidency or governorship, the parties would have needed to print only one kind of ticket for the entire state. If members of Congress were also up for election, then there would have to be separate tickets printed for each of the congressional districts. If seats in the state legislature were contested as well, they would require the printing of different tickets in each of the legislative districts. And so forth, until, in many instances, the parties were printing hundreds of different tickets throughout the state, each one appropriate for a small number of polling places. Such a system required an extensive administrative organization within the party in order to arrange the proper manufacturing of these tickets. It also necessitated close cooperation with printers, usually the editors of city and county newspapers that had become publicly aligned with that party.[21]

The ticket system also required the stationing of party workers for the distribution of tickets at the polls on election day.[22] Although some of these workers were little more than hired hands, most had a substantial reason

---

[20] This is largely because the party professionals attending conventions were much more aware and responsive to policy issues than the public at large. This fact, plus their direct experience with the conduct of elections under the ticket system, made insurgency both easy and policy-oriented. As a result, the policy stances of the major parties were pulled away from one another by the need to accommodate their respective, policy-oriented activists.

[21] For an account of how the Coshocton *Age* printed tickets for the Republican party, see S.R. no. 1313: M.D. no. 38, Pt. 2 (1866): pp. 383–5.

[22] While the vast majority of tickets were distributed by party agents at the polls, there were exceptions. The most common alternative, as already mentioned, was the printing of tickets in newspapers aligned with one of the parties. Less frequently, party organizations distributed tickets directly to voters at their homes before the election was held. In rare instances, men would also write out their own tickets where none were available at the polls.

to favor their party. Many, for example, enjoyed the patronage of elected party officials by holding government jobs, drawing public pensions, servicing government contracts, or enjoying special licensing privileges of one sort or another. Others were committed to their party for ideological reasons. Whatever their motivation, they were stationed at the polls, where they directly participated in the voting. One of the most common forms of participation was aiding illiterate or semi-literate voters in selecting their tickets. As one illiterate Ohio voter reported, "When I get a ticket from a good democrat I takes 'em."[23] In all these ways, the ticket system shaped the physical setting of the nineteenth-century polling place, providing the context within which the remainder of election laws were interpreted and enforced.

ENFORCEMENT OF LEGAL REQUIREMENTS FOR VOTING

In contemporary elections, voting eligibility is restricted by age, residency, and citizenship. In the nineteenth century, eligibility was similarly restricted but the list was somewhat longer; in addition to age, residency, and citizenship, voting was sometimes or often restricted by race, ethnicity, gender, mental competency, and literacy. During the Civil War and Reconstruction, loyalty to the Union government was a requirement for voting in the border states and the South. While these restrictions are interesting in their own right, the focus here is on how they were enforced. The most important aspects of enforcement are (1) the evidence required to demonstrate voting eligibility and (2) the officials who must evaluate that evidence.

With respect to evidence, it should be remembered that much of the United States during the nineteenth century was a preliterate society; until the turn of the century, in fact, there were many counties in which a quarter or more of adult white men could not read or write.[24] This meant that voters were

[23] S.R. no. 1313: M.D. no. 38, Pt. 2 (1866): p. 496. For numerous examples of party agents aiding men who were illiterate, semi-literate, and, in a few instances, simply forgot their glasses, see S.R. no. 1270: Contested Congressional Election in the Seventh District of Indiana: M.D. no. 11, pp. 9–10, 21, 27–9, 32, 35–6, 39, 41, 43, 59, 61, 63. Henry D. Washburn vs. Daniel W. Voorhees, election held in October 1864. These were all Republican voters at the Hamilton Township precinct in Sullivan County or at the Cloverdale polls in Putnam County. There were 242 depositions given by Republican voters at these two polling places; thirty-five of those men signed with their "mark," indicating they could not write their name. As evidence of the level of illiteracy in this township, this should be considered a lower bound; the actual level was probably much higher (pp. 8–45, 53–69).

[24] For a brief analysis of literacy rates reported in the 1850 census, including an explanation of why they were probably far too low, see Richard Bensel, "The American Ballot Box: Law, Identity, and the Polling Place in the Mid-Nineteenth Century," *Studies in American Political Development* 17 (Spring 2003): 9–10. For a map depicting literacy rates in 1900, including a discussion of that distribution, see Richard Franklin Bensel, *The Political Economy of American Industrialization, 1877– 1900* (New York: Cambridge University Press, 2000), pp. 34–7.

unable to keep records of when they were born or how long they had resided in a town or neighborhood. Since government agencies seldom kept records of these things, there were no certificates that could be presented to election officials as demonstrations of a voter's eligibility. This was less true of citizenship, where the federal government provided naturalization papers when immigrants became American citizens.[25] However, since native-born citizens were not given such certificates, election officials had to know when and whom to ask for papers. A major complicating factor was that, in most instances, there was no voter registration prior to an election.[26] For this reason, the determination of voter eligibility took place at the polls and was carried out by the "judges of election" (this was probably the most important reason why they were called "judges").

To understand just how voter eligibility was determined, it is useful to recall how the polling place was arranged. Voters gathered outside the voting window, waiting for their turn to hand in a ticket to the judges. When they made it to the front of the line (sometimes there were lines, sometimes there were just crowds of people), voters would step onto the platform and face the voting window. When a voter presented himself, he was always asked his name. Most judges were chosen as representatives of the major parties; sometimes there two, sometimes three, but they were almost always drawn from opposing parties. The judges were thus in a position to monitor both the qualifications of individual voters and each other's official behavior. In addition to the judges, who were stationed inside the polling place, the parties also stationed volunteers called "challengers" who would stand outside on either side of the voting window.[27] These challengers could, as the law allowed, "challenge" the right of a voter to cast his ticket if they doubted that the voter satisfied the suffrage qualifications of the state.[28] For

[25]   These documents were not by any means infallible proof of citizenship. For example, in Philadelphia during the Civil War, when alien status conferred an automatic exemption from military service, one immigrant was reported to have said that he was not afraid of being drafted because "I ain't naturalized." However, he still voted "[u]pon my nephew's papers; he is of the same name.'" S.R. no. 1199: M.D. no. 17 (1862): p. 175. There are many instances in other elections where naturalization papers appear to have been passed around at different precincts, thus allowing different men to vote on one set of documents.

[26]   For a history of registration laws in the various states between 1865 and 1910, including descriptions of the kinds of election frauds that they were intended to eliminate, see Joseph P. Harris, *Registration of Voters in the United States* (Washington, D.C.: Brookings Institution, 1929), pp. 65–89, 232–9.

[27]   Andrew W. Young, *The Citizen's Manual of Government and Law* (New York: H. Dayton, 1858), p. 54. When asked whether there had been "any republican challengers at the polls" in Newton Township in Licking County, Ohio, one of the judges of election replied, "Yes, sir; as thick as crows all day." S.R. no. 1313: M.D. no. 38, Pt. 2 (1866): p. 100.

[28]   Many, if not most, polling places were very crowded and the positioning of the challengers was part of a broader pattern that usually separated partisans outside the

example, challengers often objected that the voter was of foreign birth and had not been naturalized. When challenged, the prospective voter had to demonstrate, to the satisfaction of the election judges, that he indeed met the criteria named in the challenge. In this case, the voter was asked either to demonstrate that he had been born in the United States or, if he conceded his foreign birth, to present his naturalization papers. Election judges could also challenge voters on their own initiative but usually preferred to leave this role to the challengers.

Challengers, like everyone else outside the voting window, carried out an entirely private role; election law said only that any citizen could challenge the qualifications of any prospective voter.[29] Anyone, regardless of whether or not they belonged to a party organization, could play this role; while the parties selected men to act as monitors at the polls, these challengers still acted in a purely private capacity.[30] Challengers, like the election judges, were usually chosen from the ranks of party professionals who had resided in the community for years. They knew many of the voters on sight, including their party allegiance, residency status, and age.[31] Unfamiliar faces were sometimes greeted with suspicion by the challengers and judges of both parties until the voter indicated how he was going to vote; at that point, the opposing party would formally challenge his qualifications. But this gets a little ahead of the analysis. First, two features must be discussed: (1) what evidence of his qualifications the prospective voter could be expected to bring to the polls, and (2) how the election judges evaluated that evidence. At a bare minimum, the voter presented his person to the judges. The judges

voting window. For example, one Baltimore election clerk described what he considered normal and fair practice in this way: "What I mean by an open poll is, to have one party stand upon one side, and the other party upon the other side, and an open way between them." S.R. no. 1060: M.D. no. 4 (1859): p. 22.

29   When a reform party challenger in Baltimore's Thirteenth Ward "appealed to the judges inside the room whether we [the reform party] were not entitled to one side of the window, and whether they would not give us one side," the "judges said they had nothing to do outside of the window." S.R. no. 1060: M.D. no. 4 (1859): pp. 80–1.

30   This arrangement was in some respects parallel to the American court system, with challengers acting as attorneys for their respective parties (one prosecuting and the other defending the voter) and the judges (although seldom objectively) evaluating the merits of the voter's credentials. In this adversarial system, altruism was rare and was received skeptically. For example, when Samuel Null, a Pennsylvania man, reported that he had taken "steps to find out illegal votes on both sides," with some of his investigations involving visits to family homes and farms, he was asked, "What induced you to start out on this Quixotic crusade?" Null replied that he "thought it a duty to my country." And so it was, but almost no one but Samuel Null performed this duty in the middle of the nineteenth century. S.R. no. 1431: M.D. (no number, bound between nos. 24 and 25 [1868]): pp. 171, 178.

31   As a reform party challenger in Baltimore's Thirteenth Ward testified, "I knew almost every one in the ward who was entitled to vote. I challenged them, and they were put down when I challenged them, for the judges would not take their votes." S.R. no. 1060: M.D. no. 4 (1859): p. 81.

could, for example, estimate a voter's age by examining his ability to grow a beard. Ethnicity could be guessed at by observing his attire and his accent when he spoke.[32] Clothing and speech were rough guides to both the likely party leanings of the prospective voter and the probability that he was of foreign birth.

In the nineteenth century, almost all states restricted voting to men. This restriction strongly influenced the way voting was conducted. For one thing, many of the polling places were located in buildings where women – at least respectable women – were seldom found. Saloons and livery stables, for example, were usually off-limits to women in this strongly Victorian age. For another, the polls on election day were frequently places in which liquor was both freely available and consumed to excess. The parties often provided, either as courtesy or as bribe, free drinks to prospective voters, challengers, and election officials.[33]

As a result, the street or square outside the voting window frequently became a kind of alcoholic festival in which many men were clearly and spectacularly drunk.[34] For this and other reasons, verbal expression at the polls was much more coarse than the polite conversations that characterized mixed company. In fact, the crowds gathered around the polls often insulted voters who appeared to be supporting the opposing party. These insults easily moved into various forms of physical intimidation as members of the crowd, either individually or in groups, blocked the passage of prospective voters

---

[32] Asked whether any "foreigners" had voted in his community, a man in Kentucky, a naturalized foreign-born citizen himself, answered that he knew "one John Conner, who voted for W. C. Anderson. . . . I judge him to be a foreigner from his language and appearance." S.R. no. 1061: Contested Congressional Election in the Fourth District of Kentucky: M.D. no. 3, p. 24. James S. Chrisman vs. William C. Anderson, election held on August 1, 1859. Also see S.R. no. 1431: M.D. no. 7 (1868): p. 35; S.R. no. 1431: M.D. (no number, bound between nos. 24 and 25 [1868]): p. 236.

[33] The leading authority on the legality of election practices, George W. McCrary, complained, "The too common practice of providing liquors to be used to influence voters in a convention, primary election, or regular legal election, is a practice which the law will not tolerate." However, the only punishment he could find was to render void any contract in which the intent was to procure and distribute liquor to voters. *A Treatise on the American Law of Elections* (Keokuk, Iowa: R. B. Ogden, 1875), p. 139. Since these arrangements could usually not bear scrutiny on many other grounds, rendering such contracts unenforceable in a court of law was equivalent to no punishment at all.

[34] A close connection between alcohol consumption and unruly conduct by crowds attending the polls was commonly understood. For example, when Louis Valle, a voter at St. George's market in St. Louis in 1858, was asked whether that polling place had been "peaceable and quiet," he replied, "Yes, sir; no whiskey to be had." S.R. no. 1062: M.D. no. 8 (1858): p. 745. Some men were so drunk that they subsequently could not remember whether or not they had voted. See, for example, S.R. no. 1431: M.D. no. 7 (1868): pp. 355–6; S.R. no. 1431: M.D. (no number, bound between nos. 24 and 25 [1868]): pp. 20, 53.

to the voting window, implicitly threatening violence if the voter pressed his way forward.

Violence and intimidation were usually restricted to the immediate vicinity of the polling place; otherwise, potential voters were free to go about their business. It was only when men approached the polls that partisans began to construct them as allies or enemies. The social setting around the precinct then became a highly charged ethnic, religious, and ideological battleground in which individuals were stereotyped as friend or foe on the basis of clothing, accent, or skin color.

Under the informal conventions of the period, election etiquette required only that a "man of ordinary courage" be able to make his way to the voting window. This was the general standard by which normal jostling was distinguished from excessive violence.[35] Those men too timid to meet this condition could not rightfully claim, under the social practices and understandings of the time, that their right to vote had been denied.[36] However, if conditions became too threatening, thus dissuading a "man of ordinary courage" from pressing his way through a hostile crowd, then most observers would agree that the election results were invalid at that precinct.[37] As might be presumed, this standard was difficult to apply in practice.

---

[35] See, for example, this question posed to a doctor who had gone to the polls in Baltimore's Nineteenth Ward: "Will you please state any remarks made by any of the crowd calculated to intimidate a man of ordinary courage, and to prevent his exercising the right of suffrage as a freeman?" This was the general standard by which "normal" jostling was distinguished from excessive "violence." S.R. no. 1060: M.D. no. 4 (1859): p. 177; also see p. 179. In his *American Law of Elections*, McCrary set down this rule: "Slight disturbances frequently occur [at elections], and are often sufficient to alarm a few of the more timid, without materially affecting the result or the freedom of the election. The true rule is this.... To vacate an election ... it must clearly appear that there was such a display of force as ought to have intimidated men of ordinary firmness" (p. 314).

[36] When asked to give his age, weight, and height, a man who had been prevented from reaching the voting window in Baltimore's Eighteenth Ward answered, "I am a little over fifty; weight, from 212 to 215 pounds; and am about six feet high." When asked, "Are you not a man in the full vigor of manhood and strength?" he replied, "I should think I was, sir." This exchange occurred after the witness had said that he did not attempt to vote "because I was satisfied that it would be useless." Another voter in the Nineteenth Ward was similarly asked for his height, age, and weight, answering, "I am six feet high, and 44, or 45, or 46 years old; somewhere along there ... [my weight is] 270." He was then asked for the state of his health, responding, "Very good." However, when requested to "describe what persistent efforts you made to get up to the window to vote," he stated that he "did not make any at all." S.R. no. 1060: M.D. no. 4 (1859): pp. 153, 154, 247. A lawyer working for the reform coalition in the Tenth Ward testified that he asked "considerable numbers of native-born citizens" who had reform tickets "to vote, persuaded them to vote, endeavored to influence their manhood, but, looking about, they would say they had wives and children, and would not like to risk their lives in a useless attempt" (p. 203).

[37] On occasion men were actually killed. For example, a voter was murdered at the polls in Baltimore's Fifteenth Ward in 1859. For an emotional and graphic account of his

In fact, one the strongest arguments against women's suffrage in the nineteenth century was that the polls were "no place for a woman." The response, though less persuasive to most Americans in the period, was that the presence of women would have compelled men, in effect, to clean up their act, resulting in at least a much higher standard of public decorum at the polls and, possibly, more honest elections.[38] Both arguments, of course, could be true at the same time. In reality, however, elections were one of the most purely male venues in American society; women were almost never seen within the immediate neighborhood of a polling place on election day.[39]

To return to our main topic: One of the primary responsibilities of a judge of election, in addition to receiving tickets and depositing them in the ballot box, was the evaluation of voter eligibility. In carrying out this responsibility, however, judges had very little to work with in terms of hard evidence. Birth certificates, for example, would have made the determination of age relatively easy. But most states did not officially record births, and such certificates were simply unavailable at most polling places. In practice, election judges usually relied on a close physical inspection of the prospective voter, called up a collective recollection of the voter's personal history, or simply accepted the voter's word that he had reached the required age for voting.

In all these matters, the prospective voter could be asked to swear that he met the qualifications for voting; he could, for example, be asked to take an oath that he was in fact a natural born citizen or had reached twenty-one years of age.[40] "Taking out the book," as the process of swearing was called when the Bible was presented to the voter, resolved many disputes over voting

---

death, given in testimony by his brother who was wounded in the same incident, see S.R. no. 1060: M.D. no. 4 (1859): pp. 139, 140.

[38]   As it was, expectations with reference to acceptable public behavior were usually low. For example, a judge of election in Baltimore in October 1859 declared that, in his ward at least, "I do not believe there was a soul there who did not have perfectly free access to the polls . . . there was some little scrambling, &c., but the police did their duty in an admirable manner . . . the consequence was that after some fighting, and after arresting a man and committing him to jail for striking two men," everything was quiet and orderly. S.R. no. 1060: M.D. no. 4 (1859): pp. 99, 101.

[39]   In the thousands of pages contained in the contested election hearings, there was only one instance in which a woman was reported to have attended a polling place. This occurred in the 1866 congressional election in Mount Vernon, Ohio, when the wife of a man who had apparently suffered a disabling stroke escorted her spouse to the polls with the help of his male friends. S.R. no. 1313: M.D. no. 38, Pt. 2 (1866): p. 198. For a general survey of gender and participation in politics in the nineteenth century, see Mary Ryan, *Women in Public: Between Banners and Ballots, 1825–1880* (Baltimore: Johns Hopkins University Press, 1990).

[40]   See, for example, S.R. no. 1016: Contested Election for Delegate from the Territory of Nebraska: M.D. no. 28, p. 3. Bird B. Chapman vs. Fenner Ferguson, election held on August, 1857; S.R. no. 1402: Contested Congressional Election in the Eleventh District of New York: M.D. no. 27, Pt. 1, pp. 131–2. Charles H. Van Wyck vs. George W. Greene, election held on November 3, 1868.

qualifications by simply placing the burden on the voter.[41] If the voter lied under an oath given to an election judge, he could be fined or imprisoned. Oath taking was probably most commonly used in the border states during the Civil War and the early years of Reconstruction; election judges in the border states were enjoined to prevent men who had "sympathized" with the Confederacy from voting. Since sympathy often involved purely private thoughts that had never been on public display, requiring prospective voters to swear that they had indeed never harbored southern sympathies at least made a pretense at enforcement. Given the number of men who actually refused to swear such an oath, that pretense clearly had some impact.

Generally speaking, oaths had one major defect: They were only as good as the underlying threat of discovery. If, for example, it could be demonstrated under more intensive investigation that a prospective voter had not reached the qualifying age under election laws, then the voter who swore a false oath ran at least some risk of prosecution. However, many men who presented themselves at the polls simply did not know the answer to the questions posed to them by election judges. They did not know, for example, when they were born and thus when or whether they had reached the required voting age. This was true for perhaps 10 percent or so of the population but varied widely by region. In some parts of rural Kentucky, for instance, it seemed as if almost no one knew how old they were during the years just before the Civil War. And many, if not most, oaths were sworn by voters who were unknown to the election judges; many of these men, once the election had taken place, could not be located. They simply merged back into what was often a chaotic social cauldron in which anonymity cloaked, to the point of invisibility, those who lived a transient existence. For these men, false oaths were only one element in the social negotiations that they pragmatically navigated at the polls.

One of the most difficult voting requirements to enforce involved mental competency. Most laws made "idiocy" a disqualification, but even under the best of circumstances, idiocy was often hard to determine. And the mid-nineteenth century was not the best of circumstances; because there were very few psychiatrists or social workers in the United States, very few cognitively impaired adults had been officially identified as idiots. Even fewer had been identified as mentally ill. For these reasons, election judges had to fall back on their own judgment, strongly shaped by community norms and collective understandings of the mental abilities of prospective voters. It appears that they were far more reluctant to declare their neighbors insane (of normal intelligence but mentally unstable) than to view them as imbecilic.

In most cases, election judges applied two different kinds of standards. The most general standard was whether or not the voter was capable of handling

---

[41] For examples, see S.R. no. 962: M.D. no. 68 (1857): pp. 195, 233; S.R. no. 1402: M.D. no. 3 (1868): pp. 174–5, 389–91, 421–2.

his own affairs; this was a very broad and ambiguous test because most of the social transactions involved in normal lives were relatively simple. For example, many prospective voters with borderline mental capacities lived with their parents on farms and had little, if anything, to do with the outside community. The most complex social interaction they ever attempted was, in fact, facing the election judges when voting.

The second standard was a "rough and ready" intelligence test based on factual questions (e.g., Who is president of the United States? or What year is this?) or mathematical problems involving simple arithmetic. Because so many voters were illiterate, an inability to read or write was never taken as evidence of idiocy. And given the very low educational attainments of much of the population, the answers to factual questions or mathematical problems had to be interpreted carefully. Sheer ignorance, for example, did not bar a man from voting. But the inability to be educated, if the opportunity was offered, did constitute a disqualification.[42]

In all these instances, election judges were forced to rely on evidence immediately available at the polls. That evidence could usually be classified under three different headings. The first was the claim made by the prospective voter himself, often backed by a sworn oath that the information he provided was true. The second was close inspection of the prospective voter's physical appearance, attire, speech, and demeanor. The third was the joint recollection of the election judges, challengers, and bystanders as to the social characteristics, such as racial identity and age, of the prospective voter. As we see below, much of what transpired in and around the polling place was deeply influenced by the ways in which party

[42]   Many of the points made in the text arose in a hearing investigating the conduct of a Kentucky election. The specific issue raised in this hearing was whether a voter by the name of Steven Coyle had enough "sense" to vote. The witness had known Coyle for twenty years and was first asked, "Has or not Steven Coyle enough sense to know the difference in the principles and issues of the political parties, and to choose and vote understandingly?" Answer: "I think not." Question: "Can he or not count ten in number?" Answer: "I don't think he can." Question: "Have you or not tried to learn him to count, and could you do it?" Answer: "I have tried to learn him to count money and numbers, and could not do it." Question: "Has he or not been condemned by the circuit court of this county as an idiot, and placed as a charge on the State?" Answer: "Such is my understanding." Question: "Has or not Steven Coyle enough sense to be a good work hand?" Answer: "He is a good farm hand, and has enough sense to know how to do it." Question: "Has he or not a capacity susceptible of improvement, and has his mind not been purposely neglected that he might be a State charge?" Answer: "His mind is susceptible of improvement, and has improved considerably in the last few years. My opinion is that his mind was purposely neglected that he might be a State charge." Question: "Is he now a condemned idiot and a State charge?" Answer: "He is not." While the conclusion that should have been deduced from this evidence is not obvious, the example does illustrate the kind of questions the election judges would have posed in determining whether a voter should be disqualified for mental incompetency. S.R. no. 1061: M.D. no. 3 (1859): pp. 57–8.

agents and election judges examined the evidence men brought with them to the polls.

American elections in the middle of the nineteenth century were both notably uniform and extremely diverse. They were remarkably uniform in that, despite the wide discretion with which the individual states could design suffrage requirements and the mechanical characteristics of the polling place, most of the legal requirements for voting were very similar across the nation. Election officials, for example, were assigned comparable responsibilities. Party tickets were almost identical in form. And for localities in which wood frame or brick buildings existed, the physical structures in which voting occurred were remarkably uniform. However, the practice of elections varied quite a bit across the United States. The major reason for this diversity was variation in the socio-economic setting in which elections were conducted. Despite the relative uniformity of legal requirements and physical structures, this diversity decisively shaped the way in which election officials carried out their responsibilities and party organizations competed for support. The following chapter describes some of the most common characteristics of election practice in the United States, including the printing and distribution of party tickets, appointment of election officials, and some aspects of the determination of suffrage eligibility. Subsequent chapters analyze variation across the primary venues of voting: the rural East (including both northern and southern states), large cities, and the western frontier. Because election practice dramatically altered during the Civil War, a separate chapter describes these changes. A concluding chapter summarizes the findings of the book.

2

Structure and Practice of Elections

The physical arrangement and design of ballot boxes, voting windows, and party tickets would have been recognizable to American voters throughout the nation. These material elements of the election process gave rise to practices that influenced the formation of individual voting decisions and shaped the way in which those decisions became registered as formal votes. Here we examine how these practices and the structure of voting were exploited by party agents as they sought to turn the process to personal and partisan advantage.

Election practice emerged out of the interaction between, on the one hand, the degree of familiarity between party agents and voters and, on the other, the formal requirements for voting set down in election law. With respect to the latter, the Constitution of the State of Virginia stipulated:

1. Every white male citizen of the commonwealth, of the age of twenty-one years, who has been a resident of the state for two years, and of the county, city or town where he offers to vote for twelve months next preceding an election – and no other person – shall be qualified to vote for members of the general assembly and all officers elective by the people: but no person in the military, naval or marine service of the United States shall be deemed a resident of this state, by reason of being stationed therein. And no person shall have the right to vote, who is of unsound mind, or a pauper, or a non-commissioned officer, soldier, seaman or marine in the service of the United States, or who has been convicted of bribery in an election, or of any infamous offence.[1]

In thus defining suffrage eligibility, Virginia made at least ten different kinds of distinctions between various individuals inhabiting the state. The adjective "white," for example, distinguished "white" people from all other races. The

---

[1] George W. Munford, *The Code of Virginia* (Richmond: Ritchie, Dunnavant, 1860), p. 38.

noun "citizen" drew a line between citizens and aliens. The disqualifying attributes of "unsound mind" and "pauper" categorized individuals with reference to mental competency and economic self-sufficiency. In different ways, the residency and age requirements made time a defining element. Past personal conduct underlay the disqualifications due to convictions for bribery or "infamous" offenses.[2] Each one of these distinctions compelled party agents and election officials to identify, in some way or another, the category into which a prospective voter fell.

Of all the distinctions made in Virginia election law, gender was probably the least problematic. Although government authorities did not regulate or record gender classifications, Americans viewed sexual categories as one of the most fundamental distinctions structuring their society. As such, gender was founded on physical differences between the sexes that could be almost invariably confirmed on inspection of the individual's person. Although it was certainly possible to "pass" as a member of the opposite sex, even under extremely challenging conditions, men gathered in and around the polling place simply did not believe or otherwise anticipate that any woman would disguise herself as a man in order to vote.[3]

In fairly sharp contrast, military service was one of the best documented characteristics in American society. The federal government kept detailed records of officers and enlisted men through which ineligible voters could be identified. The problem was that these records were not usually available to election officials and they thus could not prove that a man approaching the voting window was serving in the army or navy. As a result, wherever military units were stationed in the United States, soldiers often donned civilian clothing and passed as otherwise qualified residents of the locality. One major impact of the distinction embedded in election law was to compel military men wishing to vote to wear civilian clothing. Another was to make groups of men approaching the polling place together at least suspect if they both appeared to know one another and were unknown to election officials and party challengers.[4] In fact, such

---

[2] Virginia's suffrage restrictions were similar to those of many free (as well as other slave) states. See, for example, Alexander Keyssar, *The Right to Vote: The Contested History of Democracy in the United States* (New York: Basic Books, 2000), pp. 33, 61–3, and Tables A.4–7 and A.9.

[3] No one personally approaching the voting window was ever challenged on grounds of gender, and no instance of a physical inspection of a potential voter's primary sex characteristics has been discovered in the contested election hearings. With respect to passing under extremely difficult conditions, see Lauren Cook Burgess, ed., *An Uncommon Soldier: The Civil War Letters of Sarah Rosetta Wakeman, Alias Private Lyons Wakeman, 153rd Regiment, New York State Volunteers* (New York: Oxford University Press, 1994).

[4] See Chapters 5 and 6 for examples drawn from forts on the western frontier and encampments in the border states during the Civil War.

groups of men were often suspect for reasons other than possible military service.[5]

With respect to military service, government documents could prove only that a man was ineligible to vote. When confronted at the polls, a man would naturally contend that such a record did not exist because they were not in the army or navy. With respect to foreign-born men, however, government documents could prove that a man was eligible to vote, at least with respect to citizenship. Foreign-born men were expected to retain possession of the documents certifying that they had become citizens. On demand, they would present these documents (commonly referred to as their "papers") to election officials.[6] Lacking papers, a man was either a native-born citizen or an unnaturalized alien. Election officials were rarely certain which was the case when men with strange accents and wearing odd apparel approached the polls.

Somewhat similarly, most states made a felony criminal conviction a disqualification for suffrage, and records of criminal convictions were kept by government authorities. However, as evidence that a man was ineligible to vote, these records were simply unavailable to election officials at the polls.[7] So how could an election judge or challenger identify a man as an ex-convict? In most cases, such men could be identified only if the judges or challengers knew them personally. For example, in the 1859 election in Baltimore, a

---

[5] For example, railroad gangs were sometimes brought to the polls by party agents even though they could not meet the residency requirements of the community in which they labored. Similarly, as detailed in Chapter 4, party agents sometimes "colonized" a constituency by housing adult men in boarding houses just before an election. These men were brought to the polls in groups because these party agents wanted to make sure that they voted (and voted correctly) and because their sheer numbers increased the chances that they would be allowed to turn in their tickets (e.g., they could physically force their way up to the voting window even as supporters of the opposition party vigorously protested their presence). Compared with situations such as these, occasions when parties brought qualified voters to the polls in a noisy show of partisan solidarity were rarely reported in the hearings. In any event, a ritualized display of partisan unity (i.e., men marching en masse to the polls) is entirely consistent with some of the practices through which party agents shepherded and monitored men who had been enticed to vote. Put another way, opposition party agents probably viewed such ritualized displays as possible smokescreens for depositing fraudulent votes. And, in fact, that is the way in which they were almost universally described in the hearings.

[6] This is described in Chapter 4.

[7] In the 1868 congressional election, a man by the name of Nehemiah Lord voted in Liberty, New York. A Democratic politician subsequently charged that Lord had been "convicted and sentenced to State prison; his sentence was never commuted, I believe; I wrote to the superintendent of the prison and ascertained that fact." While such correspondence might demonstrate the ineligibility of a voter, election judges clearly could not wait for the return mail before ruling on a man's right to vote. Ser. Rec. (hereafter S.R.) no. 1402: Contested Congressional Election in the Eleventh District of New York: Mis. Doc. (hereafter M.D.) no. 27, Pt. 1, p. 129. Charles H. Van Wyck vs. George W. Greene, election held on November 3, 1868.

reform party challenger in the Eleventh Ward alerted the judges that Daniel Hinton, whom he had known for more than a decade, "was not entitled to vote... because he had been sentenced to the penitentiary and had served out his term." The challenger knew that this voter had been convicted because Hinton had been "sentenced when I was deputy clerk of the criminal court."[8] However, if a man was not personally known by those attending the polls, there was no way to determine whether he was disqualified by a criminal conviction.

As a result, very few voters were challenged on the ground that they were convicted felons. Contextual evidence, including the criminal records of many of those involved in partisan activities in and around the polls, strongly suggests that this was one of the most laxly enforced suffrage restrictions. Even more poorly maintained were records documenting whether or not a man was a pauper. In fact, the term was simply left undefined in most states. Where election officials had a clear understanding, either under the law or in practice, the category usually identified an inmate of the county poor farm or a recipient of outdoor relief. But many men resided on poor farms or received relief only sporadically. In fact, party agents often arranged for their release or provided alternative means of support to such men just before an election so they would be eligible to vote.[9]

With respect to disqualification on grounds of having an "unsound mind," the government kept fairly careful records of men who had been committed to an asylum or had had someone appointed by a court to look after their affairs. But these records were usually unavailable to election officials and, in any case, documented only a fairly small percentage of men who were recognized to be mentally incompetent.

For most of the distinctions set down in election law, the government simply did not keep formal records. This was true for race, age, and residency. All of these were determined by election officials at the polls upon oral interrogation of the voter, physical inspection of the voter's person, and

---

8 S.R. no. 1060: Contested Congressional Election in the Fourth District of Maryland: M.D. no. 4, p. 61. William G. Harrison vs. H. Winter Davis, election held on November 2, 1859.

9 See, for example, the testimony of William Weil, who stated that Louis Christman, the director of the Bucks County poorhouse, lodged Frederick Frash with him just before the October and November elections. Weil said that Christman had asked him to make a bedstead. When Weil told Christman that he could not do it without assistance, Christman sent Frash, a former carpenter with a "sore leg" who normally lived on the poor farm, to work and live with Weil. Christman said that he thought Frash could help Weil make the bedstead, but, if not, "it would be all right," meaning that the director would pay Weil for Frash's board and room in any case. Frash stayed with Weil just long enough to vote in the October election, returned to the farm, came back to Weil's house just before the November election, voted, and then returned to the farm once more. S.R. no. 1431: Contested Congressional Election in the Fifth District of Pennsylvania: M.D. no. 7, pp. 195–6. Caleb N. Taylor vs. John R. Reading, election held on October 13, 1868.

mutual consultation with bystanders who opposed or supported the voter's claims.[10]

COMMON ASPECTS OF THE AMERICAN POLLING PLACE

The most common element in voting was the party ticket. Containing the party's nominees for political office, these tickets were distributed by party organizations in the public area outside the voting window.[11] Individual party agents picked up these tickets from the printer and prepared them for use. In most instances, this preparation included cutting up the large sheets on which the tickets were printed. If separate tickets were required for different races, the tickets were bundled together, usually with string. Consolidated tickets containing all races were sometimes twelve to fifteen inches long and thus a little awkward to handle. Party agents often folded these in order to make them easier to carry. In addition to convenience, folding a ticket gave the voter some privacy with respect to his preferences. However, this privacy should not be overestimated; party agents attending the polls closely observed with whom the voter associated just before approaching the voting window and were also very aware of the often subtle differences in the quality of the paper and printing associated with the various tickets. From this information, in addition to whatever personal knowledge they might have of the voter's identity and political affiliation, party agents usually knew which ticket was to be cast before the voter reached the window.[12]

Most of the party agents distributed "regular" tickets containing the official nominees of one or another of the party organizations. However, almost all those distributing tickets outside the voting window were more interested in the success of one or more particular candidates on this ticket while ambivalent or indifferent toward the others. While this sympathy was sometimes based in ideological affinity or policy positions, on most occasions

---

[10] Most of the enforcement of suffrage requirements occurred at the polling place, and the usual result of fraudulent attempts to vote, when detected, was that the ticket was not accepted by the judges of election. Only rarely were fraudulent voters actually prosecuted for their actions. For two exceptions, one for being under age and the other for presenting counterfeit naturalization papers, see S.R. no. 1431: M.D. no. 7 (1868): pp. 118, 163–5.

[11] The design and distribution of party tickets are described in Chapter 1.

[12] When asked how he knew that the men he had named had voted a Democratic ticket, a Republican in Philadelphia gave five reasons: "First, because they were brought by the democratic precinct politicians; second, because they received their tickets from those having charge of the democratic tickets; and third, because the tickets they voted were tickets with democratic headings, and I saw them; fourth, because democrats vouched for them; and fifth, because the democratic election officers received all their votes." S.R. no. 1431: Contested Congressional Election in the Fifth District of Pennsylvania: M.D. no. 7, p. 85. Caleb N. Taylor vs. John R. Reading, election held on October 13, 1868.

ticket distributors were more personally interested in the success of their favored candidate. In some cases, this interest could be traced to prospects for
a patronage appointment that the candidate, if victorious, would control.[13]
In other instances, the party agent was employed by a particular candidate or
his organization. Either way, the party agent was consequently more loyal
to that candidate than to the party ticket as a whole. Where this was the
case, ticket distributors sometimes carried an array of tickets. One of them
would be the regular ticket of the party to which they belonged. Others
would be modified tickets in which their favored candidate's name would
be written in or pasted over the printed name of a competitor.[14] If the voter
wished to vote the regular party slate, then the distributor would provide
that ticket. If the voter did not want to support the party slate but was willing
to back the agent's candidate (often persuaded to do so by friendly cajoling,
a drink of whisky, or a small bribe), then the distributor would provide an
appropriately modified ticket.[15]

With respect to modified tickets, one of the most interesting cases arose in
an Indiana congressional election in October 1868.[16] The Republican party
in Wayne County was divided into factions, one favoring and the other
opposing George Julian. The anti-Julian faction was so hostile to the party's
congressional nominee that they arranged to have Republican tickets printed
with the name of the Democratic candidate, Jonathan S. Reid, substituted
for Julian. This was done without any agreement or collaboration with the

---

[13] On the importance of patronage to the maintenance of antebellum party organizations,
see Mark W. Summers, *The Plundering Generation: Corruption and the Crisis of the
Union, 1849–1861* (New York: Oxford University Press, 1987), pp. 23–36.

[14] For example, Republicans working for Charles Van Wyck, a candidate for Congress in
New York State, arranged for Democratic tickets to be printed with Van Wyck's name
in place of the Democratic nominee. These tickets were then distributed to Democratic
voters, most of whom apparently received five dollars for voting them. S.R. no. 1402:
Contested Congressional Election in the Eleventh District of New York: M.D. no. 27,
Pt. 2, pp. 3–5. Charles H. Van Wyck vs. George W. Greene, election held on November
3, 1868.

[15] For example, an agent working for a Democratic candidate for alderman in Detroit
distributed both Republican and Democratic tickets to voters; these tickets had only
one name in common, that of the candidate for alderman. S.R. no. 1060: Contested
Congressional Election in the First District of Michigan: M.D. no. 7, p. 38. William
A. Howard vs. George B. Cooper, election held in November 1858. In Wallkill, New
York, the distributors of Democratic tickets were offered five dollars for every ticket on
which appeared a "paster" with the name of the Republican candidate for Congress.
Individual distributors were given a different colored paster so that each could be
rewarded appropriately. The Republicans also tried to make the same arrangement,
offering two instead of five dollars apiece, with respect to one of the local offices. S.R.
no. 1402: M.D. no. 27, Pt. 1 (1868): pp. 184, 188. For other negotiations of a similar
character, see S.R. no. 1402: M.D. no. 27, Pt. 2 (1868): pp. 12, 17.

[16] The following account is drawn from S.R. no. 1432: Contested Congressional Election
in the Fourth District of Indiana: M.D. no. 15, pp. 6, 42–3, 87–8, 126–7, 155. Jonathan
S. Reid vs. George W. Julian, election held on October 13, 1868.

Table 2.1. *Modified, Scratched, and Straight Ticket Votes in the South Precinct of Wayne Township, Wayne County, Indiana, October 13, 1868*

Total votes received for
    John S. Reid, Democratic Candidate for Congress: 670
    George W. Julian, Republican Candidate for Congress: 479
Straight party tickets (including congressional contest)
    Democratic: 507
    Republican: 470
Straight party tickets (with the exception of the congressional contest)
    Republican (with Reid printed or pasted in place of Julian): 110
    Republican (with Reid written in): 46
Scratched tickets (with mixed party votes for races besides Congress)
    Voted for Reid: 7
    Voted for Julian: 9
Tickets in which no candidate for Congress was supported
    Otherwise Democratic: 1
    Otherwise Republican: 31

Source: S.R. no. 1432: Contested Congressional Election in the Fourth District of Indiana: M.D. no. 15, p. 42. Jonathan S. Reid vs. George W. Julian, election held on October 13, 1868.

Democrats, and men recognized as Republican ticket distributors gave out the modified tickets at the polls. Most of this insurgency was apparently confined to the south precinct of Wayne Township where the impact was quite dramatic (see Table 2.1).

A total of 1,181 tickets were turned in to the judges at South Precinct. The large majority (977 of 1,181, or 83 percent) were "straight" tickets in which votes were cast for all offices and for only one party. Even so, the proportion of modified or scratched tickets was much higher than for most precincts in most elections in the United States. Anything above 5 percent usually indicated a concerted effort by ticket distributors and other party agents to break up a party slate. Usually, this was an attempt by party agents to infiltrate the opposition party slate by substituting one name in an otherwise straight ticket (e.g., Democratic agents substituting one Democratic name in an otherwise straight Republican ticket). One of the interesting aspects in the present case is that party activists were attempting to defeat their own candidate by substituting an opposition name into otherwise straight Republican tickets. They were remarkably successful in this effort. Of those tickets that supported Republicans for all races (aside from the congressional contest), almost a quarter (156 of 626) backed the Democratic candidate.

These tickets were modified in three primary ways. First, most of them were tickets in which the name of the Democratic candidate, John S. Reid, was simply printed in place of the Republican candidate. Otherwise, for all intents and purposes, these tickets would have looked identical to "regular" or unmodified Republican tickets. While very convenient for Republicans who wished to bolt to Reid while supporting the rest of the party slate, such tickets could have easily deceived other men who simply wanted to vote Republican for all offices. For example, one man who had intended to support Julian reported that, in fact, he had probably cast a ticket backing Reid. As he later recalled, "I obtained it from one Smith, whose first name I do not remember; he works for Bratz, Perry & co., in this city.... I was told afterward that said Smith was dealing out tickets that had Reid's name inserted instead of Julian's." Although apparently literate and somewhat concerned about the outcome of the election, this man had failed to examine closely the ticket he voted.[17]

The second kind of modification occurred when Reid's name was "pasted" over Julian's name on what was otherwise a straight Republican ticket. The only difference between the tickets in the first two categories would have been that those with pasted "slips" (as they were called) would have been more easily recognizable, in both appearance and texture. To be deceived by such tickets, even illiterate voters would have had to pay less attention than normal to the ticket they turned in to the judges.[18] Generally speaking, most men appear to have paid little attention to their tickets, either implicitly trusting those who distributed them or having been somehow paid for their vote. Even so, many men at this polling place were probably already aware that irregular tickets were in play.[19] As one of the voters later recalled, "there

[17]   The anti-Julian faction evidently intended to deceive voters. For example, a storekeeper reported the discovery of modified tickets (i.e., with Reid on them) among those he had put out on his counter as a convenience for Republican voters. He concluded that he had inadvertently distributed modified tickets among the regular ones he had intended to distribute. The modified tickets had either been surreptitiously planted among those on his shop counter or misrepresented when originally given to him. In this case, both a fellow partisan and common voters had been deceived. S.R. no. 1432: M.D. no. 15 (1868): p. 263.

[18]   With respect to such possibilities, the testimony in these hearings is sometimes unreliable. For example, men who were apparently illiterate (because each signed his testimony with his mark) sometimes reported that they had "read" Julian's name on the ticket they turned into the judges. This is possible, at least in the sense that they might have recognized the form of the letters as signifying his name, but a more likely explanation was that they were reluctant to confess their illiteracy in an open hearing. S.R. no. 1432: M.D. no. 15 (1868): pp. 132, 142. Other illiterate voters confessed that they did not know for whom they voted (pp. 202, 232). For instances in which an illiterate voter had someone else read his ticket for him or specifically asked the distributor whose name appeared in the congressional race, see pp. 149, 205, 266. Other men simply could not say whether or not they had voted for Julian, either because they could not read or did not examine their ticket before turning it in to the judges (pp. 156, 168, 176, 201, 213, 219, 226, 242, 253, 268, 273, 277, 280, 320, 327, 329, 337, 349, 350).

[19]   Rumors that modified tickets were being distributed to voters surfaced very early. For example, reacting to these reports, Daniel Moorman procured a number of Republican

was a cry of 'spurious ticket' in the crowd." Other men, however, found out about the existence of modified tickets only after they had voted.[20]

The third kind of modification entailed writing Reid's name in place of Julian's. This modification involved "scratching," or crossing out, the name of the regular party nominee and writing in the name of the opposition candidate. Although the context suggests that many otherwise Republican tickets were printed with no candidate listed for Congress (so that "scratching" would not have been necessary), the testimony is not conclusive on this point. If this were the case, the voter or ticket distributor could have written in either Reid's or Julian's name. This interpretation would help explain the otherwise abnormally large number of tickets with no candidate listed (because the voter simply failed to write in a name for the office). It would also help explain why there were no (otherwise) Democratic tickets with Julian's name inserted (because Democratic tickets were not printed with no candidate in the congressional contest).[21] In any event, all the "scratching" in the congressional race involved Republican tickets. And these would have been the least deceptive of the three types of modifications; the modification would have been obvious even after the most cursory examination of the ticket.[22]

tickets during the morning hours, closely examined them to make certain that no modification had been made, and then distributed them to his employees. He claimed that several of "the leading hands" had told him that most of his employees were Republican, and although they had not asked him to do so, he distributed the tickets as a kind of public service. S.R. no. 1432: M.D. no. 15 (1868): pp. 266–7.

[20]   Inattention to the modern American ballot similarly produced erroneous votes in the 2000 presidential election when the infamous "butterfly ballot" apparently misled thousands of Democrats in Palm Beach County, Florida, to mark a choice for Patrick Buchanan instead of their party's nominee, Albert Gore. In that case, however, intentional deception can be ruled out because the ballot was designed by a loyal agent of the Democratic party. The problem arose out of a failure to anticipate just how little energy most voters are willing to devote to the study of the ballot's form and content. Even the slightest ambiguity in ballot design can produce numerous mistakes by individual voters, most of which are never traced or detected. For an analysis of the butterfly ballot and its consequences, see Howard Gillman, *The Votes That Counted: How the Court Decided the 2000 Presidential Election* (Chicago: University of Chicago Press, 2001), pp. 21–4.

[21]   Only thirty-two tickets, about 2.7 percent, did not indicate a vote for Congress. Of these thirty-two, all but one backed the Republican candidate for governor. Since the governor's race headed the ticket (i.e., was the first contest listed) and was used as a short-hand method of estimating party strength in a precinct, this pattern meant that almost all the tickets that did not express a choice for Congress were probably "Republican" tickets that, other than the congressional race, backed candidates for that party. Given the contextual evidence presented in the hearings, these were probably tickets that had been printed with a blank entered in the congressional contest, a blank that had never been filled in.

[22]   As noted in the table, there were also sixteen tickets that were "scratched" for one or more offices, aside from the congressional race. These tickets were probably not manufactured by the anti-Julian faction because they broke disproportionally for

As a result of the machinations of the anti-Julian faction, Julian ran behind Reid by 191 votes at this precinct even as the Republican candidate for governor was running ahead of the Democrat by about 150 or so. This kind of swing between individual races was extremely rare in the middle of the nineteenth century and was facilitated by an organized rebellion against the regular Republican nominee. The same tactics, executed by Democratic agents at this poll, would probably have encountered much more resistance among men who regarded themselves as Republican loyalists.

Like individual party agents, local political organizations often cared more about the fate of their own candidates than they did about the national part of the ticket. In such cases, these organizations would accommodate voters who would support them only if they could split their ticket. For example, in 1859, a reform coalition was formed in order to contest American party control of the city government of Baltimore. While most of the voters to whom this coalition appealed were Democrats (and the Democratic party provided most of the organizational muscle), a sizable minority were Know-Nothings. For that reason, the reform committee in the Ninth Ward printed two different tickets, one with the name of the Democratic candidate for Congress, William G. Harrison, and another with the name of the American party candidate, H. Winter Davis. Since control of the House seat was secondary to cleaning up the municipal administration, reformers handed out both tickets at the polls.[23]

Opening and Closing the Polls

In the larger cities where the residence of the voter was frequently some distance from his place of employment, the polls usually closed before these men would return home. To accommodate those who wished to vote before going off to work, the polling place was usually opened early in the morning.[24] As a consequence, voting was particularly heavy during the first hour of the election. The rhythm was somewhat different at rural precincts where voters usually lived somewhat further away from the polling place. There voting was more evenly spread throughout the day with men sometimes arriving at the polls just before or at dusk.

With respect to opening and closing the polls, election practices were often informally adjusted to meet what were viewed as extraordinary conditions. On the frontier, where the distance to the polling place was often great and changing weather conditions could make travel problematic, election

---

Julian (nine to seven). Instead, they probably reflected spontaneous (i.e., unorganized) ticket modification by men who, for whatever reason, wished to "split" their tickets between candidates sponsored by the two parties.

[23] S.R. no. 1060: M.D. no. 4 (1859): pp. 34–5, 56.
[24] This was, for example, the case in Philadelphia. S.R. no. 1431: M.D. no. 7 (1868): pp. 89–90.

statutes were sometimes liberally interpreted or disregarded all together. For example, in Florence, Nebraska, the judges held the polls open until seven o'clock, one hour past the closing time mandated by law, so that "eight or ten voters out on the prairie making hay" might be able to vote.[25] In this case, the judges viewed "making hay while the sun shines" as a reasonable excuse for casting tardy ballots.

Many states set dawn as the time for opening the polls and sundown as the time for closing them.[26] This was particularly useful in rural and small town precincts in which ascertaining the correct time, as told by a watch or clock, might be difficult. S. E. Higgins, sheriff of election, recollected how he told the time in Crab Orchard, Kentucky:

The voting was commenced about fifteen minutes after six o'clock, by the watch – my own watch. The polls closed at about fifteen minutes after seven o'clock in the evening, by Mr. Carson's watch, my own having stopped, and I then took his. I think there were a couple of votes cast after the judges said "close the polls." Young Humble rode up and asked if there was time to get in a few votes he had out, and the judges agreed to hold up until he could get them in....I think the sun was probably shining a little when they voted....When the officers of the election agreed to let the two men vote, a number of bystanders of the opposite party contended that it was not right to do so, as it was beyond the time fixed by the constitution for the closing of the polls. I thought they allowed them to vote to keep down a fight....The sun was shining on the houses when they voted.[27]

Anticipating service as a party challenger at the Jamestown, Kentucky, polls, William H. Haynes made careful preparations for the election: "On Sunday night the clerk of the election came to my house to stay all night; asked me

[25]   S.R. no. 1016: Contested Election for Delegate from the Territory of Nebraska: M.D. no. 28, p. 3. Bird B. Chapman vs. Fenner Ferguson, election held in August 1857. A voter at that precinct supported the decision to keep the polls open: "I understood the object to be to permit voters who were out on the prairie making hay and at work down on the ferry boat to come in. I knew the men; they were old residents here, and I supposed they were legal voters. I am not certain they were all citizens of the United States, but I supposed they were and had a right to vote. It has been the custom here to keep the polls open until the voters were all in that we knew of" (p. 5).

[26]   See, for example, Munford, *Code of Virginia*, p. 82: "The poll shall not be opened at any election sooner than sunrise, and shall be closed at sunset." Virginia also extended the voting period for state and local elections if the weather was bad: "if the electors who appear at any place of voting cannot all be polled before sunset, or if it shall appear to the commissioners that many of those entitled to vote were prevented from attending by rain or rise of water courses, they shall keep the poll open for three days, including the first . . ." (p. 82).

[27]   S.R. no. 1063: Contested Congressional Election in the Fourth District of Kentucky: M.D. no. 11, pp. 103–4. Response of Anderson to Chrisman in James S. Chrisman vs. William C. Anderson, election held August 1, 1859. Crab Orchard was a hamlet of some 350 people with a church, an academy, eight stores, and a locally renowned mineral springs. When Higgins said, "the sun was shining on the houses," we can probably assume that light was no longer directly hitting the ground below.

if I had a watch; I had one; we got an almanac and set my watch right at sundown; on Monday morning of the election I could see the first rays of the sun as it was rising, and I examined my watch and found it was precisely right; I have a good watch, I think."[28] Haynes was a particularly conscientious participant; most party agents and election officials would have, like Sheriff Higgins, simply watched for the sun to appear and to disappear from the sky.

Selection of Election Officials

At some precincts, judges of election were elected in the morning, just before the polls opened, by those men who happened to be present.[29] Because the selection of judges was anticipated, the attendance of these men was, of course, no accident; they were there in order to participate in the selection of the judges. Some of the negotiations attending these pre-election proceedings were quite complex, reflecting a mixture of community norms, notions of fair play between the party organizations, and the formal provisions set down in the statutory code. Sewell Coulson, a Republican, described just such a hodgepodge of factors in the 1864 election of judges at the Hamilton Township polls in Sullivan County, Indiana:

When the inspector of the election, Major Griffith, announced to the persons collected there that he was ready to receive nominations for judges, Mr. Hansill nominated James A. Beard; my brother Uriah Wilson nominated Joseph Martin, postmaster of the town of Sullivan; and Thomas McIntosh nominated Porter Burks. Beard and Burks were democrats; Martin is a republican. Before the vote was taken for the

---

[28] S.R. no. 1063: M.D. no. 11 (1859): p. 228. While Jamestown was the seat of Russell County, the village held only six stores and about 200 inhabitants.

[29] Although most officials had been appointed prior to the day of election and had previously agreed to serve, absences were fairly common. Most states appear to have provided for the filling of vacancies by men who happened to be present at the opening of the polls. See, e.g., Munford, *Code of Virginia*, p. 84. The first official duty of these officials was to swear an oath to carry out their responsibilities faithfully. In Virginia, this oath was comparatively brief: "I do solemnly swear, that in the election about to be held, I will faithfully and impartially discharge the duties appertaining to my office, according to law. So help me God" (p. 84). For an example of such an election of officials in Cincinnati, Ohio, see S.R. no. 1431: Contested Congressional Election in the First District of Ohio: M.D. no. 16, pp. 8, 97. Benjamin Eggleston vs. P. W. Strader, election held on October 13, 1868. And in Wayne County, Indiana, see S.R. no. 1432: M.D. no. 15 (1868): p. 303. The usual practice was for one of the judges to be sworn by one of the other judges. The first judge, who was usually formally or informally designated the "chairman" of the election officials, then swore in the rest of the officials. The author has in his possession a written document from the March 4, 1884, election in Puckwanny Township, Brule County, Dakota Territory, in which the oaths are written down and signed by the three judges in this fashion. Although the oaths are also written down for the two clerks, the latter are unsigned. Except for the signatures of the other two judges, everything is in the lead judge's handwriting, and he designated himself as "chairman."

election of the judges considerable discussion was going on about having a mixed board, in which the inspector, Mr. Samuel R. Hansill, James W. Hinkle, and myself, participated. The inspector seemed to think that each party should be represented on the board. Mr. Hinkle and myself insisted on it as a matter of right; we asked it as a matter of favor to let us have one member of the board, to settle all disputes in regard to the fairness of the election. Mr. Hansill got up on a store-box (I think) and spoke in very violent language against Martin serving on the board. I then proposed to put Mr. Hinkle or some other of our friends on the board. Mr. Hansill replied that he would not trust Mr. Martin, Hinkle, or any other black abolitionist, on the board. At this time somebody to my left said that he withdrew the nomination of Porter Burks. Mr. Hansill urged that the vote on Beard be taken, and he was the first man elected. Mr. Hansill then insisted that the vote be taken on Porter Burks; his name was put to vote, and no vote was taken upon the nomination of Martin, or any other republican.

Before these votes were taken, the inspector read the law, to the effect that the bystanders had the right to elect the judges. The balloting occurred outside within a few feet of the voting window. The crowd participating in the selection of judges was quite large, extending from the window out some ten or fifteen yards.[30]

In most precincts, however, judges, inspectors, and clerks were appointed before election day by local government officials, usually in consultation with the major party organizations. Most of these election officers had served in prior elections and were thus well aware of the customs and norms that had developed over the years. While new disputes inevitably arose over the qualifications of both old and new residents, veteran election officials usually tried to interpret these disagreements in terms of their shared experience. Where this experience did not provide a conclusive decision, they often logrolled their differences, admitting doubtful voters on both sides in roughly equal numbers. Serious problems arose only where one of the parties either swamped the polls with men who were transparently unqualified to vote or, on capturing the election machinery, turned away clearly eligible voters simply because they would have supported the opposition.

The Ballot Boxes

In most precincts in the United States, each voter cast but a single ticket naming candidates for each office to be decided in the election. When voters wanted to split their ticket, they either searched for an irregular ticket in which one or more candidates were drawn from the opposing party or erased

---

30   S.R. no. 1270: Contested Congressional Election in the Seventh District of Indiana: M.D. no. 11, p. 49. Henry D. Washburn vs. Daniel W. Voorhees, election held in October 1864. Because the two judges selected in this proceeding were both Democrats, Coulson and his fellow Republicans were disappointed in the result. For another example, see S.R. no. 1432: M.D. no. 15 (1868): pp. 5–6.

a candidate's name and wrote in an alternative. The situation was different where more than one ticket was employed in an election.[31] In many such cases, the additional tickets were dedicated to contests, such as amendments to the state constitution, which did not involve party slates. But some state election laws required a separate ticket for every governmental level.[32] In these places, multiple tickets required multiple ballot boxes and split ticket voting took another form.

In the October 1862 general election in Philadelphia, for example, there were five separate boxes. One was for state offices in which tickets named candidates that both ran statewide and for Congress. County tickets were deposited in the second, municipal tickets in the third, and ward tickets in the fourth. In the fifth box were placed tickets for the "division," or precinct. If a man voted a "full" ticket, he handed the judge of election five tickets, one for every level of government. If a man voted a "straight" ticket, he not only handed the judge five tickets but the tickets would also name candidates running under the same party label. The parties facilitated straight ticket voting by preparing "bundles" of the appropriate tickets. Voters would then hand these bundles to the judges as their votes, the judges sorting the tickets into their respective boxes.[33] Party agents supporting insurgent candidates would prepare their own bundles, mixing and matching candidates in whatever manner that appeared to maximize their prospects. They could also prepare bundles of tickets in whatever way voters wished, as long, of course, as those bundles contained candidates whom the agents supported. Personal campaigns, backed by relatives and friends of local candidates, sometimes offered many alternative bundles in which the only common candidate was

[31] Separate boxes were required, for example, when voter eligibility varied for federal and local offices so that two individuals might vote in a national election but only one might be eligible to vote in a local contest in the same election. For examples of differing suffrage requirements for national, state, and local offices, see Keyssar, *Right to Vote*, pp. 29, 30–1.

[32] In the 1864 general election in New York City, there were five boxes, one each for presidential electors, state offices, member of Congress, assembly district, and city and county races. S.R. no. 1269: Contested Congressional Election in the Eighth District of New York: M.D. no. 7, Pt. 1, p. 302. William E. Dodge vs. James Brooks, election held on November 8, 1864.

[33] S.R. no. 1199: Contested Congressional Election in the Third District of Pennsylvania: M.D. no. 26, pp. 101–3, 114–16, 134–6. John Kline vs. Leonard Myers, election held on October 14, 1862. Also see S.R. no. 1199: Contested Congressional Election in the Fifth District of Pennsylvania: M.D. no. 17, pp. 84, 110–11, 131. Charles W. Carrigan vs. M. Russell Thayer, election held on October 14, 1862. Even under the multi-box system, there was often just one physical box. For example, at one Pennsylvania precinct, there was a box, three feet long, fourteen inches high, and about a foot wide, with three holes in the top for national, state, and county offices, respectively. At another precinct, the box was very large: six feet long, nine inches square, and divided into eight compartments (pp. 136, 146–7). For descriptions of other types of boxes, see pp. 152, 158.

the one they supported. This tactic in effect separated that candidate from any party slate.

Perhaps the major change from the single-box system was that the voted tickets left no record of these strategies. Since each of the several boxes in the multi-box system held tickets of only one type, it was not possible to determine how voters who voted for one candidate, say, for Congress, voted for other offices. It was also not possible to reconstruct the strategies of party agents who offered tickets to voters coming to the polls. In a single-box system, irregular, printed tickets left behind physical evidence of preparation and distribution outside party channels and, thus, of an organized insurgency. If supporters of a Democratic candidate for Congress, for example, distributed irregular tickets naming Republicans for every office except Congress, those tickets would show up during the counting of the vote. Under a multi-box system, the counting of the tickets could uncover no evidence of such a strategy.[34] Whether this difference, in fact, made irregular election strategies more common than under single-box systems is hard to say, but it appears to have changed, at least slightly, the sociology of the polls. Negotiations between voters and the distributors of tickets were, for example, more subtle and complex in multi-box elections where bundles of tickets were given out to voters.

Poll Books

When voters presented themselves and handed in their tickets, one of the election judges would ask their names. The most important duty of election clerks was to record these names in poll books that, in turn, provided evidence both as to the identity of those who voted (thus preventing men from voting twice in an election) and as to the number of those who voted (as a control on the number of tickets voted by these men). However, there were several problems with this system. First, spelling was erratic because the clerks received the names of voters orally, usually secondhand from the judges who had asked the voters their names at the window. Uncommon names, particularly those of immigrants from Southern or Eastern Europe, were often phonetically interpreted by clerks in ways that defied any precise connection with the person who had presented himself at the polls; for many names thus set down in the poll books, it was simply impossible, once the election had been completed, to say that the entries evidenced that a particular person had actually voted. This problem was compounded by the fact that many nineteenth-century voters were illiterate and thus could not

---

34   This is not entirely true. The "county" or "state" ticket," for example, could have more than one candidate on it if more than one office at that level of government were at stake in the election; in such cases, irregular tickets could still appear at the polls, along with other strategies typical of single-box systems.

spell their names for election judges.[35] A third difficulty operated from the opposite direction: The names of some men were so common that precise identification of particular individuals was impossible.[36]

Aggravating both problems was the fact that the polls were sometimes very busy, so busy that the writing down of names was precluded altogether. At one polling place in Baltimore, for example, 246 voters presented themselves in the first eighteen minutes after the window had been opened. As the clerk of election later testified, it was simply "a matter of impossibility" to record their names. After consulting the election judges, the clerks made simple checks or scratch marks next to the numbers in the poll books, thereby indicating that someone had voted.[37] And, as with many things in and around the polling place, this kind of congestion could be manipulated to advantage by the party organizations. In Baltimore, for example, an experienced election judge in the Thirteenth Ward testified that an elderly leader of the Americans was "walking about the street [during the 1859 election]...[he] hallowed every now and then, 'Now's your time; natives wade in'; and every time that created an excitement and rush to the window." By this, the judge interpolated, the American leader meant, "Now press in, boys; force in your votes, if possible, under the excitement."[38] For all these reasons, poll books often did very little to discourage men from voting more than once at different polls or even at one very busy polling place. Nonetheless, election

[35] Part of the problem was that people were often much less concerned with the spelling of their own surnames than would be the case today. This was a perennial difficulty for those who prepared city directories, as this following excerpt from an editor's preface illustrates: "Absolute correctness in a Directory is unattainable. Most frequent are errors in the orthography of names, and they are generally attributable to the fact, that different members of a family frequently spell their name in different ways. This is especially the case with some of the descendants of our immigrant population, who, in far too many cases, regardless of the sacred duty of preserving their family names inviolate, change them to suit their own tastes, or to facilitate pronunciation, without using the means provided by law, for doing so." *Columbus City Directory for 1880* (Columbus, Ohio: G. J. Brand, 1880).

[36] Attorneys for the defendant in one election case contended: "In a large city, and amongst the Irish population particularly, how many persons are found bearing the same names? By a reference to the [city] directory, it will be found that there are persons by the half score and score bearing the names found upon the poll-books. It would be, therefore, idle to rely upon such testimony [as to the identity of particular individuals]." *Brief of the Argument by Cooper & Marshall, for Mr. Barrett* in S.R. no. 1062: Contested Congressional Election in the First District of Missouri: M.D. no. 8, p. 42. Frank P. Blair, Jr., vs. J. R. Barrett, election held in August 1858.

[37] S.R. no. 962: Contested Congressional Election in the Third District of Maryland: M.D. no. 68, p. 231. William Pinkney Whyte vs. J. Morrison Harris, election held on November 4, 1857. Similar congestion was reported to have occurred at a Philadelphia precinct just after the polls opened and later during the "dinner hour." S.R. no. 1431: M.D. no. 7 (1868): pp. 37–8. Morning congestion was also reported in Cincinnati. S.R. no. 1431: M.D. no. 16 (1868): p. 112.

[38] S.R. no. 1060: M.D. no. 4 (1859): pp. 143–5.

clerks assiduously kept these records, forwarding them to the county along with summary accounts of the votes cast at the precinct.

Poll Taxes

Many states imposed poll taxes as a requirement for voting; in effect, they were a capita tax on adult males. These taxes influenced the polling place in several ways. They could, for example, be costly to poor men, thus discouraging their participation in elections. However, party organizations often paid the levy.[39] In 1862, poll taxes in Pennsylvania were as low as twenty-five cents. This was sufficiently inexpensive that the major deterrent to voting was the sheer inconvenience of making a trip to the county assessor.[40] As in other things, the party organizations stepped into the breach; agents for one of the major parties sometimes paid the taxes for individuals they knew to be loyal partisans and delivered the receipts to the voters. For the very poor, for whom the tax was both inconvenient and prohibitively costly, party agents would foot the bill in anticipation that their solicitude would be rewarded at the polls. For some voters, such as the residents of a county poor farm, the payment of the poll tax was merely a technical requirement for voting men who were already largely dependent on an elected party official (the steward of the farm). In many instances, these men did not even know how much their tax had been or who had paid the levy. In most cases, poll taxes did not so much discourage voting as strengthen party organizations as party agents mediated the satisfaction of eligibility requirements and subsequently, as a by-product, monitored the participation of individual voters in an election.

At the polls, election officials used the tax assessor's roll (a record of poll tax receipts) as a check against whether or not voters had paid the levy and, thus, were qualified to vote. The tax assessor's roll could also be used as proof of residency, in effect becoming a primitive registration list.[41] However, a

[39] See, for example, Summers, *The Plundering Generation*, p. 60.
[40] Although many caveats must attend the estimate, the average daily wage for an adult male in manufacturing in the East in 1862 was probably around $1.50 or so. That would have made the poll tax roughly equivalent to one-sixth of the daily wage. For the daily wage of all manufacturing workers in the East and a brief discussion of gender and age differentials in the manufacturing sector, see Clarence D. Long, *Wages and Earnings in the United States: 1860–1890* (Princeton, N.J.: Princeton University Press, 1960), pp. 104–8, 132–3. Table A-3 in this source reported the daily wage for all workers in manufacturing as $1.32 in 1862.
[41] S.R. no. 1199: M.D. no. 17 (1862): pp. 53–6, 60, 101, 115–16. In the 1868 election, a Republican clerk at one of the Philadelphia polling places complained that sixty-one men voted whose names were not on the tax assessor's roll. Much of the difficulty arose from inaccuracies in the list (e.g., misspelled names) or illegible entries. Many of these men voted after having been "vouched for" by Democratic election officials. S.R. no. 1431: M.D. no. 7 (1868): pp. 35–6. Also see pp. 65, 84–5. It should be noted that the tax assessor's roll could demonstrate only residency and payment of the poll tax. With respect to other eligibility requirements, including proof that a man was a citizen

man who did not appear on the roll could still vote if he presented a tax receipt, indicating payment of the poll tax, or swore an oath that he had paid the tax.[42] In addition, the tax assessor's roll usually possessed the same kinds of spelling and identity problems that plagued the poll books. As a result, the roll only partially discouraged voting irregularities at the polling place.

Property Qualifications

By the middle of the nineteenth century, property qualifications had been abolished almost everywhere in the United States except in Rhode Island, where they were imposed on foreign-born voters, and in New York, where blacks had to possess a "freehold estate of the value of $250" before they could vote.[43] The New York requirement remained in force up until passage of the Fifteenth Amendment and was still operating after the Civil War had ended. David Redfield, a Republican inspector of election at Tompkin's Hotel at Mape's corner, described how this freehold requirement worked in the 1868 congressional election. About a dozen black men had voted and every one of them had voted Republican. When challenged by Democrats, each voter swore before election officials that he owned enough property to meet the suffrage requirement. Although Redfield believed that they were all qualified to vote, their oath was the only evidence any of them presented at the polls.[44] Since the law stated that the property a black man held had to be worth at least $250, these voters could not simply produce a deed demonstrating ownership; the oath was required to back up the voter's claim that his property was worth that much money.

On the Marking of Tickets

Party organizations and their agents monitored their ostensible supporters in many different ways. When they supplied voters with tickets at the polling place, for example, all they had to do was follow those voters as they made

or had reached twenty-one years of age, the roll either contained no information or was not conclusive.

[42] As with most eligibility requirements, enforcement was sometimes lax. At one precinct, for example, a man was allowed to cast a ticket even though he had not paid his taxes. A Republican serving as an election official told his colleagues that he "would let him go, and he [the official's name was Cadwallader] would see the tax was paid; he did not pay it at the time." S.R. no. 1199: M.D. no. 17 (1862): pp. 173–4.

[43] South Carolina also imposed a requirement of a freehold of 50 acres or a town lot if a man had not been a resident of an election district for six months. Keyssar, *Right to Vote*, pp. 29, 130–1, 330–5.

[44] Regardless of whether they were challenged, black men were required to swear a separate oath based on this property qualification. S.R. no. 1402: M.D. no. 27, Pt. 1 (1868): pp. 90, 92–3.

their way to the voting window and handed in their tickets.[45] Strong partisans often made this task easy by waving their tickets over their heads as they moved through the crowd. Other men, however, would conceal their tickets, folding them in their hands or putting them in their pockets. For these voters, there was no guarantee that the ticket turned into the judge was the one they had picked up from the party agent. Concealment presented major problems to those agents who had provided voters with material favors of one sort or another in return for the promise of their support. Party challengers, of course, stood by the voting window and could monitor the ticket once it reappeared, but they still needed some way of telling one folded ticket from another.

Although they often traded places back and forth with those distributing tickets at the polls, challengers themselves seldom distributed tickets to voters.[46] Although an explanation for this separation of roles never appeared in the hearings, the most important factor was probably that the sometimes extended negotiations between party agents and voters that attended the distribution of tickets, if carried on by challengers, would have been both dilatory and awkward. Negotiations with voters, if conducted by challengers, would have been dilatory in that they would have held up the voting by other men. Standing just before the window, a voter carrying on a conversation with one or the other of the party challengers would have made access to the window difficult for other voters. The combination of roles would also have been awkward because the bargaining between voter and agent would have necessarily taken place in the presence of a challenger belonging to the opposition party (who usually stood just a few feet away on the other side of the window). The conversation between agent and voter would have entailed

---

[45] One of the most extreme examples of such monitoring occurred at one of the precincts in Wayne County, Indiana, in the 1868 congressional election. The polls were fairly crowded, and Albert Prescott, who was very interested in having James Buhl vote a straight Republican ticket, closely watched Buhl's every move as he made his way to the election judges. As they stood in line for about fifteen minutes, Prescott was just in front of Buhl, who had his arm extended over Prescott's shoulder, holding his ticket so Prescott could see it at all times. Buhl seems to have been just as interested in Prescott's vote, because he was monitoring the latter's ticket in a similar fashion. S.R. no. 1432: M.D. no. 15 (1868): pp. 127–8.

[46] Samuel Brent, a Democratic partisan in Mount Vernon, Ohio, gave a typical description of this interchangeability of roles. "The evening before the election it was arranged in General Morgan's office, by the candidates interested, that, among others who were to be at the polls, I was to be there with a list of the democratic voters in the township, furnished me by the democratic candidate for judge, and as the voters were called it was my duty to check them off on this list, which I did for a time. At other times I relieved the person appointed to keep the poll, and sometimes I challenged votes, being at the polls from the time of opening till closing, except about an hour at noon." S.R. no. 1313: Contested Congressional Election in the Thirteenth District of Ohio: M.D. no. 38, Pt. 2, p. 212. Columbus Delano vs. George W. Morgan, election held on October 9, 1866.

an open declaration of the voter's support, almost certain to provoke at least a counter-offer or argument from the opposing challenger or a challenge on grounds of bribery or some other infraction. Because negotiations between party agents and men approaching the polls would be embarrassing, if made public, ticket distributors tended to hover around the perimeter of the crowd of men surrounding the window.[47] They rarely operated very close to the window itself.

One of the more complicated transactions occurred in the town of Minnisink, New York, during the 1868 congressional election. Peter Belcher, a farm hand employed by a man named Colonel Wisner, had heard a rumor that $800 "came in town" just before the election and that $10 would be offered to each man who voted the Republican ticket. On the day of the election, Belcher approached one of the Republican agents, George Schoonover, and asked him whether the rumor was true. Schoonover and another Republican, Henry Wadsworth, took Belcher into a tavern and treated him while they discussed the matter. During this conversation, Belcher described himself as a Republican but also a poor man who deserved some of the money that was in play. In addition, he told them that he was afraid to vote the Republican ticket because Colonel Wisner, his landlord, was a staunch Democrat.

Strengthening his case for a larger bribe, Belcher added that Wisner had promised him "a present" if he voted a straight Democratic ticket.[48] Wisner, in fact, was working the polls for the Democrats at the same time Belcher was negotiating with the Republicans. For this reason, Schoonover and Wadsworth prepared Democratic tickets for Belcher, leaving intact the Democratic headings so that they would be recognizable but scratching off the Democratic candidates and writing in Republican names in their place. However, Schoonover balked at the price of Belcher's vote. Belcher told him, "I would vote the Grant ticket for $10; he asked me if $3 wouldn't be big in my eyes."

The polls in Minnisink were located in a room above the tavern. After he had negotiated a price with Schoonover ($6 or $10; it isn't clear), Belcher was taken outside under a nearby "horse-shed" where the tickets were prepared and the money changed hands. After that, Belcher went back into the tavern and up the stairs. Although he passed through the room where votes were being taken, he continued through a series of doors until he reached a back room where he knew Democratic agents, including Colonel Wisner, would

[47] In Mount Hope, New York, the 1868 congressional election was held in the back room of Osmer Green's tavern. Out in front of the tavern, about five or six feet from the front stoop, a Republican ticket distributor conducted his negotiations with incoming voters, offering five-dollar bills along with their tickets. S.R. no. 1402: M.D. no. 27, Pt. 1 (1868): pp. 176–7.

[48] Belcher later that day received a dollar from Colonel Wisner; he described this as a loan.

be. There were four Democrats in the room, five including Belcher. Belcher showed them his "counterfeited" tickets and the bribe. One of the Democrats gave Belcher clean tickets in exchange and Belcher went to the polls and voted them.

This account, pulled out of Belcher in an extended interrogation and partially corroborated by Wadsworth, would seem to be a case of political entrapment, a snare arranged by the Democrats.[49] Supporting such an interpretation was the fact that the Democrats after the election offered $100 to anyone who would swear an affidavit that they had taken a bribe from the Republicans at this precinct. On the other hand, Belcher was illiterate and probably not capable of the complex machinations that this plot – if it was a plot – required. In that case, an alternative explanation could be that, after receiving the Republican bribe, he became frightened that Colonel Wisner would discover his defection and throw him off his farm. Thus Belcher could have been (and probably was) afraid of his employer, could have accepted a Republican bribe in good faith, and, just a short time later (possibly after encountering the Colonel in the upstairs polling place), could have reneged on this bribe by cooperating with the Democrats. Whatever the truth of the matter, Belcher had received money from both parties in return for his vote.

Most challengers became adept (or so they claimed) at recognizing even small differences in the coloring or texture of competing party tickets. Much of this variation was unintentional; the size and shape of tickets offered at the polls varied quite a bit simply because there was little or no coordination between the parties. Given the absence of standardization, in fact, it would have been surprising if the tickets offered to voters had been similar in appearance. Even so, parties sometimes intentionally designed their tickets so that they could be readily distinguished from those used by the opposition. Since differences in color and size were features easily spotted, even from a distance, they were common ways in which tickets were marked.

There were several reasons for marking a ticket. First, distinguishing features were intended as aids to illiterate voters who might otherwise mistakenly vote for the opposition. Since tickets were sometimes left in piles unattended by party officials, illiterate voters could pick up and vote a ticket belonging to the party they opposed if there were not some way of distinguishing between them. Party agents distributing tickets at the polls were also not above misrepresenting their offerings if they thought voters could not detect the deception. For the purposes of reducing deception or voter error, a masthead in the form of a vignette or portrait would serve almost as

---

49   Wadsworth corroborated both the conversations between Belcher and the two Republicans and the preparation of the tickets. He refused to answer the question of whether he had paid Belcher a bribe. S.R. no. 1402: M.D. no. 27, Pt. 1 (1868): pp. 193–5, 198–9.

well as color or size, and, in fact, mastheads were the most frequently used method of distinguishing tickets.[50]

However, parties also marked tickets in order to facilitate bribery or intimidation. One of the more interesting cases involved a Republican party agent, Charles H. Coe, who had entered into extended negotiations with three members of a family in Knox County, Ohio. Coe had apparently bribed the mother of a man who had just reached twenty-one years of age and was thus eligible to vote for the first time. He began his testimony in the third person, disguising the fact he was the one who had bribed her.

> I know the gentleman who offered Mrs. Beach $10 to make a Union man out of her son William [S. Beach, a hotel-keeper in Centreburg, Knox County]. Before she was entitled to the $10 his ticket was to be marked, to satisfy the gentleman who offered her the $10 that he did vote the Union ticket. I marked the ticket myself; also gave one to his father, marked, written on the back of them, "our country." The ticket the son voted was written straight; the one the old gentleman voted was written backwards. It was done in order to keep them from gouging, as we knew the old gentleman was a Union man, for fear he would vote the marked ticket that was marked for his son, and then Mrs. Beach claim the $10. When the votes were counted out of the box, the tickets were both there....

Coe marked the father's ticket because he did not want to pay for a vote that would have been cast for the Republicans without a bribe. He was afraid that the father would have taken the son's ticket and cast it himself. The son then would have voted any way he wished and the mother still would have pocketed the money. This was a little too much for the attorney for the Democratic candidate, who rather sardonically asked, "Have the goodness to state the name of the pious person whose anxiety for the morals of Young Beech [*sic*] induced him to give Mrs. Beech [*sic*] $10 to get her son to vote the republican ticket." Coe readily admitted that he had

> offered it myself.... I didn't pay any bribe. I made her a present of $5 for keeping her son as pure as she did, and am to pay the other $5, or make her a present of $5, when he (William) keeps entirely from the bad company that he was about to fall in with. The mother always told me her son was a Union man.

Despite the mother's attestation, Coe had suspected that young Beach was about to stray from the party fold.

> I had heard the son (William) say that he wouldn't vote for Columbus Delano or any other man that was in favor of niggers voting.... There were [in the bad company he was keeping] two or three of his associates that frolicked and caroused around,

---

[50] However, even in a hotly contested election the parties sometimes fielded very similar tickets. See, for example, S.R. no. 1060: M.D. no. 4 (1859): pp. 125–6. Since a party's tickets could vary in form when cast in the same polling place, there was, of course, no reason for them to be identical in shape from precinct to precinct. And, in fact, they varied quite a bit (pp. 234–40).

who were democrats, and he was inclined to run with them. . . . [They were a] young blacksmith – I don't know his name; he works with Higgins; Ira Barr, who made his boasts that he was going to make a democrat of him. . . . We did not know how he stood, nor what his politics were; but we saw him often in bad company, and feared he would be led astray, and this was done in order to bring him in the way he should go at an early day [i.e., in his first election].

And he had indeed gone astray. When Coe examined young Beach's ticket when the votes were counted,

Columbus Delano's name was so badly erased the ticket was worn through; also our Union candidate for sheriff, (Steele) Cassell, the candidate for auditor and probate judge, were all erased with pencil mark, and no insertions.

As a result, Coe paid the mother only $5 because she had not "accomplished her work [in that William] voted a Union ticket with more than one-half erased."[51]

While Coe's negotiations had been conducted away from the polling place on a day prior to the election, most bribes were settled on within sight of the voting window while men were turning in their tickets. These transactions were often facilitated by manufacturing tickets of a distinctive color or size.[52] Because these features were easily seen at a distance, they aided the party in making sure either that those they had bribed actually executed their part of the transaction or that those who otherwise favored their candidates were enabled to vote. Waving the marked ticket over their heads, voters supporting the dominant party would be given easy passage to the voting window. Once there, the party's challengers would give them every assistance in meeting the questions of election judges. Lacking this "safe conduct" pass, voters of the weaker party would find the crowd around the voting window comparatively hostile and opposition party agents ready to challenge their qualifications.

In antebellum Baltimore, American party gangs so thoroughly dominated the area around many precincts that possession of a red-striped ballot was the only way a voter could reach the voting window. Other voters were simply shoved aside or, in many cases, violently assaulted. In such situations, the weaker party was compelled either to abandon the contest or resort to

---

[51]   S.R. no. 1313: Contested Congressional Election in the Thirteenth District of Ohio: M.D. no. 38, Pt. 1, pp. 32–6. Columbus Delano vs. George W. Morgan, election held October 9, 1866.

[52]   Distinctive tickets could also facilitate intimidation. For example, in 1844 colored tickets were evidently used in order to monitor voting by mill workers in Fayetteville, North Carolina. Whiggish mill owners had told their employees that a Democratic victory would force their factories to close and, just in case workers were still inclined to stray, use of colored tickets made secret voting impossible. Harry L. Watson, *Jacksonian Politics and Community Conflict: The Emergence of the Second American Party System in Cumberland County, North Carolina* (Baton Rouge: Louisiana State University Press, 1981), pp. 285–6.

subterfuge, mimicking the color and form of the dominant party's ticket.[53] In some elections, however, a party might use a variety of mastheads. For example, in Coshocton, Ohio, the opposition Democratic party provided tickets with five different devices, one that pictured an eagle as a phoenix rising from a fire and four more: "Two of them had the American eagle upon them; one a semi-hemisphere with a flag floating from its apex; the other the temple of liberty. Then there were some we cut out of a newspaper." In such an election, imitation would be impractical because party agents would not be able to visually distinguish between their own and opposition tickets in any case.[54]

In all these ways, the material ticket shaped the sociology of the polling place as a symbolic affirmation of a voting intention. As a focus for negotiation between a party agent and a voter, the ticket was marked, distributed, and monitored. As a focus of contestation between the parties, the ticket was the pivot on which a challenge might be launched. Never, in the thousands upon thousands of accounts of challenges made before the voting window, did a party challenger impeach the qualifications of one of his party's supporters. Thus, the effectiveness of a challenger in advancing his party's interests depended to a large extent on how well he could distinguish between tickets carried to the window by voters.

Counting the Tickets

Election day ended with the counting of the votes, usually in the same room as that in which the votes had been received.[55] In one sense, the tabulation of votes lies outside the scope of this study; most ordinary voters had gone home and the proceedings were almost entirely in the hands of party agents and election officials. However, from another perspective, the casting of tickets by ordinary voters was but a prelude to the actual voting. For one thing, the

---

[53] In the vernacular of the polling place, these were sometimes called "mongrel" tickets. An election inspector in Goshen, New York, stated that such tickets "are almost always found at the polls." S.R. no. 1402: M.D. no. 27, Pt. 1 (1868): pp. 81, 89. Imitation tickets became so common in California that the state legislature passed a law requiring that "every ticket be of paper, uniform in size, color, weight, texture, and appearance." The legislature also required that each party register their masthead design with election officials, prohibiting anyone other than that party from using the vignette on tickets. Philip J. Ethington, *The Public City: The Political Construction of Urban Life in San Francisco, 1850–1900* (New York: Cambridge University Press, 1994), pp. 228–9, 291. Also see Glenn C. Altschuler and Stuart M. Blumin, *Rude Republic: Americans and Their Politics in the Nineteenth Century* (Princeton, N.J.: Princeton University Press, 2000), pp. 75–7. Imitation tickets were particularly useful in challenging the dominant party's hold on patronage employees. See, for example, S.R. no. 962: M.D. no. 68 (1857): p. 809.

[54] S.R. no. 1313: M.D. no. 38, Pt. 2 (1866): p. 387.

[55] For a description of the procedures and practices associated with voting and counting the votes in Philadelphia, see S.R. no. 1431: M.D. no. 7 (1868): p. 124.

acts of voting that took place during the hours when the polls were open created the context within which the counting of tickets took place; when disputes arose over whether or not certain tickets should be counted, the plausibility of alternative interpretations was usually grounded in what had transpired during the day when the tickets had been cast. In addition, the resolution of those disputes sometimes involved creative counting methods that partially vitiated what must have been the actual tally.[56]

An extreme example of such creative counting occurred in the First Ward in New York City on November 2, 1858. The election was held in a tavern that day. The voting had been carried out in a small back room that had been divided by a screen. Voters passed through the bar on their way to and from this partitioned space. In his testimony, William Stokley, one of the canvassers, described the enclosed area in which the voting and counting occurred as about "ten feet wide by nineteen feet long.... [A two-foot-wide] table [holding the ballot boxes] was in the middle of the room...against the partition, and we [the election officials] behind the table...." Although the bar was closed to paying customers, liquor passed freely between the barroom and the men inside this space both during the hours when the polls were open and afterward when the counting of the tickets was conducted. Stokley, by his own admission, was not a teetotaler:

I drank on that day when I thought I wanted it; I did not go out during the canvass to drink, but did drink; did not leave my seat, there was plenty of drink around me – a row of glasses, seven or eight; if I had drank all of it I should have been unable to stand; took all that was offered to me and put it on the floor behind me; it was a pretty jolly time; that is, if you understand what it is to be jolly on election night.... My share of that jollity was not so pleasant; I had some six glasses on the floor; I don't think I swallowed a spoonful in all; I meant to keep sober, and they wanted to get me drunk.

[56] One of the most common problems encountered was a discrepancy between the number of votes cast and the number of names that had been written upon the poll books. Where there were too few votes, election officials simply assumed that some voters had not voted for that office or offices. This assumption was probably incorrect, but at least it was plausible. Where there were too many votes, there was no obvious explanation (unless duplicate tickets were discovered folded up with each other). The way most officials solved this problem was to put all the tickets back in the box and randomly draw out the requisite number of excess votes. These tickets were then destroyed and the count was appropriately adjusted. But other methods of reconciling the totals were also used. In one Pennsylvania election, for example, Isaac Hurst, an election clerk, simply "ate up thirteen tickets, to make it come out even with the other election.... He didn't tell me what kind of tickets, whether republican or democrat; he just said he ate them." Since Hurst had only one arm, he pulled on folded tickets with his teeth in order to open them up when the votes were counted. This practice seems to have led naturally to his eating them in order to correct the count. S.R. no. 1431: Contested Congressional Election in the Twenty-first District of Pennsylvania: M.D. (no number, bound between nos. 24 and 25), p. 48. John Covode vs. Henry D. Foster, election held on October 13, 1868.

One of the other witnesses also reported that Stokley had been drinking "pretty freely" both during the day and that night, "He had taken plenty; [but was] not exactly overpowered, so far as I know."[57]

After midnight, as the counting proceeded, a dispute arose over the origin of twenty-four tickets for the congressional race that had mysteriously appeared in the ballot box in which only votes for a judicial election were supposed to have been placed. These twenty-four tickets were, according to the poll books kept by the clerks, in excess of the number of tickets that had been cast during the day. Stokley, who had been carefully observing the counting process, accused one of the participants of having planted the tickets:

I saw the hand of a man on the board [of the table], his other hand hold of the front of the chairman's hat, pulling it over his eyes; at that moment the box was emptied over this man's hand, the tickets emptied out of the judiciary box. I objected at the time. I said you will find more tickets there than that box calls for, I guarantee. It was a pleasant little time; bad language used, swearing, revolvers out. . . . It lasted some time, two or three hours. . . . From the time we commenced our canvass till we got through it was one continuous trouble.

The room was full of people. The space could not hold more than ten or so and those that could not get inside stood in the entrance. Nothing separated spectators from the election officials except the narrow table in the center of the room. These spectators, in Stokley's words, "could very easily reach either of us [the canvassers]." On several occasions, Stokley sent to the station house, requesting a detachment of officers in order to clear the room. At times there were almost a dozen or so officers in attendance but at other times there were none at all. Whenever the police left, "the row began again, the men coming back a little more drunk." The dispute over the surplus ballots apparently erupted during one of the periods when the officers were absent from the room:

The revolvers were drawn upon each other, and general threats were made; but the spite was pitched upon me. I was called modestly a know-nothing, and told that I ought not to live, because I insist on my country not being disfranchised, and am in favor of Americans holding office – [that I] would starve them [immigrants] if I could . . . they [the Democrats] insisted on Mr. Sickles having these 24 votes. . . . [There were] thirty or forty outside clamorous; every man who could get into the door shook his fist at me; can't tell how many threatened my life; there was a knife brandished over the head of a man that I saw, but he could not reach me if he wanted to; only one door to get in at, and that was always full . . . sometimes you would not see the men, only the arm or hand. I saw three revolvers at one time. I can't name the persons who held [them]. . . . They threatened to kill me if I didn't sign [the official statement

---

57 S.R. no. 1103: Contested Congressional Election in the Third District of New York: M.D. no. 6, pp. 54–5, 73–4, 122–3, 146. Amor J. Williamson vs. Daniel E. Sickles, election held on November 2, 1858.

of votes cast at that polling place]. I shouldn't leave the room alive without I did sign it.

In the midst of this violent and threatening display, Stokley secretly instructed one of the clerks to append a protest to the statement of votes and then ended the controversy by signing the document.[58]

In other precincts, where the parties had reached a detente of sorts, the process through which the ballots were counted was more mundane.[59] After the 1860 congressional election in Philadelphia, for example, the process of counting the ballots began as soon as the polls were closed. The judge of election and the two inspectors opened the ballot boxes and laid out the tickets. They then placed the tickets in piles. For each of the parties, there was a pile for "straight" or "full" tickets (those in which none of the candidates had been erased or marked off). There were additional piles for tickets that had been "split" in one way or another; the usual way in this particular election was for a "sticker" with another candidate's name to have been pasted in one of the places where the regular party nominee had appeared.[60] But split tickets could also be created by marking out the regular nominee and writing in an alternative candidate. Similarly, voters could abstain with respect to a particular office simply by erasing the regular nominee's name and failing to indicate a choice. Because they usually constituted but a small fraction of all the votes cast, these split tickets, whatever their form, were set aside at the beginning of the count.

Once the tickets were separated into piles, the full tickets for each of the parties were counted into groups of ten. Each group was counted at least twice, the first time by an election official affiliated with one party and a second time by someone affiliated with the other party. At the end of the second counting, the stack of ten was "twisted" in such a way that the ballots adhered to each other and the clerks were instructed to mark a large "X" on the tally sheet. That "X" indicated ten votes for every candidate on the party ticket; as can be seen, this procedure considerably simplified the canvassing in that only one tabulation was required for recording the vote of many offices. The split tickets (also called "scratched" or "slip" tickets, depending on how the voter marked his choice) were then counted individually and similarly bundled. However, since split tickets were much less numerous, these bundles usually held fewer than ten tickets. While the counting process

[58]   S.R. no. 1103: M.D. no. 6 (1858): pp. 49, 54, 74, 109, 146.

[59]   At the end of voting, the election officials were usually very hungry and often ate before counting the votes. When they went to supper, they took the ballot box with them and monitored each other while dining. In one Indiana election, for example, the election inspector locked the ballot box and placed it alongside his chair while all of the officials ate at the same table. S.R. no. 1432: M.D. no. 15 (1868): pp. 61–3.

[60]   Because these stickers were usually colored, the tickets on which they were pasted were easily distinguished from the straight tickets.

was relatively simple, the multiple tabulations of each bundle and careful inspection of each ticket took a lot of time. In the third division polling place of the Sixteenth Ward, for example, the counting started at about 8:30 in the evening and was not finished until after midnight, when all the official papers had been signed and the bundled tickets had been placed back in the ballot boxes, which were then sealed.[61]

In Boston, the tickets were counted at hourly intervals while the polling place was open. The following account came from George W. Bail, a letter carrier and clerk of election in the Twelfth Ward (commonly known as South Boston):

The inspectors received the votes and checked the names of the voters as they voted; and after the close of the polls, counted those ballots that had not been previously counted. The warden and myself assorted and counted the votes during the day, and after they were counted I recorded them, as fast as I could, during the day...it was the intention to empty the ballot-boxes every hour; it might have varied a little either way. They were emptied on to a table by the inspectors; the table was directly in their rear, at which the warden and clerk sat.

Bail stated that there were at least seven different, printed tickets cast at this precinct. The two most common tickets contained the regular Democratic and Republican slates. In addition, there were tickets with the headings "constitutional union" and "independent people's," as well as another ticket headed as "democratic" with an eagle vignette and two labeled "people's." Each of these tickets presented different, sometimes overlapping, slates of candidates. In addition to "straight" (unaltered) tickets, there were also "scratched" tickets in which one or more of the candidates' names had been changed or erased. After dumping the ballot boxes out on the table, the tickets were sorted into piles, one for each of the types of unaltered tickets and one for each of the types of scratched tickets. When a pile reached a certain size (possibly ten, but Bail did not say what the threshold was), the tickets

[61] The third division of the Eleventh Ward and the first precinct of the Nineteenth Ward followed procedures almost identical to that described in the text; in both places, the counting was also not completed until after midnight. S.R. no. 1141: Contested Congressional Election in the Third District of Pennsylvania: M.D. no. 27, pp. 27–8, 31–2, 33, 35, 40–2, 44–6, 49, 56. John Kline vs. John P. Verree, election held on October 9, 1860. The laborious counting procedures meant that at least some of the officials spent a very long day at the polls. For example, one inspector in the Sixteenth Ward recalled that he had left home to go to the precinct between 7 and 8 o'clock in the morning and had been at the polls all day: "I hadn't anything [to eat] but what was provided by Mr. Murphy, the keeper of the house; that was before dinner, and it was what they call 'lunch.' [This was somewhere between 9 and 11 o'clock in the morning.]...I believe I had a drink whenever I felt like getting it, which was not very often." There was water in the room and, in addition, "spirituous liquors" were "brought in glasses...[I also had] pie and milk, but I can't say at what time; it was in the afternoon." However, he didn't remember any drinking while the tickets were counted (pp. 36–7).

of that type would be tied up and the number of votes so cast recorded by the clerk. The election officials posted the running count of these bundled votes on a blackboard, tallied in such a way that bystanders and, of course, the officials themselves could see what the voting had been up until the last hourly count.[62]

In Philadelphia, the ballot box was counted at hourly intervals in such a way that discrepancies between the number of tickets and the number of voters could be detected. As in Boston, the procedure for counting the tickets was quite elaborate, involving a second set of inspectors and clerks whose sole task was to tabulate the tickets at these hourly intervals. When voting was light and the precinct was heavily tilted toward one party, it was often possible to tell who had voted the minority ticket during the last period. At one precinct, for example, two of the Democratic election officials were known to have cast the only minority party ballots because no others showed up in the boxes. Under the 1861 law that mandated these hourly tabulations, the interim counts were to be publicly announced; thus, as in Boston, all partisans attending the polls were aware throughout the day of how the election was running at that precinct.[63]

Viva Voce Voting

In some states, such as Kentucky and Missouri, voters verbally announced their choices in the polling places instead of using tickets.[64] While the law required the voter to announce publicly his preferred choice for each race, practice varied quite a bit from the statutes. The primary reason for variance was that voters, whether or not they were literate, found it difficult to memorize the names of the candidates for office. As aids, the parties furnished

---

[62] S.R. no. 1198: Contested Congressional Election in the Third District of Massachusetts: M.D. no. 14, pp. 24–5. John S. Sleeper vs. Alexander H. Rice, election held on November 4, 1862. In Roxbury, Norfolk County, where the votes were also counted at hourly intervals, the "ward officers would take a portion [of the counted tickets] and put them in their pockets; if they were perfect [straight] ones the vote distributors [party agents outside the polling place] would come for them, and they would be given to them to use over again on the same day. The imperfect ones would be used for waste paper." This procedure meant that the same ticket could be legally cast several times in one election (p. 53).

[63] S.R. no. 1199: M.D. no. 17 (1862): pp. 57, 61–2, 95–6. The act required hourly tabulations only in the city of Philadelphia. Frederick C. Brightly, *A Digest of the Laws of Pennsylvania, 1700–1872* (Philadelphia: Kay & Brother, 1873), p. 582. For other examples of these hourly compilations of votes, see S.R. no. 1199: M.D. no. 26 (1862): pp. 97–100, 104–13, 117–33, 139–42.

[64] For a brief overview of viva voce voting in the United States, see Paul Bourke and Donald DeBats, *Washington County: Politics and Community in Antebellum America* (Baltimore: Johns Hopkins University Press, 1995), pp. 3–4, 6–13. The last states to abandon oral voting were Arkansas (in 1854), West Virginia (1861), Missouri (1863), Virginia (1867), Oregon (1872), and Kentucky (1891).

printed slates of candidates that could be read by the voter to election offi-cials. However, if a voter was illiterate, these printed slates were clearly of no use. In those cases, election officials accepted the printed slates as the voter's choices.[65] Most of the time election officials apparently accepted the simple declaration of the voter that he was voting for one of the party slates, implicitly naming each of the candidates on one of those slates. This method was faster because election clerks could simply record votes by party at the polls, later allocating the number of votes so cast to each of the candidates on the party slates. For voters, particularly illiterate ones, this practice dras-tically simplified the act of voting; all they had to do was name the party they supported.[66]

One election conducted by voice voting was held in August 1859 in the Big Glades precinct of Pulaski County, Kentucky. William H. Todd acted as sheriff, a position roughly equivalent to that of election judge in other states, and described how William Davis had voted:

William Davis . . . handed me his ticket, entire democratic, including Chrisman's name for Congress, and I cried the ticket democratic [without naming the individual can-didates on the ticket]. . . . I asked Mr. Davis who he voted for, and he handed me the democratic ticket; he did not call out the names, but remarked, here's my vote; all the votes were taken in this way, except when they failed to vote the entire ticket of either party.[67]

[65] For example, see the following testimony from William R. Bowman, of Boyle County, Kentucky: "My politics are democratic; I voted with a ticket at the election; I went to town late in the evening, and went into Mr. Burton's store, and called for two tickets; Mr. Staley, a democrat, was with me. Mr. David Gregory handed me two tickets and I handed one to Staley and I told Mr. Gregory to scratch off Chrisman's name from mine, and add Josh. Owens' name for senator. He did so; I took the ticket, handed it in at the polls, and told them I voted that ticket. It had Chrisman's name scratched off; I called no names at the polls at all. . . ." S.R. no. 1063: M.D. no. 11 (1859): p. 64. Recognizing that mute voters would not be able to announce their choices, Virginia law allowed "dumb persons entitled to suffrage [to] vote by ballot." Munford, *Code of Virginia*, p. 39. In presidential elections, the voter was required to provide a ticket listing the electors for whom he wished to vote and, in addition, announce his choices before the election officials. His name was also written on the back of the ticket he voted (p. 84).

[66] This was, for example, the practice in Missouri. Outside the county of St. Louis, "the general system of conducting elections . . . is to take the votes *viva voce*, or by presenting a ticket to the judges of election, who hand it to an officer, whose duty it is to cry in an audible voice the names of the candidates voted for, and the offices for which they are voted, and the clerks make the proper entries in the poll-books, in accordance with that announcement, all of which is done in the presence and hearing of the voters." From a ruling by Judge James R. Lackland, St. Louis Circuit Court, Eighth Judicial Circuit of Missouri, September 10, 1858, S.R. no. 1062: M.D. no. 8 (1858): p. 13.

[67] S.R. no. 1061: Contested Congressional Election in the Fourth District of Kentucky: M.D. no. 3, p. 16. James S. Chrisman vs. William C. Anderson, election held on August 1, 1859. Also see p. 44.

The procedure at a precinct in Wayne County was roughly similar. There, as one of the judges of election recounted, the votes were generally given in by tickets that were received through a voting window. The sheriff then read the names of each of the candidates on the ticket. The major difference between that practice and a normal ticket system was that the choices were orally relayed to the clerks in a way that made known to bystanders the voter's choices and, incidentally, provided an opportunity for error on the part of the election official who announced those choices.[68]

Because viva voce voting entailed a very public display of a voter's preferences, we might naturally conclude that adoption of a ticket system would be motivated by a desire to make votes less visible. Although tickets were themselves open to public view, even if folded and handed directly to election judges, there were many ways in which voters and parties could frustrate the monitoring of votes by the opposition. So it was at least possible, in the words of a Missouri judge, that the ticket system enabled "indigent and dependent citizens [to] freely vote in secret without fear of injury from overbearing and oppressive landlords and employers." Having made that case, however, this judge went on to say why he believed that the employment of the ticket system in the city and county of St. Louis was not motivated by a desire for secrecy:

I put the policy of our ballot system upon other grounds which seem to me more consistent with the dignity and independence of the citizen. It is well known that the old viva voce method of voting as early as 1842, when this county and city contained a population of only some forty or fifty thousand, became too cumbersome and expensive to be allowed to remain; for although the polls were kept open for three consecutive days, it became almost impossible to take all the votes in that time.[69]

So it was logistical necessity, not the integrity of voting, that motivated the change from voice voting to tickets. This interpretation is strongly supported by the way in which the reform was instituted; when a voter turned in his ticket in St. Louis, the ticket would be marked with the number appearing next to his name in the poll books. Thus, every voter's choice could be identified when the votes were later counted. While the system may have made it marginally more difficult, compared with viva voce voting, for those outside the voting window to identify a voter's choice, the fact remained that election officials were fully aware of how all men voted.

The specific procedure under which viva voce elections were conducted probably had some impact on what is known as straight-ticket voting (in which the voter supported the same party's candidates from the top to the

---

[68] In this instance, a dispute arose over whether or not the sheriff had read the name of the Democratic candidate for Congress. S.R. no. 1063: M.D. no. 11 (1859): p. 644.

[69] From a ruling by Judge James R. Lackland, St. Louis Circuit Court, Eighth Judicial Circuit of Missouri, September 10, 1858, reprinted in S.R. no. 1062: M.D. no. 8 (1858): p. 14.

bottom of the ticket). Voters could deviate from a straight ticket in one of two ways: either by failing to cast votes for one or more races, usually toward the bottom of the ticket where candidates for minor offices were listed ("roll-off") or by voting for the opposition in one or more races ("splitting" the ticket). If voters, as seems to be the case in Kentucky, simply turned in a party ticket that was then read aloud to the clerks, there would seem to be little reason for voting behavior to differ much from procedures in which the voter turned in a party ticket that was deposited in a ballot box. But if voters were compelled to announce their vote orally, either from memory or by reading aloud from a party ticket, both roll-off and split-ticket voting might have increased dramatically, again compared with a ballot box procedure. Roll-off, in particular, would have been aggravated by failure to memorize adequately the names of candidates for minor offices. Split-ticket voting, less certainly, might have risen as voters tended to identify candidates who were familiar to them, regardless of party. Given the low literacy rate among white adult men in Kentucky, reliance on a paper party ticket, given by the voter to an election official, was probably a necessity if viva voce voting were to be conducted at all. But in Oregon, where literacy rates were much higher, elections may have been conducted in such a way that voters themselves announced their choices to officials.[70]

Liquor, Corruption, and Bribery

As men moved about the polling place, party agents would often offer them liquid refreshment, almost always whisky, as an enticement to vote their ticket. In some cases, these libations came out of a common jug or barrel. In others, the party agent would provide a small sum of money so that the voter could purchase his drink at a nearby saloon. In some cases, one or both of the parties offered almost unlimited drinks to voters who, as a result, were thoroughly inebriated by the time they turned in their ticket. One such man was Aaron Sharp, who resided in Mount Vernon, Ohio, when the 1866 congressional election was held. Although he didn't "claim to belong to any party in particular," Sharp also said that he had been inclined to vote for the Democratic candidate. However, Balivar Church, a friend of his, had spent the night before the election with him.[71] They evidently drank all that

---

[70] S.R. no. 1062: M.D. no. 8 (1858): pp. 11–12. Bourke and DeBats analyse both roll-off and ticket splitting in Oregon viva voce elections but do not describe how voters made their choices known to election officials. *Washington County*, pp. 201–8.

[71] As the following exchange indicates, Sharp's residence might have been a boarding house. "Q. Was there a girl at your house that helped you and Church drink the liquor? A. No sir; there was no liquor in the presence of the girl that I know of; the girl had gone to bed before we got there. Q. Did Church pay any particular attention to the girl that night? A. Not as I know of; the girl had gone to bed when we got home. Q. Was the girl understood to be a little easy in her virtue? A. I guess she had

night. About four in the morning, a Democrat named Bates came by Sharp's house, intending to accompany him to the polls. As Sharp put it, "Bates came to the door and waked me up, and I lighted a candle and let him in; we all three came down street together; Bates asked me when I came in to go down street with him, and Church said I wasn't going down until he went." Both Church and Sharp were feeling the "influence of [the liquor] considerably."

Church had evidently been pressuring Sharp to vote for the Republican nominee, and the three of them "went into the Kenyon house tavern." They continued to drink: "we had a big jug full; there were several together who had it ... I didn't see it paid for; I was called in to drink in the bar-room, and also in the alley, by the stable." The men who supplied the liquor "called themselves 'the boys in blue'" and the drinking was apparently sponsored by the Republican party. During this time, Bates and Church competed for Sharp's attention. "[Bates] wanted to speak with me; and he took me to one side once or twice, but Church followed us right up, and he (Bates) didn't get a chance to tell what he wanted." In the end, Church won this competition and Sharp "voted the ticket they call the 'boys in blue'; I didn't read the ticket; it had a picture on; Church told me that it was the right one, and I shoved her in; it didn't make much difference with me then how I voted."[72] But, as Sharp had earlier explained, he voted Republican only because he was drunk.

Although some men reported that they had been paid a hundred dollars or more for their votes, their accounts seem suspect. Individual votes were simply not worth more than a dollar or so in the vast majority of elections.[73]

---

that name. Q. What was her name? A. Sarah Black. Q. How long had she been at your house? A. I could not tell you exactly how long she had been there; she had been boarding there for three or four weeks, until the time she took sick." S.R. no. 1313: M. D. no. 38, Pt. 2 (1866): p. 223.

[72] When asked whether Bates kept "a 'doggery,'" Sharp replied that he "kept a grocery – yes, sir; a saloon, as it is called" where, in previous elections, Sharp had often drank before voting. But on this election day, Bates's "grocery" was closed for some reason and the Democrats were apparently not treating voters. Although Sharp did not say so explicitly, this seems to be the reason that Church was able to persuade him to vote the Republican ticket. The Republicans were treating voters and the Democrats weren't. S.R. no. 1313: M.D. no. 38, Pt. 2 (1866): p. 224.

[73] In a close election, however, the price of a man's vote could skyrocket. David Finch, a self-described "cripple," described how he had been approached in a saloon in Middletown, New York, on the day of the 1868 election. Late in the afternoon, three Democrats came down from the polls and urged him to vote. Finch told them he "didn't care" which party won because neither one suited him. Finally, after much coaxing, he agreed to go. The bidding apparently rose to over twenty-five dollars, at least that was what Finch said a Republican offered him not to go to the polls with the Democrats. In fact, even as Finch approached the voting window, this Republican was whispering in his ear that his offer was still good. S.R. no. 1402: M.D. no. 27, Pt. 1 (1868): pp. 156–7.

At least a dollar was the most common sum men reported as the going rate for votes at most precincts in the middle of the nineteenth century.[74] In lieu of cash, party agents sometimes gave voters a pair of shoes, pants, or bushels of corn.[75] In other cases, they paid men money in order to defray the alleged costs of their transportation to the polls. The small sums involved in all these instances, along with the at least remotely plausible explanations offered for their payment, tended to be accepted as a normal part of election day ritual. And while the practice was obviously rife with potential abuse, party agents would publicly, if reluctantly, acknowledge that their employers routinely gave them "walking around money" to be used at the polls on election day.[76]

Party agents usually knew the men whose votes they solicited and attempted to protect these men from those working for the opposition party. In 1866, for example, a Republican agent, J. W. Everich, shepherded a family of poor men to the polls in Zanesville, Ohio:

One, or both of the Wagners, told me that John English, John Taylor, and George W. Griffee were after them, trying to get them to vote the democratic ticket; that Griffee gave Jim a picture to do so; I told them to keep out of their road entirely and not to let them see them, and not let them buy their vote; they said they always voted the Union ticket; that they had never voted anything else but once [when] John Roberts hired the old man to vote the democratic ticket; brought them from the country in a

---

74   In his own research, Mark Summers concluded that most voters "would settle for a dollar or two, though ten dollars became the customary rate in New Jersey...." *The Plundering Generation: Corruption and the Crisis of the Union, 1849–1861* (New York: Oxford University Press, 1987), p. 56. More generally, see pp. 51–4. Although primarily concerned with election practices in the Gilded Age, also see John Reynolds, " 'The Silent Dollar': Vote Buying in New Jersey," *New Jersey History* 98 (Fall-Winter 1980): 191–211.

75   For example, John Sanders, of Deerpark, New York, swore that the Republicans had given him a pair of boots in return for his vote. S.R. no. 1402: M.D. no. 27, Pt. 1 (1868): p. 196. In Greensburg, Pennsylvania, a Republican similarly attempted to bribe a man with a pair of boots. S.R. no. 1431: M.D. (no number, bound between nos. 24 and 25 [1868]): p. 365. For a similar instance in which two brothers, former residents of a poorhouse and of borderline intelligence, were bribed with a pair of pantaloons and plug of tobacco, see p. 409. According to the Democratic ticket distributor at this polls, the Republican who enticed the brothers "threatened to shoot them if they did not keep their contract." For another example of shoes used as an enticement for political support, see Altschuler and Blumin, *Rude Republic*, p. 68.

76   Virginia, like all states, made the bribery of voters illegal. "If any free person, directly or indirectly, give to a voter, in any election, any money, goods or chattels, under an agreement, express or implied, that such voter shall give his vote for a particular candidate, such person shall be punished by fine not less than twenty nor more than one hundred dollars. And the voter receiving such money, goods or chattels in pursuance of such agreement, shall be punished in like manner with the person giving the same." In addition, all those convicted of bribery lost their right to vote. Munford, *Code of Virginia*, pp. 38, 811–12. However, as was the case with betting on the outcome of an election, such laws were simply unenforceable.

buggy and promised to give them a dollar, and wouldn't [pay them]; they done little chores for me, and I had given them presents heretofore, and if they would keep out of their road, and not allow any of them to buy them or cheat them by giving them a copperhead ticket, telling them it was a Union one, and wait for me until I called for them in the morning, I would give them each a sack of flour – not to vote the Union ticket, but because they were poor, and I could stand it.

Because Everich claimed the Wagners had always voted Republican, "unless stolen off by the other party," his intervention merely protected the purity of their vote.[77] The sacks of flour were but an act of charity that incidentally (albeit in a timely way) offset enticements that might be offered by the Democrats.[78] On the other hand, Everich considered any attempt by the Democrats to seduce these Republican voters to be a violation of interparty comity and thus immoral.

Although party agents often vigorously pursued their quarry, few were as industrious as a Republican named Marion Keever in Licking County, Ohio. One of his targets was a fifty-six-year-old lifelong Democrat named Daniel Bixler. Asked how large a family he had, Bixler responded as best he could: "they say I am the father of fourteen children. I have one wife." Although he acknowledged that it was "wrong" to sell his vote, Bixler was not afraid of going to the penitentiary and frankly admitted that he had "done it in order to get the pay." From his perspective, this kind of transaction was permissible for someone "in my condition...as I was poor." Bixler's knowledge of politics was even more impoverished than his pocketbook. When asked, "Which was you in favor of in 1864, Jeff. Davis or Lincoln?," he responded, "That is a hard question for me to answer."

The difficulty probably lay in the fact that he knew that Lincoln had been a Republican, and thus, in order to be consistent in his testimony, he should have chosen Lincoln's opponent. However, Jefferson Davis had not run against Lincoln, although this was implied in the question, leaving Bixler in a bit of a quandary. Keever had also exploited his ignorance by incorrectly describing the Democratic candidate for Congress, George W. Morgan, as "the rebel Morgan, the man who had the guerillas." By identifying the Democrat as the Confederate cavalry raider, Keever made Bixler's vote for the Republican Columbus Delano easier to solicit. Bixler's antipathy to the "rebel Morgan" also indicated that his willingness to entertain Jefferson Davis as a competitor to Lincoln did not originate in hostility to the Union cause during the Civil War.

---

[77] S.R. no. 1313: M.D. no. 38, Pt. 2 (1866): pp. 673–4.

[78] James O'Connor, a hotelkeeper in the town of Goshen, similarly reported that he received four barrels of flour from an anonymous donor, ostensibly for distribution to the poor (which he claimed to have done). In return, it was implied, the Republicans expected him to support their candidates. S.R. no. 1402: M.D. no. 27, Pt. 1 (1868): p. 182.

But Bixler's gullibility was best evidenced by the bargain he and Keever had struck. As Bixler recalled the transaction, Keever had come

down to my house and wanted to know if I was going to that election. I told him that I supposed I would; that I had hardly time. He said I had better go up; I told him I supposed I would some time during the day; then he wanted to know who I was going to vote for; I told him I didn't hardly know until I got up into town, and some man would give me a ticket that I could put dependence in; then he told me if I would vote for Delano he would give me five dollars, and he would pay me one dollar and a half for a corn basket which he said would make six dollars and a half; would buy me brick to build a chimney; also he said he would give me a tree of winter apples and ten or fifteen bushels of drying apples, and that three stores – Graves's, Moore's, and Conaway's – would give me seventy dollars for voting for Delano, and he would see that I got a due bill if I did not want to trade it all out at one time.... I went to the election with him.... He came after me in a buggy at my house.

Bixler dutifully voted for Delano. Since he could not read his ticket, he did not know whether or not he had voted for the rest of the Republican slate. But Keever evidently welched on his end of the bargain because Bixler reported, "He has not paid me anything only the apples." This was not surprising, of course, since Keever had offered far more than what was probably the going rate for a man's vote in that election.[79]

A. M. Stewart, a Democratic precinct worker also in Licking County, related an even more generous transaction than the bargain Bixler had made. This agreement involved a Samuel Spencer and his father-in-law, William Burns. After the election was over, Spencer had come to Stewart's house

on a visit ... we got to talking about Mr. Burns; I asked him if [Burns] had returned from the west; he said he had not, and was not going to. I asked him how he ... came to vote for Delano last fall; he answered me by saying, "I will tell you; I have never told anybody else, but will tell you." He said Burns, his father-in-law, told him that if he would vote for Delano he would give him the use of the little farm, the house, and garden, for twenty years free of rent, and a cow; and said he, "I was hard up, and I done it." ... [Prior to that, Samuel Spencer had been a] democrat always, from a boy up, an outspoken one; he told me also the cause of his [voting Republican] was that he was hard up and had no place ... he said he would never do it again; that he would see them all sunk in hell and the whole Burns family on top before he would do so again....[80]

Reading between the lines, the bargain described in this narrative was probably made in good faith. The father-in-law, wishing to move west, most likely wanted to leave the family farm in his son-in-law's hands regardless of how the latter voted. Although Burns was a Republican and probably had desired his party to win the congressional seat, the dominant motive in transferring

[79] S.R. no. 1313: M.D. no. 38, Pt. 2 (1866): pp. 30–1.
[80] Ibid., pp. 54–5.

control of the farm to his son-in-law was probably to provide for his daughter, who had apparently not married well. The election agreement was merely an accessory to this transfer. On its face, however, this bargain was just as ridiculously one-sided as Bixler's negotiation had been.

In the same election, John Evans described how he himself had been persuaded to vote for Delano. Realizing that Evans was a Democrat, James Wright had taken a Democratic ticket and pasted a sticker with Delano on it over the name of George W. Morgan, the Democratic candidate. He then approached Evans and "said Mr. Delano had a very nice buck, and I [Evans] have a very nice ewe, and I might take it up and put it to his buck." Wright went on to say that Delano's buck had taken "the first premium at the State fair" and was thus regarded, in the words of the questioner, as "the best buck in the State of Ohio." When asked if he had been induced to vote for Delano by that promise, Evans replied, "I don't know whether I was particular," but went on to say, "I was a little on that; I thought I could make something by that, as I was a little hard up." So, in return for the promise that Delano's buck would service his ewe, Evans accepted the altered Democratic ticket. Even so, he reported that he had unsuccessfully "tried to work the name off with my finger."[81] This account appears plausible, especially if Evans's ewe were as described and the agreement, when finally worked out with Delano himself, had included transfer of some of the resulting progeny.

While individual votes were usually not worth more than a dollar or so in the open market surrounding the voting window, election officials in charge of the ballot boxes and the tabulation of votes at the end of the day were worth much more. For example, John R. Hargin, an inspector of election in New York City, reported that an agent of the Tammany Hall organization had taken him aside on the morning of the election and said,

"Here, put that in your pocket," handing me some money. I asked him, "What is that for?" "What a damned fool you must be!" he said, "put that in your pocket; take all you get and say nothing." I put the money in my pocket; there were several gentlemen present, and I didn't hide it a bit; they saw it. As I was about going in [to the polling place], says he, "Now, I want to talk to you." Says he, "When votes is on the boxes, don't you trouble yourself much about that registry." Says he, "Let your word be 'down'" [evidently, "down" into the box]. After I came inside I told Jenny [another election official] what had occurred; he shrugged his shoulders a little bit, and didn't pay any attention to it, apparently. Mr. Irving [the Tammany man] came a little back, and says, "Don't forget, now." He sung out "Down with," several times himself.

[81] Ibid., pp. 57–8. Evans rented a place from Wright's nephew and did not have his own farm. These landlord and kinship connections probably explain how the Republican agent knew Evans owned a ewe. Because he signed his testimony with his mark, Evans was probably illiterate.

Irving was rather clumsily attempting to bribe Hargin in order to have him approve men as voters when their names did not appear in the registry.[82]

Unlike Hargin, most election officials were already heavily committed to their respective parties and candidates. In most instances, these officials had been nominated by their respective party organizations, and many of them had held patronage positions as a reward for service to the party. Even without a bribe, many of them would at least slightly tilt the voting process toward their side of the contest if they were certain that their actions would go undetected. Those who were too scrupulous to do so were probably not open to bribes. In any case, the only real check on abuse of their authority was the presence of officials from one of the competing parties. In many accounts in the hearings, election officials reported that they left the polls on election day only in order to respond to the "call of nature."[83] They usually had meals brought to them while the voting proceeded or, in many cases, did not eat until the polls had closed. For many officials, their duties began at sunrise when the polls opened and continued into the early hours of the next morning. During all this time, they continuously monitored each other's activities in order to make certain neither party gained advantage over the other.

Money and Patronage as the Currency of Politics

Money and patronage motivated many of the party agents who distributed tickets, challenged opposition voters, and served as election officials behind the voting window. Although they tended to work only with candidates of a single party, many of these agents were otherwise more or less freelance operatives who offered their services for a fee.[84] They sometimes claimed, for example, that they had privileged access to groups of men, either because of ethnic or religious affinity or through an employer. If properly compensated and directed through this agent, these groups of men could be induced to

[82] Later, as canvasser, Hargin unfolded ballots for the congressional race and found that many of them had been folded around one another in order to cast two votes as one. S.R. no. 1269: M.D. no. 7, Pt. 1 (1864): pp. 189–90, 193.

[83] The most explicit of these references appeared in the testimony of Meredith Ambrose, a judge of election in Booneville, Kentucky, who related that he "was absent at one time while the election was progressing, from five to ten minutes. I walked about fifty paces back and forth to attend to a call of nature – I mean, to urinate." S.R. no. 1432: Contested Congressional Election in the Eighth District of Kentucky: M.D. no. 13, pp. 617–18. Sidney M. Barnes vs. George M. Adams, election held on November 3, 1868.

[84] On patronage as an intensely personal, even apolitical search for a "position" by men who controlled blocks of voters, see Altschuler and Blumin, *Rude Republic*, pp. 40–5. Note that "apolitical" here refers to principles and policy, not party organization. On the kinds of campaign activities and demonstrations arranged by party professionals, see pp. 61–2, 67–9.

throw their votes to one or the other of the competing candidates. In other cases, they would advertise their extensive contacts with unidentified men who had access to such groups, promising both to make them available to the candidate and to insulate the candidate from all unsavory contact or connection with this seamy underside of practical politics. Most of the examples presented below arose in the nation's larger cities where the mobilization of voters and the mounting of a visible campaign were more expensive and complex operations than in rural areas.

Because candidacies could be launched late in a campaign, merely by printing and distributing the necessary tickets, the ticket system made possible a wide range of strategies at the polls. For example, in the 1858 election in New York's Third Congressional District, Daniel Sickles, the Democratic candidate, offered Henry Farrington, an attorney and member of the American party, an arrangement through which the latter could mount an independent campaign. While modestly supported, Farrington's candidacy promised to split the opposition in such a way that Sickles would be elected. As Farrington himself testified, the inducements offered him included

an arrangement ... whereby all my expenses of the canvass should be paid by [Sickles] himself or friends, and in case of Mr. Sickles succeeding in his election, he was to concede to me certain appointments – I mean concede to me and my political friends. No particular appointments were specified; generally understood to mean custom-house or navy yard appointments. ... [Although] ... the official return only credited me [Farrington] with three, four, or five votes, [he had] a conversation with Mr. Sickles on the evening of the election and after the votes had been canvassed, and in that conversation Mr. Sickles remarked to me that I had passed votes enough to elect him – that is, that I had received votes enough to secure his election; he did not estimate the number of such votes. The result of the canvass was supposed to be known at the time of such conversation; it was between 11 and 12 p.m.

William Ellsworth, who had aided Sickles's campaign, testified that Farrington had felt that Amor Williamson, the major candidate opposing Sickles, had betrayed the Americans (Know-Nothings) by forming a close connection with the Republican party. For that reason, it was Farrington who offered to stand for election if, in the words of the questioning counsel, "he could afford to pay the necessary expenses, such as printing, getting up meetings, &c ... [stating] that he was too poor to pay for such expenses, and ask[ing] to have a portion of them defrayed by Mr. Sickles." Sickles then agreed to this arrangement.[85]

Given the depth of his involvement in the campaign, Ellsworth was probably in a position to know how and why this bargain had been struck. In addition to his major role in the Sickles campaign, Ellsworth had handled the operations associated with Farrington's candidacy, "printing tickets, posting and printing handbills, erection of stands for tickets, employment of men

[85] S.R. no. 1103: M.D. no. 6 (1858): pp. 37–8, 93–4.

to attend those stands, expense of holding several Farrington meetings, and folding of tickets, advertising, &c." However, when it became clear in the last days before the election "that it would be impossible to rally a vote on Farrington as a separate candidate," the Farrington operations were more or less shut down and his supporters were "advised to support Mr. Sickles directly as the best means of defeating Williamson." Thus, after Farrington was abandoned, the men recruited to work for him turned their attention to Sickles.[86]

In total, Ellsworth had employed almost 200 men on election day "to distribute tickets; tend to polls; employed to do all they could to secure Mr. Sickles's election . . . some stayed at poll, and some hunted up voters for Mr. Sickles."[87] Most of these men, 134 in all, were paid five dollars each; the remainder received more money. One particularly valuable man received fifty dollars in gold; "about ten" others received twenty or more dollars. In several of the wards, for example, he employed men to discover the names of residents who had voted in prior elections but had since moved away.[88] Another man was "employed to go about in a horse and wagon to see if the ticket men were at posts and electioneering men were busy." In total, Ellsworth estimated that he had spent somewhere between six and eight hundred dollars employing men in the campaign.[89]

---

[86] Farrington's bargaining position was clearly weak because his support was thin and he lacked a supporting organization. In effect, his candidacy was merely the creature of one of the major parties competing in the race. The situation was very different in the Eighth Congressional District in 1864, where a three-way race developed between Republican William Dodge; a regular Democratic candidate, James Brooks; and Thomas Barr, a war Democrat backed by Tammany Hall. All three candidates were viable contenders, although Barr could not have won unless Dodge had retired from the race and thus consolidated the prowar vote. Barr, in fact, tried to get Dodge to withdraw in his favor. When this failed, he asked the Dodge campaign to provide him with funds that would then be used to split the Democratic vote. Barr requested $5,000 but received only $2,000 from the Dodge campaign. In requesting the larger amount, Barr may have been asking Dodge to match a competing bid from the Brooks campaign; the latter had offered Barr $5,000 to withdraw from the race. S.R. no. 1269: Contested Congressional Election in the Eighth District of New York: M.D. no. 7, Pt. 2, pp. 34–7, 40, 46–8, 60. William E. Dodge vs. James Brooks; election held on November 8, 1864. For other revealing testimony on the costs associated with the Republican campaign, see pp. 145–6, 148.

[87] S.R. no. 1103: M.D. no. 6 (1858): pp. 86–7, 97, 103.

[88] At first glance, a list of such men might have been used to produce fraudulent votes for Sickles. Because the names would have appeared in previous poll-books, voters using them would have seemed to be legitimate residents. However, because the parties were, in effect, responsible for monitoring their opponents, such a list could also be used to detect illegal voters recruited by the opposition. In fact, such a list could be used to both abet and discourage illegal voting at the same time. S.R. no. 1103: M.D. no. 6 (1858): pp. 87, 102.

[89] Simple arithmetic $[(134 \times 5) + 50 + (10 \times 20) + (30 \times \text{more than } 5)]$ suggests that he could not have spent less than $1,070; however, the larger point is that Ellsworth

I paid some on the day of election and some next day; the day after election I paid one hundred and sixty-five dollars to men I employed at the polls. . . . I don't recollect whether I did or not [pay money to someone to induce them to vote for Mr. Sickles at that election]. I may have done it and may have not; I paid money to get in votes for Mr. Sickles, that was what I was employed for to do, I suppose . . . I may have held out various inducements for persons to vote *for* Sickles, but I never offered any money directly.

However, when asked if he had employed "any persons not residents of the district to come into the district that day for the purpose of voting for Mr. Sickles," Elsworth declined to answer the question. He also would not say whether or not he had personal knowledge of men "who were not residents or voters in the district coming into it with the avowed and express purpose of voting for Mr. Sickles." When asked whether or not he had "repeatedly stated to persons that you knew of a large number of illegal votes having been given for Mr. Sickles at that election," Ellsworth unhelpfully responded, "I don't recollect." When the question was repeated, he was more direct, "I decline to answer that question . . . [b]ecause if I should answer it might make me liable to criminal prosecution. I don't know what I said." At this point, counsel for Sickles requested that the commissioner instruct Ellsworth that he would not be liable to any criminal prosecution for any answer he might give to these questions. Ellsworth still would not budge, "[f]or good reasons – my own, and nobody else's." After again refusing to answer questions related to the bribing of voters, he added, "I do not wish to compromise any friend of mine by any act of mine regarding any statement I may make."[90]

On a somewhat smaller scale, John Wildey also organized part of the Sickles election operations. Proprietor of a porterhouse (tavern), Wildey was evidently an independent political agent. Even after deciding to back Sickles, for example, he received an offer

to support Mr. Williamson. . . . As I was coming through Beekman street a gentleman by the name of Preston – I think he is in the employ of Mr. Williamson – I think he is in that office, foreman or something – says "You're just the man I wanted to see, Jack. Has your brother been to see you?" (My brother is a machinist, and does work for Mr. Williamson and all the printers. He has a place in Ann street.) I said "No; what about?" "Mr. Williamson is a candidate for Congress and would like to have your support." I stated to him I was a very warm friend of Mr. Sickles, and was going to support him. He wanted to know if there wasn't any inducement he could offer for me to support Mr. Williamson that campaign; he was a nice man, &c. I told him not; if there was any other man, with the exception of Mr. Sickles, running I might talk to him. He said he was sorry; he knew I was a good worker up there in the ward;

    probably did not know how much he actually spent and was evidently eager to underestimate the total.
90   S.R. no. 1103: M.D. no. 6 (1858): pp. 88–9, 91–2, 94–6, 98.

he knew I could help Mr. Williamson, if I would . . . I gave him to understand that I was going to vote for Mr. Sickles; bade him good bye and left.

Wildey also received an offer from representatives of Hiram Walbridge, who was running a strong race as an Anti-Lecompton Democrat.[91] However, Wildey had a very poor opinion of the men who approached him on Walbridge's behalf and did not give this offer much credence.

In regard to Mr. Walbridge, the parties who spoke to me were Henry and Benjamin Wood and a Mr. Thompson, a gambler. Mr. Thompson got in debt all around the ward and did not pay up; had open account in porter-houses and did not settle up. Several young men in the ward Thompson had hired to distribute tickets, &c., he was to give $10 per day; he forgot to pay them. Mr. Thompson offered me $200 to support Mr. Walbridge, and to make me chairman of a meeting for which they afterwards got H. N. Wild; he stated to me he was going for Walbridge to get his son as a cadet in West Point. . . .

After reaching an agreement with Sickles, the Democratic candidate gave him between two and three hundred dollars. Wildey also received another two hundred to two hundred and fifty dollars from the treasurer of the Eighth Ward committee. With this money, he paid "men to stand at the ticket boxes and distribute tickets . . . to paint banners to string across the street . . . for posting bills . . . to help put up banners." On election day, he paid "in the neighborhood of $200 or $250," keeping "a book . . . showing the names and amounts; paid them $5 each, and told them at the time I was paying for services, and they could vote for whom they saw fit."

In addition to erecting stands for speech making, hiring musicians, and purchasing torches for processions and meetings, Wildey "procured banners to be painted [in] the whole third congressional district; put them up in every ward. Two in some wards; a large number." He also

had fifty transparencies painted; cost me fifty cents apiece; and the banner in Broadway cost $55 for painting alone, without canvas or ropes. . . . I would give [Mr. Sickles] bills and he would give me money or a check; some bills went direct to him, as music, and he paid it to my knowledge. Mr. Sickles never give me one dollar at that election to pay me, or for me to induce votes, or to spend in any way I thought fit, but all for expenses incurred as I have named. . . . I was a member of the ward committee, and the money I got from the treasurer of the committee went [to pay men for distributing ballots]; the ticket distributors get $5 per day. . . . [They served] the whole democratic ticket for Congress and for all other offices voted for at that election. . . . Certainly, it is the custom [for all parties at every election to employ and pay men to attend the polls and distribute ballots to voters]. Every party does

[91]   An Anti-Lecompton Democrat was one opposed to the proslave constitution promoted for the Territory of Kansas by the Buchanan administration. Such Democrats were also called "Anti-Administration Democrats" and were usually allied with Senator Stephen Douglas of Illinois.

it. . . . Four or five men of my company were working the American ticket, and I think they told me they got $3 [for distributing Williamson's ticket]. . . . [92]

While Wildey was not paid for his services, he did want a favor. Two or three weeks before the election, he had told Sickles that he

was an applicant for the situation of inspector of fire apparatus. I wanted Mr. Sickles to try to get me that situation from Mr. Cooper, street commissioner, and if he couldn't get that, a place in the custom-house, or anything else he could get me to do, and he then stated he had no influence with Mr. Schell [because Schell was opposed to him].

At the time of the hearing, Wildey, in fact, held a position in the customhouse to which he had been appointed about a year after the election. But in what seemed flat contradiction of his other testimony, Wildey stated that he was "satisfied I did not get it through Mr. Sickles. I never spoke to Mr. Sickles about a place in the custom-house."[93]

While Wildey seems to have received what he wanted in this campaign, other men were not so fortunate. The major risk in offering these kinds of political services to a candidate was that they might welch on their end of the bargain once they were elected. In 1864, Stephen Geoghan, a professional political agent, thought he had come to a satisfactory understanding with James Brooks, the Democratic candidate for congressman from the Eighth District in New York City. When Brooks failed to deliver on his end of the agreement, Geoghan turned against him and testified for the Republican, William Dodge, when the latter contested the election. As a consequence of his falling out with Brooks, Geoghan gave a particularly revealing account of how such an agent operated at the nineteenth-century polls. Aside from his political avocation, Geoghan had a very checkered work history, but his primary source of income for the last eleven years had come from ownership of two liquor stores. At least one of these was a bar and played a part in his election operations.

Geoghan worked but one precinct, attending the polls continuously on the day of election. As he put it, "I wouldn't take time to eat my meals, for fear I would lose the voting." His primary tactic, perfected in previous campaigns, was to prepare a list of men who had died in the precinct but still appeared on the voting register. Again in Geoghan's words, "I know them to be dead; but we substitute a man to vote their names, and keep them on. We've got to do that, you know, to help a friend." And this "efficient aid," as the counsel later restated the matter, is what he had performed for Brooks in the 1864 election. He estimated that he had produced "in the neighborhood of twenty or thirty" votes for the Democrat out of 340 tickets cast at that precinct.[94]

---

[92]   S.R. no. 1103: M.D. no. 6 (1858): pp. 66–7.

[93]   Ibid., pp. 68–72.

[94]   In the terminology of the period, Geoghan was a "striker," someone who could produce, for a favor or a price, a bloc of votes for a particular candidate. Such men

Geoghan voted only once because he "was too well known" to attempt to vote on the names of dead men himself. On other hand, when asked how many men he had induced to vote illegally, he replied, "All that ever I can get. I couldn't give you any regular statement, for everybody I can get to vote I make them vote. It's a business I practice."

Geoghan estimated that other professionals operating at his precinct produced an additional thirty or forty illegal votes. Some of these men were evidently rival agents, and there, in fact, was quite a bit of competition associated with his avocation. For example, his response to how "many fights do you suppose you have been in in the course of your life" was "[a] great many. In the course of the election I'm the whole time fighting generally; I fight with my nails election day." As for those who had voted on the identities of dead men, they had all disappeared. Geoghan felt that was only natural; as he put it, "Well, we can't keep them in the house [his tavern], because it wouldn't pay to support them and keep them idle."

Geoghan's motives in delivering this testimony were a little unclear at first. He was obviously not an advocate of "clean government" exposing wrongdoing at the polls. And he seemed to be unrepentant; in fact, there was more than a little self-satisfaction in the way in which he described his political operation. While allowing that "there is always little quarrels in politics," he also denied revenge as a motive. It was only toward the end that he came to the bottom line.

Well, sir, I will tell you. When I went for Mr. Brooks the day of the election, I went for him and did all I could to carry the district for him, and kept my house [bar] for him all day; I spent my money and used my liquor. Mr. Brooks was elected, but he forgot to come and ask me whether it cost me anything for it. I thought it was my duty [to testify as he had], when he wasn't gentleman enough to come and ask me how much it cost me. Mr. Stewart came and asked me how much it cost me, and I told him "Nothing, sir." I busied myself greatly in his election; that is all the circumstances that there is about it; a man that is worth nothing after election is worth nothing before it.

Brooks could not have missed this attack on his political integrity; it was delivered in the hearing on his own contested election, and Brooks may have been personally in attendance.[95] What Geoghan had evidently wanted was a generous "gift" in recognition of his political prowess; cash payment on a formal "bill" for his services delivered by one of the candidate's underlings

---

usually participated in lower class social networks as leaders of street gangs or criminal entrepreneurs such as the proprietors of bordellos. Summers, *The Plundering Generation*, p. 57.

[95] While there is no evidence in the transcript that Brooks was present when Geoghan testified, many contestants attended their own hearings. In some cases, contestants even acted as their own attorneys.

reduced him, as he saw it, to a mere employee.[96] In addition to a generous gift, there had to be some sort of social recognition of his able services by the candidate.[97]

Both Democrats and Republicans played this game. Most of the time Democrats played with other Democrats and Republicans with other Republicans. But sometimes agents crossed the line. When this occurred, neither the agent nor the candidate knew each other very well, and the risk of deception was usually fairly high. One such cross-party arrangement was negotiated during the 1866 congressional campaign in the Thirteenth District of Ohio. The most important player on the Republican side was George Johns, a federal employee in Washington, D.C., apparently in the House of Representatives, who was closely allied with Columbus Delano, the Republican candidate. As Delano's unofficial representative, he went into a saloon owned by Patrick Lamb, a local Democratic agent.

I asked the gentlemen who were with me if they would have something to drink. A glass of ale was taken, and I gave a five dollar bill in payment. Lamb was not then present, and there being only a small boy he could not make the change. I told him it would do another time, but Lamb coming in shortly, the change was made. I had no conversation with him on this occasion, but I had heard him spoken of and referred to by others as a "Fenian." Later in the evening, after the close of the Butler meeting, he met me in Hughes' & Nichols's confectionery saloon, in this city; he took me one side and said that he had a considerable number of friends who were laborers, whom he wanted to get to vote for the republican party. I think he mentioned the number as between eighty and one hundred and twenty, and professed to have a considerable list of them – that it needed some work and attention and time to get them to the polls. He said that if he had fifty dollars to pay for his time and labor, and to pay his expenses, he would go and see them up and down the canal. He mentioned that they were at work on the canal, some at Hebron, some at Hanover, and at other places. I told him I would give him some money for that purpose, and gave him twenty dollars, and told him I would give him more if necessary. I gave him no more then, but delayed for the purpose of making inquiries into his standing. He afterwards came to me on two or three occasions and I gave him small sums of money, probably ten dollars at a time, but I kept no memorandum or account of it.

---

96 For an instance in which a party agent attempted to extort his employer (claiming he was just trying to pressure his party to pay a legitimate bill for his services), see S.R. no. 1431: M.D. (no number, bound between nos. 24 and 25 [1868]): pp. 211–13. For a case of entrapment in which a Republican posed as an indigent Democrat in search of a bribe, see pp. 251–5, 402–3.

97 S.R. no. 1269: M.D. no. 7, Pt. 1 (1864): pp. 448–52, 472, 477–8. Dodge, the challenger in this contest, had astutely granted this social recognition by receiving Geoghan at home in his parlor. In his own testimony, however, Dodge attempted to deny any relationship with Geoghan. Perhaps appalled by the social connection that Geoghan was now claiming, the Republican candidate called Geoghan "an unscrupulous and desperate politician" and said that a "man who keeps two grog-shops" cannot be accorded "the highest respectability." S.R. no. 1269: M.D. no. 7, Pt. 2 (1864): p. 147.

Widely known as a political operative who could be "hired," Lamb's methods did not stand much scrutiny. Nevertheless and perhaps precisely because of his reputation, Johns concluded that he was man with whom he could do business.[98]

Lamb's testimony, however, indicated that they had done a little more business than Johns was willing to admit. Lamb began his narrative by saying that he had been in his saloon in Newark, Ohio, when a local leader of the Republican party had called him outside "across the canal."[99] In their conversation, the Republican, a Mr. Hagar,

asked me how many Fenians we had in Licking county; I told him we had about ninety-eight. "Well," he says, "there are a couple of gentlemen coming from Washington here to-day and have about seven thousand dollars to electioneer for Mr. Delano. I suppose the majority [of your men] don't care who they get in, and you might as well have four or five hundred dollars to get them over if you can." "I don't know as to that, Mr. Hagar; the majority of them [the Fenians] are democrats, and I don't know what influence four or five hundred dollars might have." "Well," says he, "I will bring them up and introduce them to you." I told him not to bring them up until evening.

That evening, Lamb was in his saloon when Hagar, George Johns, Major Caffrey (the editor of the Republican paper in Licking County), a Mr. Crow, and Charley Griffin arrived.

Mr. Johns called in some refreshments; I waited on him. They came to about fifty cents, he threw out a five dollar bill and told me to keep the change, as he would see me again.

This account, of course, differed from the one Johns gave. Johns had said that Lamb had not been present when he had presented the five-dollar bill. Of the two versions, Lamb's was the more believable, particularly in light of what subsequently transpired.

Mr. Hagar called me in the back room and said: "Mr. Lamb, those are the men who have the pot which will make the Fenians crawl." Mr. Crow asked me if I would not come and hear him speak, as he was around lecturing to his Irish Fenian friends; they had never been on the right track, and he wanted to put them on. . . . I heard Mr. Crow speak a few words and then retired to my place of business again.

[98] The Fenians were a clandestine organization dedicated to the overthrow of British rule in Ireland. The "Butler meeting" was evidently an address given by Ben Butler, then a Massachusetts Republican. S.R. no. 1313: M.D. no. 38, Pt. 1 (1866): p. 242.

[99] Before this conversation, another Republican had said to Lamb, " 'Here, Pat, you don't care a damned who is elected to Congress.' I said, 'Not a great deal; I have to work Sundays and every other day.' 'I should think, Pat,' said Mr. Wilson, 'that you could influence a good many in the Fenian party; you are an officer of the Fenians and a saloon-keeper,' and he would send men around to me with money; and the next man that came to me was Mr. Hagar." S.R. no. 1313: M.D. no. 38, Pt. 2 (1866): pp. 39, 41.

From Lamb's perspective, Johns had ostentatiously displayed his party's resources by refusing change on his five. The invitation to Mr. Crow's lecture was, in turn, an opening gesture toward Lamb; his attendance, however brief, signaled his receptivity. As Lamb returned to his saloon, he told one of his friends that

> it was unnecessary to go up [to the lecture], as there was a regular sucker speaking and we could make a sucker out of it too. Mr. Crow returned down in the morning and asked me how his speech suited the Fenians. I told him very well; that he had converted twenty or thirty. I had drawn a list of men, some of whom were on the Potomac river – were not here [in Newark, Ohio] at all; he asked me for the list. Mr. Crow read the list, and seeing that he had done so well here, said, "I suppose you want some money; one more speech will bring them all over."

Lamb, however, wanted to dispense with any more lectures.[100]

> I told him it was the money we wanted now. Mr. Crow called in some refreshments, and I waited on him; he left his carpet-sack with me, said he would be back in a few minutes. He was not but a short while gone, when he returned with Major Caffrey and called me out into the room. He, Mr. Caffrey, handed Mr. Crow something under the table, and Mr. Crow pulled it out and handed me a fifty dollar note, and said he had accomplished what he went after – the money; Mr. Caffrey said, put that in your pocket.

At this point, the negotiations became almost continuous, with Lamb, on the one side, trying to get as much money as he could from the Republicans, and the Republicans attempting to withhold payment for as long as they could. It did not help matters that the Republicans had grossly exaggerated their resources and now were very likely short of funds.[101]

> Mr. Caffrey said, he supposed I must have some carriages and horses; I told him yes; I could electioneer only on Sundays [perhaps because his saloon would be closed

---

[100]   From Lamb's account, it is not entirely clear whether he would have delivered his Fenians to the Republicans if the price had been right. However, his narrative does indicate that, if the price was not right, he intended to take the Republicans for all he could get without giving them any votes in return. This, in fact, was exactly what one of Lamb's friends, John McKeever, advised him to do. "I was in Lamb's one evening and Crow came in, and he asked if the boys were all right in Newark; he was going to Zanesville. Mr. Lamb told him they were all right." McKeever then asked Lamb what business he had with Crow. Lamb "said he had offered him money and asked me what he should do. I told him to take all the money he could get, and then discover on him. That is the discourse I had about it ... he told me that they were trying to give him money to buy votes, and I told him it would be wrong to buy votes, but to get all the money he could." S.R. no. 1313: Contested Congressional Election in the Thirteenth District of Ohio: M.D. no. 38, Pt. 2, p. 111. Columbus Delano vs. George W. Morgan, election held on October 9, 1866.

[101]   In his earlier conversations with Lamb, Johns had "presumed, he said, there was six or seven thousand dollars – Mr. Hagar said there was seven thousand dollars – to buy votes in this district for Delano. He called me to one side at the bazaar, and laid his hand on me and said, 'It is no trouble at all for us to get money.'" In addition, "'You can have any [patronage] position you are capable of holding.'" S.R. no. 1313: M.D. no. 38, Pt. 2 (1866): p. 41.

that day]. He told me Mr. Erasmus White would furnish me with all the horses and buggies I needed. On Sunday I went and got a carriage, two-horse carriage; then went to the Preston House and inquired for Mr. Johns; I told him it was necessary I should have some funds, if I was going on that expedition. He gave me two twenty dollar notes, forty dollars, and told me to leave some in Hanover, if I had any left, as [money] was scarce. He said the bank was not open; that he would have plenty to-morrow. I got three and myself in the carriage, and then went to the bazaar, and I went after Mr. Johns to introduce him to my friends I had in the carriage. He paid for what refreshments we had, and said "Lamb will satisfy you to-morrow." We went down to Hanover and returned; the team was not in very good order, and White said I could not have any more teams there. I went up to the bazaar and saw Mr. Johns, and he said: "Lamb, how much money can you get along with to-day?" I told him, seeing it was circus day and the folks were all in, it was very necessary that we should have a couple of hundred dollars; he told me he would not have it until he returned from Mount Vernon, but told me to wait in the bazaar, and he said he would go and see how much he could raise. He came back and said he had paid out a check this morning, and said he had but fifteen dollars, which he gave me, and told me, "You meet me at 8 o'clock to-night, and tell them to meet me at the depot when the train came in from Mount Vernon," and he would satisfy them; he would give them ten dollars each. There were three or four of them. During the day I met Major Caffrey, and told him I must have a suit of clothes; he told me to go to Charley Griffin, he had the pot. I went to Charley and told him I must have a suit of clothes; I told him I had fifteen dollars I would pay on them; he said all right, and went to Miller & Rhodes. Charley told them to charge the balance of the suit of clothes to him or the committee.

This was the last straw for Lamb. The Republicans were, from what he could see, either dribbling out money in what he considered an insulting fashion or, more likely, unable to make good on their commitments.

I saw there was no chance to carry out my principles, so I got out cards to warn all my Irish friends to beware of all traitors and not to be bought for money. Mr. Wells and Hunter got out the cards for me.[102]

As was the case with many such arrangements, Delano's agents were not particularly interested in the fate of the rest of the Republican ticket. Lamb reported that he had been instructed that "[a]ny friend that I could not get to vote for Delano to hand him a democratic ticket with Morgan's name cut out and Delano's name pasted on it, that was authorized by Mr. Johns." These instructions either assumed that Lamb's "friends" could not read or, if they could, would not notice the alteration in the congressional race.[103] In the end, Lamb reported that he had received "a hundred and five dollars of Delano money and the clothes," plus use of the carriage. As was the case with almost all such arrangements, all the details, including the transfers of money, were handled

---

[102] S.R. no. 1313: M.D. no. 38, Pt. 2 (1866): pp. 39–41.
[103] Ibid., p. 41.

by Delano's agents. The congressional candidate never entered into the negotiations.[104]

Most cross-party arrangements seem to have been negotiated prior to the election. For example, Colonel Rockwell Tyler, a New York Republican working for General Van Wyck, his party's candidate for Congress, reported an offer that his party received

> a few days before election [when] a republican meeting was held at Callicoon Depot; there were some of the leading democrats attended the meeting. In the early part of the evening a democrat made a proposition to furnish a certain number of votes at certain price. He said he would furnish 50 voters for $150. I told him I would refer him to the general, and if he concluded to do it, it would be all right, I supposed. He and I approached the general and made known the proposition, and he refused at once to appropriate any money for that kind of business. This democrat again called my attention to the matter, and wanted I should again consult the general and say that he could furnish these 50 votes, he thought, on more reasonable terms, provided he would pay something in advance. I carried the message to Mr. Van Wyck, and he again objected, saying that he would not give a dollar or a farthing for the purpose of buying votes. This man is considered to be a man of influence both in his own town and Fremont. . . . I have heard others say [that he is capable of influencing or selling 50 or 25 votes]. He . . . works through other parties . . . and I think, if he commenced early enough, he could for $150.

Although Tyler appeared to have regretted the rejection, he had probably bungled these negotiations by bringing General Van Wyck into them. Once the Republican candidate was personally involved, the Democratic agent could turn around and offer disclosure of the deal to his own party for what would probably have been a much higher price. This was particularly likely if money had changed hands before the election was held.[105]

While many arrangements of convenience between candidates and political operatives were reported in the hearings, there were only a few instances of a betrayal once an agreement had been reached. One of these occurred in Port Jervis, New York, during the 1868 election where a Republican working

---

[104]   Ibid. For Charley Griffin's attempt to put the Republican dealings with Lamb in the best possible light, see pp. 37–8.

[105]   S.R. no. 1402: M.D. no. 27, Pt. 1 (1868): p. 115. Van Wyck, however, was not entirely aloof from the nitty-gritty side of retail electioneering. On the day of the election, Andrew Bell saw him become personally involved in the voting at Mamakating Precinct. When Jacob Fritz, a carpenter and a "man of not very great intellect," came up to the voting window, Van Wyck "pulled him back." Fritz then again attempted to go to the window, only to be drawn back once more by Van Wyck. At this point, Fritz told Van Wyck, "if I must vote for you . . . take the ticket and fix it yourself." And so Van Wyck took Fritz's Democratic ticket, crossed out the Democratic nominee's name, and wrote in his own. Fritz then voted that ticket. Bell reported that Van Wyck spent the entire day at the polls. S.R. no. 1402: M.D. no. 27, Pt. 2 (1868): pp. 7–10.

the polls reported that his Democratic counterparts had offered to defect for a price:

[At] about ... 10 or 11 o'clock on election day men who had been working very hard for the democratic ticket got dissatisfied with something that didn't work right on the part of some of the leading democrats there, and they bolted from their work, came over to some of our men and made a proposition that they would go to work for us for a certain amount of money. We wouldn't entertain any such proposition, and when some of the leading democrats found out what was going on [they] took these bolters off and walked them around a block or so and finally brought [them] up at a fire-engine house and there the difficulty was settled by these democrats furnishing them with the *means* to go to work with. They received money for the purpose of going to work at the polls. When they came back they told our men that they had done better than their proposition to us. Their proposition to us was $50 to the crowd. One of them controls quite a number of votes in our town.

This Republican added, perhaps sincerely, "We declined to entertain the proposition out of principle."[106]

As in this case, the utility of such men depended on how many votes they could deliver and the certainty with which they could deliver them. In some cases, a particularly industrious party agent would negotiate agreements with voters before the election was held and then serve as one of the judges of election at the polling place where these men would vote. Dr. O. N. Ellis described how such an arrangement played out in the 1866 congressional election in Dresden, Ohio, where L. Rambo, a Republican, served as one of the judges. Standing just outside the voting window, Ellis saw Rambo with an "inkstand in his hands playing with it. I told him at the time to be careful; that he would spill it on the table." At the time, Rambo was standing at the voting window and the table was turned lengthwise so that one end was against the window as well. As it turned out, Rambo intended to spill the ink on the table. Then when a man identified only as "young Ogle" turned in his ticket to Rambo at the voting window, Rambo put one of his fingers into the spilled ink and pressed what would have been his fingerprint on to Ogle's ticket. In that way, when the judges counted the ballots, Rambo was able to identify which one Ogle had voted. According to Ellis,

he stated that he was deceived, or thought he was deceived, in the way in which some of the voters were voting, who had promised him they would vote for Mr. Delano; that he had suspicioned this young Ogle as being treacherous, and he concluded he would find him out if possible; that he marked his ticket; that he took the ballots out of the box on counting them, and upon opening the ticket made the discovery that he had voted the entire democratic ticket, and that if all the men who had promised him to vote for Delano had done so, he (Delano) would have had from thirty to forty majority in Jefferson township.

106 S.R. no. 1402: M.D. no. 27, Pt. 1 (1868): p. 100.

Rambo was evidently an employer as well as a Republican agent. Later when "Mr. Rambo's men or hands from the factory came . . . in a body" to vote, Ellis reported that Rambo suspected that two of his men were carrying Democratic tickets. In fact, Ellis reported that these men "were known to be true and tried democrats and had given their word and honor [to Ellis] that they would vote" for the Democratic congressional candidate. When each of these men voted, Rambo apparently substituted Republican tickets for the one they turned in. On each occasion, the

ticket was separately dropped upon the floor out of sight of the electors, under the window. After considerable searching on the part of Rambo two tickets were deposited in the ballot-box. I remonstrated strongly with Mr. Rambo, as well as other citizens who were outside, and spoke to Lewis J. Lemert, our oldest sitting judge, who told Mr. Rambo that he must hereafter desist, or to change places and allow him or one of the other trustees to receive ballots.

Rambo appeared to have marked these tickets as well. In this case, the Republican judge seems to have known the political allegiances of his employees and was again checking to see whether they had indeed lived up to their promises to support the Republican candidate.

During this same election, John Whartenbee, a twenty-three-year-old voter who claimed to be a staunch, lifelong Republican, stated that he had "asked Rambo himself if he would give me a new suit of clothes if I would vote for Delano; he spoke pretty low; I don't remember what he said; it was down in the warehouse, and a dance was going off, and he came up and commenced talking to me, and there was another man came up and commenced talking to him; I don't recollect what he said or anything about it." Why Whartenbee expected Rambo to bribe a fellow Republican was not clear. As it turned out, when Whartenbee voted, he voted a Democratic ticket because his brother Jerow "told me if I didn't vote it there would be a fuss in the family." Jerow and another man "pushed me right up to the polls" and made him turn in the ticket. Once he had done so, they immediately pulled him away from the window.[107]

---

[107]   S.R. no. 1313: M.D. no. 38, Pt. 2 (1866): pp. 568–70, 576–8. Family members could be very intimidating. For example, O. P. Fulton and Josiah Strickler, bystanders at the South Huntingdon Township precinct in 1868, reported that a somewhat drunk Jacob Keller stood by the voting window the entire afternoon until the polls closed. According to them, Keller swore he would kill and, somewhat redundantly, disinherit his son if he attempted to vote the Republican ticket. When Samuel appeared, Jacob pulled him away from the voting window while "threatening to knock his brains out," adding that if he voted the Republican ticket, "he should never [again] come inside of his father's house, and that he would lose five hundred dollars." The money was apparently the inheritance that the father would otherwise leave the son. Samuel did not vote in this election. S.R. no. 1431: M.D. (no number, bound between nos. 24 and 25 [1868]): pp. 102, 184.

Economic Intimidation

While party agents could bribe or otherwise entice men to support their ticket, they were usually not in a position to punish voters for the choices that they made.[108] This was, however, not the case with employers. A landowner or factory owner could use his power over employees or tenants to influence their voting decisions. This was most commonly and notoriously the case with freedmen in the South following the Civil War. But northern employers could also intimidate their men by threatening to discharge them from their employment. For intimidation to be effective, it was not necessary that this threat be explicit; when a man was sufficiently sensitive to the prospect of unemployment, all that was required was a public announcement by his employer of a party preference.

Such was the case with a non-English-speaking laborer who, in a somewhat confused account, maintained that his employer (at a chemical factory) had issued a circular informing his workers that they would either vote the Republican ticket or he did not want them to work for him anymore. The circular was written in German and began with the salutation "To the workmen of my factory." In the body of the text, along with rhetorical condemnations of southern rebels and effusive praise for the Republican program, appeared these passages:

The true patriot has now no other choice but to vote for the candidates who are pledged to continue this war to the proposed end – to support the present administration; and among these I hope to number all the free men of the factory, as I should not like to have any others around me, nor will I suffer any others around me.

In ordinary times, I have not troubled myself much about party measures and party questions; but at present the thing has become serious. Now the saying applies, "he who is not for us is against us." Today I deem it a right to demand of you to give more credence and confidence to me, an experienced and well-informed man, who would consider himself disgraced to press upon his less-informed fellow-citizens any false views of vagabond demagogues of every kind, and often interested and bribed journalists who endeavor to propagate false and infamous views.

The owner ended his appeal with the names of the candidates he endorsed. After reading the circular, the employee reasonably concluded that he would be fired if he voted the Democratic ticket. He voted for the Democrats anyway and subsequently attempted to collect his wages, believing that he would soon be dismissed for failing to support the Republicans. His foreman instead

---

[108] There were exceptions, of course. Where a man wished to be employed in a patronage job or already was so employed, he could be denied the position. There were also certain other kinds of favors that elected party officials might be in a position to dispense or to facilitate, such as the granting of military pensions. In Civil War Philadelphia, enrollment in the draft lists was a possible consequence of voting, imposed by Republican agents if men voted the Democratic ticket (see Chapter 6).

told him to go back to work.[109] While employers often publicly announced their political preferences before an election and sometimes offered inducements to their men to vote a particular ticket, there appear to be few instances in which dissenting employees were discharged.[110]

Another, more indirect way of exercising economic influence was to simply deny time off so that workers would be unable attend the polls. But this tactic, too, seems to have been rarely exercised. For example, in 1862, the foreman at a chemical factory in Philadelphia reported that the firm "gave each man time.... It has been the practice on all elections to have an hour for himself to poll his vote ... the business [of voting] is arranged so one comes off at this time, and one on." Although the owner implicitly approved the practice, the foreman stated that he granted the time off on his own initiative: "I did it without asking ... he did not instruct me; I have so much power. I have been in the habit before." In any case, the practice "was customary before I came. I did the same.... Men have been there 33 to 35 years; they know it is customary and make it a rule. They know they would be liable to be charged with it." Although the last passage evidently meant that the men's pay was docked if they took time off to vote, the employees' participation in the election was otherwise not discouraged.[111]

Economic intimidation was generally uncommon at the polls for several reasons. In the first place, most of the issues raised and fought over by the major parties did not involve, at least directly, class-based claims. Employers might be irritated by the rhetoric of certain candidates but rarely aroused by the platforms on which they ran. Second, the lack of class-based claims meant that workers in a factory or shop were internally divided in their partisan allegiances. Religion and ethnicity, for example, were as important as class status in the formation and recognition of partisan identities. When workers voted, many of them would naturally support whatever the owner's position might be, so the stakes were relatively low from the latter's perspective. Finally, employers themselves were divided in their partisan affiliations. There was no possibility, at least in most elections, that a monolithic upper-class solidarity would or could confront workers. An employer who

---

[109] S.R. no. 1199: M.D. no. 17 (1862): pp. 71–7. For the full text of the circular, see pp. 198–200.

[110] Employers were probably more likely, in return for votes, to offer material incentives of one sort or another to their workers than to threaten them. Since good workmen were simply more valuable as employees than they were as partisans at the polls, threats to fire them were probably both unbelievable and, to the extent that they demoralized the men, damaging to a firm's operations. For an exceptional instance in which a man accepted a thirty-dollar loan from his employer as an inducement to vote the Republican ticket and then was fired when he voted for the Democrats, see S.R. no. 1431: M.D. no. 7 (1868): pp. 354–5.

[111] S.R. no. 1199: M.D. no. 17 (1862): pp. 78–9. The owner did, however, announce his own preferences to his men in a circular distributed in the factory. See note 109, above.

heavily intervened in the electoral choices of his men would be isolated and, most probably, publicly pilloried. Finally, most employers were simply not equipped to monitor the polls in such a way as to detect and thus to enforce their political dictates. Party agents, who were far and away the most adept at these practices, rarely consented to be made the cat's paws of wealth and privilege; to do so was simply far more costly, in terms of public opinion, than anything an individual employer could offer. The parties had their own and more important fish to fry.

On the Poor Farm

As a group, the most economically vulnerable men in the United States were probably not workers but the residents of poor farms, operated in most cases by county governments as a refuge of last resort for those who were unable to support themselves. These farms were in effect small "welfare communities" that offset part of their expenses by raising crops and livestock and making at least some of their own clothing. Many of the residents were disabled or elderly men who had been abandoned by their families. Others suffered from mental problems of one sort or another, dementia most commonly. And most of these men were barely literate, if able to read and write at all.

Whether appointed by county commissioners or elected in their own right, the superintendents of poor farms were political officials who could exercise great influence over how paupers would vote if they went to the polls. Because farm administrators were in a position to observe the physical and mental capacities of their inmates, they usually exercised wide discretion in determining who was eligible for public aid. Since inmates were dependent on this aid for their sustenance, farm officials could use their discretion as a political reward for voting correctly or as punishment for supporting the opposition. Because farm residents lived in secluded locations, isolated from most other citizens, it was often difficult for outsiders to determine whether or not the inmates were actually intimidated by their keepers. But overt intimidation was probably unnecessary in any event. In such a closed, dependent community, it was probably obvious to the inmates that one of the conditions for public assistance was voting for the party that nominated or appointed the farm officials. Most citizens apparently presumed such was the case, and the votes of those living on the county farm were consequently viewed with great suspicion.[112]

One such instance involved the inmates of a poor farm in St. Louis County, Missouri, in 1858. These men voted at the Gravois precinct, located at the

---

[112] As was the case with Virginia, some states simply denied suffrage to all paupers, a category that earlier in the nineteenth century appears to have included at least some men who resided outside poor farms and received little, if any, public support. Later, the term more narrowly and specifically applied just to those who received public relief. Keyssar, *Right to Vote*, pp. 61, 134–5.

coal scales near the Gravois Digging, evidently a coal mine. Wagons carried men between the county farm and the coal scales so that they could vote. About a 120 men were taken to the polls in this way, and, so the report went, only one was given the "privilege" of selecting his own ticket. This was an "old man," 106 years old, who "selected the American," or Know-Nothing, ticket. All of the other men evidently voted Democratic.[113]

The line between what would be considered routine assistance by party agents and excessive influence by poor farm superintendents was sometimes hard to discern. The inmates themselves, for example, often claimed an independence that is difficult to warrant on inspection of the context in which they cast their votes. For example, David Shepherd, a seventy-three-year-old resident of the Westmoreland County poorhouse, stated,

I was always a republican. They tried to change me all they could; tried different plans, but couldn't do it. The Irish and Dutch [Germans] were all democrats to get the good-will of the boss. . . . They [inmates who did go to the polls] were all democrats, of course. If they did not vote that ticket they could not go to the election; so I think. . . . When the republican paper came there [to the poorhouse] he [the steward] would keep it back from me.

But when the November election came along, Shepherd said that he "went in with Mr. Sullenberger [the steward's father-in-law and, like the steward, a Democrat]. He gave me a drink, and told me to wait till he could get a [tax] receipt; then he took me up to the polls and I voted." From the context, it seems clear that, despite his self-described stubborn independence, Shepherd threw over his Republican loyalties in return for a drink.[114]

Similar instances arose in connection with the 1864 congressional election in the Sixteenth District of Pennsylvania, where George Widle was the steward of the Bedford County poor farm. As described by one of the witnesses, a

[113]   Relating a conversation he had had with someone who had closely attended the voting at the Gravois Precinct, the man giving this report had not himself seen the inmates vote. S.R. no. 1062: M.D. no. 8 (1858): p. 447. For a similar report in which "paupers from the county farm" were brought to the polls at the Cheltingham Precinct in an election in 1862, see S.R. no. 1198: Contested Congressional Election in the First District of Missouri: M.D. no. 15, p. 199. Samuel Knox vs. Francis P. Blair, Jr., election held on November 4, 1862. In this case, however, the superintendent of the farm and the inmates voted for Blair, the candidate who had complained of such voting four years previously. One of the concerns related to poor farm voters was their heavy concentration in precincts where the farm was located. The 1865 revision of the Missouri constitution got around this problem by stating that "no person shall be deemed to have gained or lost a residence . . . while kept at any poorhouse. . . ." Thereafter paupers would have voted where they had resided prior to their institutionalization. A. F. Denny, *General Statutes of the State of Missouri* (Jefferson City: Emory S. Foster, 1866), p. 27.

[114]   Also note that the tax receipt was illegal in that Shepherd should have been assessed at least ten days before the election. S.R. no. 1431: M.D. (no number, bound between nos. 24 and 25 [1868]): p. 225.

"considerable number of the paupers voted" for the Democratic ticket under Widle's direction.[115] Some of the things that Widle did could be considered routine party activities. For example, Widle promised the men in his charge that, once they had voted the Democratic ticket, he would treat them with whisky. Because men who earned their own living were often given liquor after they had voted, this promise could have been considered normal party politics. The problem, of course, was that paupers were usually not in a position to purchase their own liquor, and at least some of them may have been at the farm precisely because they were alcoholics. In such a context, the promise of whisky was much more than a courtesy extended to normal voters.

Widle also paid the poll tax for his men and distributed the receipts to them. When his charges appeared at the polls, they could then present these receipts as proof that the tax had been paid.[116] Finally, the steward procured Democratic tickets that he then distributed to the inmates before they voted. Both of these actions, when performed for voters who earned their own living, were normal services intended to facilitate the turnout of partisans at the polls.[117] The problem was that the steward's services could be viewed as actions that made his charges vulnerable to political pressure; if they had been ineligible to vote, for example, they could not have been intimidated into supporting one of the parties.[118]

In at least one instance, Widle appears to have offered an additional incentive that probably came out of the poor farm's budget. One of the paupers, James Sheeder, reported that, for the first time in his life, he voted Democratic in the 1864 election because "I was a pauper and needed a pair of pants. I asked for them, and he [Widle] told me he would not give me any unless I voted the democratic ticket." Two of the poor farm employees subsequently stood at the voting window and "watched me till I had voted the democratic ticket."[119] Of the nineteen paupers from the Bedford poor farm,

---

[115] S.R. no. 1271: Contested Congressional Election in the Sixteenth District of Pennsylvania: M.D. no. 117, p. 21. William H. Koontz vs. A. H. Coffroth, election held on October 11, 1864.

[116] The steward of the Westmoreland County poorhouse, in cooperation with the commissioner's clerk, similarly arranged for the payment and distribution of receipts to inmates just before the 1868 congressional election. S.R. no. 1431: M.D. (no number, bound between nos. 24 and 25 [1868]): pp. 189–94, 273.

[117] S.R. no. 1271: M.D. no. 117 (1864): p. 22.

[118] Many if not all of the inmates literally had nowhere else to go if they had been forced to leave the farm. For example, Enoch Armitage "had been working for Harvey Gates, who lived in Hopewell township. I fell off a wagon, or rather was thrown off and badly injured, and was sent to the poor-house after my money was all gone. I was with Gates twenty-one days before I was injured; had no family." S.R. no. 1271: M.D. no. 117 (1864): p. 23.

[119] Sheeder's testimony was sometimes confused and contradictory. For example, after reporting, "I might have told some persons that I had fooled Widle and voted the republican ticket, but I could not swear so," he then said, "I did tell Mr. Armitage

sixteen voted the Democratic ticket, while only three cast Republican votes. One of the Republican voters claimed to have deceived Widle into thinking that he would support the Democrats. Another reported that "Widle all along wanted me to vote the democratic ticket, but I would not do it. I don't think he treated me well for that season."[120]

Most poor farms were almost autarchies with domestic economies largely isolated from the surrounding community. Such was the case in Gettysburg, Pennsylvania, where John Culp, the son of the steward, lived in the Adams County poorhouse for eight years. During that time, Culp became well acquainted with the inmates and was thus in a position to report in detail their roles within the institution:

Daniel Shuner acted as nurse in the house; Henry Gipe worked about the house and on the farm – whatever was to be done; Patrick Mulligan attended to the cattle; they had sometimes as much as thirty head of cattle, sometimes not so many; George W. Morgan worked on the farm and about the house; would carry water, and scrub, and whatever the women wanted him to do; George Luther, when he first came the first summer, attended to the garden. I do not think he did anything after that; he was an old man. The other men named were there in the year 1864. Christian Spaidman was a tailor.... All the paupers who were able to work were required to work at such labor as the steward [his father] put them at.... All the persons whom I have mentioned were paupers at the poor-house, supported by the county. Morgan and Gipe worked most all the time. The tailor had work all the time. The others worked only occasionally.... The poor-house farm contains about 300 acres. The most of the work on the farm is done by the people of the house. David Beecher helped to work the farm; he ploughed and harrowed.... On a farm of that size two good hands could do the work, except in harvest. They always had two hands hired on the farm. The paupers helped, from time to time, as needed. David Beecher worked pretty constantly; he was crazy part of the time. The number of paupers averaged about one hundred and fifteen.[121]

Another inmate, R. G. McCreary, made clothes for the residents:

I am sixty years old. I am a tailor. I live at the poor-house. I make the clothes for the men. I was in a store at Petersburg seven years ago, and took sick with rheumatism; was sick six months, and came to the poor-house on account of my sickness. I make the clothing. I have been at the poor-house seven years.... The directors allowed me take in work from the country, and they allowed me to draw the money. I have a bargain now with the directors. I get twenty dollars a year and my boarding. I did not get anything before. This year they allow me to draw the money for any work I

that I had got the democratic ticket from Widle, but that I had fooled him and voted the republican ticket." The offer of a pair of pants, however, was corroborated by another inmate. S.R. no. 1271: M.D. no. 117 (1864): pp. 23–4.

[120] Ibid., pp. 22, 32.
[121] Ibid., pp. 209–10.

may do for other persons. I do not do much work for outside parties. I must do the poor-house work.[122]

Charles Scham was fifty years old and had been in the poor house for almost nine years. In describing his tasks, he stated, "I carry water and wood, and make fires in the wash-house, and in the furnaces, in winter, and in the crazy people's ward, at the poor-house, and attend to the crazy people, and take care of them."[123] Other men, such as Andrew Kuntz, who was blinded by cataracts, were unable to work.[124]

As was the case in Bedford County, the steward paid the tax for these men, distributing the receipts to each of his charges. With the help of his son-in-law, he then transported them to the Cumberland Township polls in a wagon. As one man attending the polls put it, "they and Cornelius Daugherty kept the men together, supplied them with tickets and voted them."[125] The poorhouse staff apparently inspected the tickets of at least some of the inmates before they were cast. Charles Scham, for example, reported that the steward and his son-in-law went "with me to the tavern where they voted, and we went up to the table, and he asked me to let him see my ticket, and I showed it to him, and then handed it in."[126]

Some of the men in the poorhouse would have voted the Democratic ticket anyway. William Keafer, for example, testified, "I voted of my free will."[127] Many others were ambivalent or apathetic; they could have been easily persuaded in the normal course of events in and around the polling place. Given their straitened circumstances, small favors such as a new pair of pants or a shot of whisky loomed far larger in their lives than the comparatively abstract act of voting. Thus, the number of instances in which men were actually compelled to vote a ticket that they in reality opposed was probably small. With reference to the voting of paupers, the major complaint often rested, at least implicitly, on their insularity from the remainder of the community. This insularity meant that the staff of the poor farm was in a position to perform the small favors that produced votes and, simultaneously, to deny

---

[122] Ibid., p. 209. Given his surname, it was somewhat surprising that McCreary reported that he had been born in Hesse Darmstadt, Germany.

[123] S.R. no. 1271: M.D. no. 117 (1864): p. 99. Another pauper, John Armstrong, also worked at the poorhouse: "I plough and harrow, and help to plant corn; now I am digging post-holes. . . . I work under the steward. I have never drawn any wages. I applied for some once, but got none. I had cradled alongside a man that got two dollars and a half a day, and thought they might give me some money." This other man was apparently a hired hand, not an inmate (p. 209).

[124] Ibid., p. 99.

[125] Ibid., pp. 98–9, 100. Judging from one of the receipts, which was for eight cents, the tax was not very heavy. Another inmate reported his tax as a dime (p. 209). In one of the previous elections, the election officials had not permitted the paupers to vote, but the circumstances were not described in the hearing (pp. 98, 100).

[126] Ibid., pp. 98–9.

[127] Ibid., p. 99.

that opportunity to the opposition. Given that opportunity, the opposition would have almost certainly practiced the same kind of politics.[128]

CONCLUSION

The connection between the material life of ordinary men, in the form of personal networks embedded in communities bounded by ethnic and religious identities, and the demands of economic elites, in the form of a widely shared understanding of how a political economy could and should operate, was made in the public space just outside the voting window. In this public space where subterranean social cleavages and elite superstructures met, party agents were the only men who were required to speak both the dialects of ethnocultural identity and the refined language of political economists. Working both sides of the road, they knew how to tap the spigots of wealth and privilege even while mobilizing the passions of men in the street. Sometimes their specialized skills went to the highest bidder; sometimes they were true only to their party or to a particular candidate.

In some ways the act of voting in mid-nineteenth-century America was clearly undemocratic. The men who voted were often illiterate and uneducated. Even if they had not been swayed by petty bribes or intimidated by violence, the connection between their votes and public policy decisions was extremely tenuous at best.[129] The enforcement of eligibility requirements was haphazard when elections were quiet and fairly administered, ferociously biased when they were not. And at the end of the day, even if the arithmetic was formally correct, the actual count sometimes bore little relation to the numbers of men who turned their tickets in.[130]

---

[128] While noting that reformers often painted a picture of the "masters of poor-houses marching paupers to the polls and instructing them how to vote," Alexander Keyssar skeptically terms this "a vivid, if implausible, image." *Right to Vote*, p. 61. There are, however, enough instances of abuse, both alleged and documented, to suggest that such things sometimes happened in exactly this way. Keyssar estimates the number of paupers denied suffrage rights under state laws as in the "hundreds of thousands" (p. 135).

[129] Few voters, however, were as absentminded as Ephraim Dally: "I voted in Hilliar township, Knox county, Ohio, for Columbus Delano; that is, I intended to vote for him. I voted a tax receipt by mistake, instead of a ticket for Delano." S.R. no. 1313: M.D. no. 38, Pt. 2 (1866): p. 199.

[130] Many poll books were reprinted in the contested election hearings during this period as either one side or the other (and sometimes both) attempted to prove that opposition supporters had voted illegally. Although arithmetical accuracy was usually not at issue, the votes tallied in these poll books can be independently verified. Although this was not done systematically, a very high proportion, ranging between a quarter and a third, of poll books in rural Kentucky (to take just one example) contained errors in simple addition. Although these errors were usually minor, they still suggest that a significant number of reported county returns did not even reflect the actual number of votes recorded in the poll books.

But in other ways the act of voting was profoundly democratic, in some cases for the very reasons that might be cited on the other side of the ledger. Illiterate and ignorant men, steeped in poverty and lacking any other claim on social respectability, were not only permitted to cast their tickets, they were enticed, cajoled, treated, and blessed as they did so.[131] They were not confused or alienated by competing claims and policy demands that had little apparent relevance to their daily existence. Instead, they were assigned identities by party agents that had a direct connection to the personal relationships and communities in which they lived. Writing some time ago, Ronald Formisano put the matter this way:

Researchers in elite sources have overestimated the information and interest possessed by mass publics on issues which generated intense elite engagement. It is time that historians confronted the brute fact that "large portions of the electorate do not have meaningful beliefs, even on issues that have formed the basis of intense political controversy for substantial periods of time." Recognition of the citizenry's limitations implies a realism which can complement, indeed intensify, commitment to a Jeffersonian belief in the development of an informed citizenry.[132]

The upper echelons of society can understand and respond to competing policy platforms and the political economic logics on which they rest. Almost everywhere in the world, suffrage laws and practices have guaranteed these echelons at least some role in democratic governments. However, only in a profoundly democratic system are those who are thoroughly unable to comprehend public policy alternatives and political economic logics placed, at least formally if not in practice, on an equal footing.

[131] Speaking of the 1830s, Mary Ryan contends the "electoral antics" of party agents that brought men to the polls "were defiantly democratic acts." "Civil Society as Democratic Practice: North American Cities during the Nineteenth Century," *Journal of Interdisciplinary History* 29 (1999): 559–84.

[132] Ronald P. Formisano, *The Birth of Mass Political Parties, Michigan, 1827–1861* (Princeton, N.J.: Princeton University Press, 1971), pp. 11–12, 35. However, Formisano neglected the role of party agents in mediating the disjunction between mass political culture and the political economy of public policy while overstating psychology, as opposed to material networks of employment and community, in tracing the development of group attitudes. Even so, his observations were important and original modifications of more traditional interpretations of nineteenth-century voting.

3

Social Construction of Identity in Eastern Rural Communities

From a very general perspective, there were three different venues for voting in the middle of the nineteenth century. For example, many men in the nation's largest cities voted at precincts where party challengers and election officials did not personally know them. With highly transient populations in each neighborhood and very large numbers of voters at each polling place, those attending the voting window usually had little more than a man's physical appearance by which to judge their qualifications and partisan allegiance. While the physiognomy and attire of would-be voters could be visually inspected, reliance on the information thus revealed involved very different practices from those in older, more settled rural communities. In sharp contrast with the latter, the ways in which it was decided who was eligible to vote and which party ticket they might be carrying usually involved stereotypes that did not rely on detailed, contextual histories of an individual. To apply these stereotypes, the crowds surrounding the voting window frequently questioned those approaching the polls, backing up their interrogations with verbal intimidation and physical force. In some cities, such practices appear to have generated the armed political clubs that commandeered precincts in their neighborhoods. Political anonymity thus came at a very high price.

A second, very different venue for voting characterized the western frontier. Situated within an ever-changing social landscape sparsely populated with men constantly moving about in search of good land and economic opportunity, precincts along the line of settlement were places in which anonymous individual voters confronted the petty but nonetheless intense interests of those who ran the polls. As formal organizations, parties were probably less important on the frontier than anywhere else in the nation. But government institutions, such as military forts and other federal installations, were correspondingly more salient factors. Parties primarily influenced frontier politics through these institutions, the latter usually allied with the administration in Washington. And these institutions, particularly military installations, housed large numbers of adult men, especially when compared with the small civilian populations in the region. Although they were usually not legally eligible, the temptation to vote federal troopers along with anyone else who might happen to be traveling through on the way to somewhere else was often irresistible.

However, most men voted in relatively settled, older rural communities well removed from the frontier. Precincts tended to be small, and election officials, party challengers, and bystanders usually recognized the individual identities of men approaching the voting window. Although those attending the polls might have to confer with one another before reaching a consensus, there was usually abundant collateral information that could be brought to bear, for example, on a man's age, mental capacity, residency, and citizenship. Because they were individually known within a widely shared social context, most men carried their social and political histories to the polls; for that reason, they were usually received and recognized as individuals, not as members of larger social categories or classes.[1] To better understand the social and political context in which the act of voting usually occurred in rural neighborhoods east of the frontier, examples of election practice, drawn from instances in which the residency, age, mental competency, and racial identity of individual voters were at issue, are discussed in this chapter.

RESIDENCY

All states had residency requirements for voting, specifying a certain number of weeks or months in a county as a suffrage qualification. Most of the time, these requirements were unproblematic; voters had lived most or all of their lives in a locality, and the election judges, being longtime residents of the community themselves, knew it. However, many other Americans were on the move in the nineteenth century. Much of that movement took the form

---

[1] These three great venues do not, of course, exhaust the variety of environments in which Americans voted in the middle of the nineteenth century. Territorial elections in long-settled, rural New Mexico, for example, combined thick contextual knowledge of individuals at the polls, the heavy influence of federal intervention in the form of trooper voting and general political oversight, and ethnic stereotypes that often disadvantaged the relatively numerous Hispanic population. In these ways, New Mexico elections tended to exhibit some of the salient characteristics of all three venues at the same time. However, there was significant clumping of social contexts and conditions around these types of environments, enough clumping to make them convenient and meaningful categories for the analysis of American political practice. This and the immediately following chapters take up each venue in turn, beginning with long-settled, rural eastern communities, continuing with the largest cities in the nation, and ending with sparsely populated, transient frontier districts.

of long-distance migration to the western frontier. In terms of residency requirements, this migration raised problems in that sparsely and newly settled frontier communities had indistinct boundaries and neighbors often could not vouch for those who lived next to them. In fact, they sometimes did not know whether anyone lived sufficiently close to them to be considered a "neighbor." But the problems in ascertaining residency within densely settled, older communities were often just as serious. In the latter, many men, particularly young men, were constantly on the move as they searched for temporary employment as farm hands, lumberjacks, or other kinds of seasonal workers.

In fact, many adult men were transients who in effect orbited around a central place or lodging that they might call their residence or, less formally, their home. Although they might return to this residence very infrequently, judges of election normally expected that every man would have one, and, thus, the problem was to identify which of a number of possibilities might be a man's residence when he was challenged at the polls.[2] Election judges considered many different things to be evidence of residence, including where a man's wife lived (if he was married), where his parents resided (if unmarried), where a man worked (if employed), and how he represented himself (calling, for example, one place or another "home").

Common practice held that men in transit could keep a residence in one community, for the purposes of voting, if they "intended" to return to that community once their employment was finished.[3] They also had to keep some sort of physical presence in that community. This placed a lot of stress on the laborer's intention, and election judges were often skeptical of the personal plans retrospectively described by men presenting themselves at the polls. One common example, generally typical of the period, involved western migration to the frontier. Adult men would often explore opportunities in the West before returning to move their families to states such as Iowa or Minnesota. If they decided not to migrate, they returned home and again took up residence. But did they, during the weeks or months they spent in search of opportunities in other states, always "intend" to return permanently to their homes? Most election judges ruled that they did, citing the residence of the wife as a substantial and continuing commitment to the community. Similarly, owning a substantial piece of property, such as a farm large enough

---

[2]   Determining residency appears to have been easier in states that imposed a poll tax. For example, antebellum New Jersey assessed a poll tax of fifty cents on all "the white male inhabitants aged 21 years and upwards." The tax records were considered conclusive evidence of both age and residency. Ser. Rec. (hereafter S.R.) no. 1103: Contested Congressional Election in the Third District of New York: Mis. Doc. (hereafter M.D.) no. 6, pp. 39, 64. Amor J. Williamson vs. Daniel E. Sickles, election held on November 2, 1858.

[3]   See, for example, George W. McCrary, *A Treatise on the American Law of Elections* (Keokuk, Iowa: R. B. Ogden, 1875), p. 53.

to provide at least a modest income, was deemed objective evidence of an intention to return.[4]

One voter, Samuel Reed, was an itinerant "practicing physician." After Reed had voted in the August 1859 Kentucky election, his right to do so was called into question in a hearing. Testifying in his support was John Potts, who confirmed that Reed "had a trunk...some medical books...some corn...and...some medicines at my house [in Creelsburg]; he had all his property, so far as I know, except his riding horse, in Creelsburg. He kept those articles (except his horse) in the precinct at my house and at my father's for more than sixty days prior to the last August election." Sixty days' residence in a community qualified a man to vote under Kentucky law. Having established that Reed had kept what appears to have been almost all his worldly possessions in Creelsburg, attention then shifted to Reed's intentions. Potts was thus asked whether Reed had told him "when he left his goods with you that he was going to Cumberland county for a few days, and was going to return to Russell county, and only went to Cumberland county to board for a few days or until he could make arrangements for board in Creelsburg." All of this Potts obligingly confirmed.[5] Because Reed had left behind material belongings sufficiently valuable that it could be presumed that he would not abandon them, the decision was a relatively simple, if informal, application of the law: Reed was, under the collective understanding of the community in the middle of the nineteenth century, a resident of Creelsburg at the time of the election.

Borderline cases, where the laborer had neither a wife nor property, had to be decided on other grounds.[6] For many young men, the family residence was the default home of the transient laborer; parents were usually willing to swear that their sons regularly lodged with them between jobs and stored belongings in the family residence when moving about the region. The really difficult cases involved unmarried, unpropertied transients who had either

---

[4] Would-be voters who had returned home had to demonstrate, by their oath, that they had never "intended" to settle elsewhere. See, for example, S.R. no. 1063: Contested Congressional Election in the Fourth District of Kentucky: M.D. no. 11, pp. 273, 303–7. Response of Anderson to Chrisman in James S. Chrisman vs. William C. Anderson, election held on August 1, 1859.

[5] S.R. no. 1061: Contested Congressional Election in the Fourth District of Kentucky: M.D. no. 3, pp. 227, 231. James S. Chrisman vs. William C. Anderson, election held on August 1, 1859.

[6] Such men presented the toughest cases for both election judges and those who reviewed their decisions. A report by the Committee on Elections to the parent House of Representatives described them as "persons who have no property, who have no family, or whose family moves with them from place to place, who have no place to return to from temporary absences, the domicile of whose origin is in another country, and has been in the most solemn manner renounced [via naturalization proceedings], and the ordinary business of whose life consists in successive temporary employments in different places." Quoted in McCrary, *American Law of Elections*, p. 428. Also see pp. 429–30.

broken relations with their families or wished to vote in jurisdictions where their families did not live. They usually had but one recourse under the law: to prove that they, on a regular and continuing basis, had their "washing" done by someone in the community, regardless of where they were employed.

Washing clothes was a specialized occupation in the nineteenth century. Unmarried males often employed one woman to do their washing, leaving with them clothes to be washed while picking up those that had been cleaned. The home of this washing woman was often accepted as prima facie evidence of residency, an "intention to return" if only to pick up one's clothes. Thus, farm laborers were said to have maintained a permanent residence in the community as they moved around the region sleeping in the fields, barns, or corn cribs of their employers.[7] Thus, for the many transients who owned little more than the proverbial "shirt on their backs," the community understanding was that a man's residence was wherever he had that shirt washed.

James Haley of Boyle County, Kentucky, for example, considered his home to be "wherever I keep my washing." However, Haley had been incarcerated in another county after he had been charged there as an accessory to a shooting. Until his release, he could neither deliver nor collect his "washing" in Boyle County. Furthermore, there was little evidence that he regularly had his clothes washed in Boyle County even when he was free. In his own words:

I was bailed out of jail; went to court, and the grand jury found no indictment.... I had not worked a day in three weeks previous to that time, to my recollection.... Principally [during that time] I was drinking whiskey, and the balance of the time, perhaps, I might have been playing cards, or perhaps something else. One week of the time I was near Bradfordsville, Marion county; one week in Boyle, and one week in Lincoln.

Haley had been released from jail on June 13, 1859. Since this release was within the sixty-day residency period required to vote in a precinct, he had to claim that, while in jail, he "intended to return" to Boyle County where he later voted. But given his habitual wandering, it was hard to say what could have substantiated such an intention. When asked what he had done to make a living in the year prior to the election, Haley said,

I have worked in Lincoln, Casey, and Boyle [counties].... The biggest portion of my time I have spent in Lincoln county, in Stanford, whilst in jail; I was there

---

[7]   As with many other aspects of election practice, reliance on washing as a primary indicator of residence had a long history. For example, in 1809 and again in 1810 a young Harvard student cited the fact that he had "his washing and mending done" at his father's house as evidence that he was qualified to vote in that town despite the fact that he was otherwise away at school. Luther S. Cushing, *Reports of Contested Elections in the Massachusetts House of Representatives, 1780–1834* (Boston: Dutton and Wentworth, 1834), pp. 56–7, 66. For a brief bibliography on social mobility in the United States during the nineteenth century, see Paul Bourke and Donald DeBats, *Washington County: Politics and Community in Antebellum America* (Baltimore: Johns Hopkins University Press, 1995), nn. 43, 44, p. 377.

forty-three days. The balance of the time I was harvesting around there. I cradled in the neighborhood for sixteen days after I got out of jail; but my washing was still at Yates'. I came on to Mr. Helm's, and expected to cradle there also; but he concluded to have no more grain cut, and I then came on to Yates', and staid about there until the election.

Haley then added, "I have been trying to make arrangements to live without work during the last twelve months. . . . I have picked up an idea that I could win my living" through gambling. Haley had been permitted to vote by the election judges after describing his circumstances under oath at the polls. After he voted, Haley immediately left town once more because "[t]here were several men here after me with pistols, &c., and I thought best to get out of danger."[8]

Several similar cases appeared in the hearings on the 1859 election in Kentucky. The first involved a William Sharp, an itinerant farm hand who claimed a residence with his uncle in Jamestown, Kentucky. When the uncle, Joseph Coffey, was asked to verify Sharp's claim, he responded very carefully:

. . . my house has been his home ever since he returned from Illinois, some year and a half, or two years, it may be three; he has had his washing done there all the time, except one shirt at Lewis Johnson's; sometimes he would stay about nine days at my house and work for me, and then he would go round about in the neighborhood and work, and return to my house and get his clothing; he was at my house all the time, except some two or three months, when he was off in Adair or Hart county tending a crop for some man.[9]

By identifying the all-important location of Sharp's "washing," Coffey's testimony substantiated his nephew's orbiting employment pattern as centering on his uncle's house. When the uncle reported that his nephew's parents were both deceased, that fact eliminated the possibility that their residence might have served as Sharp's "home." The remaining possibility, that Sharp might have had a wife and that her residence should have determined his voting eligibility, was precluded by the implicit evidence that he was not married.

While William Sharp could present a strong case to the election judges, the same was not true of Jesse Wright, a "poor old man" whose wife was dead and whose children had apparently abandoned him. Obviously destitute, he scraped out a meager living as an itinerant farm laborer. Up to about a month before the election, he had lived in Wolf Creek Precinct, Russell County, Kentucky. After that, however, he had been in Wayne County, although it was not clear what he was doing there. During that time, Wright had left his meager belongings with Hardin Wilson, a neighbor, and had told Wilson he would return for them when "he had got a place" over in Wayne County.

---

[8] S.R. no. 1063: M.D. no. 11 (1859): pp. 52–3. Shortly after the election, Haley was indicted "for false swearing on your application to vote." The outcome of that indictment did not appear in the record.

[9] S.R. no. 1061: M.D. no. 3 (1859): pp. 242–3.

Wright, however, had come back to Wolf Creek the day before the election and announced that he would vote there. Wilson told Wright that "he was knocked out of his vote." Wright protested by saying "no – that he had come back on purpose to vote; that that was his right place to vote at; that he claimed that place as his residence. He said that he claimed that as his residence, as he had his washing done there. Mrs. Hart, who lived in my [Wilson's] yard, had done washing for him. He said the people in Wayne told him that was his right place to vote." Wright may have been aged, destitute, and abandoned by his family, but he understood community practice well enough to cite his "washing" as his residence. In addition, the authorities in Wayne had identified Wolf Creek as his proper polling place, the implication being that he should be allowed to vote at one place or the other.[10]

The community understanding that a man's residence was where his washing was done was quite possibly founded on social practice; if you wanted to leave a message for a man who was known to be somewhere in a community but you knew not where to look, you would probably leave that message with a person whom you knew would, sooner or later, come into contact with that man. His "washing woman" was, in many cases, the only person an itinerant laborer was certain to contact periodically.

The most mobile men in America were undoubtedly those who worked aboard the trains. One of those men was James Boyd, who was employed six days a week on a local freight running a scheduled route between Pittsburgh and Conemaugh in southwestern Pennsylvania. He would spend one night in Pittsburgh and the next in Conemaugh, repeating the pattern again and again. When starting out, he "took breakfast in Pittsburg, dinner at Derry, and supper at Conemaugh," reversing the order on the return run. He was never off duty except on Sundays and "once when [he] had a sore heel." Otherwise he was always on the road. Boyd claimed none of the above cities and towns as his residence when he voted in October 1868. Instead, he showed up at the polls at Irwin's Station, "on account of my relations living there, and I had been living there myself" in the past. He also stated that he went to "Mr. Hiester's," either a hotel or boardinghouse at Irwin's Station, on Sundays or when he was injured. However, although he had eaten a meal in the community, he had not spent a night in Irwin's Station in the ten days prior to the election. The only other claim he had to residency there was that he passed through, without stopping, each day he was working. If Boyd had been allowed to vote at that precinct, he probably

---

10   Ibid., p. 245. Since one of the major charges in this election contest was that many nonresidents had voted, there are numerous cases in the hearings. For other examples, see pp. 266, 275–7. Also see Joseph McNeil's rambling testimony in defense of his right to vote in S.R. no. 1063: M.D. no. 11 (1859): p. 32. For another itinerant farm laborer's attempt to establish residency, see S.R. no. 1431: Contested Congressional Election in the Fifth District of Pennsylvania: M.D. no. 7, pp. 331–2. Caleb N. Taylor vs. John R. Reading, election held on October 13, 1868.

could have, with equal ease, claimed residency in Pittsburgh, Conemaugh, and even Derry.[11]

All of the men described in this section were compelled to declare a residence in order to vote. For most of them, this declaration was a fiction in that they didn't really "belong" to any community. Instead, they had fragile and tenuous links to individuals who, for their part, actually "belonged" to a community. Through their links to washing women, friends, parents, and wives (some of them estranged), itinerant men could then claim other people's communities as their own. The letter of the law never captured or addressed the complexity of the social and economic world in which men lived. The usual assumption at the polls was that every man had a residence somewhere, although that residence might not be in the precinct at which he presented himself. Thus, to refuse a man a vote on the basis of residency usually meant that the judges of election had to figure out where he should, in fact, vote.[12] Emotional ties associated with parents and wives also helped to fill the gaps. But most of the practices, customs, and norms that governed residency decisions at the polls had slim basis in formal election law. They constituted, instead, shared traditions that had evolved into a kind of popular "common law" in their respective communities.[13] Thus, some men came to have "residences" solely because they wanted to vote.[14]

Age

Most states did not officially record the births of their residents in the nineteenth century. That meant that most men did not have a certificate of birth that they could present to election officials in order to document that they had reached the qualifying age (twenty-one years old in most cases). When

---

[11] S.R. no. 1431: Contested Congressional Election in the Twenty-first District of Pennsylvania: M.D. (no number, bound between nos. 24 and 25), p. 271. John Covode vs. Henry D. Foster, election held on October 13, 1868. For other examples of itinerant train workers, see pp. 246–7, 249, 268.

[12] See, for example, the election-day saga of seventy-two-year-old Daniel Delaney, who was sent back and forth between two polling places because he had been assessed in one community and had an estranged wife in another. The judges in each precinct thought he should vote at the other. S.R. no. 1431: M.D. (no number, bound between nos. 24 and 25 [1868]): pp. 317–18.

[13] For additional examples of residency-related decisions at the polling place, see Richard Bensel, "The American Ballot Box: Law, Identity, and the Polling Place in the Mid-Nineteenth Century," *Studies in American Political Development* 17 (Spring 2003): 15–17.

[14] This is a bit of a twist on James Scott's notion of state-created "legibility" in that here the state declared a principle (i.e., a man must have a residency in order to vote), and the people, through informed practice and knowledge of particular instances, made the principle legible. *Seeing Like a State: How Certain Schemes to Improve the Human Condition Have Failed* (New Haven: Yale University Press, 1998), pp. 2–3.

a young man presented himself at the polls, the election judges construed his age in diverse ways, including his willingness to swear that he was old enough to vote. For a man known to the judges, they could compare their individual recollections, thereby constructing a kind of shared social history of his birth and youth with reference to major events in the community. One elaborate and interesting example of such reasoning appeared in testimony taken in Monticello, Kentucky.

The election had been held in August 1859, and the question posed was whether John Rollins was twenty-one years of age when he had presented himself at the polls. To qualify, Rollins had to have been born sometime on or before August 1, 1838. One witness was certain that Rollins was, in fact, not twenty-one when he voted, offering the following deductive argument as support for his belief:

I am well acquainted with [John Rollins]; and if he was born in the year of 1838, he was born in the last days of that year. I know that David Gibbs was executed in this county for the murder of Roger Oatts, and my recollection is that [the] execution was on the 22d day of July, 1838. I saw [his] mother after the execution of Gibbs and she was then pregnant ... but her pregnancy at that time was just discernible. His mother's name is Polly Rollins, or was then – she being an unmarried woman when her ... son was born. My recollection is, that he was born in December of the date 1838.[15]

At first glance, the execution of David Gibbs and the physical appearance of Polly Rollins seem to be unrelated facts. While executions were rare and noteworthy events in rural counties, pregnancies were common and normally unremarkable. Thus, this witness was using the execution to reference the period around which John Rollins had to have been born in order to qualify to vote; against that backdrop, he was recollecting how Polly Rollins appeared at that time. To bring the point home, he was asked, "At or about the time David Gibbs was hung, was or not the pregnancy of Polly Rollins discoverable?" To which he responded, "I think not."[16]

A second, illiterate witness proceeded in much the same way, only adding that John Rollins was "represented to be an illegitimate son of Stephen Gibbs ... [who had left] this county in the year 1838, and has not been in this county since he went to the west."[17] A third witness added a little more

---

[15]   S.R. no. 1061: M.D. no. 3 (1859): pp. 53–4. John Rollins had voted in a rural precinct in Wayne County, outside Monticello.

[16]   Ibid., p. 54.

[17]   Ibid., p. 55. This witness also reported that Polly Rollins had later married William Russell, "who now lives near to me." When women were brought into a hearing, either in absentia or in person, their reputed virtue was often considered relevant information. In this instance, the witness was asked, "Is she not now a reputable and straight woman?" He responded in a way that might not have been entirely satisfactory to his neighbor, "As far as I know, she stand fair at this time" (p. 55).

detail in what was a now familiar account:

David Gibbs was hanged in this county, for the murder of Roger Oates, on the 2d day of July, 1838. . . . I saw . . . Polly Rollins, on that day. . . . I resided within four miles of said Polly. She at the time was residing with Mrs. Gibbs, the mother of the said David, and was an unmarried woman, and was not married when her said John was born. When I saw her on the day [of the execution], if she was pregnant I did not notice it.

This witness gave a slightly different date for the execution of David Gibbs, but that was immaterial to the age of John Rollins.[18]

What is more noteworthy is that Polly Rollins was living with the mother of David Gibbs at the time of the execution. From that fact and by reading between the lines, we can deduce that Stephen Gibbs, the reputed father of John Rollins, was also David's brother. And since he left the county at about the same time as David was executed, never to return (and thus abandoning Polly as she became an unwed mother), we might suspect that the two brothers were both implicated in the murder of Roger Oatts. This would explain why Polly was living with Mrs. Gibbs when David was hanged; Mrs. Gibbs was Polly's (unwed) mother-in-law and became the grandmother of John Rollins at his birth.[19] It also explains why Polly's appearance was noteworthy; she was seen with the mother of an executed man and known to be romantically involved with a brother who was probably an accomplice in the murder. All of these witnesses resided within several miles of the former Polly Rollins (now Mrs. William Russell) and considered themselves neighbors. Several of them were illiterate and gave varying dates with reference to the birth of John Rollins. But they understood how the physical appearance of a woman changes over the course of a pregnancy, knew that the execution of David Gibbs had occurred relatively close to the time of the election, and had, inadvertently as it was, noted Polly's physical appearance at the time of the execution. From this information, they were able to deduce the age of John Rollins in their testimony.[20]

---

[18] S.R. no. 1061: M.D. no. 3 (1859): p. 66. Although none of these witnesses had served as a judge of election when John Rollins appeared at the polls, the hearings presumed that a similar, collective social history to the one emerging in testimony would have been available to the judges. For that reason, the evidence and interpretations presented by witnesses in the hearing were intended to gauge whether the judges had properly or improperly allowed John Rollins to vote.

[19] Two more witnesses corroborated the accounts appearing in the text. The first was a neighbor who had visited Polly Rollins shortly after the birth of her son. Since this was in February of the year following the execution of David Gibbs, John Rollins had not been twenty-one years of age at the time of the 1868 election. The second said much the same thing, reporting, "If [John Rollins's] mother was in the family way [at the time of the hanging], it was hardly perceivable." S.R. no. 1061: M.D. no. 3 (1859): p. 69.

[20] Later in the hearings, the Gibbs execution allowed William McGee to estimate the age of Stephen Loveall by way of a very similar triangulation between the execution

The same congressional election produced another instance of disputed age, this one involving the qualifications of William Massongal.[21] Terry Sizemore testified that he had told Massongal that he was under age on the day of the election. The basis for this assertion was Sizemore's recollection of the relationship between Massongal's birth and the birth of his daughter: "I have a daughter named Rebecca who will be 21 years of age the 8th day of the present month [November 1859], and my daughter Rebecca is near twelve months older than [William] Massongal. I was at the house where he was born on the evening after his ... birth, and saw him, and know that he is younger than my daughter Rebecca for the period mentioned above."

Sizemore went on to say that he had lived about two and a half miles from the Massongal home when William was born "and was well acquainted with the family, as they were my neighbors at that time. His mother worked at my house one day." This would have been rather strong testimony, except that Sizemore was illiterate and there was no written record of his daughter's age. When asked to provide corroborating evidence, Sizemore was compelled to admit that he only knew his daughter's age "merely as a matter of recollection" and had "no circumstance by which to fix" the date. A noteworthy event, such as the execution of David Gibbs in the previous example, would have given the community a reference point by which to determine Rebecca's age. In the absence of such a temporal landmark, even though Sizemore may have well been right about the twelve-month interval between the two births, his testimony still hinged on whether or not he, in fact, knew just how old his own daughter was at the time the election was held.

Sizemore's testimony was challenged from another direction. When J. J. Sheppard was asked his opinion of the "general character of Terry Sizemore," he gave a confused response: "He stands as a drunkard; it's good, so far as I know." Sheppard was then asked, "Does he not live among and keep company with a pack of low-down whores?" Sheppard replied, "I don't know; his associations are bad with loose women." Asked whether Sizemore was "regarded as an incorruptible, honest, and truthful man," Sheppard gave another confusing response: "I never heard anything on that subject. He is regarded as an honest, truthful man. I never heard anything said against his

and the births of his daughter and Loveall: "Loveall ... was born the 5th or 6th day of December, 1838; I am enabled to remember the date of his birth from the age of my daughter Anne Jane; I have a record of my daughter's birth, made about the time of her birth; I cannot read myself, but it was read to me recently, giving her birth on 20th December, 1838, and I know it is correct. My daughter was born in December after David Gibbs was hung ... in the summer of the year 1838." His account was corroborated by his wife, who again mentioned Gibbs's execution. S.R. no. 1063: M.D. no. 11 (1859): pp. 621–2.

21 William Massongal's name was also spelled Massingil, Massengill, and Massangal in the hearings, and several witnesses referred to him as "John" Massongal as well. Since all these names referenced the same person, the alternate spellings have been changed to William Massongal to eliminate confusion in the text.

truthfulness or honesty, nor anything any way on that subject."[22] Another witness, John Goddard, was more direct: "As to his moral character, I do not consider his being of the best by a long way, and has great room for repairs. . . . If he was drunk, I think it [his testimony under oath] d—d uncertain; and if sober, he might swear the truth." W. M. Burton similarly concluded that Sizemore was not to believed under oath because he was a drunk and "generally considered a naturally worthless man."[23]

Taking the stand after Sizemore had stepped down, Jesse Cox was also asked whether he could help determine Massongal's age. Although he started out well, Cox was ultimately of little help:

I am acquainted with William Massongal, and have known him from his birth, and I don't think he was twenty-one years of age at the late August election. My daughter Celia was born on the 10th day of February, 1842, and said Massongal was born in the fall or winter before said period. I had my family record examined last night by one of my neighbors, and Celia's age is so recorded. I lived in the neighborhood [within five miles] of the father of said Massongal, who is now dead, at the time of his birth.

He was then asked whether he knew Massongal's age "as well as you do that of your daughter Celia?" To which he answered, "He was at the breast of his mother, who came to my house when my daughter Celia was born, and was a little over two months of age then." However, Cox was illiterate and did not know his own age, although he said he was "over fifty." Everything then hinged on the accuracy of the "family record." Although he did not say so in his testimony, most records of events such as births, deaths, and marriages were kept in the family Bible. Someone would make these entries for illiterate families around the time the event occurred and the Bible could then be consulted by a literate friend or acquaintance when required. In the absence of official documentation, these records were considered rather strong evidence.[24]

William Massongal came up again in these hearings, but this time attention was focused on the character of his mother, Nancy. The witness, James Selby, testified that he "lived within four or five miles of [Nancy Massongal], and been acquainted with her and the family for going on two years. . . . I have been [at their house] frequently and stayed all night. . . ." Selby was then asked whether he was "acquainted with the general character of the said Nancy Massongal." To which he responded, "I hear it spoken of frequently about borrowing and not paying." Asked whether "her general character" was "good or bad," he went directly to the point: "I know nothing of her whoring with any one." However, based on his "knowledge of her character," he reported that he "would have . . . doubts" with reference to

---

[22] S.R. no. 1061: M.D. no. 3 (1859): pp. 68–9, 317–18.

[23] S.R. no. 1063: M.D. no. 11 (1859): pp. 647–8, 650.

[24] S.R. no. 1061: M.D. no. 3 (1859): pp. 72–3.

believing "her fully on oath." The questioner then returned to the mother's character: "Is it generally reported and believed in your neighborhood that Nancy [Massongal] is a whore?" To which Selby replied, "I don't know that it is." This was probably a good thing because he was then asked, "Does she neighbor and stay with you of nights occasionally?" Selby responded that she "has stayed with me three nights." Pushing home a doubtful point, the questioner then asked, "How often have you stayed with her?" The answer was, "Two nights that I know of." Although these visits were evidently with his family in tow, the counsel was apparently attempting to connect Selby to Nancy Massongal in a way that would have besmirched both of their characters.[25]

Nancy's character was indirectly brought up again during the hearings. This time Ezekiel Cecil testified that he was "acquainted with" William Massongal because "he is said to be my [illegitimate] son...he was, I am confident, born in the month of December, 1837." Cecil said that he remembered Massongal's age because "I was quite young...and the law [would have] laid a heavy fine on me if it was mine; and [I] was told that unless the mother proceeded against me in two years after the child's birth I would be relieved, and I recollect that I watched the time very closely until the two years were out." Cecil had married in 1843 but could not figure out how old Massongal had been at that time: "I have not counted it. I was married in 1843; he was born in 1837; you can count it."[26] In Cecil's case, his possible legal responsibility led him to focus intently on Nancy, her son's birth, and the date at which the statute of limitations would run out. Since he would presumably not volunteer such information in support of a partisan cause (his spouse, for example, must have been at least irritated to have her husband's premarital exploits discussed in a public forum), Cecil's account probably carried more weight than that of most of the preceding witnesses.[27]

---

[25] Since William Massongal had voted for Chrisman and since the strongest evidence supporting his eligibility with reference to age was provided by his mother, Anderson's attorney was attempting to smear the mother's reputation and thus impeach her testimony. Ibid., pp. 307–8. As in other testimony reported in this chapter, we are much less interested in the accuracy of the witness accounts than in, first, the ways in which common people could marshal evidence of the ages of their children and neighbors and, second, how they attempted to reconstruct that evidence in the presence of election officials.

[26] S.R. no. 1063: M.D. no. 11 (1859): p. 292.

[27] Pregnancies produced by sexual relations outside marriage often became well ensconced in the community's collective memory and/or publicly archived in legal records. For example, Joseph Miller, a justice of the peace in Bucks County, Pennsylvania, had conclusive proof that Henry Reinheimer, who voted in the 1868 election, was not of age: "The record I spoke of, and now hold in my hand, is the information filed with me, as a justice of peace, charging the crime of fornication and bastardy on his father, Aaron Reinheimer. In that information she [his mother, Levina Giffen] makes oath that he was born on the 4th of February, 1848." S.R. no. 1431: M.D. no. 7 (1868): p. 16.

However, the person who was in the best position to triangulate William Massongal's birth with other events in the community was probably his mother. After having her character closely examined in these hearings, Nancy finally appeared in the flesh. Like most of the other witnesses, she began by forcefully stating her conclusion: "To the best of my recollection, he [William Monroe Massongal] was twenty-two years of age last Thursday, (1st day of December, 1859). The record of my children's ages has been lost. The only way I have to come at his age is by counting back by the ages of my other children." While this would have meant that William was eligible to vote in the 1859 election, it soon became evident that Nancy was not able to count "back by the ages" of her other children.

She had given birth to thirteen children, "seven living and six dead." The usual interval between these births, she reported, had been in "general near two years; this is my recollection." Sarah had been the oldest, born the "first of June; I can't tell the year." Elizabeth had been the next oldest, born the "first day of March; I don't know the year." Both Sarah and Elizabeth were dead. Then came Delany, who was still living and had been born the "6th day of July; I can't tell the year." After Delany came Matthew, also living and born the "third day of October; I don't know the year."

William Monroe, whose age was in dispute in this hearing, appeared fifth in the birth order. He had been born on the "first day of December; I don't know the year." Nancy had previously "moved from the upper part of Missouri to Morgan county, Tennessee, when I had only one child. I then remained there on the same place [in Morgan County] that my son William Monroe was born until all my children were born. I then moved to Kentucky, going on three years ago, to the place where I now live." After William, came Polly, born the "third day of May; I don't know the year."

Up to this point all of Nancy's children had been reported as having been born early in their respective months, usually the first or third day. However, Louisa, seventh in line, "was born in June, sometime about the middle; I don't know the year." Serepta Susanna, the eighth child, was born "sometime along in January; I don't know the year." The ninth was given her mother's name; she "was born the 11th day of February; I don't know the year." John was tenth, but Nancy confessed, "I don't remember when he was born." Dempsey was eleventh, but, as was the case with John, she admitted, "I don't know the month Dempsey was born, nor the year. Those who died, including John and Dempsey, who died from the breast, I did not pay so much attention to them. My next was named Franky Ann; she was my last living child; she was born the last day of January; I don't know the year. My next and last child was named Adam; he is dead; he was born the first day of December; I don't know the year." In sum, Nancy Massengill was able to recall the birth order of her thirteen children but could not provide the year for any of them.

However, Nancy did give an age for Adam: "It [*sic*] is dead. If living, it would be about seven years old. I can't give the month. I laid six months confined after its birth." Although she could not recall the date of her marriage, she could give the date of her husband's death: "He will have been dead three years the 25th day of January next." She said that she was able to calculate the time that had elapsed since Adam was born "[o]n account of my husband being dead, and the time he died." Adam "lived five months and three weeks after its birth" and "died about three years before my husband died." Thus, Nancy's estimate of what would have been Adam's age at the time of the hearing appears to have been roughly accurate. Since there were eight birth intervals between Adam and William and since she had reported that the usual interval had been about two years, William would have been about twenty-three years old at the time of the hearing, give or take one or two years. While it seems unlikely that she would have been able to fabricate her testimony in such a way as to support her son's eligibility to vote (e.g., she signed her testimony with her mark, indicating that she was illiterate), she may have been aware that there may have been legal consequences. When she was asked whether she knew "that it is a violation of law for a young man to vote before his majority," she reported, "That's what I have heard folks say."

Although Nancy Massongal would not have been present at the polls when William voted and, even if she had, the judges would probably not have allowed her to present such a complicated account as evidence of her son's age, the primary question here is what kind of materials the community had available when age became an issue.[28] In other words, how would the judges of election, when and if William were challenged at the polls, have constructed his age when he himself did not know when he had been born? Nancy's character, as was evident from earlier testimony, would have been a factor because it would have, at the minimum, colored the reputation that her son brought with him to the polls. However, the sheer physical limits on Nancy's reproductive capacity would have counted in his favor; the number of children that she had borne, along with William's place in the birth order, made it very likely that he had been of age when he presented himself at the polls. All of this testimony, of course, would have been moot had the "record of my children's ages" not been "lost." This, in all likelihood, had been the family Bible.[29]

---

[28]   S.R. no. 1063: M.D. no. 11 (1859): pp. 312–14. As in all these contested elections, this hearing was held several months after the polls had closed. For a description of these hearings, see Chapter 1.

[29]   As in this case, Bibles and other written records could disappear or be destroyed. This had happened to James Crawford, who reported that the family Bible "was burnt up when the house burnt up." This left Crawford uncertain as to the date of his son's birth. "I know when he was born, the month he was born, and the year, but I can't say the date. He was born 1845, the 21st or 22d day of May; I can't tell exactly."

As evidence of age, family Bibles were themselves subject to contextual interpretation. In 1866, a young man named Job Evans cast his first vote in an election in Knox County, Ohio. Dr. J. N. Burr, who had delivered all six children in the Evans family, stated that he knew Job was twenty-one because he had written down in his day book the date on which he had been born as "October 20, 1844. Job Evans, visit, obstrt.....$5.00." This journal recorded the date of the delivery, the family to which the child was born, and the amount owed the doctor. If the family had paid in cash, this entry may not have been made. The mother, in opposition to the doctor's testimony, stated that the family Bible recorded Job's birth date as October 5, 1846. However, there were some problems with the Bible. In the first place, when the entries for the eldest children had been copied from an earlier record (probably another Bible), "there was a mistake [made] in their ages [i.e., the wrong year was entered] ... by the man that wrote it down." The family still had the page on which the births had originally been recorded, in each case the morning after the birth. But the portion of that page on which Job's birth had originally been recorded "was lost about three years ago this spring, when we were cleaning house." So the mother, who was incidentally incriminating her son as an illegal voter, could demonstrate Job's age only by referring to the copied entries for her children, some of which she admitted were erroneous. Why she chose to incriminate her son as an illegal voter was unclear. As she put it, "I hadn't a particle of thought or care about it [the election]. I am not a politician; I did not meddle with it."[30]

Andrew Hill voted in the 1859 Kentucky congressional election at the Parmleysville Precinct in Wayne County. His mother, Katherine Winchester, was asked how old Andrew had been when he voted in that election; her testimony again indicates just how complicated such a question could become in antebellum Kentucky.[31] In opening the questioning, counsel asked whether she was "the same person that is usually called Katharine Hill by your neighbors." Answering in the affirmative, she added that her "son was born the 20th day of March. I am no scholar and don't recollect the year in which he was born, but to the best of my knowledge he was twenty-one years of age the 20th day of last March [1859]. I was married in my sixteenth year, and my oldest son was born in my seventeenth year, and he, my oldest son, will be twenty-five years old the 16th of February next [1860]. I have a

However uncertain he was of the date, the father was certain that his son had been twenty-one years of age when he voted on October 9, 1866. And so he had been, if his recollection was correct. S.R. no. 1313: Contested Congressional Election in the Thirteenth District of Ohio: M.D. no. 38, Pt. 2, p. 617. Columbus Delano vs. George W. Morgan, election held on October 9, 1866. For another example, see S.R. no. 1061: M.D. no. 3 (1859): p. 134.

[30]   S.R. no. 1313: Contested Congressional Election in the Thirteenth District of Ohio: M.D. no. 38, Pt. 1, pp. 54–5, and Pt. 2, p. 252. Columbus Delano vs. George W. Morgan, election held on October 9, 1866.

[31]   Her testimony appears in S.R. no. 1061: M.D. no. 3 (1859): pp. 295, 297–8.

daughter only between the said oldest and the said Andrew Hill, and their age is in the Bible. She will be twenty-four years old the 10th day of next May [1860]." Apparently, Andrew's birth was not recorded in the Bible; otherwise, his age would have been immediately substantiated. When asked how old she was, as a way of verifying the date of her marriage and the birth of her oldest son, she answered that her "mother told me that I was married in my sixteenth [year] and had a child in my seventeenth year, and my oldest child will be twenty-five the 16th of next month. I don't know how old I am; count it yourself." She was then asked how she knew the age of her oldest child. To this, she responded, "Well, I just kept his age along by what my mother told me of my own age." After proceeding in this way for a bit, the questioning then returned to Andrew. His mother again confirmed that he "will be twenty-two next March agreeably to what little I know about it."

Katherine had had eleven children, all of whom were still living. She had been married twice before she wed Douglas Winchester, her current husband. Her first marriage was to a Joseph Owens, who "took another woman and went off." She had had one child by him. Her second marriage was to an Andy Bultram, by whom she had borne six children before he died. Between Bultram's death and her marriage to Douglas Winchester, she had borne four children out of wedlock; these were her youngest. Her union with Winchester, now three years and counting, had been childless. When asked why her son went "by the name of Hill" when, by her account, she had been married to Bultram when he was born, she said, "Because people just call him that. All my boys go by the name of Hill. I was a Hill before my first marriage." In closing, she was asked whether she knew where Andrew was. She said that she didn't know. Counsel then asked whether he had "not run away so soon as he had voted." His mother replied, "No, sir; he has not run away; the last I heard of him, he was living on the lands of [Joseph] Dolan, with his brother-in-law, in this county." Although the election judges would have not had the opportunity to question Andrew's mother – because women almost never went anywhere near the polling place on election day – it is fairly clear that neither she nor her son knew how old he was. The extensive questioning of her family history was an attempt to triangulate his date of birth by referencing the ages of her other children and the dates of her marriages. While her evidence must have been mildly titillating to a Victorian audience and painfully revealing for her, her testimony left Andrew's age just as mysterious when she had finished as it had been before she began.

Another witness, John Lewallen, could corroborate much of Katherine Hill's account. Lewallen began by addressing her age: "I suppose she is somewhere near forty; this is only guess work. . . . Her oldest child's name is Bailey; I am of opinion he was born in 1834; this is also guess work; I do not know the month or day of the month. . . . Her second child's name is Ceily; she was born in 1838. . . . The next one is named Andrew, and I think he was born in the spring of 1840. After this I moved from the place where I was then living, and lived about fourteen or fifteen miles from Mrs. Hill, and I do not know when the balance of her children were born." After saying that she had first taken up with a man named Owens, he stated, "I don't know whether he left before or after the child was born; I heard that they had parted several times, and then they would live together again." He didn't know how long it was before she began living with [Bultram] but said that it "was a right smart while." However, there were two Bultrams involved with Hill: "It was talked that she cohabited with a William [Bultram] a short time after Owens left; this was not Andrew [Bultram], the reputed father of Andrew Hill . . . after she commenced living with [Bultram] she had children pretty fast." Lewallen's account would have made Andrew under age at the time of the election.[32]

Even more titillating was the testimony presented as an attempt to impeach Katherine Hill's character. The mildest criticism was offered by Andrew Lewallen: "I am acquainted with her; I never heard tell of her being sworn until since the last election. If she was mad at me I would fear her, but if she was friendly with me I should not be afraid. . . . I heard three of my neighbor women say that she had told a barefaced lie on them. These are all the reasons I have for saying that I would not believe her on oath."[33] John Lewallen was much more damning. Asked whether he was "acquainted with the general moral character of Catharine Hill," he replied, "Yes, sir; I am; and it is not good." Asked whether he would believe "her on oath if she had anything at stake" (e.g., possible prosecution of her son for underage voting), Lewallen answered, "I would not like to." When asked whether "her character [has] been ever since she was a girl that of a prostitute and bad whore, ready for every call," Lewallen agreed, "That is her character."[34]

Lewis Davenport agreed, relating that "she lives about three miles from me; I have known her from six to ten years." He then added, "Her general character in my neighborhood is that she is a prostitute." As to her reputation

---

[32] S.R. no. 1063: M.D. no. 11 (1859): p. 610. Also contradicting her testimony was William Dobbs, a farmer familiar with the family, who related, "Andrew Hill came to my house in July last; I wanted to hire him to work, and asked him his age, as he looked small; he answered me, as I now recollect, that he was eighteen years of age (18); his two younger brothers were with him, and I thought them small for plough boys; I had talked to Katy Hill or Winchester before the boys came to my house, and she stated that the boys were all under her, and that if I hired any of them she must have half of the pay, and the other half must go to the benefit of the boys to buy clothes, &c. I am not sure that it was Andrew who answered my question about his age; but if not him, it was answered for him by one of the others in his presence" (p. 632).

[33] S.R. no. 1063: M.D. no. 11 (1859): pp. 605–6.

[34] Ibid., p. 608. After defaming Katherine Hill in this way, it came as no surprise that Lewallen thought she was not a credible witness: "Any woman that has the reputation in her neighborhood that she has I cannot believe her on oath." When asked whether his "opinion of her . . . constitute[d] general character," he replied that his "own opinion of itself would not amount to general character if the neighborhood were not of the same opinion" (p. 610).

since her last marriage to Douglas Winchester, Davenport reported, "I don't know how long she has been married to her last husband; not more than two years, I think; since her last marriage I have heard no one say that he had had intercourse with her, though I think she is believed still to be a prostitute." His opinion of her "general character," based on her sexual history as he understood it, led Davenport to conclude, "I don't think I could believe her on oath." This was only mildly qualified by his admission that he had "heard her testify on oath; and I never heard any one say that she was not to be believed on oath, though I have heard a few persons say they would not believe her on oath."[35]

Katherine Hill's sexual behavior was brought into this hearing in order to impeach her credibility with respect to her family's history.[36] Even if she had been viewed by the community as someone who should be believed under oath, all that she could retrieve from her family's history were a few birth dates in the family Bible (none of them pertaining to Andrew) and the serial appearance and disappearance of the various men with whom she had cohabited. Did she actually "know" her son's age? Probably not but, then again, no one did.

The years in older rural regions were marked by the passage of routine as well as extraordinary events. Extraordinary events provided widely shared temporal landmarks against which members of the community could shape a collective memory of personal histories and circumstances.[37] However, when

---

[35] Davenport had served as an election clerk at one of the precincts in Wayne county. Ibid., pp. 616–17. William Dobbs concurred: "I know her; she has been living in my neighborhood for some time, I suppose about three miles and a half from me; her general moral character is *bad*.... From my acquaintance with her general character, I could not believe her on oath about any matter that I did not know myself to be as she should state it.... I don't know that I ever heard her testify on oath, but I have heard divers persons say that they would not believe her on oath." Ibid., p. 633. However, Dobbs himself was rumored to be a counterfeiter. See the next note.

[36] Because most women led relatively private lives, with few public transactions in which they participated independently of their families or, after marriage, their husbands, the most signal evidence of their moral character was their sexual reputation. With men, moral character was more complex. John Goddard, a voter in Monticello, Kentucky, was asked whether he would agree that "the rumor" as to William Dobbs being in a "scrape of that sort" (i.e., counterfeiting) "did not amount to general character." He replied, "As to general character, my notion is, that it takes several items to make up one; and although one item might make a part of a general character, I cannot say that one item would make a general character." Ibid., p. 648. A woman would not have enjoyed such a second chance.

[37] In 1866, William McCullock's son voted in a congressional election in Knox County, Ohio, and the father was later asked to substantiate his son's age. In response, he stated that his son had been "born on the 5th of May, 1844 or 1845 – the year of the great frost that killed the corn and wheat." Although McCullock had been requested by subpoena to produce the family Bible, he reported that he possessed neither a family Bible nor any other written record of the births in the family. He signed his testimony with his mark. S.R. no. 1313: M.D. no. 38, Pt. 2 (1866): p. 135.

events gracing the passage of time were routine and repetitive, people could not offer anything to election judges except their honest and well-intended belief that they or those they knew had reached the required age for voting.[38] That had been the case with Katherine Hill's intimate, self-enclosed history of her family.

As the primary chroniclers of their family's history, mothers were responsible for remembering important events, including the dates of births, deaths, and marriages. According to the mother of Daniel Bowers, nothing very remarkable seemed to have happened before or after he was born. Although she was not entirely sure he was of voting age, she guessed that he was old enough:

...the way I counted the years, it would make him twenty-two the other month. He was born where Mr. George lives; we lived there till the next spring after he was born. Then we moved where Bob Daily lives now; lived there a year. Then we moved on Sonash's place, and was there till fall. From Sonash's we moved to the saw mill, and were there fifteen years; we left there in the spring. Then we moved down to the creek one year; then we moved to where we are now; and again next spring we will have been there three years.... We were at the mill fifteen years and a half.

Since all the reference points were very prosaic events, at least from the perspective of those outside the family, there was no way to substantiate the mother's information except by way of internal coherence. And there a somewhat liberal interpretation of her account might have made Daniel twenty-one when he voted (even a liberal reading needed the crucial half year added to the time spent at the saw mill in the last passage). A skeptical attorney asked Bowers whether she knew of anyone else who had moved in the year when Daniel was born. She named a neighbor, A. L. McFarlane, who had left for Pittsburgh. When McFarlane was later called to testify, he said that he had moved on April 1, 1848; if so, Daniel Bowers was underage at the time of the election.

However, McFarlane was subsequently trumped by Joseph Skelly, tax collector for North Huntingdon Township. Skelly recalled that he had discussed Daniel's age with his mother, and in that conversation "she told me there was a boy buried at Long Run church, if I would go up there I could see his age;

---

[38] Somewhere in between the extraordinary and the routine was the evidence offered by Samuel Ogle's mother. She had no record of his birth but knew that he had been born on February 29 because his birthday came around only every four years. That fact led her to believe that he had been born on that date in 1848 and was thus eligible to vote. While not conclusive when considered alone, her information at least narrowed down young Ogle's age to some multiple of four. S.R. no. 1431: M.D. (no number, bound between nos. 24 and 25 [1868]): p. 95. For other examples of men who had only a vague sense – if that – of how old they were, see S.R. no. 1313: M.D. no. 38, Pt. 2 (1866): pp. 50–1.

that this boy's name was Philip J. Howell, son of Andrew Howell. I went to the church-yard, found young Howell's tombstone, which showed his age to be fourteen years and six days when he died, November 28, 1860.... She told me when Philip J. Howell was borned, she went to his mother's to see him, and that her son Daniel at that time was between five and six months of age." That would have made young Daniel well over twenty-one at the time of the October election.[39]

In urban areas where members of the community had much more difficulty constructing a shared understanding of a man's history, age almost became a moot issue. Robert Roden, who voted at the corner of Thirty-first Street and Second Avenue in New York City, sounded very much like a rural Kentuckian when responding to a question. "Do you want me to say what I believe from others, or from my own knowledge? I can't give that [date of birth] on any personal knowledge. I can't swear that I was born in Ireland either."[40] Even if election officials and bystanders could have reconstructed Roden's age, the large number of men approaching the voting window would have precluded much discussion of the issue. But in the long-settled rural regions of the United States, they might have helped Roden make his case, most likely using some of the same techniques and shared understandings that underpinned the other examples in this section.

MENTAL COMPETENCY

Most states made mental competency a requirement for suffrage. This requirement can be divided more or less neatly into two categories: mental capacity and mental illness. In the vernacular at the polls, these categories usually descended into simpler concepts of "idiocy" and "insanity." In either case, election judges and challengers were almost always compelled to rely on a subjective understanding of the complex social history of the men who appeared before the voting window.

Aside from the law, the community usually had several reasons to suspect the participation of men of low intelligence. One, of course, is that the mentally disabled did not understand or did not understand very well the issues involved in the election. That meant that their choices were either somewhat arbitrarily made or, worse, easily influenced by others. Another reason was that the ethical compass of those with weak mental capacities,

---

39 Because the mother was illiterate, she had no written records to refresh her memory or independently corroborate her account. S.R. no. 1431: M.D. (no number, bound between nos. 24 and 25 [1868]): pp. 185–6, 372.

40 The reference to Ireland bore on whether or not he needed naturalization papers to vote. S.R. no. 1269: Contested Congressional Election in the Eighth District of New York: M.D. no. 7, Pt. 1, p. 17. William E. Dodge vs. James Brooks, election held on November 8, 1864.

as understood in the community at large, was often skewed or even missing altogether. Nevertheless, almost all such men comprehended some things well enough to display at least some characteristics of normal intelligence. Under sustained questioning, however, their responses revealed very serious contextual misunderstandings and fallacies that would have been obvious to any election official.

Some men had always been of low intelligence and their limitations were widely recognized within the community. John Andrews, a voter at the markethouse in Mount Vernon, Ohio, was such a man. When Andrews "was six months old, lying in a cradle; his sister was playing with a horn around him, and when she blowed it seemed to enliven him; finally she put [the horn] right against his ear and blew it, and the child gave a scream and lay under the doctor's hand for six months, and could not raise its head, and has never got over its injury." This incident left Andrews profoundly deaf and, as a result, he could not speak. His father, who was himself illiterate, reported that Andrews could neither read nor write, that he had no conception of religion, although he attended church, and that he was almost completely ignorant of politics, even though he voted. But Harvey Cox, a Republican partisan who had done "all I could" for his party's congressional candidate, gave a much more favorable view of Andrews, saying that he "lives neighbor to me. I think he rode down [to the polls] in my wagon. . . . I am not able to tell you [who gave him a ticket]; likely I did. I supplied those generally who were in my wagon [with Delano tickets]. . . . I believe he has [sense], as far as I know. I know he is a good hand to work. He has worked some for me. I see him pretty much every Sunday (dressed up) going to church. I have seen him riding around Sundays on horseback with the young men, and am informed that he was going to see the girls. . . . He would answer me [in conversation]; I suppose he could hear me. I had to talk pretty loud to him. . . . I have not been acquainted with him only about a year . . . he has ordinary [mental] capacity. I suppose his present condition results from want of education."[41]

Others had become senile after living most of their lives as friends and neighbors of the other men frequenting the polls. In such cases, the determination of mental capacity involved a painful disruption of fraternal relations. Such was the case with an elderly voter who, from the evidence, appears to have suffered from dementia. This voter, known to us as A. M. Bolton, had been carried to the polls in a community just north of Cincinnati, Ohio. The election was held in October 1856, and the Republican party had just nominated a presidential candidate for the first time. The men gathered around the voting window knew Bolton fairly well, and the questions posed to him

[41] S.R. no. 1313: M.D. no. 38, Pt. 2 (1866): pp. 210, 212. Although Cox's testimony appears to have been perjured, any attempt to demonstrate that fact would have run up against the extreme difficulty of communicating with Andrews.

were, at least in the beginning, intended only to be helpful. He was first asked what ticket he wished to vote. He answered, "I don't know." One of the men then tried to prompt him by asking whether "he did not wish to vote against slavery." Bolton replied once again, "I don't know." Bolton was then asked whether he recognized several of the bystanders with whom he had been acquainted for decades.

As they were individually pointed out to him, he answered "no" in each instance. At that point, one of the men "asked him if he wished to vote the whig ticket." While Bolton agreeably answered "yes," there was a serious problem with this question: The Whig party had disappeared as a formal organization and none of the leading presidential candidates could be unambiguously identified as a Whig nominee. Bolton had apparently been asked whether he wished to vote the Whig ticket because he had formerly identified with that party and because, even with his failing faculties, he could remember some things in the remote past. However, former Whigs had divided their affections in this election between Millard Fillmore, the candidate of the American party, and John Fremont, the Republican nominee. Thus both Fillmore and Fremont could be said to be Bolton's choice. While one of the men went to retrieve a Fillmore ticket, another man put a Republican ticket in Bolton's hand and raised his arm so that the election judge could reach it. The election judge then accepted the ticket, depositing it in the ballot box, and Bolton's vote was counted for the Republicans.

What had begun as a collective and sincere attempt to determine how this elderly man wished to vote had ended as a partisan exploitation of Bolton's incapacity. And that is how it comes to our attention. The Democratic congressional candidate claimed that Bolton had not really intended to vote for his Republican opponent. Instead, as one witness who had known Bolton for many years reported, he "did not know what he was doing . . . he did not know his old acquaintances, those whom he had known for fifteen or twenty years. . . . Both physically and mentally, Mr. Bolton is emphatically a child. I doubt very much if he would have known his own wife if she had been there. This is the result of old age."[42] What is of interest here is not whether Bolton was mentally competent, but how the men surrounding the voting window went about determining how he wanted to vote. Their reluctance to exclude an elderly neighbor whom they had known for years illustrates how difficult it was to apply the law impartially; they wanted him to be able to vote, gave him every opportunity to indicate his choice, and divided over his competency only when he was simply unable to perform the rituals necessary to the act of voting.[43]

[42]   S.R. no. 961: Contested Congressional Election in the Third District of Ohio: M.D. no. 4, p. 82. Clement L. Vallandigham v. Lewis D. Campbell, election held on October 14, 1856.
[43]   A similar case involved an Isaac Baughman, an eighty- or ninety-year-old voter in Knox County, Ohio. Baughman was brought to the polls by several Democrats, and,

Senility also seemed to have overtaken Hiram Willey, a sixty-four-year-old voter at a precinct near Zanesville, Ohio. Willey had voted for the Republican candidate for Congress because he thought "he was the best man... [and] I thought he would do right, and make the best laws." However, he confessed that he could not identify "the leading principles" of either party and that he did not know whether or not the Republican candidate supported the tariff, backed "giving the negroes the right to vote," or "acts with the Democratic party." When asked whether the Republican candidate was "in favor of taxing United States bonds," Willey responded, "I can't tell that; I can't read any; I don't know what he is." When describing the Democrats, he said only that their leading principle was to "Go ahead at election generally."

Willey had a rough recollection of the Civil War, replying in response to questions that the conflict had been between "[o]ur people and the rebels," that the rebels "live in the south," and that the war had been "[a]bout the niggers I guess.... I suppose they wanted to free them." But he could "hardly tell" who had begun the war and did not know which side the Republican candidate had taken in the conflict. But Willey could say that he owned eighty acres of land located about "two miles on the right of the Marietta road, at the corner to George Gibbons." Some of the most interesting questions concerned religious belief. Asked whether "men live after they die," Willey confessed that he did not know. He then identified "religion" as "[t]o be good, and do good" and "the reward of good, or the punishment of evil" as "[t]o do good, I guess; if do bad, go to the bad place.... I suppose they call it hell."[44] Whether or not Willey's mental incapacity met the statutory requirement for voting was clearly a matter of interpretation. But his answers to the questions on religious belief seem to indicate that he had not lost his moral compass.

A similar case involved Calvin Hill, a sixty-one-year-old voter in Mount Vernon, Ohio, who had apparently suffered a stroke (his wife called it a "sunstroke") some five years earlier. When asked to testify on his own behalf, Hill displayed almost total ignorance of even the most mundane political events and personalities:

Q. Who did you vote for for governor of Ohio at the October election, 1866?
A. It appears to me it was Delano. [Delano, in fact, had been the Republican congressional candidate.]
Q. Who did you vote for as minister to England at the last October election? A. I don't know as I can tell.
Q. Who did you vote for as clerk of the court of common pleas for Knox county at the last October election? A. I don't know.

although challenged, the election judges accepted his ticket without asking him his name or posing any other questions to him. S.R. no. 1313: M.D. no. 38, Pt. 1 (1866): pp. 47–8, 50.
[44] S.R. no. 1313: M.D. no. 38, Pt. 2 (1866): pp. 520–2.

Q. Who did you vote for as sheriff for Knox county at the last October election?
A. I can't tell.

Q. Was the Hon. Columbus Delano a candidate for governor of Ohio, or for the office of President of the United States, at the last October election?   A. I can't understand; I am ignorant about it; I don't know.

Q. In what county does the Hon. Columbus Delano reside when at home?   A. I thought that it was in this county.

Q. Is this county in the State of Indiana or the State of Kentucky?   A. I thought this was Knox county; I thought it was in this State.

Q. Please spell the name Hill.   A. H-i-l-l.

Q. Please tell me how much nine and seven make when added together? A. Sixteen, I believe.

Q. For what office was Columbus Delano a candidate at the last October election? A. Why! wasn't it for – wasn't it for governor?

As was the usual practice in these interrogations, the attorney who was trying to prove the witness was an idiot concentrated his attention on literacy, counting, and political facts. The attorney trying to disprove the charge ordinarily focused his attention on livestock, family, and domestic events. And such was the case here, ending with a few questions that the Republican counsel believed would be easy for Hill to answer:

Q. How old are you, Mr. Hill?   A. Sixty-one, I believe.

Q. Where were you born?   A. We come, I believe, from the State of Vermont; I was born there, I believe.

Q. Where do you live now?   A. I live up here in the upper part; on the flat, in the upper part of town, up above the foundry.

Q. Whose foundry is it?   A. Cooper's foundry, I believe is the name.

Q. Have you ever been married?   A. Yes, sir; I believe I have.

Q. Have you any children?   A. Why, I expect I have.

Q. How many?   A. There is one living at home; Judson and Sarah; and we had – why, we had others.

Q. Do you belong to the republican or democratic party?   A. I used to; I believe I used to vote the republican ticket, I believe.

Q. Did you vote for General Morgan for Congress at the last October election? A. Not that I know of.

Q. Which did you like the best, Mr. Delano or General Morgan?   A. I didn't know much about any of them.

Q. How long have you lived in Mount Vernon?   A. I guess it is six years; pretty near.

Q. During our last war, were you in favor of Jeff. Davis or Lincoln?   A. It appears to me I voted for Lincoln.

But these last responses provided an opening for the Democratic counsel, who eagerly pounced on Hill once again:

Q. Was Jeff. Davis the opposing candidate to Mr. Lincoln?   A. I don't know as I can tell.

Q. Please state what division of Lincoln's army Jeff. Davis commanded during the late war? A. I don't know.

Q. Is Jeff. Davis or Columbus Delano the present governor of Ohio? A. I can't tell.

Along with two other men, Lydia Hill had escorted her husband to the polls. She reported that her son, Robert J. Hill, had once been appointed guardian for his father because he was incapable "of managing his affairs." However, Robert had since moved away and he "left it in such a way that my daughter will be appointed in his place by and by." She also stated that her husband has belonged to the Republican party "ever since the fugitive slave law was passed." However, his current mental condition

is frustrated by times; at other times he talks quite rational. He reads the Tribune and Republican paper some, and then asks me to read it to him. Seems very anxious to find out all he can. The reason why I accompanied him to the polls was because I thought he had a right to vote; at least that was my impression.... He knew he was putting in the republican ticket. He told me before he started from home that if he voted at all he would vote the republican ticket. Said he would not vote any other ticket.... He was not well at all; he was very much out of health. His mind was about as usual.... He don't do anything about managing our affairs, except to chop wood and do chores about the house. He does that readily when he sees it is needed.

When asked why she had also accompanied him to the hearing when he was called to testify, she replied, "One thing was, he hasn't been down street for more than a year, and he didn't know where the place was, though he could have found it, but said he wanted me to go along."

Marshal Bean had been one of the Democratic challengers at the polling place Calvin Hill attended and had objected to his vote:

I was engaged in the inside of the polls in looking over the list of doubtful and illegal voters which we had there, when Calvin Hill's name was called. I arose and told Mr. Reeve that I objected. He then had the ballot folded in his hand, and was ready to place it in the ballot-box. He looked at me, and immediately thrust it into the box, and rather coolly told me I was too late. I replied, "Mr. Reeve, you should certainly give us a chance to question a man." He replied, "That man is old enough to be your father." I told him it mattered not; that I challenged him on account of imbecility, and that he had at least ought to give us a chance to establish it. He made no reply. We had some controversy and talk in reference to it, others joining in.[45]

So, unlike Bolton, Hill had encountered some opposition when he voted. Given the strong evidence of his mental incapacity and the widespread community recognition of his condition, this opposition was not particularly

45 Ibid., pp. 152–3, 198, 215, 265. This was not the only occasion in which Reeve quickly dropped a Republican ticket into the ballot box just as one of the Democratic challengers was raising an objection. For another instance, see p. 211.

surprising. What is noteworthy, however, is the strong support Calvin Hill received, despite his obvious ineligibility. His wife's claim that he had a "right" to vote, for example, appears to have been based on his mental competency prior to his stroke. In other words, his prior competency somehow overrode or otherwise negated the strong evidence of current mental impairment. In addition, she had the aid of friends who probably knew him before the stroke and, like her, relied on that memory as they accompanied him to the polls. Finally the judge of election, while he was almost certainly motivated by partisan feeling as well, was clearly predisposed to accept Hill's ballot. If Hill had been a stranger, his reception might have been far more hostile.[46]

The problem was usually different with men who were mentally ill. Most communities appear to have tolerated very wide ranges of behavior as more or less normal, interpreting only truly bizarre conduct as "insane." James Egan of Greensburg, Pennsylvania, may have stood right at this boundary between the insanely bizarre and the extremely eccentric. Dr. Robert Brown, a practicing physician, had known Egan since he was a child and thought him "capable of judging between right and wrong.... I think that he would be able to judge in regard to the party, and am satisfied he would know the ticket he would vote." Brown had lived across the street from the Egan residence where James lived with his mother and had given him music lessons, finding Egan to be a capable pupil. The doctor also reported that he had seen Egan go to the post office, run errands, and, for a time, "breaking bark" at a local bark mill. However, he could not say that Egan was "entirely of sound mind."

One of the attorneys then asked the doctor, "Has he not, since coming to man's estate, made indecent exposure of his person in public places for a few cents?" The doctor, both protecting his young friend and, perhaps inadvertently, denying that he had participated in such a transaction, replied, "I have never seen him do so." But this behavior was apparently common knowledge, for counsel persisted in asking, "Don't you know that ladies living in his neighborhood have been afraid to pass where he was alone?" To this the doctor yielded, "I have heard, but I don't know."[47] In terms of prevailing community standards, James Egan was probably sane and probably possessed enough intelligence to rise above imbecility. Because he was presumed to be capable of distinguishing "right from wrong," a reputation for

---

[46]   In his *American Law of Elections*, McCrary suggested that "the vote of a man otherwise qualified, who is neither a lunatic nor an idiot, but whose faculties are merely greatly enfeebled by old age, is not to be rejected" (p. 41). In practice, such a rule favored the suffrage rights of the elderly even when their mental faculties were as impaired as younger men who had been deemed lunatics or idiots. Seen from another direction, the rule merely reported what seems to have been the prevailing disposition of judges, as social practice, throughout the nation.

[47]   S.R. no. 1431: M.D. (no number, bound between nos. 24 and 25 [1868]): p. 363. The following witness, Henry Kettering, endorsed Egan a little more strongly (pp. 363–4).

indecent exposure, absent a criminal conviction, was apparently not enough to disqualify him from voting.

The problem, of course, was to properly distinguish the truly bizarre from the merely eccentric. In some cases, men in and around the polls would turn to a professional for advice. For example, when asked to describe the mental state of an elderly man named Benjamin Rutter, a physician in Putnam, Ohio, replied,

Well, I don't know that I can exactly; I can give you the facts; the facts are simply these: the old gentleman, in passing through a crowd, generally has a farm to sell, and offers it for sale to any one, old or young, and at times returns from Zanesville with the statement that he has sold his farm. Next day, perhaps, he is in offering it for sale in a similar manner, and returns from Zanesville, having sold the same farm. This I have know him to repeat four or five times in two weeks; that is all, except that the old man is full of fun and is looked upon as a very silly old man.

In the eight or nine years he had casually known Rutter, Dr. Erwin had never seen him in a "sane condition." Asked to give a professional diagnosis, Erwin stated, "I should suppose it be monomania" but that he was "not well enough acquainted with him to say" what had produced the condition. The doctor could not find the "medical terms to explain it; monomania is generally produced by the mind dwelling on one subject till he becomes insane." As for the "difference between an insane person and an idiot," Erwin acknowledged that there "is a difference; an idiot is really in a state of imbecility continually." Rutter, in his professional opinion, was not an idiot but was instead "affected with insanity in the form of monomania." Simply put, Erwin believed that Rutter's "monomania" was simultaneously the cause and primary symptom of his insanity.

The county sheriff, B. F. Leslie, had a somewhat simpler and more convincing explanation. The sheriff stated that he was somewhat acquainted with Rutter and usually saw him "twelve to twenty times a year." In the sheriff's opinion, Rutter's "actions...denote that he is wrong in his mind somehow...there has been a uniformity in his actions and language since I have first known him. Well, his mind is pretty badly affected, seems to me on one subject...in reference to gaining possession of his land and selling it." So far his description was very close to that of Dr. Erwin. As to the degree of mental incapacity, Leslie

thought the old man was in a condition that his person ought to have been taken care of by his friends; as to the management of his business, I had understood that his wife and son, or son-in-law, had entered into a contract with him to take charge of his business. I further thought that was a very proper arrangement; the old man was not competent to attend to it, from monomania or insanity on that subject. I believe further that the other parties failed to come up to their contract, and the old man was worse on that account.

In other words, his wife and son had relieved the old man of his property but had failed to take care of him. In fact, Rutter's difficulties with his family, in the sheriff's opinion, had been the cause of the old man's insanity:

> I only know what he has told me himself – what I heard in a conversation, once with his wife. He claims that his son, who works the place, will not provide him with sufficient clothing, food, and necessaries of life; and for that reason he wants to annul the bargain, get back the place, and dispose of it. He complains of having been beaten several times and driven from home; his wife says that he comes and goes when he pleases, demands his meals at unseasonable times, and is a source of great trouble to them. I have heard others say the old man was not used right.

According to the contract between the old man and his family, the son was "to furnish his father with a comfortable support during his natural life, including all the necessaries of life, in consideration for which he was to . . . have the use of [Rutter's farm] during the old man's life, as I understood it." But Rutter complained that his son had not kept up his end of the bargain, claiming that "he would not buy him shoes and clothes; he was almost naked, and in rags."

  The sheriff had had only one conversation with Rutter where the topic had not concerned his land and family. In that conversation, Rutter had "talked about his courtship and marriage, and seemed to relate it as intelligently as any other person would; it was only a short conversation." Otherwise, one way or another, Rutter would bring up his grievance against his family, asserting that "his son Bill and his wife had took up together, and were selling everything off the place; wouldn't let him have any money to buy anything, and wouldn't buy anything for him; then he would show me his old shoes and hat, and told me they were the best he had." The sheriff repeated that he had "heard the old man say several times that 'Bill and his mother had took up together,' and that he intended to marry another woman" but apparently was not quite certain whether or not Rutter was charging his son and wife with incest. Leslie concluded that Rutter was in no condition "to attend to any ordinary business," aside from the purchase of "some cheap clothing for himself, or something of that kind."

  When Benjamin Rutter was called to testify on his own behalf, the old man corroborated much of what the doctor and sheriff had reported:

> I have told you all I wish to say. I was nearly naked; I was so. I was without hat or shoe, and with my daughter's brother's son I ventured my life in going through Columbus, and I brought him back. It was Edmund, they called him; Jack, he was named after my father. They put the meadow on the buckeye in grass at times, you see. It has been a long time. I got the land in a swap. I don't know as there is any use in saying anything more about it. I got it from Bush's son, and a fifty dollar note he gave to a store-keeper, and I borrowed fifteen dollars from a neighbor and raised the house, and afterwards threw it down, by the Lord, I did. I have no more to say. I don't know what they will do with Bill and Jim. They must go to Columbus, or

else there is no law. Lawyer Spencer lives in Somerset. I would let the old woman go clear, because she put me in the poor-house. We only had eleven children. I can beat you singing a song to the ladies. I have seen a heap of this world. I was raised with a tory when I was a boy. What they will do with him – what business has he to write for my children to put their names on my record? I have no more to say about it, gentlemen. I lived with old Daniel Horn, and when he went to die he said, (after he was buried.) I was talking with somebody; then Jake Horn wanted to go in with the administrator. I know my name is here on the books. What are you laughing for? I am telling the truth. I am getting hard of hearing, and if I was to go into a new country I would be judge of the country. It is the valuablest piece of land in the bottom – best barn. I went into the woods there. I am going to have a book made of my lifetime. I may get a horse from Jim, for he treated me before I had any writing at all. I never had any writing with my children – none of them. Nothing more to say about it. I don't want to hear people sing in the court-house. I reckon it will soon be dinner time for me. I must get me some shoes. I don't know where he lives. He is not going to give me ten dollars; I expect to get two or three, though, I want the pay, not the order. . . . I am a single man yet. I have a lady promised, to take next week. The woman that marries me will be the richest woman in the world. I was never to be drowned. I shot a squirrel from the top of the tree and he dropped six inches. I then put two poles together, clumb a sapling, and got him down and went around the hill and got an Indian pony – and the book of my lifetime will be the most curious book ever seen, and I will swear to it all. I don't know the use of this writing. I had the book all wrote, and Jake Springer's daughters tore it up and swept it out. I don't like to be in the poor-house. Her and Bill done that. It wasn't Jim. When they came to take me out, they asked me if I hadn't gone crazy. I told them all the men in the town couldn't set me crazy. They never go to any meeting, and she was baptised by the Duners. I used to be a wild, rattling boy.

Rutter was then asked, "If five or six of the girls want to marry you, how are you going to make choice between them?"

Why, I can pick out which one I like to have. If you were in the same fix, I would like to know what you would do. When I get home, I will go to the cupboard and hunt, but there won't be any chickens there. George Rutter sold my father's place and had a man driving the team and he didn't charge a cent; and he laid me down 8– dollars. He built a stone house and barn; I will go right down by that settlement. My father wasn't in his right mind. I was six years old when my mother died. McCoy was a tory and the curiousest man I ever saw. He would not vote for President. I lived there three times, and at last got the place on shares. He turned the horses in the field until his time was up.

Toward the end of his rambling, Rutter was asked whether he voted for James Brown or John Smith, both fictitious names, in the 1866 congressional election. Rutter replied that he had "voted a Jackson ticket. I didn't look at any of the names. I don't want you to abuse me. I am an old man. I am not dead. They shall go to Columbus, but I will let her go clear, for she had no better sense."

Samuel Hamilton, one of the voters at that polling place, recounted how Rutter had come to vote in that election:

He voted the republican ticket. . . . I was standing near the polls when Jeremiah Zigler and Josiah Gardner brought him near to the place of voting in a buggy; they helped him out of the buggy, and he went to the place of voting; there was some disturbance about who he was going to vote for. I being very well acquainted with Mr. Rutter, went to him and asked him what ticket he wanted to vote; he told me he wanted to vote the republican ticket; he then pulled a ticket out of his pocket and showed it to me; I told him that was right if he wanted to vote the republican ticket; I saw him put that same ticket in the hole where they put them in, and the trustees took it from his hand. . . .

Hamilton also reported that Rutter had lived in the community since at least 1830 and had always voted at that precinct. But "since he became deranged," Rutter "wasn't in the habit of going there unless he was taken by some political party." Hamilton thought Rutter's mental condition had been caused "some twelve or fourteen years" ago "by drinking whiskey; I have seen him have many a whiskey fit." Up until the Civil War, Rutter had voted with the Democrats but since then had cast a Republican ticket. The men who had brought him to the polls in the 1866 election had thus been Republicans.[48]

If a man had been committed to a lunatic asylum at one time or another, this information was usually considered decisive evidence of his mental incompetency. However, William Ray voted in Muskingum County, Ohio, even though he had spent three months in the state asylum in Columbus and a couple of weeks afterward in the county infirmary (this appears to have been the county poorhouse where, according to Ray himself, he was sent for "swearing at Liza"). His commitment to the asylum had been ten years prior to the election and he had gone to the infirmary some three years later. David Handshy, the judge of election at Ray's polling place, believed that he had never been released from the infirmary but, instead, "ran away." Handshy also said he didn't "believe he is of sound mind" but, for reasons that were not stated, did not consider him an incompetent voter: "If I had thought so at that time I would not have received [his vote]." One of the other judges had agreed to accept Ray's ticket on the grounds that "we were incapable of deciding whether he was insane or not." When Ray testified on his own

48 S.R. no. 1313: M.D. no. 38, Pt. 2 (1866): pp. 537–8, 544–6, 549–50, 614–16. While Rutter appears to have been completely consumed by his "monomania," other men were only intermittently unbalanced. In such cases, a community would sometimes incorporate or exclude them from political affairs depending on their state of mind. See, for example, testimony concerning Abram Fulkerson, Jr., who may have been schizophrenic. When mentally stable, he had been asked to serve as clerk of an election and performed his role competently. The rest of the time, however, he wandered around the neighborhood in a deranged state of mind. S.R. no. 1063: M.D. no. 11 (1859): pp. 35–6, 55.

behalf, he acquitted himself fairly well, demonstrating a greater than average range of political knowledge and interpretation.[49]

While William Ray was at least intermittently well aware of the political reality surrounding him, other men were not. One of these was Silas Dibble, who lived in Granville Township, Licking County, Ohio. After the election was contested, Dibble's mental competency was challenged in the following exchange with counsel for the Democratic candidate:

Q. How much are seven and nine?   A. Three.
Q. Seven and four?   A. Five.
Q. Nineteen and six?   A. Six.
Q. How much do one and eleven make?   A. Four.
Q. If you take one from three how much remains?   A. Two.
Q. Add three to seven?   A. Five.
Q. What is your name?   A. My name is Silas Dibble.
Q. Spell Dibble.   A. I aint much of a speller.
Q. Try; give us a trial.   A. (No answer.)
Q. With what letter does your name begin, S or T?   A. S.
Q. Are there one or two r's in your name, Dibble?   A. Two.
Q. Who did you vote for for President at the October election, 1866?   A. Delano.
Q. Who did you vote for for governor at the October election, 1866?   A. Delano.
Q. Who did you vote for for sheriff at the October election, 1866?   A. For Delano.
Q. Who did you vote for for justice of the peace?   A. I did not vote for justice of the peace.
Q. Who is governor of the State of Ohio?   A. Mr. Delano.
Q. Who did you vote for for Congress at the October election, 1866?   A. Delano.
Q. Who is mayor of the city of New York?   A. I don't know, sir.
Q. In what State does Mr. Delano live?   A. I don't know, sir.

When cross-examined by the Republican attorney, Dibble was presented in a slightly better light.

Q. Have you ever seen Mr. Delano?   A. No, sir.
Q. Why did not you vote for General Morgan for Congress?   A. I did not want to; did not feel like it; did not like him a bit.
Q. Which do you like the best, Mr. Delano or General Morgan?   A. Mr. Delano.[50]

However, this attempt to demonstrate that Dibble had some reason to prefer Delano had been fatally undermined by the previous exchange in which Dibble had indicated that this same Delano was simultaneously running for president, governor, and sheriff, as well as Congress.

Luman Dibble, Silas's father, testified that his son "has never been able to have much development. He learned his letters when he was young, but could not remember them." The problem seemed to have worsened, along with his physical health, as Silas grew older. In any case, the father stated

---

[49]   S.R. no. 1313: M.D. no. 38, Pt. 2 (1866): pp. 655–7, 661–3.
[50]   Ibid., pp. 22–3. Not surprisingly, Dibble signed his testimony with his mark.

that Silas was "able when he was young to walk down street until this last fall, but his legs have entirely failed him . . . years back we were in the habit of giving him money to go down into town to purchase articles with. We have several times trusted him to get into the hack to go up to Pataskala, where we have a brother living, and he could pay his fare on the cars." Otherwise, the family had never "trusted him at any time to conduct any kind of business on his own account."

Attracted by the excitement, Silas had evidently attended the polling place for much of the day. Toward late afternoon, his father went looking for him.

When I went down after him, about 4 o'clock, I found him on the inside of the place where they were voting. I spoke to – said to him, Come Silas, it is time to go home. Some one said, Silas, have you voted? No, said he; they won't let me vote. He came to me at the door, and I took hold of him, and started down the town hall steps. After I had got three or four rods from the steps some one called to me; I stopped and looked around, and one of the members of the board of trustees, Jason Collins, said to me, I want you to take Silas back into the hall. I heard some one say, as I went into the hall door, they are going to look at the law, and see if he is not a voter; he went inside and sat down.

Father and son had lived all their lives in Granville Township. The men in and around the polling place must have known Silas for years and, thus, must have been well aware of his mental state. Although Silas was thirty-three years old and, perhaps aside from his mental condition, met all the eligibility requirements, he had never voted in an election. On this occasion, however, the father reported that he "saw some of the board take a law book, statutes of Ohio, I suppose, and examine it. I understood, but not directly, from the trustees that they did not like to take the responsibility of allowing him to vote." The primary reason they were uncomfortable was probably the social context in which they would have to rule on Silas's mental competency. On the one hand, after calling Silas back into the polling place, it would obviously be cruel to rule him incompetent. And yet to decide the son was eligible in front of his father (who was painfully aware of his son's disability) would have been almost equally crass and manipulative. Having boxed themselves in, the

trustees called in three physicians to consult with, Dr. Bryan, Dr. A. Follett, and Dr. Sennett. The consultation was private. After conversation, one member of the board said he could vote and handed him a ticket; I believe one of the members of the board, Dr. Sedgwick, handed him the ticket.

It is not clear whether the doctors personally examined Silas. Since they may have already known him, such an examination was probably unnecessary in any case. And since both the medical and legal criteria for imbecility were almost hopelessly vague and indeterminate, their discussion must have been whether or not the community would have wanted them to rule Silas eligible (not whether Silas was, in fact, an imbecile). The relevant community at this polling place was heavily Republican. All three judges of election in Granville Township, for example, belonged to the party. And the ticket that Dr. Sedgwick, one of the clerks, gave to Silas was a Republican ticket. Silas obediently "handed the ticket to Gilmore Granger, one of the trustees, and he put it into the box."[51]

It is not clear whether the judges of election thought they needed every vote they could find (and thus violated what had been the prevailing customs and norms that had previously kept Silas from voting) or whether, Silas having spent the day at the polls with them, they felt that a friendly gesture of social inclusion was in order. Since these two possibilities are not mutually exclusive, there is, of course, no particular reason to choose between them. What should be clear, however, was that this kind of close inspection of a voter and sensitivity to community opinion was possible only in a rural or small town precinct. In a large city, the judges would have taken the ticket and that would have been that.

Like Dibble, Nathaniel Martin voted for the first time in the 1866 congressional election. And, like Dibble, Martin had a protective father. In fact, Martin's father "[f]or a number of years . . . kept him away from the polls by not letting him know he was of age, until the excitement got very high. He [Nathaniel, the son] found out, and his brothers got him to voting. . . . [His brother] Richard came with him to the polls this fall." Although Martin had been given the nickname "Doc," the clerk attending the polls reported that Nathaniel did not know his own name. For that reason, the clerk had "been in the habit of telling his name for him when he came to vote" so that he might be properly entered in the poll book. Although Martin lived on the family farm, the clerk also related that he had "heard his father say he could not trust him to feed his horses."

Richard Martin gave a slightly more favorable evaluation of his brother's mental competency. When asked "the state of [Nathaniel's] mental faculties," Richard replied, "I don't know that I could tell you. He is not really imbecile in all things." Since this was hardly a ringing endorsement, Richard was asked, "In what particular point is he imbecile?" He replied,

I hardly know how to answer that question. He can work. . . . He can chop and he can plough; he can do as much as any other man at rough farm labor; he would not have the same judgement that I or other men would have. If we would set him to laying up fence, if we would lay the work for him he could go on and lay up the fence. His memory in most things is decidedly good; for instance, if he or I were doing a piece of work to-day and anything should happen, as the horses running away, and if I should ask him about it in a number of years, he would remember it and tell all

---

[51] Ibid., pp. 23–4. Silas was apparently not offered an opportunity to choose between a Democratic and Republican ticket.

about it . . . His memory in some things is good. We have our mail twice a week, and he knows when mail day comes, and Sundays, as well as anybody.

However, Richard did admit that his brother was illiterate and, although he had been given the opportunity to learn to read and write, just seemed to be unable to do so.

When called to testify on his own behalf, Nathaniel Martin started off well by correctly recalling his name and identifying Delano as the man he had supported in the congressional election (although he thought he had voted for Delano in the spring of 1865 when, in fact, no election had been held then). But things went more or less downhill from there. When asked to identify the current year, Nathaniel answered, "Six, I guess." Although he could count to twenty without error, he gave more or less random answers – all incorrect – to simple addition problems. When asked to identify Columbus Delano, he answered, "United States, I guess." When this response sparked a request to identify "United States," Nathaniel consistently replied, "Delano, I guess." Politics was not something with which Nathaniel was particularly comfortable:

> Q. Who is General Morgan?   A. Don't know that.
> Q. Who told you to vote for Delano?   A. I told myself.
> Q. Who gave you the ticket?   A. Some men.
> Q. Did you read it?   A. No, sir.
> Q. Who run against Delano for Congress?   A. I guess Morgan did.

The questioning then returned to simple math problems, again with apparently random responses. When asked to say his "A,B,C's," Nathaniel responded, "B, C, F, G, A, P, Q, R, S, T, W, Y, U." He also named "F" as the first letter of the alphabet and "H" as the last. But, in what must have been a bit of a surprise to the Democratic counsel, Nathaniel came pretty close in his attempt to spell Delano, responding "D-e-l-n-o-w." The questioning then returned to politics:

> Q. Who did you vote for for Congress in the spring of 1868?   A. Lincoln.
> Q. Who in 1869 [the current year was 1867]?   A. John Brough, I guess.
> Q. What is a candidate?   A. State, I guess.
> Q. What is an office?   A. State of Ohio.
> Q. What State is this?   A. Newark, I guess.
> Q. What county is this?   A. State, I guess.
> Q. Who did you vote for for auditor of this county last fall?   A. I don't know.
> Q. Who did you vote for for justice of the peace last fall?   A. Squire, I guess.
> Q. Where does Delano live?   A. In the United States, I guess.
> Q. Where else?   A. I don't know that.
> Q. Who did you vote for for sheriff last fall?   A. Delano, I guess.
> Q. Who did you vote for for recorder last fall?   A. Don't know that.
> Q. Who did you vote for for treasurer last fall?   A. John Brough, I guess.
> Q. Who is John Brough?   A. John; our State, I guess; John Brough.
> Q. Who is governor of Ohio?   A. Todd, I guess.

Q. Who is Todd: A. United States, I guess.

Q. Who did you vote for for Congress in the year nineteen hundred? A. Don't know – Delano, I guess.

Q. How much does one and one make? A. Two.

Q. How much does one and two make? A. Eighty.

Q. How much is twice one? A. Ninety.

Q. Who did you vote for for governor last fall? A. Todd, I guess.

Q. Who did you vote for for President of the United States last fall? A. Lincoln, I guess.

The cross-examination by the Republican attorney stressed domestic topics with which Nathaniel clearly felt more at home:

Q. Who do you live with? A. Martin.

Q. Spell the name of Martin. A. Louis Martin, Dick Martin, and Mart, I guess.

Q. Have you got any sisters? A. One.

Q. What is her name? A. Jane.

Q. Did you ever have any money? A. No, sir.

Q. Can you work? A. Yes, sir.

Q. What do you work at? A. Farming.

Q. What do you do on the farm? A. Plough and fix up the fence.

Q. Have you ploughed any lately? A. No, not yet.

Q. Are you going to plough any pretty soon? A. Yes, pretty soon. [This testimony was taken about the middle of April.]

Q. What are you going to plant or sow on the ground that you are going to plough pretty soon? A. Corn, I guess.

Q. Have your folks got any wheat in the ground now? A. No, sir.

Q. Have your folks got any sheep now? A. Yes, sir.

Q. Have they got any little lambs this spring? A. No, sir.

Q. Have they got any horses? A. Yes, got two.

Q. What color are they? A. Gray.

Q. Do they match pretty well? A. No, sir.

Q. Which is the best of the two? A. Both just alike, I guess.

But when the questioning returned to politics, the light began to dim again:

Q. Where do you go to vote? A. To house.

Q. Who lives in the house next to where you live? A. A man.

Q. Did you ever hear of Jeff. Davis? A. No, sir.

Although Nathaniel Martin was clearly mentally deficient, no one challenged his right to vote. As the clerk said, "I don't know really whether I could say what constitutes an idiot." This uncertainty effectively gave his brother Richard, a stout Republican, twice as many votes as most men.[52]

---

[52] Ibid., pp. 42–3, 107–8, 113–16. For very similar interrogations of Jessie Whitehead and William Dickerson, see pp. 103–5, 108–11. Like Martin, Dickerson was much more comfortable with domestic affairs on the family farm than he was with arithmetic and politics. Another man, Riley Garlinghouse, was brought in a wagon to the polls by his employer, Franklin Gilbert, with whom Garlinghouse also lived. Although Gilbert

No one would challenge these voters' sanity on the basis of such interrogations. And an objective bystander might have judged at least some of them to be above imbecility. On the other hand, Dibble and Martin had clearly handed over almost all of their affairs to members of their family and were probably not in any condition to take them up again.[53] For them, the act of voting itself must have been a mysterious event, only dimly comprehended if at all.[54] That such men possessed and exercised the right of suffrage was profound evidence of an extremely strong societal commitment to democratic principles.

We should not, however, believe that this tolerance was entirely due to some abstract virtue of democratic incorporation. Many of these cases featured a party agent bringing a mentally disabled man to the polls and guiding him through the voting process before the opposition could challenge the man's sanity or intelligence. In other cases, competing party agents believed that each had the man's support and thus failed to challenge him. One particularly revealing instance of the latter was recorded at a precinct in Westmoreland County, Pennsylvania, where Abram Bennett, a distributor of Democratic tickets, complained that Cornelius Gintelsberger had voted for the Republican congressional candidate. As Bennett explained, Gintelsberger had shown up at the polls and asked for a Democratic ticket. As he proceeded to the voting window, however, he was challenged on "sanity" by John Covode, who was working the precinct for the Republicans and was himself the Republican congressional candidate. When Gintelsberger agreed to discuss his ticket with Covode, the Republican withdrew his challenge, took him aside, and apparently pasted his own name (John Covode) over that of the Democratic candidate. Having thus, through threat of a challenge, induced Gintelsberger to vote for him, Covode allowed him to return to the voting window. Having tacitly admitted that Gintelsberger was a qualified voter by giving him a ticket when he first entered the polling place, Bennett could not conscientiously turn around and declare him incompetent when Covode was able to intimidate him (and may not have wanted to since Gintelsberger was, aside from the congressional race, voting the Democratic slate). That many, if not most, party agents would have similarly subordinated enforcement of suffrage laws when those conflicted with a larger vote total somewhat vitiates any broader commitment to democratic incorporation.[55]

did not believe that Garlinghouse was "a person of sound mind," he nonetheless gave Riley a Republican ticket that he then voted (pp. 47–9).

[53]   In his *American Law of Elections*, McCrary suggested that the test of imbecility turned on whether or not "the voter knew enough to understand the nature of his act, if he understood what he was doing..." (p. 42). The reader is encouraged to reread the testimony in the text and decide whether any of these men passed that test.

[54]   For additional discussion of mental competency, including examples drawn from the contested election hearings, see Bensel, "The American Ballot Box," pp. 19–23.

[55]   S.R. no. 1431: M.D. (no number, bound between nos. 24 and 25 [1868]): pp. 408–10.

Racial Identity

Men approaching the polls were identified in many ways. If they kept company with known partisans, they were accordingly associated with that party. In other cases, an accent and/or distinctive clothing placed a man in a particular ethnic community and often, thereby, in a particular religious denomination. In addition to native-born Americans belonging to one of the mainstream Protestant faiths, the men who manned the polls were also, in many instances, foreign-born Catholics. In fact, part of their utility to party organizations rested in their ability to identify fellow ethnics or communicants. But all these men were, without exception, white.

Because blacks were categorically prohibited from voting everywhere except New England (aside from Connecticut) and New York (if they met a property-holding qualification that applied only to their race), no black distributed tickets, challenged voters, or administered the voting process in the vast southern and western reaches of the United States.[56] This meant that blacks, as potential experts on identifying members of their race, were unavailable to the whites who ran and monitored elections. And although many whites believed they could accurately distinguish black men from white, they often had to do so without the kind of corroborating social information that might be offered in supporting, for example, a man's claim to nativity or adulthood. Many blacks were, in fact, strangers to whites even though they lived in the same community, often in close proximity. As a factor in structuring the polling place, racial identity was thus equally problematic in rural and in urban polling places. For that reason, racial identity could as easily be incorporated into an analysis of any of the three voting venues. It is included here because the cases illustrate the limits of a thickly textured social consensus in the dominant white community, even in long-settled rural areas of the nation.

Race was one of the most important distinguishing social characteristics in American society in the nineteenth century, primarily because slavery made the distinction between whites and blacks the basis for distinguishing between free men and those held in bondage. Native Americans were similarly distinguished from whites, declared to be members of quasi-independent nations that could make treaties with the federal government, and promptly despoiled of their lands and heritage. Both race and ethnicity were somewhat differently bound up in the discriminatory laws that denied Chinese

---

[56] In fact, there are so few references to blacks in the contested election hearings that we can safely conclude that they were rarely, if ever, found at polling places in states where they could not vote. Even in states where blacks could vote, they were sometimes discouraged from participating. Jean H. Baker, *Affairs of Party: The Political Culture of Northern Democrats in the Mid-Nineteenth Century* (Ithaca, N.Y.: Cornell University Press, 1983), p. 245. In fairly sharp contrast, the hearings demonstrate that ineligible white men often frequented the polls despite their ineligibility.

immigrants American citizenship and confined them to the lowest rungs of the employment ladder. Until adoption of the Fifteenth Amendment to the Constitution, the states could restrict suffrage on the basis of race, and most states in fact restricted voting to whites. However, like gender, race was rarely a contentious issue at the polls.[57]

Because extremely high stakes were involved in racial identity, most Americans became very adept at recognizing the physical and social characteristics that marked someone as a member of one group or another. This recognition, arising out of shared beliefs in racial physiognomy and reinforced through constant reference to group opinion, socially constructed individual identities in ways that irretrievably placed almost all Americans in one racial community or another. There were problems with this classification only at the margin, a margin inhabited by those whose ancestry left them with ambiguous features that could not be socially constructed through community recollections of the person's genealogy.

When questions involving racial identity arose, there was no precise way of determining who was white. If births had been officially registered, the determination of racial identity could have been made a governmental function. Prospective voters could have been asked for their birth certificates at the polls, thereby precluding the otherwise necessary physical inspection of the voter. As it was, when prospective voters with ambiguous racial characteristics presented themselves at the polls, election judges improvised, trying to match up their understanding of the law with the evidence immediately at hand.

When four such men approached one of the polling places in Hamilton, Ohio, for example, the election judges relied on their collective interpretation of the community standard for racial identity, personal knowledge of the family lineage of the voters, and the personal statements of the voters themselves in reaching a decision. One of the election judges, Thomas Millikin, later testified in the contested election hearing. When asked "whether any persons of color or mulattos voted at" the election, Millikin replied, "There were such persons; their names were Alfred Anderson, John M. Mitchell, Reuben Redman, and James E. Robbins." He was then queried as to the "appearance of these men ... with regard to color," to which he responded, "There was in each a visible admixture of African blood." He was then asked whether he was "at the time of said election personally acquainted with each of the colored persons" he had named, and "if so, what [was his] opinion of the proportion of African blood they respectively contain[ed]." Millikin answered:

[57] For example, when a "mulatto man" presented himself at the window in Florence, Nebraska, his ticket was summarily rejected, evidently without incident. S.R. no. 1016: Contested Election for Delegate from the Territory of Nebraska: M.D. no. 28, p. 4. Bird B. Chapman vs. Fenner Ferguson, election held in August 1857.

I was well acquainted with Anderson, tolerable well acquainted with Mitchell, and slightly acquainted with Robbins. I was not personally acquainted with Redman. I cannot give any very satisfactory opinion upon the subject. In regard to Anderson I would think he had more white than black blood. In reference to the others, I would think it doubtful whether the white or black blood predominates. At the election the votes of these persons were admitted upon their own evidence as to color; no other evidence on that subject being offered.

When asked whether any of these men had been "sworn as to the proportion of white blood they contained," Millikin said, "Yes; Robbins and Redman, as appears by the poll books. The others do not appear, from the poll books, to have been sworn. Anderson had been sworn at a previous election, and was not sworn at this." The attorney for the Republican candidate then asked why Mitchell was not also sworn, "If you had doubts as to the white blood predominating in him," Millikin replied, "I have no recollection . . . whether he was sworn or not; I have forgotten the circumstances attending the reception of his vote, but think it was received upon the statement of Anderson, as they came to the polls together and voted." In sum, the judges had allowed these men to vote because they had represented themselves as possessing "more than half white blood" and thus eligible under the law. Given their physical appearance, these representations were considered at least plausible by the judges.[58]

One of the men whom Millikin had allowed to vote, Alfred Anderson, testified later in the hearing. Asked how long he had lived in Hamilton Anderson answered, "I have resided here from 1839 to 1844, and from 1852 to the present time. My father was James Shannon, reputed to be a white man, and my mother was Mary T. Anderson, now wife of Robert G. H. Anderson, who, from her statement, I presume had one-fourth part of African blood in her veins. Her father was a white man and her mother was Indian and African. James Shannon is brother of Wilson Shannon, late governor of Kansas. About the other persons, called colored, I know nothing save from appearances." When asked whether there was "any visible admixture of African blood in" either Reuben Redman or John Mitchell, Anderson responded in the affirmative with respect to Reuben but that, in Mitchell's case, "In my opinion there is none." Anderson was then asked whether Mitchell "associate[d] with white or colored persons." He answered, "With both. He goes on the river, and in his business relations he passes as a white man, and in his domestic relations he associates with colored people." When queried as to whether he knew, "from conversations with [Mitchell], as to the proportion of African blood in his veins," Anderson reported, "He has always disclaimed having any."[59]

[58] S.R. no. 961: M.D. no. 4 (1856): pp. 105–6. Also see pp. 126–7.
[59] Ibid., p. 121.

This incident is fascinating for several reasons. First, the inherent ambiguity of racial identity, at least at the margin, is on full display. Mitchell, for example, is reported as passing as a white man when at work but associating with blacks in his domestic relations. For him, at least, the community had not arrived at a collective judgment as to his race. In Anderson's testimony, he claimed a predominantly white parentage, acknowledging only that his mother was one-quarter black. However, his reputedly white father apparently never married his mother and had probably not recognized him as a son. Thus, a birth certificate, even if Anderson had had one, would not have conclusively documented Anderson's racial inheritance. This was probably true of most interracial unions. The racial identity of Anderson's father, James Shannon, was only indirectly evidenced; he was asserted to be the brother of Wilson Shannon, a former territorial governor of Kansas. The latter, we are left to assume, must have been unambiguously white, in appearance at least, in order to have held that post. Thus, his brother, James, even if he only shared one of Wilson's parents, must have been at least half-white in parentage.[60]

Second, the election judges had accepted the racial identities claimed by these four men because it accorded with the judges' interpretation of their physical appearance and collective recollection of their racial standing and lineage. Although at least some of the men were sworn, this appears to have been only a formality; they would not have been allowed to take an oath if the judges themselves had not believed that there was a probability that the men were, in fact, regarded as at least half-white by the community at large. Third, the formal standard followed in this case – that voters had to be only half-white in order to satisfy the law – was remarkably relaxed. Most states required that people, in order to be considered white, have no more than one-eighth proportion of other races represented in their genealogical history (or, more conventionally, in "their blood").[61] Finally, the whole incident illustrates just how personally difficult exercising a legitimate right to vote could be. Anderson and his friends were remarkably assertive, if not courageous. They must have known that they risked a close examination of their physical appearance, review of their standing in the community, and accounting of their racial parentage when they attempted to vote. And this examination was carried on in what was one of the most public of all nineteenth-

---

[60] Ten years later, when Charles Wright voted in another Ohio election, he similarly relied on an implicit social recognition of his father's white identity. Wright had been born before the Civil War in Loudon County, Virginia. While he acknowledged that his mother was "a mulatto," he claimed that his father "was a white man." In support of that claim, he noted that his father had been "clerk of court in Loudon county." Like Anderson before him, he too voted the Republican ticket. S.R. no. 1313: M.D. no. 38, Pt. 2 (1866): p. 24.

[61] Ohio law specified only that electors had to be "white," without formally defining the term. *Statutes of the State of Ohio*, Joseph R. Swan, compiler (Cincinnati: H. W. Derby, 1854), p. 20.

century venues – a crowded polling place – before election judges who were themselves drawn from respectable white society. Most men possessing similarly ambiguous racial identities probably chose not to face possible public humiliation by presenting themselves at the polls.

Twelve years later, in the 1868 congressional election in Cincinnati, the dangers that could accompany the assertion of a white identity were amply demonstrated. Unlike most of the polling places described in this chapter, this was an urban precinct, and to understand what happened there, we must first describe the setting.[62] The Thirteenth Ward polling place was located within a fire station, commonly called an "enginehouse." The front door to the enginehouse was about fifteen feet wide. To separate the election officials from the voters, a partition about five feet high had been placed across this opening, with the judges of election just inside. On the outside, there were challengers representing both the Democratic and Republican parties. In front of the enginehouse was an elevated platform, with a railing on either side and a gangway that extended a short distance into the street. Voters approached the judges over this gangway, exiting after they had turned in their tickets. On the sidewalk and filling the street in front of the enginehouse was a large crowd of between 300 and 400 people.

Dr. George Doherty, a physician, a Democrat, and one of the judges of election at this precinct, had expected a number of mixed-race men to present themselves at the polls. In preparation for that possibility, he had asked former United States Senator George Pugh, a lawyer who happened to reside in the ward (he lived with Doherty), to act as a legal adviser to the election officials. As Pugh recalled,

Dr. Doherty woke me by rapping on the door of my bed-room just as he was starting for the polls of the thirteenth ward. I dressed myself as quickly as I could and went to the polls; it may have been possibly ten, fifteen, or twenty minutes after the polls were opened before I arrived. I state in explanation that, on the previous day, Dr. Doherty, for himself and Mr. Corbett, the two trustees of the ward, requested me to examine the act of the legislature, in the session of 1868, to regulate voting by persons having a visible admixture of black blood in connection with the decision of the supreme court on that statute.

After studying that act, other statutes, and related decisions by the Ohio Supreme Court, Pugh concluded that

the authority of the judges of election was complete . . . to ascertain by examination of the party offering to vote, whether he had or had not a preponderance of white blood, and also whether he was actually a resident of the ward, or merely a transient person. It was in consequence of this advice Dr. Doherty requested me to come to

---

[62] The following description and account has been drawn from S.R. no. 1431: Contested Congressional Election in the First District of Ohio: M.D. no. 16, pp. 24–7, 29–35, 109–14, 116, 119, 127, 140. Benjamin Eggleston vs. P. W. Strader, election held on October 13, 1868.

the polls as quickly as I could dress myself, in order to give . . . advice as to particular cases that might arise.

Pugh reported that the processing of voters went smoothly:

[T]hose who had a visible admixture of African blood were inquired of also as to their parentage. Some equivocated and contradicted themselves to that degree that the judges rejected their votes. Others, several, stated the quantity of their African blood as low as a fourth, or an eighth, but alleged that they had Indian blood, the quantity of which, added to their admitted quantity of African blood, rendered them less than half white, and the judges rejected their votes.[63]

On this last point, Pugh advised the judges that the Ohio Supreme Court had ruled that "Indian blood disqualified as much as African." However, he also noted that several persons offered to vote "in whom I could not distinguish any sign of African blood"; with respect to these men, he advised the judges to accept their tickets. If, on the other hand, the judges thought that the men who appeared before them were of mixed race, their votes were summarily rejected. This was the case even if they offered to swear that they possessed a "preponderance" of white blood.

In effect Pugh provided a thin veneer of legal buttressing for Democratic judges who wished to reject all tickets offered by mixed race voters. Not surprisingly, in every instance these tickets would have been Republican. While the partisan dimension of the judges' behavior is interesting, the more important aspect was the way in which mixed race men experienced their attempt to vote. One of these men was Nelson Briggs, a paper-hanger and carpenter by trade, who approached the polls in the company of a Republican agent named Walker. As Briggs stood in line on the gangway, about five or six feet from where the judges were taking tickets, Dr. Doherty told him to go away from the polls because he would not be allowed to vote. At this point, Briggs was in full view of most of the crowd and immediately became the center of attention. When one of the bystanders yelled out, "Swear him," Doherty allowed Briggs to approach the enginehouse. As Briggs recollected,

Dr. Doherty swore me; and he asked me then whether I was white or colored, and I told him that I was colored. I told him that my mother was white and that her mother

---

[63]   Many, if not most, adult men in the United States had some trouble with mathematical fractions. In the genetic calculations that nineteenth-century Americans believed governed racial lineage, all of these fractions should have had even denominators (i.e., been divisible by two). But many men did not think of their ancestry in this way and, thus, could have been accused of misrepresenting or inaccurately representing their racial composition. For example, in response to the question, "How much white and how much colored blood have you?," one of the mixed-race men at this polling place replied, "I suppose it would be about two parts white – two-thirds, what you would call it." Such reports may have comprised some of what Pugh termed as equivocations and contradictions in their self-descriptions. Ibid., p. 35.

was an Irish woman; and the crowd raised in such a fury – there was pretty much all Irish there. This other judge, Corbett, he told Dr. Doherty that I was all right, to take my vote, and Dr. Doherty said he knowed his business, and said I could not vote. The crowd they rushed up and said "Down with him! Down with him!" There was three policemen came up and escorted me out of the crowd over on to eighth street, and so I went on home.

The Thirteenth Ward was a largely Irish, working-class neighborhood, and Briggs's public declaration that an Irish woman had cohabited with a black man did not go down well.

Henry Elbert, a steamboatman who possessed, in his own words, "a preponderance of white blood," was just starting to enter the gangway when Doherty first addressed Briggs. In his version of events, Doherty had held up his hand and called out to Briggs, "No use coming here; you can't vote here." When Briggs hesitated, Doherty again held up his hand and said, "Go back; you can't vote here." And it was apparently Walker, the Republican agent, who asked Doherty to swear Briggs. As Briggs was being sworn, the crowd was yelling, "Down with him; down with the nigger!" When Briggs was leaving the polls, the crowd turned and spotted Elbert, yelling, "Here's another one coming up to vote." He, like Briggs before him, was now exposed on the gangway. Gauging the hostility of the crowd, Elbert did not think it safe to approach the enginehouse and left the polls.

Charles Reeves, a tobacconist who maintained that he possessed "more white than black blood," also attempted to vote at this polling place. The judges swore him in and then refused his vote. He had voted without difficulty at this precinct in four or five prior elections, but in this one the crowd was yelling "Take him down!" as he discussed his eligibility with the judges. As one of the judges, John Clarke, later stated, "I think they [mixed-race men] had reason to fear violence" and then described a fourth incident in which a man "was dragged down off of the polls while being interrogated by the judges." One of the Republican challengers added that only the presence of the police prevented the crowd from violently assaulting these men. The police sergeant commanding the detachment agreed that only the presence of his men, stationed on either side of the voters' platform, allowed mixed-race men to even approach the judges.

However, even with the policemen in attendance, the crowd still effectively enforced the summary decisions of the Democratic judges by intimidating those whose votes were rejected. One of the clerks, for example, reported that the "crowd was very noisy and would call out, 'Don't let that nigger vote!' or, 'Take that nigger away from there!' and a great many similar remarks.... I heard no threats of personal violence, but I would not have considered myself safe had I been a person with a visible admixture of African blood." At one point when the crowd was particularly agitated, the police sergeant heard one person yell, "Take the black son of a bitch down, as he had no right up there to vote."

John Clarke blamed the Democratic judges of election for the intimidating environment surrounding the polls. The Republican judge stated that Doherty had placed his hand on the chest of several voters, pushing them away from the polls while exclaiming "You cannot be examined here, your hair is too kinky." "Quite a number" of such men were thus rejected even after they had sworn they possessed a sufficient proportion of white blood. In his defense, Doherty claimed that these mixed-race men had not been treated any more rudely by the judges and the crowd than were naturalized immigrants (by whom he apparently meant Irish men) when they attempted to vote. However, there is no evidence that naturalized voters had any trouble voting in the Thirteenth Ward on this particular day.

The embarrassment and humiliation a mixed-race voter encountered at the polls was sometimes not confined to just the man who approached the polls. For example, John Walter, an election judge at the Jenner Township polling place in Somerset County, Pennsylvania, reported that George Cristner was "mixed; his mother is a mulatto; his reputed father was a white man" and he was thus "denied the right to vote . . . on account of color." While Walter confidently asserted Cristner's genealogy and, incidentally, his mother's sexual history, a voter at the same precinct, John Johnson, was not so sure. Johnson began by describing Cristner as "a negro" but then backed up and said, "I don't call George C. Cristner a negro, but a mulatto. I don't know his father. I have seen his mother. His mother is the widow Cristner; she is pretty dark-complected; she has negro blood in her veins; she is a dark mulatto. . . . Mrs. Cristner is a sister of George and Samuel Deitz, who are black – Samuel not so black, but George quite black." However, Johnson, apparently well aware that he was under oath, once again partially retracted his testimony: "I can't say positively that Mrs. Cristner is a sister of George and Samuel Deitz, but by hearsay." Such partially informed speculation probably accompanied most debates over the racial identity of men approaching the polls. Based on rumor and innuendo, these discussions would have implicated many more people beyond the one man who attempted to vote.[64]

While cases of ambiguous racial identity appear to have been even more rare in the slave states than in the North, one did arise in the 1859 election in Clinton County, Kentucky. Despite the doubts of the election judges and other county officers, a man known as P. H. Clark voted at one of the precincts in that election. Clark was "a fellow that made his appearance in this county from parts unknown" about eighteen months prior to the election; his "parentage and genealogy were unknown in this country," and

---

[64] S.R. no. 1271: Contested Congressional Election in the Sixteenth District of Pennsylvania: M.D. no. 117, pp. 139–41. William H. Koontz vs. A. H. Coffroth, election held on October 11, 1864. The 1860 census reported only twelve blacks among the 1,762 residents of Jenner Township; Johnson had speculated on possible relationships between four of them, a third of the total, in his testimony.

after voting he "left here for parts unknown." As one witness reported, "I know nothing, nor have I heard anything, about his parentage, or race, or relationship."[65]

Nor, apparently, did anyone else. With neither a contextual basis for reconstructing Clark's genealogy nor a community history of acceptance or rejection of his possible identity as a black man, the men in and around the polls were compelled to fall back on Clark's physical appearance as a guide to his race. Constable J. A. Morrison, for example, testified that he knew Clark in his capacity "as an officer; I had him in custody not long since." When asked to describe Clark's physical appearance, Morrison reported that he "is very dark; his nose is flat, his lips are rather thick, his hair is kinky, and he has the actions and speech of a negro. I had him in custody two days, and examined him closely." He was then asked, "From your knowledge of him, do you believe him to be tinctured with African blood? If so, how much?" To which he replied, "I think he is tinctured with African blood; and have frequently said that I believe he is at least half African." Morrison then said that he did not know where Clark was "at this time," adding that "it is reported, and generally believed, that he has left this county."

Since Clark himself could not be presented as evidence, Morrison was asked to elaborate on his description. His response suggests the complex construction of racial identity in southern communities: "I suppose he has, slightly [the appearance of a mulatto]; he is rather too dark for a bright mulatto." Morrison's testimony ended with the admission that he knew nothing of Clark's actual "parentage."

A second witness, John Guthrie, stated that he "was acquainted with [Clark] when he resided in this county" and offered a description of the man: "He was dark, or rather brown. I think his hair was kinky, his lips thick, and his nose flat." Guthrie was then asked, "When you say his hair is kinky, do you or not mean that his hair is curly, more so than is usual?" To this, the witness responded, "I do mean that his hair is more curly than is a white man's hair." Asked whether he had ever "seen men of whose European blood you had no doubt that were of complexion equally, if not more, dark than Clark's," Guthrie responded, "I do not know that I ever did." Although he knew nothing of Clark's "parentage," Guthrie ventured the opinion, based on Clark's physical appearance, that he was "tinctured with African blood to the extent of one-fourth or more."

All of this was corroborated by yet a third witness, Mark Marlow, who had lived about a mile from Clark's house and had been "acquainted with him some fourteen or fifteen months" before the election was held. Marlow reported that Clark's neighbors "generally called [him] Mr. Dick's negro, as he resided on the land of Rufus K. Dick." Also acknowledging that he knew nothing of Clark's "parentage" and more or less repeating previous

---

[65] S.R. no. 1063: M.D. no. 11 (1859): p. 486.

descriptions, Marlow testified that Clark "had very much the appearance of a negro. His hair instead of being only curly, was kinky – more so than any white person; his nose was flat, and his lips thick. Both his nose and lips were more like a negro's than a white person. His actions and speech were also more like a negro's than a white person's." He concluded that Clark "is tinctured with African blood, and to the extent of one-half at least, if not more." The questioner then suggested that Clark had left the community after "a controversy was raised in reference to [his] vote"; Marlow only said that he "has gone I know not where." Asked whether he had "ever hear[d] his [Clark's] blood called in question previous to the recent election," Marlow responded, "I do not recollect that I ever did."[66]

Like the others, Abijah Guthrie said that he both knew Clark personally and believed him to be "tinctured with African blood to the extent of one-fourth at least, and perhaps one-half," describing him as "about the color of a dark mulatto; his hair was coarse and rough, pretty much like a negro's wool; his actions and speech were like those of a negro." To the extent that he merely repeated what others had already said, Guthrie's testimony was unremarkable. But he also testified, in effect, as to the opinion of his wife. Acknowledging that Clark had "frequently visited" his home, having "been there many times," Guthrie was asked, "Did or not your lady in your presence refuse to let him eat at the table where white people generally ate?" The witness responded, "Clark did come and eat at my house with some white men one morning, and my wife came to me complaining that that negro was eating with the white men, and said that the next time she would send him to the kitchen." Several things are at least implied in this exchange. First, the testimony invokes domestic social practice as evidence of racial identity. Guthrie's wife, as an interpreter of racial custom and etiquette, is thus cited in support of Clark's black identity.[67] But even more interesting is the evidently relaxed behavior of Guthrie and the other white men toward Clark. They were apparently willing to sit down and eat their breakfast alongside him, even though Guthrie represented Clark as unambiguously black. Only the wife raised an objection and that objection was raised only in private. The color line was not so tightly drawn as to clearly demarcate, in practice, Clark as beyond the pale of the white community.[68]

In fact, one witness regarded Clark's racial identity as sufficiently ambiguous that he would not have objected to his vote. Although not acquainted with Clark, P. H. Smith reported that he had "seen him once. He is tolerably

---

[66]　S.R. no. 1061: M.D. no. 3 (1859): pp. 89–92.

[67]　Another witness, Montgomery Howard, reached a similar conclusion; although Howard admitted, "I don't know Clark to be a negro or mulatto," he went on to say that he "had the appearance of being mixed blooded. From his looks, I would not like to let him eat at my table or sleep in my beds with white folks." S.R. no. 1063: M.D. no. 11 (1859): p. 486.

[68]　S.R. no. 1061: M.D. no. 3 (1859): p. 100.

dark; but I think I have seen some men who were regarded as white men that I thought were as dark as he. . . . I think I have seen men vote whose color was as dark as Clark's, whose votes were never challenged or suspected." Smith went on to say, "If I had not heard the thing [Clark's racial identity] talked about, I do not think I would have thought of such a thing; I did not notice the man particularly." However, although Smith did not regard Clark as black, he did think that his color made him an undesirable political ally. When asked whether he had not told another man that he (Smith) "would not have wanted the vote of as dark a man as Clark; and that if Anderson was elected only by Clark's vote he ought not to accept the seat," the witness responded that he "might have said that I would not want as dark a man's vote as Clark was. I don't recollect that I said Anderson ought not to accept if elected by his vote only."[69]

If members of the white community were more or less in agreement that P. H. Clark was black, it is surprising that he was allowed to vote. Although interpolation is still necessary, the best explanation arises out of the testimony of R. A. Burchett, who had been appointed sheriff at this precinct. Burchett was the official who would have "cried" out Clark's vote and thus would have been present when the vote was accepted. Stating that he personally knew Clark, Burchett went onto describe him: "His skin was very much the same complexion as that of a negro; his hair was nearly as kinky as any negro's; his nose was tolerably flat; his lips were tolerably thick; his speech and actions were like those of a negro." Like the previous witnesses, Burchett concluded that Clark was "tinctured with African blood to the extent of one-half, at least. This opinion is based on his dark color, his thick lips, flat nose, kinky hair, speech and actions." When Clark presented himself at the polls, Martin B. Owens, the Democratic judge of election, objected to his vote, "saying that his skin was too dark for him to be a good voter; that he must be of Mexican or some other descent than European; but Miles H. Davis, the other judge [representing the oppositionists], insisted that he was a legal voter; and after parleying about it for some time, some one remarked that when the judges differed the sheriff [i.e., Burchett, the witness] was to decide. Then . . . Owens remarked that he would let him pass; and thus he was permitted to vote."[70]

How Clark came to be at the polls is a mystery, but the most likely explanation is that he was recruited by the oppositionists.[71] He thus would have supported the oppositionist party slate and that, in turn, would have

[69]   S.R. no. 1063: M.D. no. 11 (1859): pp. 477–9.
[70]   S.R. no. 1061: M.D. no. 3 (1859): pp. 97–8. Burchett was also asked "[h]as or not P. H. Clark blue eyes?" To which he replied, "I think not" (p. 99). As is evident in these descriptions, most whites possessed well-developed, if sometimes personally idiosyncratic, stereotypes of the appearance and behavior of blacks.
[71]   One of the witnesses, Montgomery Howard, stated that two supporters of W. C. Anderson, the oppositionist candidate, were "trying to vote" Clark. Howard told

explained why Owens objected to his vote. This would also explain why Davis would have insisted that he was a legal voter. With the two election judges deadlocked, the sheriff of the election (Burchett) became the tie-breaking vote on Clark's eligibility. How he would have come down on that issue is not clear, but his description of Clark's physical appearance and his opinion as to Clark's racial identity suggest that he would have refused the vote.[72] But before he was asked to intervene, the two judges had negotiated a solution in which Clark's vote was accepted. Although we do not know what their discussion entailed, we might speculate that the settlement involved the acceptance of an equally dubious vote from the Democratic side that would have balanced Clark's support for the opposition. Informal agreements of this sort were common between election judges. Many judges, particularly in rural, long-settled precincts, had known each other for years and thus had ample opportunity to develop a personal relationship in which conflict-minimizing practices eased much of the stress of partisan competition. These practices roughly corresponded to the letter of the law, but the law was no barrier when personal conceptions of fair play or community values were at stake. As one result of these practices, P. H. Clark, a black man in a slave state, was allowed to vote just before the Civil War.

Many northern election judges also believed they could detect the presence of black blood and its proportion through a close examination of a man's features. When Charles Miles was challenged at the Menallen Township polls in Pennsylvania, he claimed that his mother was Swiss and his father was Italian.[73] However, his father was dead and he had not heard from his mother for the past four or five years. Since Miles apparently had no other relatives in the neighborhood, the other men at the polls had only his sworn oath and physical features as evidence. A rather brusque and unsophisticated evaluation of Miles was offered by Aaron Stewart, a voter at that township: "He was a black man; that's all I know about him." When asked to describe the color and character of Miles's hair, Stewart responded, "Just like the rest of the niggers." Stewart was then asked whether he had been "close up to" Miles, answering, "I was right by his side at the window." This drew what may have been the most crude question posed in all the hearings, "Did he smell like a darky?" Stewart responded, "I didn't smell at him." Fielding another question concerning how close one would have to be in order to determine that Miles was black, Stewart reported, "I saw him

---

them, "[I]f I was in their place that I would not vote him [because] he was mixed blooded." S.R. no. 1063: M.D. no. 11 (1859): pp. 486–7.

[72] On judicial reliance on physical appearance as evidence of racial identity, see Thomas D. Morris, *Southern Slavery and the Law, 1619–1860* (Chapel Hill: University of North Carolina Press, 1996), pp. 25–8.

[73] The following is based on testimony appearing in S.R. no. 1431: M.D. (no number, bound between nos. 24 and 25 [1868]): pp. 87, 324, 327.

to-day a distance of two hundred yards, and knew he was a negro." Stewart must have had remarkably good eyesight.

Jasper Thompson, like Stewart a voter at the Menallen Township, was a little more forthcoming but less certain as to how Miles should be categorized:

He was examined before the board, and, as near as I can recollect, said his father was an Italian and his mother a Swiss, or his mother an Italian and his father a Swiss; one or the other, I am not certain which. . . . He is rather dark, but I have seen men darker that had no negro blood in them. After hearing his statement, did not suppose him to have African blood in him; but had I not heard his examination, or statement, I might have had my doubts as to his being white or not.

So Thompson's physical examination of Miles was inconclusive, but he, as a Republican, was willing to accept Miles's self-description (as well as the Republican ticket Miles would have cast).

William Gosnell was the assessor of the township and "assessed" Miles as a "colored man." However, this was after the election, and his official opinion was thus not available at the polls when the judges were deliberating. Gosenell still offered his opinion: "I thought he was a colored man – a man of African descent. . . . He is very dark; a great deal darker than a great many who don't claim to be anything else but a negro." At this point, Gosnell was catechized quite closely.

Q. "Do you mean that he was blacker than a full-blooded African?" A. "No, sir."
Q. "Could a man that was nothing else but a negro be anything else but an African?" A. "There can be a full-blooded negro and a half-blooded negro."
Q. "Was his hair curly and kinky?" A. "It was curly and kinky."
Q. "Was his nose flat?" A. "Yes."
Q. "Lips protruding?" A. "Yes, sir."
Q. "Hadn't he, now, every possible physical mark of an African?" A. "I thought he had. I want it understood that I don't want him put down as a full-blooded African."

Here the questioning focused on the four most commonly cited characteristics distinguishing blacks from whites: complexion, hair texture, the shape of the nose, and the form of the lips. Taken alone, none of them was viewed as decisive evidence of a person's racial identity (although they are listed here in the descending order of their relative importance). They were, instead, a kind of check list that men consulted when attempting to classify persons unknown to them and thus a way of rationally discussing what was in many cases an intractably difficult problem.

Miles had voted at the October congressional election, having been approved by election officials among which the Democrats were in the majority at this precinct. This decision had provoked some controversy, particularly when Republicans taunted the Democrats for having allowed a black man to vote.[74] Apparently in response to this criticism, the election officials at Menallen Township changed their decision in the subsequent November presidential election and ruled Miles ineligible. William McGinness, one of the inspectors of election at Menallen Township, gave the most detailed account of the way Miles was evaluated in the November election. The inspector reported that there was substantial disagreement among the men at the polls, but, in the end, the election officials disqualified him because they thought he had given false information under oath. According to McGinness, Miles had sworn that he had voted for the last fifteen years (thus establishing a lengthy precedential history of having been viewed as white). However, another man, Edmund Leonard, told the election officials that Miles had told him that "he[, Miles, had] never voted in his life, except in the army [and] at the October election." The board apparently accepted Leonard's statement as a contradiction to Mile's sworn oath.[75]

McGinness himself was convinced both that Miles was black and that the physical evidence was incontrovertible. In support for that opinion, he stated that Miles "was a walnut-brown, and had greasy, ornary [*sic*], mean, dirty hair." Given the discrepancy between the rulings in October and November, this report naturally led to a question of whether or not "Miles's hair [was] greasier, ornarier [*sic*], meaner, and dirtier in November than it was in October." Consistent with his belief in naturally endowed and immutable racial characteristics, McGinness reported that he had seen "no difference" between the two elections. Since McGinness had referred to hair characteristics that could describe unkempt hair on any head, white or black, he was then asked to identify "the distinguishing features of physical difference between a white man and a black man." Here McGinness was much more original and decisive than most men: "The lesser the angle [apparently of the nose], the small ear, the white of the eye resembles a young mushroom; the finger nail is longer and narrower, and more oval than the white man. That is all I have studied about negrooligy." In response to a follow-up question, McGinness affirmed that "the white of Miles's eye resemble[d] a young mushroom."

The most apparent conclusion to be drawn from these witnesses is how capriciously and inconsistently racial criteria were applied to Miles. Pressing a little deeper, however, we can easily see that none of these men (all of them securely classified as white) exhibited any doubt that racial categories were, in some sense, susceptible to proof and therefore real features of society. Taken one step further, we can also easily see how such discussions at the polls, carried on by men who were among the political leaders of their

---

74   This was an election in which Republican support for the voting rights of southern freedmen was probably the most salient issue before the voters.

75   However, if Miles had openly voted while in the army, he must have been serving in a white unit because the Union military was segregated. This meant that military recruiters and his comrades in arms must have considered him white.

neighborhood, would significantly strengthen both the salience of racial categories in all aspects of public life while also buttressing the underlying social consensus on which their application necessarily rested. One of the most important wellsprings of racial identity and, ultimately, racial subordination was thus the practical application of suffrage laws.

CONCLUSION

In long-settled, eastern rural communities most men brought to the polls extensive individual social and political histories when they voted. In some cases, they could convincingly relate these histories as evidence of their eligibility to vote. In others, their kin and neighbors collectively constructed these histories from their own memories, with or without a contribution from the erstwhile voter. In both instances, men who usually knew each other well gathered at the polls, shared what they knew of the histories and identities of individuals who approached the polls, and thus constructed whether or not men could rightfully participate in the election. The dense social contexts in which these rural precincts were embedded enabled the enforcement – if we can call it that – of legal requirements that, in urban neighborhoods or on the western frontier, were more or less dead letters. For example, while mental capacity, age, and residency were among the most commonly contested suffrage requirements in rural and small town polling places, these same characteristics almost literally dropped from sight in the nation's larger cities. In urban polling places, ethnicity and citizenship were far and away the most contested characteristics of a voter.

4

Ethno-Cultural Stereotypes and Voting in Large Cities

In terms of political practice and material organization, rural precincts in long-settled regions of the slave and free states had more in common with each other than either had with polling places in large cities.[1] And large cities, whether northern or southern, resembled one another more than either looked like their immediately surrounding rural areas. This general divergence between rural and urban polling places arose for a number of reasons. For one thing, urban populations were much more diverse in terms of ethnicity, religious beliefs, and economic livelihoods than were their rural hinterlands.[2] This diversity, along with the emergence of ghettos that concentrated urban inhabitants in their own distinct ethnic, religious, and class communities, meant that party agents and election officials did not personally know many of the men who approached the voting window.[3] And even

---

[1] In the last decade prior to the Civil War, the major difference between the laws governing elections in the slave and free states was probably the fact that a few slave states still retained a procedure in which the voter publicly announced his voting choices in some way (see Chapter 2). Oral voting aside, there were few differences in either suffrage qualifications or the material arrangement of the polls, and most observers, when presented with the texts of election statutes from slave and free states, would have been hard-pressed to tell them apart.

[2] While most of the evidence presented in this chapter is drawn from the nation's largest cities, some examples report election practice in smaller towns. The major criterion for inclusion in this chapter is whether or not the urban center was large enough that party agents could not personally identify most of the men approaching the voting window. For a brief discussion of the differences between rural and urban voting, see Glenn C. Altschuler and Stuart M. Blumin, *Rude Republic: Americans and Their Politics in the Nineteenth Century* (Princeton, N.J.: Princeton University Press, 2000), p. 234.

[3] However, the men who served as party agents in and around the polling place still personally recognized a great many voters. One inspector of elections in Philadelphia, for example, stated that he knew "by sight" three-fifths of the 500 men who voted at his precinct. Another Philadelphia inspector claimed to be "acquainted" with 75 percent of the 400 voters at his precinct. An election judge in the same city said that

if one of them might recognize a man, the others usually could not help to establish that voter's identity.

In addition, polling places in the nation's largest cities were much closer together than they were in rural neighborhoods. In rural areas, polling places were usually at least several miles apart, and riding from one to the other was inconvenient at best. But in the largest cities polling places might be only blocks apart, with one close to where a man lived, another near the place in which he worked, and perhaps yet another somewhere along the path he normally took between home and work. The close proximity of polling places in larger cities, combined with the relative anonymity of individuals, meant that men could choose the precinct in which they might vote without going too far out of their way. These factors also meant that many men were able, if they so wished, to vote at more than one precinct in the same election. That multiple voting was very common seems beyond serious dispute, although it is impossible to estimate the incidence even roughly. However, the frequency of multiple voting was high enough to be considered a serious problem in urban polling places, while the incidence was vanishingly low in most rural precincts. This problem led a few states before 1870 to institute voter registration systems, usually but not always restricted to the largest cities in the state.[4]

Finally, even though urban polling places were usually spaced much closer together, they were also much larger in terms of the numbers of voters who attended them. In most states, a large rural precinct would have 200 or 300 voters, but a relatively small urban polling place would usually have twice that number or more. The sheer size of these urban precincts meant that processing voters, particularly during the early morning hours when men voted on their way to work, was an arduous task. Even when little or no attempt was made to screen voters for eligibility, simply writing down their names and depositing their tickets necessarily consumed most of the attention of the clerks and election judges. There was usually little or no time for the kind of extended discussions of a man's age or residency that often took place in rural areas.

In the larger cities, age and residency requirements thus became more or less moot issues because they were simply unenforceable in the absence of contextual information. The sheer number of men approaching the voting

he personally knew at least two-thirds of the 458 voters in his precinct. However, an election judge who had lived in his precinct for twenty-seven years admitted that he did not know half of the 600 voters there. Ser. Rec. (hereafter S.R.) no. 1431: Contested Congressional Election in the Fifth District of Pennsylvania: Mis. Doc. (hereafter M.D.) no. 7, pp. 342, 345, 348, 352. Caleb N. Taylor vs. John R. Reading, election held on October 13, 1868.

4 Alexander Keyssar, *The Right to Vote: The Contested History of Democracy in the United States* (New York: Basic Books, 2000), pp. 65–6, 151–2. Also see Joseph P. Harris, *Registration of Voters in the United States* (Washington, D.C.: Brookings Institution, 1929), pp. 65–89.

window, along with the fact that many of them were voting outside their own neighborhood, thus reinforced the relative anonymity of the average voter. This anonymity, in turn, strongly encouraged a reliance on stereotyped ethnic and class characteristics, such as clothing and accent, as a means of identifying voters with a particular party organization or as not qualified to participate in an election.[5] Although ethnic and religious prejudice was probably as pronounced in many rural areas, such stereotypes were usually not necessary outside the cities because much deeper familiarity with the community and its inhabitants would have made them redundant. The crowds of men attending a rural polling place already knew those who approached the polls.

Citizenship was the most frequently disputed suffrage qualification in most urban polling places both because other characteristics, such as age and residence, were much more difficult to enforce and because many of the most recent immigrants to the United States resided in the nation's largest cities. This preponderance was particularly pronounced for those who lacked the wealth to take up a homestead on the western frontier, who could not speak English or spoke the language with a very heavy accent, or whose dress and mannerisms could be most easily identified with a specific foreign-born community. Regardless of where they lived, naturalized immigrants were expected to possess papers, signed and sealed by either a state or a federal judge. Election officials could insist that such men present these papers at the polls. For all these reasons, ethnic traits were the most common characteristics with which party agents and election officials categorized individual men in urban polling places.

ETHNICITY

In some ways, racial and ethnic identities were constructed along similar lines. For instance, as discussed in the previous chapter, the identification of a man as black was based on speech and behavior, as well as physical appearance. Speech and behavior were similarly important in identifying ethnicity. However, there were differences as well. While physiological characteristics were the most important markers for establishing black identity, the attire of a man was the primary badge of ethnicity. In addition, when a man was constructed as "black," the almost universal result was his exclusion from voting. The consequences attached to ethnicity were much more

5   Experienced political agents, however, knew that appearances could be deceiving. For example, when Wesley Coffman of St. Louisville, Ohio, described Emanuel Sites, he confessed, "I did not know what his politics were; he looked like a democrat; he was a man that worked for his living, and I did not think that a man who worked for his living would vote that ticket [the Republican]." S.R. no. 1313: Contested Congressional Election in the Thirteenth District of Ohio: M.D. no. 38, Pt. 2, p. 73. Columbus Delano vs. George W. Morgan, election held on October 9, 1866.

complicated. For one thing, the terms "ethnic" and "ethnicity" were never used by election officials, party agents, and common voters attending the polls. Instead, the generic label for indicating someone of foreign birth was "foreigner." But most political discourse in and around the polls associated men with a particular nationality, identifying them, for example, as "German" or "Irish." Even so, the relationship between national origin and personal appearance was not demarcated very well; those attending the polls understood, for example, that someone of Southern European background could be quite swarthy with curly hair and thus could be taken for a "mulatto" at the polls if no collateral information was available. But while racial and ethnic identities might blur together under cursory inspection, the law was comparatively exact; blacks could not vote and foreigners could.

However, not all foreigners could vote in the mid-nineteenth century, only those who had been properly naturalized. Federal law stipulated that, in order for an immigrant to be eligible for U.S. citizenship, he must have resided in the United States for at least five consecutive years and at least one year in the state in which he applied. At least two years before he could be naturalized, an immigrant must have declared his intention to become a citizen, at the same time renouncing all allegiance to any foreign nation. As evidence of this declaration, he was issued what were universally known at the polls as his "first papers."

Persons who entered the United States at an age younger than eighteen and some of those honorably discharged from the military or navy of the United States were not required to make these declarations. For everybody else, this oath marked the onset of a subsequent two-year waiting period before the immigrant could demonstrate, by way of good character and law-abiding history, that he qualified for American citizenship. He then renounced all titles and noble orders that may have been previously attached to his name while swearing to uphold the national constitution. Meeting these conditions, he was given a document identifying him as a naturalized American citizen. These documents were issued by both the federal and, much more frequently, state courts. At the polls, these were known universally as an immigrant's "second papers."[6]

---

[6] These naturalization procedures were first set down in a federal law enacted on April 14, 1802, and remained almost unchanged for the remainder of the nineteenth century. For contemporary descriptions of the naturalization process, see Andrew W. Young, *Introduction to the Science of Government*, rev. 20th ed. (Buffalo, N.Y.: Geo. H. Derby, 1851) pp. 121–2; M. W. Cluskey, *The Political Text-book or Encyclopedia* (Washington, D.C.: Cornelius Wendell, 1857), pp. 361–5; Everit Brown and Albert Strauss, *A Dictionary of American Politics* (New York: A. L. Burt, 1892), p. 342; George W. McCrary, *A Treatise on the American Law of Elections* (Keokuk, Iowa: R. B. Ogden, 1875), pp. 44–6. Immigrants disproportionately resided in the larger American cities. A census conducted in St. Louis in 1858, for example, both reported the number of white males over twenty-one and broke them down into categories. Of the 38,387 white adult males in the city, 24 percent were native-born Americans and 76 percent

The states imposed varying requirements for voting with respect to citizenship. Many, such as Alabama and Arkansas, required only that immigrants had declared their intention to become citizens.[7] In practice, that meant that these men had to have taken out their first papers, which, if challenged at the polls, they would present as evidence of their eligibility for voting. Others, such as West Virginia, required full American citizenship. If men in such states were challenged, they presented their second papers.[8] These legal requirements made the identification of foreign-born residents at the polls one of the most important priorities of party agents and election officials.

Election judges were enjoined by law to ask foreign-born voters for documentary proof of naturalization or intent to become naturalized.[9] However, these officials had no easy way of identifying who was not a native-born citizen and, thus, who to ask for papers. By default, they often relied on the same ethnic stereotypes that partisans outside the voting window used to separate friendly and hostile voters. A heavy Irish brogue, for example, would almost always lead a Know-Nothing observer to challenge a voter, compelling the election judge to ask for "papers" and the voter to produce them.[10] In these cases, the participants did not usually have anything more to go on than their immediate observation of the voter.

Thus, in communities with large numbers of aliens who were personally unknown to those attending the polls, the physical appearance of men who presented themselves was compared with stereotypes previously constructed

had been born abroad. Of those born abroad, 51 percent were naturalized citizens (having taken out their second papers), 13 percent had only their first papers, and 36 percent had not begun the naturalization process. S.R. no. 1062: Contested Congressional Election in the First District of Missouri: M.D. no. 8, p. 946. Frank P. Blair, Jr., vs. J. R. Barrett, election held in August 1858. The 1860 census reported that 60 percent of the population of St. Louis had been born abroad, the highest proportion of any American city. Michael Fellman, *Inside War: The Guerrilla Conflict in Missouri during the American Civil War* (New York: Oxford University Press, 1989), p. 8.

7   For the laws on alien suffrage for Indiana, Illinois, Michigan, Wisconsin, Oregon Territory, etc., see Cluskey, *Political Text-book*, pp. 31–42. On alien suffrage generally, see Keyssar, *Right to Vote*, p. 33.

8   For varying state and territorial requirements for suffrage, see, for example, *American Year-Book and National Register for 1869* (Hartford, Conn.: O. D. Case, 1869), pp. 275–510.

9   In his *American Law of Elections*, McCrary noted that it was impossible to prove that an immigrant had not been naturalized. "There are in the United States many hundreds of Courts possessing the power to grant naturalization, and to require in any case that affirmative proof be offered that no one of such Courts has ever granted naturalization to a particular person, would be to require what is practically impossible" (p. 220). Thus, the burden of proof was on the immigrant to produce the papers he had been given by the court.

10 As an election inspector in Pennsylvania put it, "I don't know any better [how to identify foreigners] than by their dialect." S.R. no. 1431: M.D. (no number, bound between nos. 24 and 25), p. 27.

for members of the various ethnic communities. As these men approached the voting window, they would be asked which party they were likely to support or where they lived. If a prospective voter belonged to an ethnic group that tended to support the opposition, he would be challenged as to his citizenship at the window and thus compelled to present his papers. If he belonged to a friendly group, party agents would turn the other way or, even more often, encourage his participation in the election regardless of whether he met statutory requirements for voting.

Most immigrants who attempted to vote carried their papers with them to the polls, if they were legally qualified, or tried to bluff their way through to the window, if they were not.[11] If challenged and the state allowed men with their first papers to vote, they might claim that they had been seventeen years of age or younger when they entered the country, thus explaining why they did not have papers. If such a claim was made, then election officials were compelled to construct the age of the voter and project that age back to the year when the man had immigrated to the United States. Since many of these men neither knew nor could document their current age or the year when they had immigrated, these estimates were often uncertain.[12] Left to their own devices, election officials usually projected estimates favorable to their party's interests. If allowed to proceed, these anonymous men were usually sworn as to the information they had provided, permitted to vote, and then vanished back into the vast, amorphous sea of humanity that American cities had become by the middle of the nineteenth century.

Of course, if papers could be produced by these men, they were even more likely to survive challenges at the voting window. Knowing this, the parties – particularly the Democratic party – often provided such papers to their partisans as a kind of public service.[13] In the 1868 election, for example, a number of immigrants voted in New York who apparently had been given their second naturalization papers just before the election. They all apparently voted the Democratic ticket after their papers had been facilitated by party officials serving in official roles (e.g., as a state judge). The testimony

---

[11] Like any other document, these papers could be lost or destroyed. See, for example, S.R. no. 1063: Contested Congressional Election in the Fourth District of Kentucky: M.D. no. 11, p. 402. Response of Anderson to Chrisman in James S. Chrisman vs. William C. Anderson, election held on August 1, 1859.

[12] See, for examples, S.R. no. 1313: Contested Congressional Election in the Thirteenth District of Ohio: M.D. no. 38, Pt. 1, pp. 56–9. Columbus Delano vs. George W. Morgan, election held on October 9, 1866; S.R. no. 1431: M.D. no. 7, p. 187. For a description of the testimony in those hearings, see Richard Bensel, "The American Ballot Box: Law, Identity, and the Polling Place in the Mid-Nineteenth Century," *Studies in American Political Development* 17 (Spring 2003): 17–19.

[13] On the fraudulent operation of "naturalization mills" that sometimes produced such papers just prior to an election, see Mark W. Summers, *The Plundering Generation: Corruption and the Crisis of the Union, 1849–1861* (New York: Oxford University Press, 1987), pp. 58–9.

taken during hearings on the subsequent election contest described a number of different ways that these papers could be mass produced and conveniently distributed to the men who voted on them and, of course, without regard to whether or not the men actually could be legally naturalized. Just before the presidential election, for example, Richard Tracy, a small shopkeeper in Deerpark, received between

55 or 60 naturalization papers for distribution . . . [i]n packages done up in a small tin cream of tartar box, not locked. It was sent to my place or left by parties unknown to me. I received an anonymous letter stating I was to receive this box, and it gave me instructions how to distribute the papers. . . . The instructions were that parties would call for these papers, and it instructed me not to hand the papers to the parties, but to leave them in the box in the front shop, and the parties would get the papers themselves. I left the box in the front shop as directed. . . .

The shopkeeper did not closely examine these papers, but he did know what they were and was not surprised when men came to pick one up. As Tracy explained, "whenever I saw men coming for them I went in the back shop and disappeared" so that he could not identify who might have picked up a copy. All but fourteen were distributed to men who thus very likely became voters in the subsequent election.[14]

William McNeal, a merchant in Montgomery, said he had received a package of naturalization papers made out to William Carroll and John McHugh, who were laborers employed "on the track of the Montgomery and Erie railroad." Although the package did not contain any instructions, McNeal gave both papers to Carroll. In fact, many aliens worked as unskilled laborers on the nation's railroads. Because most of their native-born or naturalized friends and relatives belonged to the Democratic party, these aliens could easily be persuaded to vote a Democratic ticket. If the party, in addition to ties of friendship and kinship, offered them naturalization papers as well, all the better. A few men who lived in Goshen received papers from an anonymous source through the post office. Others simply reported that their papers "were brought" to them. Since naturalization papers could be received only after a personal apparance in a state or federal court, their papers were considered fraudulent and their tickets were summarily rejected.

The way in which these papers were prepared and distributed was described by Philander Banker of Middletown, who began his testimony by saying that he had known the Democratic congressional candidate, George

[14] One of the naturalization papers was in fact made out for Tracy himself, but he refused to accept it. Although Tracy was a Democrat and most of the papers were apparently intended for Democrats, one or two may have been made out for Republicans. S.R. no. 1402: Contested Congressional Election in the Eleventh District of New York: M.D. no. 27, Pt. 1, pp. 37, 73–4. Charles H. Van Wyck vs. George W. Greene, election held on November 3, 1868.

Greene, for more than twelve years. He then narrated a conversation in which Greene and another Democratic partisan attempted to involve him in the process:

> I went in the Taylor House, Middletown, about two weeks before election, and I met Mr. Greene, and I think Charles Dunning was in company. Mr. Greene asked me to take a cigar with him, and we came back from the counter to the centre of the bar-room. No person was near by, and he asked me if I knew of any men who wanted their papers. I told him I did not at that time, and he said: "Look around and find out; you are living in Middletown, and must know some, and send me their names, or give them to John Bell," which would be the same thing, and he would make it all right with me, and see that the men got their papers.

Later in his testimony, when Greene was acting as his own counsel, Banker referred to him in the second person:

> Charles Dunning was in your company at that time…you and I were in the centre of the room, and there were a number of people sitting about the room, but Mr. Greene and I had this conversation away from them, and he spoke in a manner that it would be difficult for the others to hear.

Why Banker related this conversation was unclear. He only said, "I have been [a Republican] lately, but previously a democrat; I guess you know pretty well."[15]

Because ethnic communities were relatively closed, the parties needed agents from each of the major groups at the polls. An Irishman approaching the voting window, for example, was much more likely to be identified by a fellow countryman than by a German. In addition, a fellow countryman would be much better equipped to conduct the brief interrogations that transpired before the voting window. For instance, when questioned by an Irish party agent, an Irish immigrant ran the risk of misidentifying family origins in the old country or linkages between the ostensible time of landing in the United States and events important to the Irish community (e.g., "Did you come to this country before or after – occurred in Ireland?"). In addition, those immigrants who were not residents of the district in which they were

[15] S.R. no. 1402: M.D. no. 27, Pt. 1 (1868): pp. 74–5, 78, 121, 125. James Norton, a prominent Democrat and editor of the Middletown *Mercury*, had boasted to Wilson Taylor, a Republican merchant, that "the democratic party would carry the State of New York, and this district. I [remarked] that if they did I thought they would have to do a wholesale naturalization business. He said they intended to naturalize as many as was necessary to do it. He said they would do it as an offset to the negro vote the republican party would get in the south" (p. 173). For similar use of blank naturalization papers in the 1868 Pennsylvania election, see S.R. no. 1431: M.D. (no number, bound between nos. 24 and 25 [1868]): pp. 173–4.

trying to vote could often be spotted by fellow countrymen when the latter asked the name of the street they lived on, who their neighbors were, what church they attended, and so forth.

In most communities, ethnic groups became closely identified with one of the major parties. If so, then the agents of that party who belonged to that group tended to see prospective voters sharing their nationality as "obligated" to support their organization. For example, Irishmen who served as agents of the Democratic party in major American cities almost universally denounced countrymen who supported any other party as ethnic "traitors," "renegades," or worse. While ethnicity would have been an important political quality in and around the polls in any event, both the citizenship requirements set down in election law (which made ethnicity an important attribute because immigrants might not be qualified to vote) and the ticket system of voting (which enabled discovery of voter intentions by party agents before a ticket was handed in to the election judges) strongly reinforced the salience of ethnic identities and thus strengthened the alignment of each group with one or the other of the major parties. When elections were hotly contested, ethnicity, partisan allegiance, and attitudes toward the major issues of the day frequently became conflated in ways that defied the understanding of many voters.

In the years just prior to the Civil War, St. Louis, Missouri, became one such political cauldron as the Whig party broke up over nativist and free-soil issues. Know-Nothing lodges sprung up throughout the city as native-born Protestants mobilized against immigrant Catholics. Since many of these native-born Protestants were also free-soilers opposed to slavery's expansion into the western territories, ethnicity and religion became bound up with positions for and against slavery at the polls. However, compared with other periods in the nineteenth century, party organizations were relatively unstable; factions moved from one side to another of what was sometimes a three-cornered contest involving proslavery and free-soil elements of the Democratic party and the nativist remnants of the Whig and American organizations. One of the most important of these contests involved the congressional election in the first district of Missouri in August 1858 among Frank Blair, John Barrett, and Samuel Breckinridge. Blair ran as a Free Soil candidate, although his relations with the recently formed Republican party were close. Barrett was the proslavery Democratic nominee, and Breckinridge was supported by the then fading American or Know-Nothing organization. Although all three ran what appear to have been competitive races, only the results for the two front-runners, Blair and Barrett, were contested; Blair was ultimately able to take the seat away from Barrett, who had been originally certified as the victor.

Here we are primarily interested in how the election was conducted at and around the polling place. Henry Blow, for example, distributed Blair tickets at Carondelet, a small city of 3,000 people on the banks of the Mississippi about six miles from St. Louis, and later testified as to events in and around the voting window:

When I went [to the polls] early in the morning I observed a great many persons that I had never seen in Carondelet before, and asked a number of our citizens who they were, and was told they were friends of Mr. Barrett, who had come down to attend to the election. . . . I can give the best idea of them by stating a circumstance which occurred at the polls. There was an old man that came to me and stated that he wished to vote for the best man, and asked me to give him a ticket. I asked him if he was a voter, having never seen him that I recollected of at that time, though I had. He replied he was, and I said here is a ticket I have voted myself, and gave him a ticket. He stated that he had come to me because he had no confidence in the other fellows, as he called them, and asked me where he was to vote. I told him, showed him the polls, when a Mr. Donnelly, a gentleman, I believe living in this county somewhere, I don't know where, stepped up and said to this man, you shan't vote that ticket; you are an Irishman and one of our men. He jerked him away from where he was standing and tried to get the ticket from the hands of the man, who protested against this conduct, and insisted on voting the ticket. Mr. Donnelly then indulged in such language towards me as to bring on a collision with me, which I avoided. He was very abusive. My impression was that he had a mob to sustain him in anything he might do. I was perfectly satisfied of it. Not a single one of them I knew of the party. . . . I don't think any one of the party acting with [Donnelly] were citizens of Carondelet at that time. He ordered his men to come up; I think there were four of them came up. They took the poor old fellow up, marched him off to a grocery; they carried him off; took him in their arms bodily, and took him off.[16]

One of the interesting things in this passage, in addition to the possessive attitude of the Democratic partisans toward their Irish countrymen, is the willingness of Blow to have this old man vote as long as it was the Blair ticket. He did not ask or otherwise seem interested in this voter's identity until he had been taken in hand by the opposition. When Blow again ran into Donnelly after the election, the latter attempted to establish professional relations with him:

Next day I saw Mr. Donnelly, who spoke to me on the platform at St. Louis, the platform of the railroad depot at Plum street. He remarked to me that he wished to make an explanation to me; that he had gone to Carondelet to make every Irishman vote the Barrett ticket, and I think he said to elect Judge Hackney, but that is a mere impression; that he had no intention of insulting me, but made the old man vote the right ticket – vote his ticket; but if he had it to do over again, after learning the circumstances, that he would not have interfered in that particular case. . . . About two weeks afterwards I saw the old fellow I have referred to; he was in a starving condition; he complained bitterly that they had failed to do anything for him as they

---

[16] This was not the first time men had been transported down to Carondelet. For a description of a violent St. Louis election of city officers in the spring of 1838, including a partisan struggle for control of the Carondelet polling place between the Whigs and Democrats, see David Grimsted, *American Mobbing, 1828–1861: Toward Civil War* (New York: Oxford University Press, 1998), pp. 181–3.

promised, and I have understood since that he was just passing through the village – he was a beggar.

Somewhat later in the hearing, Blow added that his "conversation was very brief with the old man; he only stigmatized them as them fellers. I supposed, of course, he alluded to the men who took him off. When I saw him he was about naked."

Offering what in effect was the Democratic defense, Richard H. Southard of Carondelet reinterpreted what Blow had described as coercion as something between forcible persuasion and political seduction:

I saw the old man take a ticket from Mr. Blow. I was standing about ten feet from Mr. Blow, facing him. Upon the old man's taking the ticket several men went up to him, and I saw some one get the ticket from him. After this had occurred the old man came close to me. There were some parties between Mr. Blow and myself at this time. I said to the old man, "that's a black republican ticket; you are a democrat, and don't want to vote any such ticket." Thereupon I asked him to go and take a drink. Upon the invitation he went along, and we both took a drink. I then gave him a Barrett ticket – a national democratic ticket. We went back to the polls; he voted. I suppose he voted the ticket I gave him. I then asked him to go and take another drink. He went and took a drink and appeared well satisfied.

However much the Blair partisans might complain, conditions at the Carondelet Precinct appear to have been fairly normal for an urban, working-class community. Although he was testifying for the contestant and therefore was attempting to cite abuses at the polls, Madison Miller, a longtime resident of Carondelet and a Blair supporter, gave what in several respects was a description of a routine election:

The place of voting was at a window; it was frequently so crowded around the window that a person could not have got through. I noticed, however, that when one of their own [Democratic] party, from outside of the crowd, would halloo out "Make way for a voter," a passageway was immediately made to afford the voter an opportunity to get to the poll.... I saw several [voters] brought up who were so much intoxicated that they hardly seemed to know what they were doing. There was another instance, where a man was brought up, but, upon being challenged, he declined to take the oath; sometime afterwards he was brought up again, evidently very much affected with liquor, but, upon being closely questioned, he declined taking the necessary oath. Towards evening the same individual was brought up so drunk that he could not stand alone, and this time he voted.[17]

---

[17] S.R. no. 1062: M.D. no. 8 (1858): pp. 450–1, 456, 548, 834–5. As in other contests, partisans also tried to characterize voting abuses as either normal politics or legitimate retribution for problems in previous elections. Describing a former election in Carondelet, for example, Edward Castello said, "I think there were but two parties at that time, whig and democrat. It was dangerous for a democrat to go to the polls and vote if they knew his politics. They had men at the polls with hickory sticks, and it was dangerous for a man to be known as a democrat" (p. 592).

Public intoxication, crowds of voters, and moderate forms of physical intimidation by the opposition party were archetypal elements of urban elections
throughout the United States in the nineteenth century. If elections had routinely been overturned on those grounds, most urban constituencies would
have been unrepresented in Congress or any other governmental body.

But we should return to the ethnic dimension of the St. Louis election.
The voting at most precincts in the city was reported as fairly quiet and
orderly. The two polling places in the Ninth Ward, however, were troubled by
more or less serious irregularities. At the eastern precinct at Miles's stables,
for example, the clerk of election described conditions that were, on the
one hand, partially attributable to the social complexion of the immediate
neighborhood and, on the other, aggravated by the partisan attitude of the
judges of election:

In challenging, there was considerable difficulty among the challengers and the people. There were a great many naturalized citizens who came there to vote, and on
introducing their papers there was a dispute between Mr. Horn, one of the judges,
and Squire McDonald about letting them vote on their papers without being sworn.
One of the challengers, sitting in the window right opposite me, demanded that they
should be sworn – every man voting on papers should be sworn. Mr. McDonald,
one of the judges of election, paid no attention to him. He persisted in demanding
there should be a decision on it; pronounced it illegal for the reason that half a dozen
persons might vote on the same papers, not only there, but elsewhere throughout the
city. They consulted together, Mr. Horn and him, and Mr. Armstrong; and Mr. Horn
picked up the statutes of the State of Missouri, and contended that they should be
sworn. Mr. McDonald was of the other opinion, and said their papers were sufficient.
Mr. Armstrong, I think, didn't take any part in the matter; if he did, I did not hear him,
there was such a confusion and noise there. A number of citizens and challengers,
on the outside in the livery stable, coincided with Mr. Horn, and requested they
should be sworn. I interfered at the time and also requested they should be sworn.
Mr. McDonald refused to do it, and I presumed at the time, it is my belief, he refused
to do so from the fact that a great many Breckinridge men or know-nothings on the
outside requested it should be done. Consequently they voted all day long without
being sworn – those who had papers to present. Some time about the middle of the
day, about dinner time, there was a number of Germans that were challenged; they
were sent after their papers, and some of them refused to go after their papers and
left in a passion, in disgust, and didn't vote, at all, or said they wouldn't vote; and
my presumption was they had come there during the dinner hour to vote in order to
prevent them from losing time while they were at work.

The problem at this precinct was both logistical and partisan. On the one
hand, it would have been difficult to conduct the election if most of the voters
were compelled to swear an oath that they were, in fact, qualified to vote.
The procedures associated with these oaths would have considerably length-
ened the time it took the average man to vote, resulting in long lines and
significant delays for all voters. The election judges therefore had a logistical
reason to ask that the challengers exercise discretion when challenging the

qualifications of a voter or requesting that an oath be sworn. On the other hand, Philip McDonald, the judge of election who opposed all oath-taking, was a Democrat; for reasons not clearly apparent in the testimony, his ruling was decisive. Since oaths would have strengthened the legal penalties against fraudulent voting and since most of such voting was being done by immigrants aligned with the Democratic party, this judge could be accused of partisan bias, and, thus, the election at this precinct was tainted.

The opposition naturally chose to interpret McDonald's position as partisan. William G. Clendenen, a Blair challenger, testified that, after he had challenged several voters as not being residents of either the city or the state, McDonald "tole me that they were judges of election, and for me to mind my own business, and that I was nothing but a pimp and puppy, and was trying to keep honest people from voting – workingmen from voting were the words he used." Henry Crouse, a challenger working for the Know-Nothings, also stated that McDonald had called him names, saying that he was "nothing but a pimp, and a gambler, and a baboon, and a monkey, and sent there purposely to challenge hard-working rough-looking men's votes."

While the name calling was clearly offensive, the description of Crouse's intentions was probably accurate. In any case, McDonald was asked to account for his conduct, in particular whether he had called "any persons who were engaged there in challenging against the national democratic party a pimp and a puppy." He replied in a way that underscored how partisan feeling and official administration of an election were inextricably intertwined:

I have no recollection of using any such language. A man placed himself there as challenger whose name I don't know. By his personal appearance I knew him to be a gambler or pigeon dropper. He made declarations which I believed were calculated to provoke a breach of the peace. He declared that he would challenge every man who came up in the garb of a working man, and made it a point to challenge all such persons. All that he challenged were refused, without they would take the necessary oath and answer the necessary questions prescribed by law. Some seven or eight such peremptory challenges were responded to by bringing the papers. Their votes, by the consent of the judges, were received. This course was persisted in by this man until his conduct became so offensive to the bystanders that I was afraid they would use violence, and I told him I would have him removed. My object in this was to prevent a breach of the peace.[18]

As can be seen, McDonald had no trouble recalling at least one of the challengers who, he surmised, might have charged that he had used the phrase "a pimp and a puppy." Judging this man solely by "his personal appearance," the election judge confidently declared that challenger to be a gambler. Gambling on the outcome of elections, in fact, was common throughout

---

[18]   S.R. no. 1062: M.D. no. 8 (1858): pp. 566–7, 633, 729–30, 880. A "pigeon dropper" was a gambler who cheated. As an aside, it might be noted that the *Brief of the Argument by Cooper & Marshall, for Mr. Barrett* observed that "[j]udges of elections are men, and often excitable men, especially when they are *Irishmen*" (p. 33).

the United States, and most of those who bet were not above trying to sway the outcome by participating in the voting.[19] So it could be that McDonald believed that Crouse was challenging working-class voters in order to win a wager that the Democrats would be defeated at that precinct. If so, then Crouse's challenges not only would have been frivolous; they would have been tainted in the eyes of the law.[20] But McDonald also defended his decisions as an attempt to protect Crouse from an otherwise impending attack by members of the crowd outside the voting window and, more generally, to preserve order at the polls. However his testimony is evaluated, the unavoidable conclusion is that the election in the eastern precinct of the Ninth Ward was not precisely or ideally conducted when measured against the strictures and expectations of the law.

While the crush of working-class, immigrant voters was taxing the election machinery and fraying partisan nerves at the eastern end of the Ninth Ward, the western precinct was beset by a very different set of problems. Patrick McSherry, a Blair agent, went to this polling place intending to distribute "free democratic" tickets. When he arrived in his horse and buggy, he found an alcoholic festival run in the interests of Barrett's regular Democratic supporters:

[I]t was raining very hard when I got there; a lot of fellows were around the polls, mostly Irish, I suppose [note that McSherry was probably Irish himself]; they all appeared to be drunk; they came out, three or four of them; it was raining very hard at the time; I had the tickets under the seat in my buggy to keep them out of the wet . . . as I stopped my horse opposite the polls, [they] remarked that there was a nice

---

[19] Altschuler and Blumin, for example, note that betting "was a widespread activity in America, and elections provided one of its most obvious and compelling venues." *Rude Republic*, p. 73. As one example of the ubiquity of election betting, see the argument between Charles Ashby and John Barrett, who was defending his congressional seat in this contested election. Barrett was conducting the questioning on his own behalf and asked Ashby whether they (Barrett and Ashby) had bet on the election, what the amount might have been, and whether or not he (Ashby) had been serious in making his wager. S.R. no. 1062: M.D. no. 8 (1858): pp. 579–80. The evidence in the contested election hearings generally suggests that party professionals were the most frequent bettors.

[20] Most states made such wagers illegal, and in Missouri gambling both in general and on elections was illegal. See *Revised Statutes of the State of Missouri*, vol. 1 (Jefferson City: James Lusk, 1856), pp. 818–19. However, because such wagers were rarely formalized in writing and because neither party to a bet, even if he lost, had any reason to report the wager to the authorities, election day betting prohibitions were largely unenforceable. For example, a Captain Bush challenged Edward Van Bergen at the Callicoon Depot polls in New York, accusing him of having wagered a bottle of wine on the election. Bush said that the bet had been arranged about two or three weeks prior to the election, the bettors and other men having drunk the wine at that time. Van Bergen simply swore that he had not bet on the election and then voted. S.R. no. 1402: Contested Congressional Election in the Eleventh District of New York: M.D. no. 27, Pt. 2, p. 18. Charles H. Van Wyck vs. George W. Greene, election held on November 3, 1868.

gentleman that was going to vote for Mr. Barrett; they made considerable noise, and I told them I had come to fetch some tickets for Mr. Blair and the free democratic party; they remarked that they didn't want any of that kind of tickets there, that they were all Barrett men there. My horse took fright; I finally got him stopped, and looked around to see if I could find no policeman to keep order; I could find none.

At that point, McSherry reported the disorderly situation to the police. When he returned to the precinct, he

saw gangs of men running to and from what I took to be a mill around the corner from where the polls were located, shouting and making considerable noise; they had all been drinking. . . . I think it used to be a planing-mill, or is now a planing-mill, belonging to Captain Wade and others. . . . [The crowd around the polls made very] loud and abusive talk to those who differed with them and were disposed to vote civilly. . . . I presume [members of the crowd] got [their liquor] in that mill, but I can't say; they were coming to and from the mill around the corner from the polls. I heard two men exclaim that that was damn fine brandy they got around the corner at the planing-mill.[21]

McSherry later admitted that the city administration of St. Louis, including the police, was in the hands of the "free Democrats," Blair's faction; thus the failure to keep order at this polling place was not a partisan decision.[22]

Another Blair agent, Edward Castello, also attempted to distribute tickets at the western precinct. His exchanges with the regular Democrats aptly describe the conflation of ethnicity, partisan allegiance, and the increasingly heated conflict over slavery in antebellum St. Louis. Castello arrived at the polling place just after noon and immediately began to look for a place to leave the "free democratic tickets" he had brought with him. As he was looking about, he was accosted by an acquaintance, John Grace, who assailed Castello because his tickets contained the name of a Know-Nothing candidate. Grace went on to charge that Blair, the congressional candidate on the ticket,

wants to make a negro as good as an Irishman; wants to bring wages down to Chicago prices, 50 cents a day; I am surprised to see you, an Irishman, at the polls with those tickets; he [Grace] was an Irishman, and every drop of blood which was in his body was Irish; that he had always taken me for an Irishman, and was sorry to see me there with them tickets in my hand.

[21] S.R. no. 1062: M.D. no. 8 (1858): p. 473. When McSherry was asked whether he had ever witnessed "a general election in the city of St. Louis at which you did not see during the day drunken men, and hear shouting and halloing," he responded, "Our elections since the riots have been conducted very peaceably . . ." (p. 474).

[22] In accordance with state law, the mayor of St. Louis had closed all liquor establishments on the day of the election. However, since the party organizations were in the habit of providing free alcohol at the polls anyway, closing the saloons did not have much effect. Ibid., p. 592.

Incensed that his ethnic identity had been questioned, Castello heatedly replied, "I was an Irishman, that my father was an Irishman, and that I believed that my mother was an Irishwoman, and that I had as good a right at those polls as any free white man or Irishman in the county or the State." Castello then said that he "had never been driven from the polls" and that, if he were prevented from distributing his tickets, it was time "that those who were in favor of free labor should come to the polls armed with shot-guns, revolvers, and bowie knives."

Clearly welcoming the challenge, Grace retorted that he and his partisans "should like to see you come that way." Castello then charged that Grace's tickets contained a Know-Nothing candidate, thus impugning his ethnic loyalty in the same way that Grace had slandered his a little earlier. One of Grace's partisans subsequently "jerked" some of Castello's tickets out of his hand by reaching around behind him. The tickets "were scattered and torn and a great huzza raised, and cries of 'Turn him out! drag him out! the damned traitor.'" At that point, Castello backed off from the crowd. Resuming his search for a place to leave his tickets, he saw some lying in a nearby drugstore. He added his remaining tickets to the stack inside the store and then approached the voting window, only to be attacked once more, with one of the crowd identifying him as "the Irish traitor, the damned Irish renegade; hoist him away from there!" Looking around the crowd, he did not recognize a friendly face but did see "Mr. Lawler, the calaboose keeper, surrounded by a party of the same crowd." He supposed that Lawler was in "a row kicked up" because he was accused of being "another renegade Irishman." The members of this crowd Castello described as "the check-shirt gentry, non-voters, unnaturalized citizens, not citizens of county or State, imported on railroads and steamboats." As he left the polls and went home to his dinner, Castello recalled that he had thought "things had come to a bad pass."[23]

As Castello's account indicates, the western precinct had been taken over by a mob composed of regular Democrats affiliated with President Buchanan's administration in Washington. But Blair's people, who were called by this mob "black republicans," were a hodgepodge of remnants from the defunct Whig and American parties, intermingled with free-soil, renegade Democrats. To call them an organized political party would be stretching the fact.[24]

---

[23] Ibid., pp. 589–90.

[24] Regular Democrats at the polls often called Blair a "damned black Republican" in an attempt to brand him with a northern, allegedly abolitionist label. Ibid., p. 648. Preferring the label "free Democrats," Blair's men almost never used the term "Republican." The one exception was Thomas Tallis, who reported that he had gone to the Gravois precinct coal mines "with some tickets; the regular republican ticket – that is, Frank Blair's ticket; Jo. O'Neil came into the office and said there were none of our tickets out there; so I took tickets out there" (p. 615).

As an alternative to partisan feeling, ethnicity could be seen as the most salient motivating factor; certainly, the way the regular Democrats made claims on voters suggests this interpretation. When Grace confronted Castello, he accused him of being a "traitor" to his Irish brethren, not a heretic within his party clan.[25] It was in the name of ethnic, not party, obligations that men around the polls suppressed the opposition. But underlying these claims on ethnic loyalty were at least two elements. One was the pull of party patronage that operated through informal networks embedded within the various ethnic communities. Patronage materially tied these communities to the formal party organizations in ways that heightened passions at the polls while playing down the broader policy implications of the outcome. The other was composed of the way in which these broader policy implications ostensibly affected the interests of the various ethnic communities. The regular Democrats, for example, charged that Castello wished to promote free black labor in competition with Irish workers, thus bringing down average wages in St. Louis to the level then prevailing in Chicago, ostensibly a free-soil city. Castello responded by charging that the regular Democrats had placed a Know-Nothing on their ticket. Since Know-Nothing lodges were invariably hostile to both immigrants and Catholics, the regular Democrats had themselves, Castello charged, damaged Irish interests.

Differences over slavery cropped up most often in connection with the charge that Blair was a "black Republican." Although free-soil Democrats were often as hostile to emancipation as were their proslavery opponents, Blair was still open to the charge that he was somehow "soft" on the issue. For example, one transplanted New Hampshire Democrat had no trouble conflating ethnicity and policy and, thus, reaffirming his political identity in his new home. As reported secondhand by another witness, "He said he didn't know what rules we had in this State; that he was after coming from New Hampshire three months ago, and that they all vote there against the abolitionists, as every Irishman ought to do, and they should do the same here, and then they would have none of them in this State."[26] From this way of looking at things, the reason Blair should be called an abolitionist had as much to do with his opposition to Irish-Catholic Democrats as it did with any position on slavery.

[25]   As one witness, Charles Ashby, reported, religion and ethnicity closely overlapped in social practice: "John Grace ... a member of the Catholic church, and an Irishman" told him that "the priest had told all the Irish they must vote for Barrett; all the members of the Catholic church, at least the members about there, to vote for Barrett." Ibid., p. 578. On the other side of the partisan and ideological fence in St. Louis were the Germans, 81 percent of whom were to vote for Abraham Lincoln in the 1860 presidential election. Fellman, *Inside War*, p. 10.

[26]   S.R. no. 1062: M.D. no. 8 (1858): p. 494. Missouri law required twelve months' residency in the state as a qualification for voting.

We must conclude that partisan, ethnic, and ideological elements all contributed to the passions of the mob attending the western precinct of the Ninth Ward in St. Louis. And members of the mob were probably even less able to disentangle these various strains than we are a century and a half later. For one thing, many of them were so inebriated that reasonable comprehension must have been beyond their grasp. One of the judges of election at the western precinct, William Bailey, testified, "About every half hour the judges could hear the crowd say: 'let us go to the mill and liquor up.'" He then went on to say that Captain Wade, the owner of that mill and the leading regular Democrat working the polls, was himself drunk: "I don't think Captain Wade's memory could serve him to remember anything that occurred throughout that day, as he was intoxicated most of the day, and gave more trouble to the judges than any other person in the crowd." Bailey then added:

Captain Wade came there [to the polls], and by his noisy conduct hindered the judges in the discharge of our duties. I requested him in a gentlemanly way to clear the polls. He replied by calling the judges a set of damned black republicans, saying that they ought to have been kicked out before then. I told him that if he did not desist I would have him arrested, whereupon he struck me in the face with his fist. The police officer McDonald attempted to arrest him. He was torn from the officer by his gang. Fearing an attack upon the polls, the judges were compelled to close before the proper time.

Wearing "white linen clothes and a big straw hat," Wade was easily recognizable as he moved about the crowd outside the voting window, but he did not "try to intimidate anybody who came there to vote" because "he was not large enough; he was too small; unless it would be by his noisy and drunken conduct."[27]

William Buckman, one of the election judges who served with Bailey, testified that "there were from one hundred and fifty to two hundred close around the window; the police had to be called every few minutes to clear the way, which was impossible for them to do on account of the small number of them there present." Buckman stated that this crowd was outside the voting window "from morning till night." The Democrats

stationed [one person] on each side of the window as challengers. Mr. Wade came and stood in the centre, which blocked up the whole window. I requested him to stand [to] one side to allow room for voters. He said he wouldn't do it. I told him he must do it, and should do it. He then stepped aside and said the judges were all a set of damned black republicans any how. Mr. Bailey then made answer; said he, "I hope, Mr. Wade, you don't call me a black republican." His answer was, "Yes, I do." Mr. Bailey made answer and said, "Then you're a liar": and Mr. Wade struck him across the face.

[27] Ibid., pp. 645–6, 648, 650–1. Bailey, in fact, supported the Know-Nothing ticket and was thus not a Republican of any sort (p. 649).

The polls were then closed ten minutes before the time specified by law because the judges wanted "to preserve the ballot-boxes" from the "mob and general riot at the window."[28]

John C. Bollman offered one reason why members of this crowd did not disperse after they had voted: "After I came from dinner I was told by the gentleman who owns the [planing] mill near the Biddle market, [that] he had two barrels of whiskey lying behind his office, and that he would get all the Irish to vote for Mr. Barrett, and that for doing so he would take them behind the office and give them something to drink."[29] However, Daniel Rawlings, the city marshal, reported that conditions at the western precinct had been fairly normal, "[a]bout the same when politics run very high, and when a little affected with whiskey or beer." Responding to another question about whether there were "as many arrests made [in the city] on that day as ordinarily during the week," Rawlings answered, "There were not as many made on that day as during the week, and about the same as on previous elections. The reason is, there is more latitude allowed on that day."[30] As far as the marshal was concerned, as long as there was no "danger as to life or limb" on election day, men could act out their politics in whatever way they wanted. This passed for political tolerance, American-style.[31]

MULTIPLE VOTING IN URBAN PRECINCTS

The relative anonymity of voters in the nation's larger cities, along with the enticements offered by one or the other of the party organizations, encouraged many men to attempt to vote more than once.[32] Because it was hard to

[28] Ibid., pp. 659, 661, 663. A third election judge at this precinct corroborated both the Bailey and Buckman accounts (p. 654).

[29] Ibid., p. 697.

[30] Ibid., pp. 940, 942. Earlier testimony from one of the election judges contradicted Rawlings (p. 664).

[31] As for liquor, the *Brief of the Argument by Cooper & Marshall, for Mr. Barrett* quoted a report issued by a committee of the U.S. House of Representatives with reference to another election case: "'if the committee are to break up every election where persons are seen *drunk*, they will have a great deal of work upon their hands.'" Barrett's attorneys then continued, "We imagine there is nothing worthy of reply in that point of the contestant's case, for we have not been favored with any law of Missouri which either disfranchises a man as a voter because he indulges to excess in drinking, or renders an election voidable on the ground that such a man has cast his vote in it . . . " S.R. no. 1062: M.D. no. 8 (1858): p. 26.

[32] Israel O. Beattie, a longtime resident of Middletown, New York, reported that he had belonged to the Democratic party for about forty-eight hours. He said, "I had just got in the ranks, and found it like taking a cold bath, that the sooner I was out of it the better." However, during that time, he had "followed the democratic doctrine – vote early and vote often." And since he had stood as the Democratic candidate for town supervisor in that election, he had voted twice for himself, "according to the rules of the party." S.R. no. 1402: M.D. no. 27, Pt. 1 (1868): p. 100.

detect, multiple voting at different precincts was probably the more common method. Even so, multiple voting at the same polling place, because it did not entail the transportation of voters around the city, was much more efficient. The latter strategy was usually possible only when the election machinery was controlled by sympathetic partisans who literally looked the other way when a man voted more than once. Sometimes, however, the crowd outside the voting window intimidated election judges into accepting tickets they knew to be fraudulent.[33]

Election judges in urban precincts relied on their memories, noting the facial expressions and appearances of each voter in turn, as the primary means of identifying multiple voters. Thus, even when a man returned to the window and gave a name different from what he had given the first time he voted, election judges would reject his ticket if they recognized him. Given the large numbers of men who usually attempted to vote at urban polling places, the memories of election judges were severely strained as they tried to call up mental pictures of those who had already cast their tickets. Exploiting this weakness, multiple voters often changed their attire, however slightly, in ways that made it more difficult for judges to recognize them.

One common practice was for repeating voters to pull their caps down over their eyes when presenting themselves before the window. For example, one witness, describing the voting in Baltimore's Eighth Ward in 1857, testified that "the boys I spoke of voted more than once, stepping back and changing their caps and coming up again." Conscientious judges would remove those caps in order to get a good look at the voter before allowing the ticket.[34] Two years later, in the Ninth Ward, American voters were reported to have changed clothes in the enginehouse that served as their party's headquarters before returning to the polls and voting again. This was early in the day; later, when their party had taken full control of the polls and driven off the Democratic election judge who might have interfered with them, American voters cast their tickets "without any restraint, without changing their garments. They would walk up to the window and vote; go off a few steps, and then come back and vote again."[35]

In some instances, men were asked to cross into a particular ward in order to vote for a candidate for local office. That candidate simply did not care whether these men had voted anywhere else in the same city. In Detroit in November 1858, a Democratic candidate, Alexander Stowell, hired a man named Charles Orvis to deliver voters to the precinct in the Fifth Ward where

[33] See, for example, Summers, *The Plundering Generation*, p. 58.

[34] S.R. no. 962: Contested Congressional Election in the Third District of Maryland: M.D. no. 68, p. 947. William Pinkney Whyte vs. J. Morrison Harris, election held on November 4, 1857.

[35] S.R. no. 1060: Contested Congressional Election in the Fourth District of Maryland: M.D. no. 4, pp. 11–12. William G. Harrison vs. H. Winter Davis, election held on November 8, 1859. Also see the testimony of the clerk of election, p. 21.

he was running for alderman. To retain his services, Stowell first had to bail Orvis out of jail because he had been charged with fraudulently conveying property. Dispensing with all pretense of legality, Orvis "came up to the polls now and then during the day with squads of men." David Smith, a broom manufacturer working for the Democratic party at the polls that day, would then lead these squads up to the voting window, crying out, "Make way for the broommakers," thus implying that these men were his employees. After they turned in their tickets, Smith would "take them up to a grocery nearby and treat them" with alcohol. As for Stowell, once the election was over, he feared that Orvis would skip bail and "leave me in the lurch." Within a day or two, Stowell "gave him up on the bail piece"; this would have presumably returned Orvis to jail, but he had already left the ward and Stowell had "not seen him since."[36]

There are a number of interesting elements in this account. First, we see once again the way in which otherwise reputable candidates and public officials would insulate themselves from the seamy side of election practice by hiring others to do their dirty work. Orvis must have worked the polls before, perhaps even for Stowell, or else the candidate would not have realized that Orvis could in fact recruit squads of anonymous, illegal voters. In addition, because he had already been arrested on an unrelated charge, Orvis must have been doubly attractive to Stowell. When Stowell bailed him out, he in effect paid in advance for his work. If he did not perform as expected, Stowell could revoke his bail, thereby placing Orvis back in his cell. If Orvis instead skipped his bail, Stowell would not, at the very least, face the possibility that his agent might stick around Detroit and blackmail him. In fact, we might suspect that Stowell revoked bail only once he knew that Orvis had already left town. Thus, it was not fear that Orvis would leave that led Stowell to revoke bail; it was apprehension that Orvis might return. As for David Smith, the broommaker, his part in the proceedings must have been more or less a charade, a public performance in which both bystanders and election officials were well aware that the men he led were not his employees. Making brooms was, for one thing, not a large industry in the nineteenth century, and Smith almost certainly did not employ many men in his operation.[37] The fraudulent character of the whole operation, from the noisy escort of these squads of men up to the voting window and thence to the grocery for liquid

---

[36]   S.R. no. 1060: Contested Congressional Election in the First District of Michigan: M.D. no. 7, pp. 37, 53–4. William A. Howard vs. George B. Cooper, election held on November 2, 1858. Although Stowell refused to answer many of the questions posed to him in the hearing, both he and Smith otherwise represented this election as completely normal. For instance, Smith maintained that there was nothing "extraordinary in voters taking a drink on election day," while Stowell averred "I did never see an election where there was not something improper done" (pp. 38, 54).

[37]   If he had, he almost certainly would have left the task of leading them to the polls to a subordinate.

refreshment, must have been transparently obvious to anyone who cared to watch.

COLONIZATION

Another, closely related practice – "colonization" – entailed the importation of men into a particular precinct just before the day of election.[38] In these cases, men were boarded in precincts that were expected to be closely contested. Thomas Howrigan, a keeper of a boardinghouse in Detroit's Second Ward, for example, testified that he had "induced [40 to 45 men] to come [to his boardinghouse] for the purpose of voting." Howrigan went on to say that his guests "came to board with me with the understanding that they would vote the democratic ticket," adding that he "would not board any person who was going to work against me politically." Despite this understanding, Howrigan was careful to state that he had "made no bargain with them. I told them to come and stay with me till after the election, and they should have what they wanted. I knew that they were all democrats and would vote the democratic ticket whatever ward they were in." In addition to their room, Howrigan offered his boarders free liquor, which they "drank five or six times each day or oftener." These men "were mechanics, laborers, sailors, and young men out of employment; and so far as I know they were legal voters in this ward" once they had resided at his boardinghouse for ten days. Howrigan reported that there were about 500 or 600 men out of work in the city at the time; the primary reason his boarders accepted his offer was because they had no employment and thus no reason to reside anywhere else when the election took place. When they moved into the boardinghouse, they carried no baggage and left within a week after the election.

As for Howrigan, he had entered into an arrangement with the Democratic party in which he was "to be made whole" by receiving both remuneration for his expenses and "a certain appointment in this city." The party consented to this arrangement in order to "carry it on ward officers." He attended the polls on election day, giving each of his men "straight democratic tickets" and

---

[38] One late nineteenth-century political dictionary defined "colonization" in this way: "In elections it is a common form of fraud to bring into a doubtful district men from other parts, and to give them some show of a residence in that district so as to enable them to vote there and so turn the result. The voters thus moved or colonized can, of course, always be spared at the points from which they are taken, so that while the total vote of the party in the State remains unchanged, it will be so distributed as to give to that party more Congressmen or members of the Legislature, as the case may be, than it would otherwise have had. This is called colonization, and its practice is confined almost exclusively to the larger cities. Lodging houses are frequently used for this purpose, and these are shockingly crowded with transplanted voters on the day preceding election, or registration, where that formality is required." Brown and Strauss, *A Dictionary of American Politics*, pp. 107–8. For examples of colonization, see Summers, *The Plundering Generation*, pp. 54, 57–8.

stood at the window when they voted.[39] Once Howrigan's men had turned in their tickets, they remained at the polls, taking possession of the platform outside the voting window and "the grounds adjacent" to it. Through their "rowdyish...violent [and] insolent behavior," they "did all in their power to prevent republican electors from passing their votes to the inspectors."[40]

A much more elaborate scheme was concocted in Fayette County, Pennsylvania, during the 1868 congressional election. One part of this plan involved John Smith, who had recently sold a "sand works" in Dunbar Township to Edwin Pechin, president of the Youghiogheny Iron and Coal Company.[41] In a separate transaction, Pechin asked Smith to hire men for his iron mill, and thus it came to pass that Smith recruited at least eight men in Pittsburgh. Smith paid their railroad fares from Pittsburgh to Fayette County and then received reimbursement from either the Democratic leader or Pechin. However, he had another person actually buy the tickets because he was afraid someone would conclude he was "importing men into Fayette County" in order to pad the Democratic vote. (The Republicans had, in fact, hired someone to watch out for "importations" from Pittsburgh.) Pechin later testified that he had hired these men only to work for him, not to vote. However, Pechin did say that he had instructed Smith "to hire only democrats, as it was my avowed policy, openly expressed, in hiring new men to take those who felt with me."[42] Other than that, the iron mill owner said he did not know how these men voted in the election.

At least some of these men boarded with a Mrs. McDowell, the wife of a Captain William McDowell. As it turned out, Captain McDowell was a

39 Despite his best efforts, Howrigan reported that one of his men "received a dollar for voting for the republican city officers"; however, "the balance of the ticket [cast by this man who had been, in effect, bribed twice by different parties] was for the democratic candidates." S.R. no. 1060: M.D. no. 7 (1858): pp. 15–16, 20, 22–3.

40 This report came from a Republican who attended the polls. Ibid., p. 27. For corroboration, see pp. 30–3. Another witness said that, in addition to Howrigan's men, the Democratic nominee running for supervisor also "had a party" at the Second Ward polling place (p. 40).

41 The following account is based on testimony that appears in S.R. no. 1431: M.D. (no number, bound between nos. 24 and 25 [1868]): pp. 28–9, 32, 36–7, 45, 62–3, 70, 109.

42 Subsequent testimony indicated that Samuel Wickersham, a former president and one of the largest stockholders in this company, had met with a number of Democrats in Pittsburgh and publicly announced his intention to hire 200 men for the same purpose, but these men would be hired only if they would vote for the Republican congressional candidate. When asked whether Pechin might object, Wickersham stated that he served on the executive committee of the company and would overrule the president. Pechin was duly informed of Wickersham's intention and had apparently prevailed. While the incident indicates the close involvement of the iron mill in politics and the potential importance of employment in mobilizing voters for a particular party, it also demonstrates that corporate interests were not monopolized by either party. S.R. no. 1431: M.D. (no number, bound between nos. 24 and 25 [1868]): pp. 403, 407–8.

political agent who usually worked for the Democratic party. Just prior to
this election, however, McDowell had apparently offered his services to the
Republicans, saying that he and his voters "had done a great deal for the
democracy, and they had not done much for him." Because the Republicans
had rebuffed his offer, McDowell was still working with the Democrats.
The Captain's men were "composed, as appearance indicated, of mountain
democrats and foreigners, with some few citizens from the settlement." The
"Mountain," also called "Irish Town," was McDowell's stomping grounds,
and the Republican challengers, including one who had lived in the precinct
all of his life, knew few of the men who lived there. Although they had only
recently arrived from Pittsburgh, Pechin's employees blended quite easily
into the local population.

On election day, Captain McDowell brought thirty-five to forty men to the
Dunbar Township precinct, marching his "brigade" up to the polls in two
ranks. As they formed about the voting window, they gave loud cheers for
Henry Foster, the Democratic congressional candidate, and were welcomed
by the Democratic inspector of elections, James McCullough, who had been
drinking rather heavily.[43] McCullough waved his arm out the voting window,
joined in the cheering for Foster, and taunted the Republicans with, "You
thought you had the mountain district." The demeanor of McDowell's men
was so physical and their discipline so perfected that the Republican challengers could not get into position to challenge them. They thus voted for the
Democratic ticket, en masse and without challenge. The Republicans could
trace at least some of these voters back to Pittsburgh, could demonstrate that
they had been screened for their political sympathies, and could substantiate
that they had fallen into the hands of a political agent who hired his services.
What they could not prove was that these men had been hired to vote and,
since they apparently would have met the residency requirement, that they
were illegal voters.

Railroad workers moved fairly often as they built new track or repaired
existing lines. Working in gangs around the country, they constituted transient communities that could be easily mobilized at the polls. Since almost
all such workers were common laborers and immigrants (most reports described them as preponderantly "Irish"), they were usually predisposed to
vote for Democrats. And agents for that party were eager that they do so.
In the 1868 congressional election in southwestern Pennsylvania, for example, John Hilliard, a division foreman directing a gang repairing track near
Uniontown, reported an incident that illustrates some of the mechanics of
their mobilization. Just ten days before the election, a Democratic agent by
the name of William Guffey brought five such workers to the home of the

---

[43] Although McCullough probably consumed more alcohol than the others, apparently
all or most of the election officials, both Democratic and Republican, had been drinking that day. Ibid., pp. 18–24, 299–301.

local assessor in order to have them assessed (for the payment of a poll tax, a precondition for voting). This was about eight o'clock in the evening, well after normal business hours. Guffey told the assessor, who probably knew better but also knew not to ask many questions, that he "had employed them to work on the [rail]road leading from Guffey's station [run by the Guffey family] to Moore's distillery." Hilliard, who had accompanied Guffey to the assessor's home, knew this to be false because he had never seen any work done on that line while he was posted in the county.

Later, while in Pittsburgh just before the November election, Guffey asked Hilliard to accompany him to "engine-house No. 4" in the city where he hoped to recruit more voters to colonize Westmoreland County. Guffey then told him that it was these firemen who had voted in the prior (October) congressional election. They had then returned to Pittsburgh where they voted again. The total cost to Guffey in that election had been twenty-five dollars "to get them drunk" and pay their railroad fares. Hilliard's response was to say, "I think these things are too barefaced" to avoid detection. Guffey replied with might have been the motto for many a political agent: "Pshaw! what is the ballot-box but a farce?" When Hilliard insisted that the "figure 4's [for the engine-house] were too prominent on those red shirts," the agent retorted that they changed "their shirts" before they voted.

The railroad foreman also reported a second, somewhat different, kind of colonization involving Guffey:

> The "floating gang" is an auxiliary force sometimes used on railroads for extra heavy work. . . . I had [charge of] a "gang" of eighteen or nineteen sent to Guffey's station by Frank Smith, roadmaster, a few days previous to the last day of assessment [before the October election]. I had not called for them at that point; neither were they needed there. Frank Smith came with them, and left eight on the way up, and dropped off ten or eleven more when he came back in the evening. I was told by Wesley Guffey that he did this to divert attention, and that they intended to use them for the election, and that Hugert, the president of the road, would bear Smith out in it. What I mean is, that Hugert would bear Smith out in having a "floating gang" on the road. This "gang" came from Pittsburg[h].

This arrangement was not much different from the one involving the Youghiogheny Iron and Coal Company. In both cases, the company arranged employment for men who then voted for the Democratic party. Guffey, however, also arranged for the preparation and distribution of fraudulent naturalization papers to the alien railroad laborers.[44]

---

[44] Ibid., pp. 276–7. Hilliard's motives in reporting Guffey's machinations were unclear. He reported, for example, that he "was and am a democrat" and had actively supported the Democratic candidate for Congress in this election. However, he also added that he disapproved of Guffey's schemes and "earnestly hope that the management of democratic principles and policies may be wrested from the vile managers that desecrate democracy in that section of country." At the end of his testimony, he stated that he was still "engaged in my customary avocation – laying . . . track" but that he was now employed by a different company, the Dutchess and Columbia Railroad,

One of the more unusual instances of colonization involved St. Vincent's monastery, to which was also attached a nunnery (named St. Xavier's) and parochial school (sometimes termed a "college" in the testimony).[45] St. Vincent's was located on some 200 acres in rural Pennsylvania but might as well have been in a small town or city. Like army posts on the frontier or work gangs on railroad lines, St. Vincent's was an institution composed largely of adult men with little or no involvement with the surrounding community. And, like army posts, factories, or railroad lines, men could be assigned quarters in a monastery just before an election in such a way as to pack a local precinct. The Republicans attending the polls in the 1868 congressional election believed this is what had happened.

That the suspect voters, in fact, came from the monastery was supported by testimony from James Smith, a Republican who lived less than half a mile from St. Vincent's. Although the road that ran by his house was but one of several that might have been used, he counted fifty-eight men from the monastery who passed over it on the way to the polls. This total included some whom he "never saw before or afterward." (Smith later said that he counted these men because he wanted to know how many voters had come from St. Vincent's.) Although he couldn't "exactly tell" how long these men had been at the monastery, Smith contended that

they can't have been there long.... I was up there the evening before the election, and there were four persons came there with carpet-bags; and I said to the man that keeps the cows – I don't know his name, but I know him. "Are you gathering your folks in?" He said: "Yes, yes, yes."

Smith claimed to be fairly familiar with the men living and working at the St. Vincent's complex:

I have been there [at the monastery] very often; some weeks two or three times a week ... [i]n their house, and working in their barn.... One morning I was up there to clip sheep for them. I sat on the threshing machine and counted some seventy to seventy-five brothers and monks together, coming from worship, out of the church.... I wanted to see how many came out; I was just sitting there; hadn't much to do.

---

instead of the Pennsylvania. Given that he was incriminating his former superiors and employers, the change of jobs was probably a good idea.

45   The following account is taken from S.R. no. 1431: M.D. (no number, bound between nos. 24 and 25 [1868]): pp. 201–3, 205–7, 209, 211, 216–21, 239. Although this was the only instance of colonization involving a Catholic monastery to appear in the hearings, the example conformed to the general pattern in several ways: (1) the availability of institutional space in which to board prospective voters, (2) a community relatively closed to outside observers, (3) a superficial display that appeared to satisfy the residency requirement, and (4) the clear alignment of the proprietor with one or the other of the major parties. This monastery's involvement in the election was detected only because the institution was located in a rural setting and the men had to travel over the public roads to the polls. In an urban context, the same activity would probably have gone unnoticed.

But after his repeated trips to the complex, he could name only four of the residents. And even then, he could give only their first names because, as he put it, "they go by the name of brothers." Since this seemed to undercut his earlier testimony, he hastened to add that he knew the "greater part of them by face." Most of the students, he reported, were "boys...quite small, some of them." What is most interesting in Smith's testimony is how little he knew about the denizens of the complex. As a Republican and, apparently, a Protestant, he just did not seem to want a close relationship with the Catholics for whom he worked. Other Republicans, those who never visited St. Vincent's at all, would have been even more uncertain about who lived there and how long they might have been in residence. From the Republican perspective, this Catholic institution was a large black hole in their community, a black hole that could have harbored any number of illegal voters.[46]

Among the hundred or so men from St. Vincent's were about two dozen laborers who were making brick for the convent (the convent had burnt down and was being rebuilt). Because every one of the laborers, the brothers, and the priests apparently voted the Democratic ticket, local Democrats were only too happy to have their support. For example, Lewis Eisaman, assessor and collector of taxes in the township, went up to the monastery and told the brothers to put together a list of men who wished to be assessed: "I told them I was not acquainted with the men, and if they would just do that it would save me going round among them." When these names were returned to him and subsequently corrected for spelling errors, the list became part of the record of qualified voters for that precinct. From his testimony, it is not clear who paid the taxes for these men, but in other, comparable circumstances the Democratic party would have covered the fees.

While there was no formal relationship or agreement between St. Vincent's and the Democratic party, the connection was nonetheless very strong. Although Rev. Boniface Wiemar, abbot of St. Vincent's Monastery, was aware of the assessment list, he also said, "I don't attend to these things [assessment and voting]...but I charged all the officials under me to have everything done legally." He stated that 101 names of men from St. Vincent's appeared on the assessment list, among them seven students, fourteen "students of the order" (apparently brothers still in the first three years of membership), and fifty-seven "full" brothers. As in many other instances, many of these men (the abbot estimated twenty-five) received their naturalization papers just before the election. As for the party, the abbot reported that the organization

---

[46]　St. Vincent's was almost an autarchic community in that the brothers living in the monastery attended, in the words of their abbot, "to the housework, farming, kitchen-gardening, and different trades – shoemakers, tailors, and all work not done by priests." Ibid., p. 219.

"knew we were democrats and [would] not need any coaxing to turn out and vote."

About a week or so before the election, the abbot had received two threatening letters.

I don't know from whom they came; one, if I remember rightly, was dated in Derry, written by a gentleman, warning me not to have anything to do with politics; giving to understand that we should be treated like Sodom and Gomorrah if we would vote. The second pretended to be written by a lady, who said she had it confidentially from a friend of her's that we would suffer very hard if we should come out to vote, and more so, if the vote should be stronger than it was usually.

In the abbot's opinion, these threats only increased the determination of the St. Vincent's community to participate in the election "because we did not like to be deterred from the use of our rights." However, the abbot also said:

Our order, the order of St. Benedict, is no political order – never was. In religious, scientific, and economical matters the priests and brothers owe me obedience, according to our rule; but with regard to voting and politics I have no power whatever to command them. I don't know, though, whether I have authority to prohibit voting, since they are citizens; likely they would not do it, if I said no. . . . They would [obey] from reverence to the abbot.

In many ways, the stakes were somewhat higher for men living at the St. Vincent's complex than they were for Thomas Howrigan's rowdy boarders or the unskilled laborers employed by the Youghiogheny Iron and Coal Company. For one thing, their devotion to the institution (the Catholic Church) was incomparably greater. The brothers had sworn lifelong devotion to their order, while the boarders and workers were up for sale to the highest bidder. For another, St. Vincent's was situated in what was, at least partially, a hostile region. The election of friendly (Democratic) political officials was a clear, instrumental policy goal for members of the Catholic community. The men in the iron mill or the boardinghouse, by comparison, probably cared little or nothing about the outcome of their elections.

While the stakes were higher, the abbot and, presumably, the other senior brothers did not monitor the votes cast by their colleagues. In rather sharp contrast, Howrigan and McDowell watched almost every move their men made at the polls, only to abandon all interest in them once they had turned in their tickets. Even so, we might suspect that the abbot was correct when he estimated unanimous support for the Democratic party among his brethren, and we also might suspect that Howrigan and McDowell would have envied the ease with which the abbot achieved this result. With respect to whether or not men were "colonized" under the auspices and protection of the Catholic Church, the testimony is rather inconclusive. They certainly could have been; although the abbot stated that he had ordered that everything be "done legally," there was abundant opportunity for his subordinates to arrange things in a way that would have brought new men into the precinct just before the election. In this effort, they would have had the full, if largely tacit, cooperation of the local Democratic establishment. Unlike Howrigan's boardinghouse or the shopfloor of the Youghiogheny Iron and Coal Company, St. Vincent's was a moral community. However, in mid-nineteenth-century politics, it isn't clear that that made any difference at the polling place.

OUT-OF-PRECINCT VOTING

While party agents sometimes had very good reasons to pack men into closely contested precincts so that the party could win a local office, it was also possible in many states for a man to vote outside his home precinct if he notified election officials that he lived somewhere else. The rule was that a man could vote, at this distant polling place, only for those candidates who were also running in his home precinct.

For example, if a man happened to be out of precinct on the day of the election but still within his state, he could vote in state races (e.g., for governor). If he were still within his home congressional district, he could also vote for congressman, and so forth. Such an arrangement was particularly useful for men whose occupations routinely kept them away from home. One such case involved Reuben Gleason, who, in the words of John Ewalt, carried "the mail from Chesterville, Morrow county, to Centerburg, Knox county, and has done so for two or three years. . . . I believe his residence was in Chesterville, Morrow county. Don't know how long he has lived there. He is an old man. . . . [However, he] voted in Hilliar township, Knox county [where he was not a resident], and voted for Columbus Delano. He voted an open [i.e., publicly displayed] ticket" and his vote was challenged on grounds of residency. The judges of election decided to receive his vote after he "cut off the county ticket and [thus] voted [only] the State and congressional ticket. He claimed he had a right to vote anywhere along the route for which he was mail-carrier," and the judges agreed.[47]

In connection with the 1858 congressional election in St. Louis, for instance, James Tooke was asked, "Does it not frequently happen that a party living in one ward votes in another?" Tooke responded, "I presume so. . . . I have voted myself out of my ward for State officers." Asked whether it is "the law that if a man votes out of his own ward or precinct, he has to be sworn that he has not voted, and will not vote, in any other ward," Tooke

---

[47] Since the two Democratic judges were in the majority, they could have decided not to receive this Republican vote at this precinct. S.R. no. 1313: M.D. no. 38, Pt. 2 (1866): p. 213.

agreed, "I believe so; they always swore me. When I kept store in the 4th ward and lived in the 10th . . . I would vote in the 4th for general officers; they would not let me vote for ward officers." This discussion had been prompted by his assertion that voters he could not recognize were likely to be illegal voters. For party challengers, the monitoring of such out-of-precinct voters was impossible.[48]

In cities and counties where out-of-precinct voting was permitted, this possibility allowed men to choose where they might cast their votes. When violence and intimidation prevented a man from voting at one precinct, for example, he might cast his ticket at another, more friendly polling place.[49] In this way, party organizations might come to control different polling places in the same city or county such that their partisans would primarily concentrate their votes at friendly precincts, avoiding those dominated by the opposition.[50]

Thus some of the pattern of lop-sided election returns, apparently indicating the highly partisan leanings of the surrounding neighborhoods, was in fact due to the differential partisan "capturing" of the public spaces through which voters had to move before depositing their tickets. For example, if voters sought out voting places controlled by or at least friendly to their party, then the concentration of votes (polarized voting) was primarily an artifact of election practice, not the ethnic or cultural predilections of the voters in that neighborhood (although those predilections may have originally have strengthened the hold of one or the other of the parties over that particular polling place). In other words, polarized voting patterns between adjacent precincts may not have indicated polarized partisan loyalties

---

[48] S.R. no. 1062: M.D. no. 8 (1858): pp. 479, 484. Henry J. Stierlin, who served as clerk at one of the St. Louis polling places in this election, suggested that out-of-precinct voting, while permitted by law, was discouraged in practice (p. 747).

[49] The state militia, for example, made it very difficult and often impossible for Democrats to vote in Savannah, the seat of Andrew County, Missouri, in the 1862 general election. In response, these men considered the possibility of casting their tickets at other precincts in the county, in one of which at least, they were told there was "perfect order." S.R. no. 1198: Contested Congressional Election in the Seventh District of Missouri: M.D. no. 13, p. 80. John P. Bruce vs. Benjamin F. Loan, election held on November 4, 1862. For the vote of Andrew County by precinct, see p. 93.

[50] For a spatial study of voter selection of polling places in nineteenth-century Oregon, see Paul Bourke and Donald DeBats, *Washington County: Politics and Community in Antebellum America* (Baltimore, Md.: Johns Hopkins University Press, 1995), pp. 268–73. While these Oregon voters apparently selected their precincts, often traveling miles out of their way to cast votes in a distant polling place, their reasons for doing so were probably not related to the possibility of political intimidation at the polls. Voters in antebellum North Carolina were similarly free to choose a precinct. Harry L. Watson, *Jacksonian Politics and Community Conflict: The Emergence of the Second American Party System in Cumberland County, North Carolina* (Baton Rouge: Louisiana State University Press, 1981), p. 328.

in their respective neighborhoods.[51] Something like this frequently occurred in Baltimore elections during the antebellum period.

BALTIMORE ELECTIONS

Before the Civil War, the most violent precincts in the United States were probably located in Baltimore, Maryland.[52] During the 1850s, the American party emerged as a major force in national politics, displacing the Whigs.[53] As the primary competitor to the Democratic party, the Americans stressed opposition to Catholics and immigrants, along with traditional Whig issues such as tariff protection and government aid to canals and railroads. As the second largest city in the slave states, Baltimore was one of the few places in the South in which sizable numbers of immigrants resided. Many of these immigrants were Irish Catholics.[54] In addition, because Maryland had originally been a Catholic colony, many native born residents, also belonged to the church. As a result, the American and Democratic parties contested elections more fiercely in Baltimore than anywhere else in the nation.

These violent elections gave H. Winter Davis his congressional seat and later assumed vast national importance when Davis, in turn, gave the Republican party control of the House of Representatives in the Thirty-sixth

---

[51]   For example, Lee Benson reported such polarized voting, with lopsided and opposing party majorities in adjacent precincts, in his *The Concept of Jacksonian Democracy: New York as a Test Case* (New York: Atheneum, 1966), pp. 291–3. If these lopsided majorities were, in fact, produced by voter tendencies to attend only friendly partisan polling places (along with fraudulent practices favoring those parties at the same polls), the resulting pattern would put in doubt at least some of the ethno-cultural analysis that Benson presented.

[52]   Between 1828 and 1861, Grimsted found 35 election-related riots in the United States that "occurred while voting was going" and 37 more in which rallies, parades, or other political targets were attacked by mobs. The total number of dead in both types of riots came to 110, while at least 341 were seriously wounded. A rough tabulation by city indicates that at least 28 men died in Baltimore alone, apparently the highest death toll in the nation. Baltimore's share of the wounded may have exceeded 50 percent. *American Mobbing*, pp. 184–5, 200–4, 226–38. Even so, Grimsted may have underestimated the casualties in Baltimore. With respect to just the 1856 municipal and federal elections, William Evitts put the dead at 14 and the wounded at somewhere in excess of 300. *A Matter of Allegiances: Maryland from 1850 to 1861* (Baltimore, Md.: Johns Hopkins University Press, 1974), p. 98. For a general description of violence and fraud in late antebellum Baltimore elections, see Jean H. Baker, *Ambivalent Americans: The Know-Nothing Party in Maryland* (Baltimore, Md.: Johns Hopkins Press, 1977), pp. 129–34.

[53]   On the rise of the American party in the city, see Gary Lawson Browne, *Baltimore in the Nation, 1789–1861* (Chapel Hill: University of North Carolina Press, 1980), pp. 200, 203–10, 234–6, 292.

[54]   On foreign immigration into the city in the decades immediately preceding the Civil War, see ibid., pp. 191–2; Baker, *Ambivalent Americans*, p. 17.

Congress. When the House convened in December 1859, no party held a majority. When the chamber moved to elect a speaker, a deadlock ensued that lasted for almost two months. On the forty-third and what turned out to be the penultimate ballot, Davis cast his vote for William Pennington, who was thus one vote short of the speakership.[55] His vote triggered a prior agreement between George Briggs of New York and the Republicans that stipulated that Briggs, also a member of the American party, would back the Republican candidate if and when his vote would be decisive. On the very next ballot, the votes cast by Davis and Briggs put Pennington over the top and thus gave Republicans control of the chamber.[56] The Republican party thus controlled the U.S. House of Representatives throughout the 1860 presidential campaign and the ensuing secession crisis, providing a dominating position from which to legislate on slavery in the western territories, to propose a protective tariff, and to conduct an investigation of the incumbent Democratic administration.

Although slavery was not even indirectly involved in the Baltimore contests (all the candidates supported slavery) and although the elections were so violently and fraudulently conducted as to leave the "true, democratic outcome" very much in doubt, Davis's victory was nonetheless an important factor on the road to secession and civil war. In the following pages, we examine some of the events in and around polling places that gave the American party control of Baltimore's two seats in the U.S. House of Representatives. Along with evidence of local election practices and procedures, the reader should also note the disjunction between the ways in which voters and party agents interacted at the polls and the national policy implications of the outcome.

The American party in Baltimore was supported by quasi-political clubs with names such as the "Plug Uglies," "Blood Tubs," "Black Snakes," "Little Fellows," "Stingbatts," "Rough Skins," and "Babes" (the latter were

---

[55]   Before he voted on the forty-third ballot, Davis appeared "very pale, and walked round the aisles on the left as if unable to keep his seat." When his name was called, "every ear was strained to catch the response. He was at the moment promenading in the rear of the members' seats when, suddenly wheeling, 'his voice fell like a falling star,' upon the house and galleries as he answered, 'Pennington.' Such a burst of applause mingled with hisses, has never before deafened the hall." New York *Times*, February 1, 3, 1860. For a complete account, see Richard F. Bensel, "The Antebellum Political Economy and the Speaker's Contest of 1859," presented at the Ninth Annual Meeting of the Social Science History Association, Toronto, Ontario, October 1984.

[56]   Davis was the only slave state representative to vote for Pennington. While he was sympathetic to several Republican policies, particularly tariff protection, one reason he voted for Pennington may have been that the Republicans promised to protect him when his congressional seat was contested. In any event, the Republicans rejected the claims of his opponent and Davis kept his seat. For a description of the committee report recommending that Davis keep his seat, see Chester H. Rowell, *Digest of All the Contested Election Cases in the House of Representatives, 1789–1901* (rpt., Westport, Conn.: Greenwood Press, 1976), pp. 168–9.

reported to be "very huge fellows"). The Plug Uglies got their name from slang for a "tough or roughneck," a term that originally referred to "a member of a city gang of rowdies active in such places as Baltimore, New York, and Philadelphia." "Plug-Uglymore," in fact, had become a nickname for the city of Baltimore.[57] The formal title of the Blood Tubs was the "Native American Association." They earned their nickname when the club drove naturalized voters from the polls in the First Ward by covering them "with blood taken from barrels or tubs."[58] In truth, many of these were little more than gangs, spawned by the competition for the spoils of political office.[59] Their headquarters were usually located near saloons or firehouses (some of the gangs were also companies of volunteer firemen) and were generally believed to be private armories in which weapons were stored.[60] When the American party was in control of the city, precincts were often situated near these clubhouses so that the gangs could operate freely in the neighborhood around the polling place.[61]

In the First Ward, for example, the polling place was located "near the Rough Skins' headquarters . . . in the worst part of the city . . . known as the Causeway [in which could be found many] baudy-houses, grog shops, &c."[62] In the Third Ward, the "lower part of the house" in which the polling place was located "was used as a tavern; in the upper rooms the meetings were

---

[57]   S.R. no. 1060: M.D. no. 4 (1859): p. 192; Mitford M. Mathews, *A Dictionary of Americanisms on Historical Principles* (Chicago: University of Chicago Press, 1956), pp. 1265–6.

[58]   S.R. no. 962: M.D. no. 68 (1857): pp. 34, 82. They got their barrels of blood from a nearby slaughterhouse. Evitts, *A Matter of Allegiances*, pp. 116–17.

[59]   Although they had been active some years previously, most Democratic clubs were evidently defunct by this election. S.R. no. 962: M.D. no. 68 (1857): pp. 34, 82, 793, 864, 865.

[60]   The captain of the American Riflemen, however, denied this was the case with his club. When asked where their weapons were on election day, he replied, "Each man connected with the company had his own rifle at his own house; I have always permitted that . . . as a convenience to the men, and as the place down there was open; they would bring them down for the purpose of drilling, and take them away again." Ibid., pp. 62, 194, 835.

[61]   See, for example, S.R. no. 1060: M.D. no. 4 (1859): pp. 80–1. In the Seventeenth Ward, the polls were held in "a tavern. . . . I believe it is the headquarters of the tiger club; they congregate there at all events, and stand around the corner; I believe the man who keeps the place is a member of the tiger club; various other clubs assemble there" (p. 165).

[62]   This description was offered by the Democratic candidate for magistrate in that ward; on the day of election, he had been wounded in the shoulder by gunfire from American thugs as they stood in the street outside their clubhouse. S.R. no. 962: M.D. no. 68 (1857): pp. 33–4. Other witnesses described the Causeway as "the five Points of Baltimore – long known for its vice and immorality. . . . There are a number of brothels all around it." The neighborhood had "a church on one part of it called the 'Causeway Mission Chapel'; and there is a foundry, and all the rest are either taverns or bawdy-houses, with some exceptions of groceries and liquor stores" (pp. 45, 226).

held of the third ward American councils."[63] In the Ninth Ward, a voter testified that:

the place selected [for the polls] was at a remote portion of the ward, at a place which it was known timid persons would not venture. It was a disorderly neighborhood, and the polls were held in a retail liquor shop, at the house of one of the candidates for constable. On arriving at the polls I found them in possession of about twenty persons apparently strangers to me, persons I did not know, but persons whom I had seen about the tobacco warehouses ... who held entire possession and control of the polls [which were] adjoining an engine-house, which engine-house was the resort of disorderly persons, and was kept as an armory and house of refreshments for those persons. ...[64]

The usual tactics used by these clubs on election day entailed the occupa- tion of the area in front of the voting window by dozens of their members. Would-be voters were then forced to make their way through the crowd in order to hand their tickets to the election judges.[65] As they moved through the crowd, club members would insist on seeing the ticket they wished to vote.[66] If it was the American ticket, the crowd would part ranks, making an open path to the window. If it was the Democratic or "reform" ticket (a euphemism for the Democratic ticket), a cry would go out, alerting other club members that a member of the opposition was attempting to vote. At one precinct, a Democratic clerk of election reported that the "watchword" used by the club members was "ink-pink, I spy" followed by a whistle. A

---

[63] Ibid., pp. 62, 65, 194. In the Sixth Ward, the election was "held in a remote corner of the ward, at the club room of the Pioneer club ... " (p. 141).

[64] S.R. no. 1060: M.D. no. 4 (1859): pp. 11–12.

[65] One witness, a special police officer appointed by the mayor, reported that when he arrived at the polling place in the First Ward, he "found a fence before the polls nine feet high, with a gangway at each end – one to go in, and the other to go out. Inside of that fence was taken charge of by a party calling themselves Rough Skins. Any man who came up to vote, not having the striped ticket, unless they chose to let him vote, they shoved him out at the other end, and drove him away." S.R. no. 962: M.D. no. 68 (1857): p. 37. Such a barricade, which funneled voters before the window in an orderly fashion, was not unusual. See, for example, pp. 105, 223, 292. S.R. no. 1060: M.D. no. 4 (1859): pp. 58–9, 64, 155–6. In Cincinnati, such an arrangement of the polls was described as "customary." S.R. no. 1431: Contested Congressional Election in the First District of Ohio: M.D. no. 16, pp. 8–12, 18, 98–100, 104, 107–8. Benjamin Eggleston vs. P. W. Strader, election held on October 13, 1868.

[66] S.R. no. 1060: M.D. no. 4 (1859): p. 11. In the Eighteenth Ward, Know-Nothing voters turned down the tops of their tickets so that Washington's portrait was clearly visible (p. 163). The American tickets in the 1857 election were easily recognized because they had a stripe running lengthwise down the back. As one Democratic election judge noted, those voters carrying this marked ticket had no difficulty making their way to the voting window. S.R. no. 962: M.D. no. 68 (1857): pp. 25, 54, 191. In an attempt to mimic the American design, one Democrat in Third Ward used a red pencil to mark his party's tickets. However, his imitations were immediately discovered, and the naturalized German voters to whom he gave these tickets were denied access to the window (p. 200).

general (and clearly hypocritical) shout would ensue: "Make way for the voters!" This was the signal prompting a general movement of members, in mass, outward into the street. The would-be voter was thus physically moved away from the window by the sheer bulk of the crowd.[67]

In some cases, a voter might make his way undetected through the crowd. As a precaution, the American club stationed two of its brawniest members just in front of the voting window, thus forcing the voter to reach over them as he attempted to hand the ticket to the election judge. As he did so, the men blocking the window would examine the ticket and, if it was not for the American party, push the voter back into the crowd, away from the window. While opposition voters struggled in front of the voting window, those displaying the American ticket "found easy access by passing through the crowd stationed to the left of the window and the wall of the house."[68]

Controlling the space in front of the window also gave a party organization a privileged position from which to challenge voters. As Joshua Vansant, an election judge in the Fifth Ward, reported,

It has been customary to give one side of the window to one party [to station a challenger] and the other side to the other. On the occasion of the late election both sides of the window were occupied by American challengers, as they are termed, and those who were acting with them, for about the first two hours. At that time a young man approached with democratic tickets in his hands, claiming his right to one side of the window, as challenger. One of the others, by the name of McAllister, denied his right to it, and when he was in the act of reaching out his hand, as I supposed to strike or push him, I caught McAllister about the shoulder and told him "it was his right to be there. That the Democrats were entitled to one side of the window." Thereupon the young man moved up to the side of the window. McAllister passed up to the left of him and in the rear a little, and I heard him exclaim: "if you challenge any American vote I will cut your damned heart out"; but one or two voted after that expression, before a yell went up "O ye natives," and they swept him from the window; he not having challenged any vote while he remained there. There was no democratic challenger at the polls thereafter, nor was there any vote challenged on the outside of the window during that day by any one whom I knew or believed to be a democrat.[69]

---

[67] S.R. no. 962: M.D. no. 68 (1857): p. 84; also see pp. 30, 82–3. Two years later, in the Twelfth Ward, the code word was "Beware!" S.R. no. 1060: M.D. no. 4 (1859): p. 88. A police officer who served in this ward testified, "There was all kinds of violence . . . and intimidation to keep away voters – mashing their hats over their faces, pulling whiskers, and some were struck" (p. 149).

[68] S.R. no. 962: M.D. no. 68 (1857): pp. 78, 95, 138; S.R. no. 1060: M.D. no. 4 (1859): p. 89.

[69] S.R. no. 962: M.D. no. 68 (1857): pp. 93–4; also see p. 78. Two years later, in the Eleventh Ward, reformers were able (just barely) to maintain their places at the window. But in the Thirteenth Ward the Americans physically assaulted and drove off the reform challenger after he had moved to disqualify dozens of Know-Nothing voters. S.R. no. 1060: M.D. no. 4 (1859): pp. 58–9, 80–1. In the Tenth Ward, the judges endorsed a request that the reformers be given one side of the window; however, when

Whether or not it was "customary" in Baltimore to allow challengers from the opposition to stand alongside the voting window was, however, open to some dispute. One witness, an American party official in the Third Ward, testified that challengers were only "allowed when they could maintain their position; it was a matter, ever since I have been a voter, depending upon what is called 'the muscle'; we old Jackson democrats never allowed the whigs there when we could help it."[70]

The Fifth Ward was apparently one of the most violent precincts in the city and the club members were more than ordinarily aggressive, even for Baltimore.[71] When one of the election judges refused to receive the tickets of obviously unqualified men, he was cursed, pelted in the face with wads of cardboard, and told that he would be dragged physically from the voting room.[72] As the day wore on, the American club became increasingly confident of its control of the area outside the voting window and boldly offered obviously disqualified men as voters to the election judges. The judges, who belonged to both parties, begged the Americans to desist:

In the afternoon the presentation of parties to the window, who were manifestly not entitled to vote, was so numerous that I implored those who were around the polls not to bring up any more of that character of voters; a few appeared to be boys not above 16 years of age; others looked like common vagrants, and one at least offered himself thrice under different names, neither of which was his right one; the attempt of that imposition became so apparent, that the chief judge, neither of the others objecting, took the tickets from some thirty or forty persons or thereabouts, I did not count them, called the names of the party offering to vote after he received them, which name was not recorded, and a feint made as though it was being deposited in the box, and the ballot was thrown upon the floor.[73]

the Americans later took control of the polling place and violated this agreement, the judges apparently did nothing to stop them (p. 262).

[70] This witness then went on to say that access to the voting window was similarly conditioned: "if you could work or fight your way up to the window, you got your vote in; otherwise you did not; I have seen persons subjected to personal violence in their attempts to vote at nearly every election I have seen since I have been a voter, about twenty years ago, and subjected to it myself when I quit the democratic party; I lost a coat the first time, after having been knocked out of the ranks five times in my approach to the window." S.R. no. 962: M.D. no. 68 (1857): p. 808.

[71] One voter at this precinct testified that "the crowd who were surrounding the polls was composed of a club called the 'St. Lawrence Club,' composed of persons heretofore known as the 'Potter street crowd' – a notorious club of desperadoes." Ibid., p. 114.

[72] Ibid., p. 94. Generally "about 5/8 of an inch in diameter, and of the thickness of a copper cent," these wads were ordinarily used in the loading of rifles or muskets. They could not possibly injure the judge but were thrown at him as an insult to his person, backed up by the clear implication that the club members outside the window were armed.

[73] Ibid., p. 95. A Democratic election judge who had served in the First Ward testified that the judges there had reached a similar decision: "In the afternoon a number of intoxicated persons appeared at the polls and insisted upon voting, and the only way the judges could get rid of them was to take the tickets and let them believe that they

By throwing away invalid tickets, the judges could minimize the number of illegal votes; however, the vote count was still fraudulent because they were in no position to aid those voters who wished to support the Democratic candidates.[74] Two years later, after an American club took possession of the polls in the Thirteenth Ward, conditions were even worse:

> The "Eubolts"...came to the polls and commenced to riot....I saw the judge of election, upon refusing to take an American vote, have a pistol drawn and presented to his head. The party who presented the pistol said the judge was a "damned son of a bitch," and he would blow his brains out; and the judge was not only threatened with the pistol presented at his head, but the whole party outside, apparently drawing weapons, threatened to kill him unless he would allow that man to vote.[75]

When election judges ensconced behind the voting window feared for their own lives, there was clearly little they could do for common voters out in the street among the members of a violent gang.[76]

At the Fifth Ward polling place, one of the election judges, George W. Mowbray, "expostulated" with the gang occupying the area directly in front of the voting window, ordering the members to clear a path for voters. He first "made an address to them as gentlemen, and requested that each party should have an avenue by forming on each side so that the honest voters could get up and deposit their ballots," but they paid no attention. Mowbray then asked police officers "to open the avenue." One of them "mingled in the crowd and appeared to make some effort, but very little." At this point the situation outside the window turned violent. Mowbray reported that

> there was a small man there whom I saw striking and beating persons at different times; he was in the melee in which Mr. Joseph Vansant was beaten; after that he changed his hat and returned; he then would occasionally fire a pistol; I saw him on one or two occasions loading the pistol, which appeared to be a horse-pistol with a

had voted; there were no police officers there to arrest them" (pp. 25, 27). On the indifference of police officers to violence and fraud around the polling place, see S.R. no. 1060: M.D. no. 4 (1859): pp. 12–16, 25–7.

[74] As Vansant testified, "I feared for my personal safety from the hour when the polls were opened until I reached my home." S.R. no. 962: M.D. no. 68 (1857): p. 95.

[75] About fifteen members, wearing "military hats" as identifying emblems, occupied the polls. S.R. no. 1060: M.D. no. 4 (1859): p. 84.

[76] While the Know-Nothing clubs were often armed, so (apparently) were many of the reform voters, although much less ostentatiously. Ibid., pp. 255–6. Although the American party heavily relied on these gangs (so much so that it could not have ruled Baltimore without their help on election days), it is not clear exactly what the clubs received in return. Although there is no evidence that the gangs were hired by the party, they did attend party rallies and marched in partisan street processions. This public recognition of what were, in effect, lower class social clubs, along with the opportunity to attack immigrants at the polls, may have been enough incentive to participate in elections without cash changing hands. Evitts, *A Matter of Allegiances*, pp. 109, 113–16, 123.

bright barrel; he was in Temple street and also at times in Fayette street; I saw several melees there.

Although fewer and fewer naturalized voters were able to make their way to the window through the nativist gang, at least some voting continued to take place. Each time Mowbray appealed to the police for help, gang members "would chuckle and laugh." The policemen took themselves away from the polls, trying "to get out of hearing" of his voice, as the election judge surmised. As in the Fifth Ward, the election judges chose to discard the tickets of obviously illegal voters. However, the club members quickly learned what was happening and came up to the voting window

amid the most profane oaths and imprecations [to] state if they, the judges, did not put those tickets in the box, what they would do. What they threatened was intimidation, that "they would mash their (the judges') heads if they didn't." They unhung the shutters from the outside, and they came at us in the attitude as if they were using a battering ram with the shutters, as we, the judges, were standing inside near the ballot-box.

This was too much even for the police officers, and they confiscated the shutters. Afterward, the police returned to their posts and stood by idly while illegal voters were brought up to the window in droves. While most of these men were completely unknown to Mowbray, he did recognize several of them. When a man offering to vote gave his name as William H. Lester, Mowbray said, " 'How do you do Mr. Coster?' upon which he backed down and went away." When, on another occasion, the nativists presented a boy as a voter, Mowbray told the lad, "You can't vote here, you are an apprentice in a type foundry round the corner." Backed up by one of the other judges, Mowbray refused his vote. But the election judges had clearly lost control of the voting window.

Every now and then the fellows at the window would, playfully like, hold up their hands with a ticket folded, and call out some name or other. Of course these votes were not taken by me, or to my knowledge. This was up to noon. In the afternoon they brought hacks there with parties in them, crowded with fellows in hacks and wagons, numerous, I couldn't pretend to give any idea of them – many with bruised faces, blacked eyes, cut heads, and the most filthy looking creatures I had ever seen in my life. One man, as he came up, said, "Adam Stuzel." I asked him were he lived. He said, "in Potter street." I perceived he was a German. One of the judges asked him for his papers. One of those who came with him and had hold of him said, "I have his papers," and put his hand into his own pocket to pull them out, and handed the papers to Judge Abbess [apparently a Know-Nothing judge, but also honest]. I looked over the papers and said, "That won't do, the papers are made out in the name of John Baldwin," and his vote was rejected. There were a great many brought there with no papers, who were foreign-born citizens without papers, and who were brought there contrary to their wishes, and they did not vote. I said to them who brought them, "Gentlemen, these men are not sons of the soil, and they can't vote without papers." After that there was a young man came there, who wished to vote, and said he lived in the ward. I asked him if he would qualify that he was a resident of the ward. He went partially away from the window, and there appeared to be some conversation among the parties around the window with him, they trying apparently to persuade him to return. He then remarked to Judge Abbess, he would be willing to qualify, and by Abbess' request I placed the book on the end of the window to him, but very reluctantly, indeed. The party of whom I have spoken as standing in front of the window, right in the centre, with his back turned toward the judges, jerked the book [this was a Bible] out of my hand, and threw it into the street, and I did not get it back again. Said I to one of the other judges, ask him for the book, and the fellow who jerked the book out of my hand said, "damn the book," and the young man did not vote. There were crowds of parties who came up after that, a perfect onslaught of voters, I might say, whose tickets were taken by the other judges, but none of them by me, and these tickets were laid on the table, back of the ballot-box, as before. The parties on the outside seeing the judges put the tickets there, cursed and swore that they should be put in the box. They directed their attention or conversation towards the two other judges particularly, with threats of violence if they did not put them in; one of the party got in on the window sill, his head being inside a foot or more, and swore that they would break up the box; I heard rallying cries of "rose-buds" [apparently a club nickname] when these little things occurred, frequently through the day, "Oh you rose-buds," and such cries....

At one point, Mowbray had a "piece of a cigar" thrown in his face. Satisfied that the voting at the Fifth Ward polling place was blatantly unfair and illegal, Mowbray abandoned his post before the election was over, turning his commission in to the mayor. As he left the polls, he was accosted by "this notorious Grahame who had been at the polls all day helping to crowd voters out by filling up the gangway [who] followed me to the corner, and wanted to know 'why I was so down on him.'" Mowbray replied that he had "'done no more than my duty.'"[77]

Party agents fared no better than election judges. Referring to the 1859 election, for example, a member of the reform central committee of the Ninth Ward reported that he

found the polls were occupied entirely by a number of the American party, I suppose twenty to thirty, and I had not been there long before one came up to me with a drawn knife in his hand, with the blade about six inches long, and said I should have blood for supper that night; I did not say anything to him, but endeavored to get my vote in, and after a good deal of obstruction I got my vote in and I remained there distributing tickets and trying to get others to vote.[78]

[77] S.R. no. 1064: Contested Congressional Election in the Third District of Maryland: M.D. no. 28, pp. 44–7. William P. Preston vs. J. Morrison Harris, election held on November 2, 1859.

[78] S.R. no. 1060: M.D. no. 4 (1859): pp. 32–3.

Although many of the men gathered around the polls were believed to be armed, rifles and knives were usually not visible.[79] The preferred weapon was, in fact, either an awl and darning needle, both of which were easily hidden in the sleeves of club members. As voters from the opposition approached the polls, they would be jostled by the crowd around the window as club members painfully and anonymously pricked them with these tools.[80] In the 1859 election, awls were so ubiquitous that they served as an unofficial emblem for the American party and were prominently displayed, evidently as weapons, in the transparencies and banners at a Know-Nothing rally held just prior to the November election.[81] At the same rally, as another witness testified:

The eighteenth ward awl manufacturing establishment – a blacksmith's shop on wheels – took a station southeast from Mr. Harris. They appeared to be making awls there; they were at work at the forge and distributing something about among the crowd.... When the awl manufacturing establishment drove past the stand one of them threw a wreath up to Mr. Harris [a congressional candidate in another district], which he took and bowed.

As this testimony indicated, the distribution of awls to party members had become a more or less formal practice. For example, the president of the "Rattlers" placed in the *Baltimore Clipper* the following announcement of an organization meeting just prior to the election: "Rattlers' American Club, No. 1, Twelfth Ward. – The original members of the American Rattlers are

79 There were exceptions, however. During the 1859 election, for example, members of the American party openly displayed weapons. A man distributing reform tickets in the Ninth Ward reported: "I saw a crowd of as many as thirty, I suppose, dressed very much alike, with blue caps, and seemed to me to be in uniform something like the fatigue uniform of soldiers, who were singing out, 'Hurrah for the Northern Liberties,' with pistols drawn, and swearing at the same time, using language that is hardly worth while to relate." A Democratic election judge at this polling place, who was later driven off from his post, reported, "There were no fire-arms discharged while I was there; there were a plenty drawn and displayed." Ibid., pp. 14, 19, 33; also see pp. 15, 36. In the Third Ward, more than forty members of the Blood Tubs marched to and from the polling place, "with guns, drums, and arms of one sort or other ... they then made a rush for the polls and apparently took possession of them ... after awhile the guns were taken away and put away ... in Pappler's pack-house, right alongside of the polls." S.R. no. 1064: M.D. no. 28 (1859): pp. 31–2.

80 For example, as Rev. L. D. Maier, pastor of the German Lutheran Church, stood in front of the voting window, the election judge held his "ticket as high as he could so that every person could see it outside ... at the same time one young man struck me on the head and another one stuck me with an awl." S.R. no. 1064: M.D. no. 28 (1859): p. 52. On the use of darning needles in the Third Ward, see S.R. no. 962: M.D. no. 68 (1857): p. 209. On the use of awls at many polling places two years later, see S.R. no. 1060: M.D. no. 4 (1859): pp. 94, 109, 112, 119, 128, 137, 160, 162.

81 S.R. no. 1060: M.D. no. 4 (1859): 191–2. For a description of this rally and the oratory of H. Winter Davis, one of the speakers, see Baker, *Ambivalent Americans*, pp. 24–7.

hereby notified to meet on Tuesday evening, November 1, at 7 o'clock, as there are traitors in the camp. P.S. – The awls will be ready for distribution."[82]

The most vulnerable voters were those of foreign birth whose attire and speech gave them away.[83] Several naturalized voters in fact testified that they had been compelled to vote the Know-Nothing ticket by threats of violence. In some cases, they had been literally dragged up to the voting window after a ticket had been forcibly placed in their hands.[84] In the Third Ward, there were "not less than fifty, and probably . . . well on to one hundred persons standing in a solid crowd around the window; a great many of whom were dressed in blue shirts, all alike . . . when naturalized voters would approach, they were threatened 'If you come in here we will stab you,' or 'We will kill you,' and other like expressions . . . those who were admitted to the polls went under the cry of 'Open the way for the natives.'"[85] In the Twelfth Ward, several witnesses testified that fifteen to twenty members of the Plug Uglies drove up to the polls in an omnibus, tore down the barricade and a part of the porch that had been erected around the polls, and displayed guns and bowie knives in a manner intended to intimidate naturalized voters.[86]

Baltimore government officials simply turned their heads when their American party colleagues kidnaped, assaulted, and robbed foreign-born men. Reporting a particularly extreme example of such abuse, Heinrich Book, who had only his first papers and was thus ineligible to vote, testified that he had involuntarily become part of the 1859 American party campaign while going about his own business:

I was cutting wood for a man by the name of McCleary, and went there to try to settle with him; then I went down to the Point, to Shoemaker's, and his wife gave me a pair of shears to get ground on the Point; and then I came up town and came to the corner of Bond street, and one of the loafers asked me if I could saw half a cord of wood for him; I said no; he insisted upon it, and I told him I could not saw the wood, for I had to go out of town; that I did not live in town, and had to go out of town.

---

[82] Ibid., pp. 195, 249. The testimony accompanying this evidence did not report who the traitors might have been or what they had done.

[83] S.R. no. 962: M.D. no. 68 (1857): p. 29. In the First Ward, Blood Tubs had brought a cannon to the polls: "[T]he muzzle was pointed down Lombard street, which seemed to command the main avenue leading to the polls. This cannon was fired at intervals during the day, and intimidated the naturalized voters so that the main body or larger portion of them were afraid to approach the polls" (p. 32). In the 1856 election, a projectile fired from a similar cannon severed a young girl's arm. Evitts, *A Matter of Allegiances*, p. 116.

[84] S.R. no. 962: M.D. no. 68 (1857): pp. 323, 325, 327, 330.

[85] Ibid., p. 178. Even if he voluntarily voted the American party ticket, a naturalized voter still might be attacked in the Third Ward. One witness testified that he was with a German Jew who, while holding an American ticket in his hand, was assaulted from behind. Unable to identify his assailant, the victim was reported as saying that a "democrat might have struck him because he voted the native ticket, or a native might have struck him because he was a German" (p. 826).

[86] Ibid., pp. 278–85.

Another loafer then came up and caught me by the collar and said if I did not go he would break my neck. They took me then to Caroline street into a house, where they searched me to see if I had any money, and took about six dollars from me; then they carried me up stairs and kept me until Wednesday morning, the day of the election; they took me around to the polls and I had to vote; and as soon as I came back from the polls another one of the rowdies took me by the collar, took my hat away, and put a cap on my head, and voted me again; then they gave me a high hat, and voted me again; I voted four or five times before I left that one poll, and then I was taken to the next poll.... They [Americans] took me through the town in a hack four times, and they voted me the first time, eighteen times; and the next time, they voted me fourteen times; and the third time, twelve times; and the last time, eighteen times [always voting the Know-Nothing ticket].[87]

Like Book, John Ritzius was also an unnaturalized resident who was abducted by American partisans. Several days before the election, Ritzius approached some men on one of the wharves, looking for employment. Promising six dollars a week, they hired him and he worked all that day. At quitting time, they persuaded him to accompany them as they went to Wilkes Street. At that point, Ritzius was confined in a "coop," a colloquial name for a room in which foreign-born men were kept until the polls opened. These men were then marched to the voting window and compelled to cast Know-Nothing tickets before they were released.

[I was first put into the coop on] Monday, about eleven o'clock, and kept there until nine o'clock Wednesday morning. First and foremost I was put down in the cellar, and another was thrown after me; we were both thrown down. The cellar was so full that we could not readily turn around in it. On Wednesday morning, about nine o'clock, three, four, five, or six were taken out from there; when we got outside of the house each one was given a ticket, and we were carried opposite the coop to the poll to vote [at the corner] of Caroline and Wilkes streets. Then we got into a hack and went to Bond street and Ensor street, and then into a street near Bel Air market, and from that came over toward Holliday street [where we voted]. There we stopped; in Holliday street we were cooped again. There we changed our clothes and had to go three or four different times to the polls to vote.... Four men were with me...all the time.... From Holliday street they [and he] were put into omnibusses, and went down to the point to Caroline street.[88]

On Monday evening, two nights before the election, William Bartlett was waylaid as he was walking away from Smith's dock,

down in Fleet street to Eden and Aliceanna streets, and was crossing the lot, when three fellows came up behind me, wheeled me round, and asked me, "Where are you

---

[87] S.R. no. 1060: M.D. no. 4 (1859): pp. 23–4.
[88] Ibid., pp. 27–8. His daughter went to the mayor, begging "hard for my release [from the coop], but Mayor Swan told her he could not do anything about it; that I had got to stay there.... My daughter and my wife went to the coop, and tried to get me released; but they told them I was not there; that I might be on Federal Hill, in some of the [other] coops" (p. 29).

going, you drunken son of a bitch?" I said "I was going home," and that "I was no more drunk than they were"; one of them says to me, "You have got to go along with us," and two of them caught me by the collar, one on each side, and I tried to get loose, and jerked them off, one fell on one side, and the other on the other side; the other fellow jerked out his blunderbuss, and says to me, "You have said enough now, say any more and I'll blow your damned brains out"; one of the fellows jumped up, and struck me over the nose, and then two of them took hold of me, and took me across two or three lots there, till they got me to Wilke[s] street, and there they carried me through a house, along a passage way, and shoved me down into a cellar; they kept me there till Wednesday about 12 o'clock before they let me out. The captain of the coop took me out with five men, put them in a room up stairs, and took me out private, and asked me what ward I belonged to; I told him "the first ward, I don't belong to this ward"; then he called one of his men, and whispered to him, then told him to carry me round by Caroline street into Wilke[s] street, so that people should not suspicion that I had been in the coop; after that I came out, I looked around to see if there was any police about at the ward polls; there was none there; so the fellow said to me, "Come along, you have got to vote"; then he took me up to the window, and the judge, I believe, asked me my name, but the fellow with me said, "I know his name, it's all right"; "Give up your ticket," says he to me; so I gave it up to the judge, and came away.

Bartlett reported that there were 150 to 175 men in this coop, which was located across the street from the Second Ward polls. It "was a pretty merry party; the fellows had blunderbusses and guns, and now and then they would come in and trip one up, and kick him in the mouth." The confined men, however, made no effort to escape: "[T]hey were very quiet; there were some old men of 50 and 60 years of age, and some right genteel looking young men, too, and all sorts of people mixed up there." Bartlett was a native-born American, somewhat unusual for men in a coop, and was apparently illiterate (because he signed his testimony with his mark.[89]

In one instance, the Baltimore police helped gather a man for a Know-Nothing coop. Henry Funk, a voter in the Sixth Ward, testified that on the Saturday night before the election he was waylaid across from the

watch-house, in Saratoga street, by Joe Creamer and another man, and was taken by them into the watch-house, and they told me they charged me with making a noise in the street, which was untrue; I was in there about half an hour; I saw no one there but one police officer; Arnold, the baker's son, came and said he had gone my security, and asked me to go with him to take a drink; he and three or four others went up Holliday street with me, and when we got to Ras Levy's place we went in, and they asked me to drink; I took some whiskey – for they knocked me down flat on my back, and poured the whiskey into me, about half a pint; I halloed and screamed, and then they clapped me down into the cellar, and came down and robbed me and took my money, five dollars all to eight cents, from me; I wouldn't give it up, and they beat me on the head, hand, and lip, and took the money away from me; then they marched me through a hole into the adjoining house, and carried

[89] S.R. no. 1064: M.D. no. 28 (1859): p. 40.

me up stairs to the second floor; there Arnold's son beat me again; Sunday morning, about nine o'clock, I took the slats out of the window, which had been nailed on the inside, and went out on the ledge and stood there; I was going to jump, and I saw a party below with bricks, and then some fellow caught me by the collar behind and drew me back, and then they handcuffed me and gave me a lashing; I saw Marshal Herring standing on the other side of the street about an hour in the afternoon; they kept me there till election day; they kept us all there like hogs in a pen; the floor was full of excrement and stuff of all kinds; I saw men brought in there who were searched and robbed; I saw one German, who was very anxious to get home, who said he lived in the country, twenty-two miles, and left his team at the market, and he made a noise to get out and they handcuffed him, and kept him so all night, and stripped him of all his clothes, except his shirt and drawers, and they took a comfort and put it around his neck and said they would hang him; and he went down on his knees and said he would be quiet, and then they let him alone; there was one of those who kept the coop whom they called "governor," another "captain," another "steward"; they kept me in the coop till Wednesday morning, and they gave me a ticket and wanted to make me vote, but I wouldn't vote, for I ran away at the time the shooting commenced; I was at that time on the first floor; two squads of six were brought down before I was brought down; and when the party who kept the coop went out with pistols and guns I saw them shoot; I followed out behind them and made my escape, holding the ticket, which was an "American tenth ward ticket," in my hand.... In the rooms where I was, a front and back room, there were some seventy or eighty persons; there were sixty-three there, I think, on Tuesday morning, and they brought right smart into the coop after that.... I saw fellows come in with revolvers in their hands, which they pointed at the men in the coop, and told them to lie down and go to sleep, or they would be shot; and they had guns at the door, and they always came in with large clubs, like watchmen's clubs, in their hands; and I saw them beat men with them too; one German was brought in with a large beard on, and Crab Ashby took a candle and set fire to his beard and burnt it off.[90]

The origin of coops was comparatively benign.[91] In the nineteenth century, it was normal, although not universal, practice for party organizations to offer what were often termed "refreshments" to their voters. In most instances, this would be a drink or two of liquor, usually whisky, kept in a room or alley just off the street or other public space near the voting window. In Baltimore, this practice was apparently a little more elaborate than it was in most parts

---

[90] Ibid., pp. 62–3.
[91] Identified in a hearing as a "cooper by profession" (i.e., a party agent responsible for organizing coops), Thomas Spencer described their origin: "Before I was a resident of Baltimore I was familiar with cooping; I was educated in the democratic school, and taught to coop before I was a voter; I came to Baltimore in 1828, and found it practiced by the democratic party, and followed it until 1840, when I quit the democratic party ... when I left the democratic party I left the profession, because I regarded it unfair to coop and colonize.... My first coop was a stable, when I was eighteen years of age; the object of the coop was to put the voters there, feed them, and take care of them until the day of election, for fear our enemies would steal them.... I cannot call to mind the year, but the last [Democratic coop] was at the old small-pox hospital." Ibid., p. 5.

of the United States; the parties would offer their supporters both alcohol and food in rooms in the period just before the polls opened.[92] These rooms held noisy gatherings that simultaneously constituted celebrations of party fortune and petty forms of bribery. Because the celebrants often drank to excess, many of the men were in a drunken stupor when they left the coops to vote the next morning. Both bribed and drunk these voters were hardly free-thinking, independently minded citizens when they turned in their tickets to election judges. As the election contests in Baltimore became even more competitive, with the parties increasingly desperate for victory, these coops apparently evolved into temporary private prisons where liquor and food were still usually offered the men but they were no longer, in any sense, voluntary celebrants.[93]

These men made quite a spectacle when they emerged from their coops and wearily marched to the polls. A lawyer who had been distributing tickets at the Tenth Ward polling place described them:

Some time after I had voted myself, when the street was comparatively quiet, I was standing not very far from the polls, and noticed Erasmus Levy taking his station at the door of his drinking shop. In the course of a few minutes there came out, in single file, a gang of men, with one of the Regulators at their head, from Levy's house. They walked very close to each other, in single file, and I think they were a body of the most wretched and degraded looking objects I ever saw. Most of them were apparently perfectly stupefied with drink. Some of them had on shirts, some none; some hats or miserable caps, some none. One man I noticed without shoes. A good many of them were in the costume of sailors, dirty, filthy, begrimed, black. They came out, and this man at the head of them, carrying them straight up the pavement, when they came near the polls, cried out, "Make way for the voters," and pushed out of the way with his hands everybody standing upon the pavement. The men went up to the polls and deposited their ballots, this man standing by and seeing them do it, as fast as they could hand them in, and they were received by the judges as fast as the judges could take them. I think Mr. Martin, the reform judge, before that took place, had left the window. I saw Mr. Hinesly, one of the other judges, strike him upon the mouth, and Martin left. These men having voted, went back to

[92]   Asked for the history of coops in the city of Baltimore, Moses Dysart, a Know-Nothing partisan, replied, "The first 'coops' I ever knew of there, were of the election of McKim and Howard; they were the first that I ever knew of; they were democratic 'coops'; in the year following the whigs commenced cooping, as they followed in electioneering what the democrats did." Asked to describe a coop, Dysart replied, "A 'coop' is a place where they fasten men up in a room; where they feed them on laudanum [opium], and whiskey, and eatables for the day of election." Ibid., pp. 2–3.

[93]   Nativist clubs came to regard the consumption of their food, liquor, and laudanum as part of a contractual agreement to support their party. Intimidation, if necessary, was accordingly viewed as merely private enforcement of their claims under that contract. Where voters balked at voting the party ticket, club members felt that they were within their rights to detain these voters until the voting had been completed. As documented in the text, these practices later took on the characteristics of violent kidnapping and imprisonment, along with the forceful impairment of the faculties of the victims.

Levy's and into his house. Shortly after, they again came out and voted, and went back into Levy's house; and shortly after, they came out again; and the whole gang went through that process before my eyes about a half a dozen times. When I say the whole gang did it, I do not mean that I recognized the face of every man; but there were some very peculiar looking men in the gang, which I noticed as they came out in repeatedly in the same succession. This marching of the voters between the polls and Levy's house was kept up until that whole party, upon a moderate calculation, had voted half a dozen times. There were twenty or twenty-five of them. The thing became really ludicrous, from the fact that when these men came out and the man at the head of them cried out, "Make way for the voters," this crowd of Regulators, the judges, and almost everybody else, laughed out publicly at the idea of their being "voters." . . . After these men had been voted in this way, passing up in Indian file as close as they could, they marched up like soldiers, and there was a large omnibus driven up into the street, and the whole concern marched in the same way into it. They were pushed and packed in, and a man by the name of John Shaney, who was pointed out to me as the president of the Regulator club, threw himself upon the top of the omnibus upon his back, with the American flag above him, and kicked up his heels in the air, not exposing his face to the crowd at the tenth ward polls, and shouted out, "Hurrah," and the omnibus disappeared, with its occupants, up Fayette street. There were one or two omnibus loads that stopped at the northeast corner of Holliday and Fayette streets while I remained – large omnibusses filled with men in the same state of beastly intoxication. They stopped at the corner, and a message was sent from the omnibus to the Regulators. Immediately one of the Regulators went up to the corner, and, placing himself at the head of the file, the fellows in the omnibus followed him in Indian file down to the polls, under the same cry, "Make way for the voters," and the same laughter of the judges and of those around. They all went up to the polls and deposited their votes with the greatest possible rapidity, the judges taking them as rapidly as they could. Then they were led back to the omnibus, and it started off to the western party of the city.[94]

When confronted with such charges, the American party responded by noting that Baltimore elections had always been violent affairs; thus, the experience in the 1857 and 1859 elections was, from where they sat, not only normal but also justified as a means of redressing past wrongs inflicted by the Democrats, who were now complaining only because they lost.[95] And as far as normal practice went, the Americans may not have been far off. In the hearings connected with the 1859 election, for example, one of the Democratic contestant's witnesses was asked whether, in elections before the Know-nothing party was created, it was a "common thing for disturbances to take place on the day of election at the polls." The witness answered, "Yes, sir; quite a common thing." The American counsel then continued, "People

---

[94] S.R. no. 1060: M.D. no. 4 (1859): pp. 204–5.
[95] There may have been a few wards in which the election was relatively peaceful. For example, a man holding the office of fish inspector testified that "there was the customary shoving and pulling [at the Sixteenth Ward polling place], but not more than is usual at all elections. . . ." Ibid., pp. 297, 309.

knocked down sometimes; cut open with bowie-knives, as in the case of Manley, the man who was killed; and other such circumstances? I will ask you this as a distinct question: You have witnessed such scenes of disorder at the polls in Baltimore before the know-nothing party commenced, have you not?" The witness again responded affirmatively, qualifying his answer by saying that the violence in the 1859 elections was the worst he had ever seen. Another witness, a longtime resident and voter, testified that the 1840 election had been particularly violent (although again, in his opinion, not as violent as the 1859 election).[96]

However, as these witnesses contended, the level of violence in the 1859 election was still unprecedented. In one of the worst incidents, William Mauer, a naturalized voter in the Second Ward, described the death of a friend: "I am a cooper by trade [in this case, a maker of wooden barrels or casks], and was at my business, and five or six men came up to me and knocked me down, and then put a [Know-Nothing] ticket in my hand to vote it; I would not; then they drawed my clothes down, and pulled me like a dead dog along; my neighbor, Charles Beckert, came to help me, and one of them said 'shoot him! shoot him!' and after that they shooted, he falled, and he is dead and buried.... [After that] I had to vote.... [The men who took him] belonged to the Rough Skin Club." When the Rough Skins came to get him, he "was not in the shop, but on the pavement.... [The men who shot his neighbor] are in jail, I believe; they were let out on bail, and put in again after...Beckert died." When he was presented at the voting window, Mauer could not tell the judges of election that he did not want to vote because he "was bloody, and could not talk; I was all swelled up."[97]

As already noted, these Baltimore elections turned out to be among the most important congressional races in American history because H. Winter Davis became the decisive vote in the 1859–60 speaker's contest in the U.S. House of Representatives. Although they thus had a significant impact on the secession crisis, the issues at stake had little or nothing to do with slavery, the major issue associated with the coming of the Civil War.[98] In the hearings held on the 1857 election, for example, the words "slaves" or

---

[96] Ibid., pp. 36–7, 68–9.

[97] S.R. no. 1064: M.D. no. 28 (1859): pp. 34–5. Another witness, Frederick C. Meyer, a native-born voter, testified, "I saw no disorder [at the Second Ward polls]; but, away from the polls, gangs of ruffians, or 'Rough Skins,' prowled about, three or four together, with clubs in their hands, hunting up voters and taking them up to the polls; the Rough Skins had complete possession of the polls, and there was no disorder there, I mean, because there was no opposition made to them, nor possible, under the circumstances, by the opposite party" (p. 43).

[98] For a discussion of the role of slavery in competition between the American and Democratic parties, see Baker, *Ambivalent Americans*, pp. 49–50. Baker generally saw the issue as a little more salient in Maryland politics than I was able to discern in the hearings on Baltimore elections.

"slavery" never appear in over a thousand pages of testimony. The only time blacks were mentioned was when "colored" was noted in connection with houses on the block lists (as prima facie evidence that no legal voter could live at that address).[99] There were but two exceptions, one involving an incident in the First Ward in which a Democrat attempted to vote: "I went up to the window...a young man stepped up to me and told me I could not vote unless I voted a white man's ticket; I told him that I did not consider that I had a black man's ticket." In the Eighteenth Ward, "One man came up to the window and asked for a ticket, and having procured one, commenced erasing the name of Henry Winter Davis. He was asked by some one in the crowd why he had done so, and his answer was, 'I will not vote for a negro.' As soon as the man used this expression, some one in the crowd struck him with the fist." Other than as a personal insult, any connection between either the Democratic or Know-Nothing tickets and political sentiment favorable to blacks does not make sense; there seems to have been complete consensus between the parties on the place of blacks in Baltimore in politics and society. The issues involved with the status of blacks were simply and entirely irrelevant to nativist hostility to foreign-born voters.[100]

CONCLUSION

But even in these instances, there was a sociological context in which men voted. For example, in Baltimore and other cities where gangs took control of precincts, working men demanded to vote their tickets in the early morning hours before they went off to their shops and factories. These working men were sufficiently numerous and assertive that most gangs waited until late morning or early afternoon before taking control of the precinct. Even after taking control, these gangs often performed the formal rituals of an election (e.g., turning in tickets and giving names and addresses) as they marched drunken aliens up to the voting window. Even though their practices were otherwise recognized as blatantly illegal, gang members still emulated the forms of a normal election. From one perspective we might think of these performances as the demonstrative execution of a contract between the party and the gang; a simple stuffing of the ballot box would not have provided such strikingly visible evidence of their faithful execution of an agreement. But an even more important aspect of these rituals is that they

[99] In hearings on the 1859 election, testimony similarly indicated that an election judge looked up the address that a man reported as his home and rejected his vote because "the house mentioned [was] marked as 'negroes.'" S.R. no. 1064: M.D. no. 28 (1859): pp. 49–50. Otherwise the record is silent on whether these blacks were free or slave.

[100] S.R. no. 962: M.D. no. 68 (1857): pp. 31, 302. In the 1859 election, some Know-Nothing activists also called their ballot "a white man's ticket." S.R. no. 1064: M.D. no. 28 (1859): p. 43.

allowed the judges of election, usually several social strata above the ruffians who ruled the precinct, to tacitly cooperate with the gangs. The judges received tickets they knew to be illegally cast but pretended that they could not prove the ineligibility of the voter. From this perspective, the rituals crafted a link between the gang and judges that could satisfy conventional social proprieties.

5

Frontier Democracy

Reflecting the thoroughly democratic impulses of American politics, precincts were created on the frontier almost as soon as places for receiving votes appeared. These places were often lonely outposts such as houses occupied by men who ran ferries across unfordable rivers, isolated homes for sheep and cattle ranchers, or forts garrisoned by federal troops.[1] Such polling places were often ephemeral because the line of settlement was a rapidly changing social landscape. Local landmarks such as ferries often disappeared as fast as they emerged when the pattern of occupation changed the paths that farmers took to market or the tracks followed by migrating settlers. Homesteaders changed their residences as well. Many were no more than squatters who could not file a claim until the land they cleared and cultivated had been surveyed. With nothing more than their sweat invested in any particular plot, they frequently moved around, searching for the best unoccupied site.

Whatever might be the pattern of occupation when the country was first opened up, the coming of the railroad, with its stations and access to eastern markets, dramatically changed the social topography. Hamlets that had formed at the intersection of dusty roads were suddenly abandoned, replaced by small towns erupting like mushrooms wherever railroad lines happened to cross. In general, the social topography of the frontier was but a great and tentative experiment as men and women, both

---

[1] In 1862, the canvassing board of Dakota Territory waited in vain for the returns from Ritson County. Finally, as John Hutchinson, the territorial secretary, reported, the board decided not to send for the returns because "[s]ufficient time had elapsed for the returns to arrive, had there been no obstructions, and I considered it impracticable to send a messenger through, because of the Indian difficulties in that vicinity, and between here and there." Ser. Rec. (hereafter S.R.) no. 1199: Contested Delegate Election from the Territory of Dakota: Mis. Doc. (hereafter M.D.) no. 27, p. 20. J. B. S. Todd vs. William Jayne, election held on September 1, 1862.

individually and collectively, responded to constantly evolving economic opportunities.

Many of the earliest landmarks to appear on the western frontier were political in nature. For example, the designation of a small hamlet as the seat of a newly formed county often meant that it would survive while neighboring communities would waste away. These hamlets were often nothing more than a few sod houses thrown up by speculators who hoped to profit if their settlement was selected as that county seat. In cases where this designation was decided in a local election, the stakes were very high for those who held tracts of land within the competing sites.

The most visible landmarks – the ones most clearly and confidently indicated on frontier maps – were military forts. Because these forts were usually the largest settlements for miles around, federal officials purchasing supplies and services dominated the markets of small frontier communities; many settlers oriented their production toward the requirements of federal forts or Indian reservations. However, although they were the largest communities in their respective regions, forts were also occupied by men who were usually ineligible to vote under state or territorial election law. Since troopers could nonetheless sway the outcome, the temptation to fraudulently participate in frontier elections was very great. It did not help that their commanding officers were often passionate supporters of the administration in Washington.

The most notorious instance in which federal intervention subverted democratic principles was in the territory of Kansas between 1854 and 1859. Most of what occurred in Kansas had only the tacit consent of federal authorities; proslavery men crossing the border from Missouri actually produced the election results. Without the sanction of a proslavery territorial administration, however, Kansas elections might have been more democratically conducted; they could not have been worse. Because Kansas territorial elections have been extensively covered in the historical literature, they are not discussed here.[2] However, territorial elections in other places and times amply illustrate the difficulties of forming democratic communities on the sparsely settled frontier.

Forts, Troopers, and Men on the Move

On his way back to Dayton, Ohio, after trying his luck in the goldfields at Pike's Peak, Charles Comly arrived at Fort Kearny on October 10, 1859. He stayed at the fort for several days, long enough to witness the election for territorial delegate in Kearny City, about two miles from the

---

[2]   For a succinct account of the manipulation of voting rules and political conditions in Kansas that allowed passage of a proslavery constitution, see Mark W. Summers, *The Plundering Generation: Corruption and the Crisis of the Union, 1849–1861* (New York: Oxford University Press, 1987), pp. 233–5, 248–51.

fort. Comly later filed a written deposition in support of the losing candidate in that election, Samuel G. Daily. In his own words, this is what transpired:

I remained near the polls all day. I saw early in the morning that frauds were being committed, hence I watched the proceedings much closer than I otherwise would. The first fraud that attracted my attention was a soldier from the fort voting. After that I noticed, I presume (I cannot be certain as to the number), eight or ten different soldiers, or men clad in the United States military uniform, who said they were soldiers, vote in regular form. After that I saw two of the same men vote again, and one of the two voted once afterwards. Each time they changed their attire, but were poorly disguised. I further noticed quite a number of emigrants, who were coming from and going to Pike's Peak, vote; among them were James Low, Stephen L. Inslee, and William Harlan, all of whom voted for Experience Estabrook, and they were all illegal voters; they were returning in company with me from Pike's Peak. I also saw a number of others vote for Experience Estabrook whom I know had left Denver City, Kansas Territory, but a short time before I did. Every emigrant that was passing or stopping there that day was urged to vote, and the most of them did so. The regular order of voting was first to visit the trading-post known as "Jack's Ranche," take a drink of liquor and a ticket, then go across the road and vote; this programme was filled by nearly every one I saw vote. During the day, at intervals, I saw Dr. Henry Jack (the proprietor of the ranche) and one of the clerks in the store engaged in making out lists of names. After writing awhile one of them would put the list in his pocket and go over to the polls and go inside, and from conversations that I subsequently heard between the parties, I am well satisfied in my own mind that the said lists were copied into the poll-books and returned as voters. The returns, if I remember rightly, gave 238 votes, all for Experience Estabrook. To the best of my knowledge and belief I do not think there were over sixty different persons at or around the polls during the day. About 6 o'clock p.m. the polls were declared closed, and the ballot-boxes were deposited at "Jack's" store. A short time after the polls were closed two men came in from Plum creek, I believe, and desired to vote; the ballot-boxes were again taken to the polls and the ballots were received.

Comly also criticized the conduct and eligibility of the election officials at the Kearny City polling place:

I am satisfied in my own mind that one of the clerks was under twenty-one years of age, and that another one of the clerks (or probably one of the judges) was an unnaturalized foreigner. This I learned through conversation with parties acquainted with them. The judges and clerks of the election were, in my opinion, all of them more or less under the influence of liquor, and one or two of them were drunk and unfit for any kind of business. As an evidence of this, one of them (I think by the name of Burkh) signed his own name to one of the poll-books or returns, and his wife's name to the other. The error was corrected before me the next day, the said Burkh declaring that, "by God he wanted people to know that his wife had a finger in that election!" Of the men around the polls during the day I do not think that more than one-half of them were residents of the county or precinct, the balance being emigrants.'[3]

This was actually the second Fort Kearny in Nebraska, the site of the first fort having been abandoned and the garrison moved to a new location on the south bank of the Platte River in 1848. A ten-square-mile military reservation surrounded the fort, which itself included several earthwork fortifications and a major depot for military supplies. Continuously occupied until 1871, Kearny was one of the most important army posts on the Oregon Trail with its primary mission being the protection of emigrant wagon trains.[4] Kearny City, where the voting took place, was very small and almost entirely dependent on the patronage of the fort and its soldiers. According to Stephen Wattles, acting sheriff of Sarpy County, the settlement held

not over eight houses – three business houses I was in; two of them used as ranches, keeping groceries, liquors, &c., the other was a drinking house or saloon. Rankins's ranch was the largest of any; it is a one story sod or adobe house, also covered with sod; it is about twenty or twenty-two feet wide and sixty long. The other houses are of the same material and one story high, but not as large; the dram shop is probably sixteen by eighteen feet, and the other buildings are about the same size....I think they were all occupied [as domiciles] with the exception of the one they call the "town house" or "state house," and I do not know whether that was occupied or not; I saw no signs of any one living there.[5]

Regardless of its size, Kearny City lacked several characteristics almost always associated with polling places in more settled parts of the country. The most noteworthy void was the absence of a competing party organization. According to Comly, there were no challengers at the polls. This explains how blatant frauds could be committed without protest. In addition, party affiliation must have been generally weak among the men who voted Dr. Jack's ticket in return for a drink. Going through what must have been a completely transparent subterfuge of changing their uniforms or clothing, troopers and transients voted multiple times. Enlisting one of his store employees as an assistant, Dr. Jack prepared a roll of names that was then copied into the poll books as an official record of the election. The whole process, petty bribes and forgeries included, ultimately produced some 238 votes for Estabrook, almost all of them illegal. Daily received no votes, legal or otherwise. In the official record, Kearny City appeared to be a stronghold of Democratic party sentiment (not surprisingly, since the Democrats controlled

---

3   S.R. no. 1064: Contested Election for Delegate from the Territory of Nebraska: M.D. no. 12, pp. 3–4. Samuel G. Daily vs. Experience Estabrook, election held on October 11, 1859.
4   Robert B. Roberts, *Encyclopedia of Historic Forts: The Military, Pioneer, and Trading Posts of the United States* (New York: Macmillan, 1988), p. 484.
5   S.R. no. 1064: M.D. no. 12 (1859): p. 54.

the White House). In reality, this was a watering-hole for thirsty men who readily traded a walk across the street for a drink of liquor in the sutler's general store.[6]

Another such watering hole was temporarily erected at Charles Hedges's store, on the Yankton Indian Reservation near Fort Randall.[7] In the September 1862 election this store was designated the polling place for Charles Mix County. Very sparsely settled by whites, the number of eligible voters residing in the county was estimated to have been between twenty and twenty-five. Only about fifteen or so apparently voted in this election. However, over a hundred votes were cast by men who in one way or another were not eligible to vote under Dakota law. Most of them were troopers from the fort who had enlisted in Iowa, others were "half-breeds of the Yankton Sioux tribe," and the remainder simply did not satisfy the residency requirement.[8]

The polling place at Hedges's store must have been chaotic, even if the following descriptions exaggerated the disorder. William Hargis, who was employed as clerk and deputy postmaster "in the store of George Hoffman, postmaster and sutler" at Fort Randall, arrived at the polls at about

---

[6] Estabrook's brief, appended to the hearing, contended that the very identity of the settlement described by opposing witnesses was in doubt. "Wherever may be the location of the 'Kearny City' visited by Wattles, and whatever may have been done there, it is nevertheless true that his 'Kearny City' is not the only one; for the history of Nebraska would show that, in the nomenclature of the numerous cities of that Territory heretofore, this name had been a favorite. One of the most flourishing cities on the Missouri, now merged in Nebraska City, was incorporated by the legislature, and entered at the land office by that name. And other cities bearing that name, as is well known to all old settlers in Nebraska, have been projected on either side of the Platte river in the neighborhood of Fort Kearny." Rapidly changing conditions on the frontier, along with the hope of settlers that the "Kearny" name would attract additional people to their own location, created the possibility that the frauds reported in the hearing were in fact committed somewhere else. If so, they would have tainted another set of returns, not the ones at issue in the hearing. Ibid., Points and Argument of the Sitting Member Appended, pp. 9–10.

[7] Fort Randall was located about a quarter-mile south of the Missouri River almost on the boundary between the Dakota and Nebraska Territories. Established in 1856 in order to police and repress the surrounding Indian tribes, the fort was across the river from the Yankton reserve. Roberts, *Encyclopedia of Historic Forts*, p. 732. Hedges evidently maintained two stores, one at the fort where he was one of the sutlers and one on the reservation; the latter store is where the voting took place. S.R. no. 1199: M.D. no. 27 (1862): p. 69.

[8] S.R. no. 1199: M.D. no. 27 (1862): pp. 70, 81. Under Dakota territorial law, soldiers could vote only if they were Dakota residents when they had enlisted; thus troopers who had enlisted in Iowa were disqualified. "Half-breeds" were ineligible because the territory, like most states in the Union, restricted voting to whites. The residency requirement in Dakota was ninety consecutive days immediately prior to the election, but proof to the contrary was, given the disorganized conditions on the frontier, very hard to demonstrate.

10 o'clock in the morning:[9]

I saw there soldiers, half-breeds and Indians, and some citizens.... All the employees of Doctor Burleigh, Indian agent, were there assembled when I arrived there. I saw a team of Doctor Burleigh's filled with Indians and half-breeds, and driven by Mr. Andrew J. Faulk, a partner of the Indian sutler at the Yankton reserve, and father-in-law of Doctor Burleigh, the agent, returning from the polls to the agency. The Indians and half-breeds were drunk.... [The soldiers at the polls] were all members of the 14th regiment of Iowa volunteers, now the first battalion of the 41st regiment of Iowa volunteers, and were then and are now stationed at Fort Randall, and are members of companies A, B and C, respectively, but mainly of companies A and C.... They did vote, and by the advice of Major Pattee, then in command of the post. On the morning of the first of September, A.D. 1862, I overheard Major Pattee tell the orderly sergeant of company A that "the men might all go plumming, and to have them go as far as Mr. Hedge's store, the place of election." In a few moments after I saw 1st sergeant Hodgdon go in the quarters and heard him tell the men that "Major Pattee wanted them to go a plumming, and that he wanted them all to go."

"To Plum" seems to have been the verb form for "political plum" (e.g., patronage appointment). In this case, the reference was probably to the consumption of free alcohol in return for votes. Since Major Pattee was an active supporter of Governor Jayne's candidacy for territorial delegate and since he urged his men to go to the polls, this interpretation of the term seems likely; because they were Iowa residents, most of his men would appear to have had little personal stake in this election, aside from the alcohol that was to be made available at the polls.

I crossed the river shortly after that, and many of the soldiers crossed with me, and they arrived at the polls shortly after I did, well armed, with rifles, pistols and bowie-knives ... to the best of my belief, at one time during the day there were at least one hundred soldiers present at the polls. They were constantly coming and going.... I saw a great many of them drunk at the polls, and they were constantly making threats against the friends of J. B. S. Todd.... I challenged one vote, that of Edward Higgins, an Iowa soldier, who swore his vote in. I then challenged Corporal Davis, and while in the act I was snatched away from the polls by Charles P. Booge, and held till the vote was deposited. Threats were made by Iowa soldiers, which intimidated me from challenging any further.... I saw a barrel of whiskey inside where the judges sat, and a large tip pail, filled with whiskey, sitting under a shed attached to the house; a tin cup was in the pail; free access was had to the pail – Indians, half-breeds and soldiers, and citizens *ad libitum*. I also saw whiskey given from the window where the votes were received.[10]

By working at Hoffman's store on the post, Hargis had come to personally know most of the men at Fort Randall. While a sutler was not required to keep a list of the officers and men in the garrison, Hargis reported that "it is a

9   Hoffman thus appears to have run a sutler's store at the fort in competition with Hedges. Ibid., pp. 60–1.
10 Ibid., p. 61.

custom, because the soldiers have to deal with the sutler, and a great deal on credit, and the books have to be signed monthly by the captain.... We had such a correct list, which, coupled with my duties as assistant postmaster, has made me familiar with the names of the Iowa soldiers." He was similarly acquainted with "a large majority of [the Yankton Reservation "half-breeds"], both by name and features." Using his personal knowledge of these men and the records he had kept as clerk, Hargis examined the poll books kept at the Hedges's store polling place. Of the eighty-four soldiers who voted there, only six had been Dakota residents at the time of their enlistment. The remaining men had cast illegal ballots.[11] In addition, he identified the names of sixteen "Yankton half-breeds" and fifteen men employed by Dr. Burleigh, superintendent of the Yankton Indian agency. Under Dakota law, the former should have been disqualified on the basis of race, the latter on lack of residency. While the illegality of the proceedings at this polling place is interesting in its own right, the more significant point is the overwhelming size of the federal presence; almost 90 percent of the adult men attending the polls were either federal troopers, employees of the Yankton agency, or members of the Sioux tribe overseen by the agency.[12]

Much of the clerk's account was corroborated by Charles McCarty, a farmer who listed Fort Randall as his residence. Intending to monitor the polls at Hedges's store, McCarty had left the fort at about 8:30 on the morning of the election. When he reached the bank of the Missouri River (from the fort the store could be reached only by ferry), he ran into George Pleach, who had already been to the polls. Pleach told McCarty that voting had begun at four o'clock that morning and that, because his tickets had been taken away from him, he was returning to the fort to get some more. They then traveled together to the polls, Pleach riding behind McCarty on a mule. McCarty described what transpired after they arrived:

We reached there about 10 o'clock, and after I had tied up my mule, went to the window where the votes were received that day, and asked Mr. Thompson, one of the judges of the election, how many votes had been cast. He replied, "fifty-two

[11] Ibid., pp. 62–3. Another witness, Thomas Johnson, himself an Iowa soldier, testified that he recognized the names of 68 Iowa soldiers on the Charles Mix poll books. Daniel Babcock, like Johnson an Iowa soldier, recognized 70 names of Iowa troopers. Several other witnesses gave similar testimony (pp. 72–3, 75–9).

[12] Because a sutler had to have permission to operate his store at the fort, Hargis, as a sutler's clerk, was himself vulnerable to federal influence. In fact, five days before Hargis gave his testimony and possibly in retaliation for the account he would give of the election, he "was ordered off [the military reserve] by Major Pattee...not to return without his permission." On the day of the election, Hargis also testified that he had "heard Sergeant (now Lieutenant) Pattee threaten a citizen by the name of George E. Naylor with exclusion from the military post should he vote for J. B. S. Todd....Sergeant Pattee...[remarked] that he stated this on the authority of his brother [Major Pattee]...." Ibid., p. 63. Naylor was evidently threatened after he had cast his vote for Todd (p. 65).

votes." I then asked him how many General Todd had received out of this number; he said "not any," and "in his opinion he ought not to have any." After a little time I observed squads of Iowa soldiers coming towards the polls. At this time there were about twenty-five persons assembled, and of this number I should think eight or ten were soldiers. Sergeant Pattee and Sergeant Mason arrived at the polls in about a half hour after I arrived. As the soldiers approached the polls they received tickets from C. P. Booge, C. E. Hedges, Sergeant Wallis Pattee (now Lieutenant Pattee), and Sergeant Mason, and also Sergeant Crumb gave them tickets. Booge and Hedges chiefly led them up to the polls. Mr. William Hargis, on attempting to challenge the votes of these soldiers, was seized by C. P. Booge and carried away from the window, and detained him. Mr. Hargis struggled with Booge, and when the soldier whom he had challenged had voted he let him go. I was standing at the window at this time, and asked Mr. Thompson why he received this vote; he replied that he did "not hear any challenge." I then challenged the votes of three of these soldiers in succession. The oath was administered to them. Mr. Thompson then remarked that he "would not swear any more, as it would take too much time," but then said he "would swear them after they had all voted." I protested that these soldiers had no right to vote, and asked him to hand me a copy of the election laws which lay on the table; he did so, and I turned to the fiftieth section, which excluded these soldiers from voting who had enlisted out of the Territory.

Appealing to the law as a higher authority than the election judge turned out to be dangerous. McCarty was immediately threatened by Frederick Carman, an employee on the Yankton reservation, who

stepped up to the polls with a revolver in his hand and swore he would shoot the next Todd man who challenged the soldier's votes. In this he was encouraged by several of the soldiers. I did not think it prudent to attempt to challenge any more under this threat, and as the soldiers crowded up I left the window. This was between 12 and 1 o'clock. I did not challenge any more that day. I saw also, while there, George Pleach challenge the vote of a soldier, when he [the soldier] was dragged away by C. P. Booge, who brought him up to the whiskey pail. There was a large pail full of whiskey setting outside under a shed attached to the house, with a tin cup in it. This pail was kept replenished from a barrel inside the room where the judges sat. This whiskey was distributed to the soldiers by Booge during the day.

This barrel was probably part of the stock normally maintained by Hedges's store. McCarty himself was offered a drink by the election judges, who presented a glass through the voting window, and there seemed to be plenty of liquor available to the Jayne partisans, several of whom became quite unruly:

I saw a soldier named James Mowder, who was quite drunk at the polls, attempt to discharge his musket; Sergeant Crumb, with difficulty wrenched the weapon from him. A majority of the soldiers were drunk and disorderly.…Isaac Smith, a member of company A, having heard that Naylor had voted for General Todd, attempted to stab Naylor with a bowie-knife, but was prevented by Sergeant

Mason, who seized him in the act, and in the scuffle Smith stabbed himself severely in the arm.[13]

Actual white settlers, those who constituted the only eligible voters, were almost entirely invisible in all these accounts.

Federal Officials

The federal government loomed larger on the frontier than anywhere else in the nation, in large part because federal officials controlled most of the civil administration. Because almost all of these officials were appointed by the president, they shared a dependence on executive favor that, in turn, facilitated cooperation between the various federal branches in the territories. Perhaps the most important result of this cooperation was the tendency to blur the distinction between civil and military administration, often to the point where the boundary between them disappeared altogether. In 1862, for example, the two branches came together behind the candidacy of William Jayne for delegate to Congress from the Territory of Dakota.

Because territorial delegates were elected, candidates had to attract votes from settlers. These settlers, in turn, were often dependent on federal purchases and contracts, a dependence that usually conferred a decisive advantage on the administration candidate for the office. This edge was normally compounded by control of the territorial machinery for conducting elections and canvassing the votes. In the 1862 Dakota election, both of these advantages were reinforced by the fact that Jayne was then serving as territorial governor in Dakota, a position from which he was able both to coordinate federal activities on behalf of his candidacy and to influence the distribution of government contracts.[14]

[13] Ibid., pp. 64–5. McCarty reported that most of the soldiers "were armed; some of them with muskets, some with revolvers and bowie-knives, and some had both these weapons" (p. 65). The territorial canvassing board later rejected the returns from Charles Mix county because "there was evidence before us of a great fraud, and from the evidence the board concluded that a large number of the votes – probably a majority – were illegal. The evidence showed that the legal and illegal votes were so intermixed as to vitiate the entire election in this county" (p. 20).

[14] William Jayne had been appointed territorial governor by President Lincoln in 1861. At the time of his appointment, he had been a resident of Springfield, Illinois (Lincoln's hometown), and a member of the Illinois State Legislature. He had been in Dakota only but a year or so when he entered the contest for territorial delegate as the Republican candidate. When the House of Representatives overturned his election, he returned to live in Springfield. John Blair Smith Todd, his Democratic opponent, had served in the regular army in both Florida and Mexico, resigning his commission in 1856. He subsequently became an Indian trader at Fort Randall, in Dakota Territory, but accepted an appointment as brigadier general of Union volunteers early in the Civil War. This military appointment had just expired when the campaign for delegate began. *Biographical Directory of the American Congress, 1774–1971* (Washington, D.C.: Government Printing Office, 1971), pp. 1184, 1822. Of the two candidates, Todd

One of the most interesting of Jayne's interventions involved James Falkinburg, a farmer who lived near Yankton, the capital of Dakota Territory. Falkinburg testified that Jayne had approached him in Yankton on the day of election

on the platform in front of the Ash Hotel; he asked me to vote for him. I told him he hadn't done as he agreed to. He asked me what he had not done that he had agreed to do. I told him that he had agreed to finish up the house belonging to me, for the use of the Dakota cavalry company; that he had used the house for that purpose two months, and that he had not done it, and that I could have rented it had it been fitted up as per agreement, and that it had been idle three months in consequence. He said that he would make that all right with me. He then went for Lieutenant Fowler, quartermaster of the Dakota cavalry company, and came back to me, in his company, where I was standing; we then held a conversation in the rear of Collamer's saloon. Jayne and Fowler told me they would give me fifteen dollars per month for the use of the building for three months, while it was lying idle, provided I would vote for Governor Jayne. This conversation was about noon on the day of the election; I had not voted at the time. And Fowler tole me to come to his office, and he would give me a voucher for forty-five dollars. I [went] a day or two after the election . . . he gave me the voucher for this sum of forty-five dollars. The only consideration . . . was my agreeing to vote for Governor William Jayne for delegate to Congress. They further agreed that they would continue to occupy the building, for the use of government, at fifteen dollars per month, and make some improvements and repairs upon it; but they have not fully completed the finishing of the building. They have continued to pay me for it under this agreement, though they have made very little use of it.[15]

In short, Falkinburg had previously rented a partially built house to the calvary in return for a promise to complete the construction. This contract had involved Governor Jayne, but he probably did not formally act as agent for the government. For some reason, the government had not followed through on its end of the bargain, and Falkinburg, when his vote was personally solicited by the governor, used the opportunity to press his claim. In response, Jayne immediately located the quartermaster of the cavalry unit, the officer apparently responsible for formally approving cavalry requisitions, and brought him into his negotiations with Falkinburg.

As was the case with many conversations concerning political deals and bargains, this one was negotiated in a saloon; saloons were one of the few buildings open to public use in small settlements on the frontier. At the time of this election, Yankton contained at most 500 people, and the small population made it possible for the governor-as-candidate to engage in the kind of nickle-and-dime politicking that in more densely populated eastern

thus had the deeper roots in Dakota Territory. However, although both had served in the federal government, only Jayne was in a position to coordinate administration officials in support of his candidacy.

[15]   S.R. no. 1199: M.D. no. 27 (1862): p. 18.

regions would have been left to subordinates.[16] The concentration of federal power and shared relationship to the administration in Washington facilitated cooperation between Governor Jayne and Lieutenant Fowler in soliciting Falkinburg's support.

Apparently using the saloon as his base of operations, the governor was quite active on election day. Another witness, a farmer named John Stanage, testified that he saw Patrick Conway, a sergeant in the Dakota cavalry, "led up to the polls, from Collamer's saloon, by Governor William Jayne." At the time, Stanage was acting as challenger for the Democratic party in Yankton and objected to Conway's vote on the grounds that Conway had resided in St. John's, Nebraska Territory, at the time of his enlistment. On being challenged, Conway displayed his ticket in such a way that Stanage could see that he intended, not surprisingly, to vote for Jayne. After the election judges administered an oath to Conway, he was allowed to vote.[17]

Parker Brown, like Conway a farmer, reported that he was either given or promised several bribes in return for his vote for Jayne. From a man named Lamson, a clerk in the surveyor general's office (a federal post), he received two dollars. In addition, Surveyor General Hill had previously promised him "a pair of elk" in Lac City, Iowa, if he would vote for Jayne.[18] But the largest bribe, seventeen dollars, came from the governor himself. In Brown's words, "Governor William Jayne came to me on the day of election and asked me to vote for him; and if I did so, he would pay me twenty dollars ($20). He then drew from his pocket seventeen dollars ($17) and gave it to me, saying that that was all he had with him; which money I received, and told him I would vote for him."[19]

Because the governor had the authority to appoint election officials at other precincts in the territory, Jayne's influence in the election extended far

---

[16]   The same type of "retail electioneering" may have been engaged in by the territorial governor of New Mexico in 1867. S.R. no. 1350: Contested Delegate Election in the Territory of New Mexico: M.D. no. 154, pp. 95–7. J. Francisco Chaves vs. Charles P. Clever, election held on September 2, 1867. For the population of Yankton, a "post-village" on the left bank of the Missouri River near the border with Nebraska, see *Lippincott's Pronouncing Gazetteer of the World* (Philadelphia: J. B. Lippincott, 1872), p. 2307.

[17]   S.R. no. 1199: M.D. no. 27 (1862): p. 24. Conway probably swore, contra to Stanage's testimony, that he had resided in Dakota prior to joining the cavalry (pp. 26, 43).

[18]   Hill evidently compelled another of his subordinates, a surveyor, to vote for Jayne. William Lyman, who challenged many of the voters whose names came up in the testimony, reported that he did not object to this man: "Mr. Mellen came up to the polls in company with Mr. Edmunds, from the surveyor general's office; before he voted I held a conversation with him (Mr. Mellen), in which he told me that he had not intended to vote, and thought he had no right to vote, but he was forced to do it. He tore off all the names on the ticket except the name of William Jayne, for delegate to Congress, and said that was all he would vote; from a feeling of delicacy under these circumstances, I forbore to interpose a challenge." Ibid., p. 29.

[19]   Ibid., p. 30.

beyond the immediate vicinity of Collamer's saloon. One of those precincts was in Bon Homme County, where the election was held at the house of G. M. Pinney. John Shober, an attorney residing in Bon Homme, reported that two of the original appointees to the election board were Jayne supporters and one backed J. B. S. Todd, his opponent. However, the two Jayne men dismissed the Todd representative and appointed a third Jayne supporter in his place.[20] Because this switch gave the governor all three positions on the election board, the Todd men suspected fraud would occur during the counting of the vote. In response, many of the Todd supporters, when they presented themselves at the polls, voted "open" tickets, displaying them to public view as they handed them to the election officials. Shober himself "saw twenty-five open ballots cast with the name of the delegate exposed to view; they were cast for J. B. S. Todd." At that point in his testimony, he proceeded to name these men.

One of the most striking aspects of this incident was the size of the community in which it occurred. Only thirty-nine votes were cast in Bon Homme County that day, so few that the witnesses were personally acquainted with all of the voters and had memorized their names before they testified at the contested election hearing. There was thus no doubt that at least twenty-six men had voted for Todd (Shober, for example, had seen twenty-five votes and voted for Todd himself). At most, there could have been only thirteen votes for Jayne in the box.[21] Most of the voting occurred before noon. During the recess for lunch,

Moses Herrick [one of the election officials] [took] with him from the house where the election was held the ballot-box containing the ballots to his [Herrick's] own house. . . . About 1 o'clock the balloting was resumed; about 5 o'clock p.m. the polls were closed, no person being in the room except the judges and clerks of election and G. M. Pinney. The judges proceeded to count the ballots, denying admittance to the electors at the polls. The judges first began the canvass of the votes by taking the tickets from the ballot-box and separating the same into two different piles, the Todd tickets in one pile and the Jayne tickets in the other. The Jayne tickets were distinguishable from the Todd tickets by their blotted surface, the ink showing plainly through the ticket. It became at once apparent that a fraud had been perpetrated, by the substitution of ballots during the hour had for dinner. There were at this time

---

[20]   The Todd man who had been originally appointed as one of the election officials arrived before the polls opened, but G. M. Pinney, the U.S. Marshal for Dakota Territory and the person who owned the house in which the election was held, refused to let him into the house. Pinney himself remained in the house "and was very officious." Ibid., pp. 34–5.

[21]   Shober claimed that two of the Jayne judges had told him that they "were determined to swindle" Todd out of his majority in the county. For that reason, the "electors requested me to stand by the window in front of the judge, and endeavor to have all our friends vote open tickets, and to take down the names of the persons voting, and for whom they voted, which I did. The persons I have enumerated saw the propriety, under these circumstances, of voting open ballots. . . . " Ibid., pp. 34–5, 50.

about twenty-five persons around the polls, and much excitement ensued. As soon as I saw the excitement, I demanded to be admitted, and to have the canvass made public, which was at that time peremptorily refused by the judges, and by Mr. Pinney, who was their spokesman. During this time, Mr. Johnson and myself were standing at the window, directly in front of the judges. Upon this refusal of admission into the room, the excitement still increased. The judges thereupon gathered up the tickets and threw them back into the box. I then again demanded admission. After some hesitation, Pinney suggested that myself and Edward Gifford be admitted; we entered together, and went up to Moses Herrick, one of the judges of election, and asked him to proceed with the canvass, which he refused to do. I then asked him to show me the tickets, whereupon he handed me thirty of the tickets to examine. I looked them over in his presence, and found that I was right in my conclusions. I then asked him to show me the other nine of the tickets, which he refused. I found fifteen tickets among the number handed me, for Jayne. I then laid them down on the table and remarked to Mr. Herrick that there was *prima facie* evidence of fraud; that there had not been fifteen votes cast for Jayne; whereupon the judges and clerks jumped up, under the lead of G. M. Pinney, and left the room, leaving poll books, ballots, and all papers connected with the election, lying on the table.

At that point, the election officials having abandoned the canvass, Shober asked all those who had voted for Todd to step forward. There were still twenty-two Todd voters – twenty-three including Shober – at the polling place. These men proceeded to elect a new set of election judges and cast their ballots for Todd, in effect conducting the poll anew. However, John Hutchinson, secretary of Dakota Territory and a presidential appointee, reported that the returns from Bon Homme County were excluded because there "was evidence that the election . . . was broken up before the judges of the election had completed the count of votes."[22]

In sum, the governor had appointed the election officials in Bon Homme County, the election had been held in the home of a U.S. Marshal (a presidential appointee), and, when the fraud they attempted to perpetrate was foiled, the (albeit irregular) returns were rejected by a territorial canvassing board that the governor controlled. The most interesting thing, perhaps, was the extremely small number of votes that were involved. At most, the Jayne supporters were attempting to record twenty-four votes for the governor, leaving fifteen for Todd. By Shober's count, Jayne could have had, at most, only thirteen votes, leaving twenty-six for Todd. The fraud, if it had cleared the canvass, involved a substitution of only eleven Jayne tickets in place of Todd votes. The underlying factor in all of this was the sparsely populated and unorganized conditions on the far edges of the American frontier; the fraud could have been detected only with a small number of voters, cooperating in the way that settlers often did. These conditions also explain how a U.S. Marshal, acting on his own authority, might exclude a duly appointed election judge; there was simply no countervailing judicial or

[22] Ibid., pp. 20, 35–6.

law enforcement officer within many miles of the polling place.[23] Finally, the belief on the part of the Todd voters that they could somehow spontaneously take over the election proceedings through vigilante action was an attitude far more likely to be widely shared on the frontier than in older and more densely settled regions to the east.

Some of the oldest areas in the West, so old and so thickly settled that they could hardly be called "frontier," were in the Territory of New Mexico. For centuries before the United States had acquired the territory, Spanish-speaking settlers had lived in the region and had created neighborhoods and communities that had many of the norms, customs, and common understandings that typified rural districts in the eastern United States. But they also exhibited some of the practices associated with the frontier, particularly the (perhaps justified) belief that vigilante justice was sometimes the only kind of justice there was. One of these places was a precinct in Rio Arriba County known as Las Truchas, where the election was conducted at the house of Don Juan Pablo Cordova in the lower part of town.[24] At this election, there were two candidates for territorial delegate, J. Francisco Chaves and Charles Clever. When the polls closed in the early afternoon, the judges counted the ballots and found 84 votes for Chaves and 59 for Clever. This result would probably have been accepted by the men attending the polls if not for the fact that there had only been 133 voters at this precinct; there were thus ten more votes than voters.

The spectators who were monitoring the count immediately noticed the discrepancy and began to speculate on how it might have occurred. The most likely possibility, of course, was that someone had stuffed the ballot box. Since the tickets had been numbered so that the names in the poll book could be matched up with them, several of the bystanders proposed that all the tickets be emptied out onto a table so that those without numbers could be identified and, presumably, removed from the count.[25] The election judges, however, refused to inspect the tickets in this way because, as they later said, the crowd was becoming increasingly excited and they feared that the people would destroy the poll books and the tickets. In the process, as one man put it, "lives might be lost."

Instead the judges proposed to replace all the tickets in the ballot box and nail it shut. With the ballots thus protected, they would then notify the probate judge of the discrepancy and allow him to examine the tickets. As the members of the crowd became more and more agitated, the box was nailed shut and given to Miguel Ulibarri, one of the judges. With the crowd

---

23   For another instance in which U.S. Marshals intervened in the voting, see S.R. no. 1350: M.D. no. 154 (1867): pp. 107–8. However, this was in Santa Fe, one of the leading cities in the West.

24   The following account is based on testimony in ibid., pp. 45, 47–8, 112–15.

25   The tickets were also numbered at another precinct, Tierra Amarilla in Rio Arriba County. Ibid., p. 41.

(now turning into a mob) in pursuit, he took the box to his house. After leaving the box in his house, Ulibarri apparently met with the other judges at a private home where they had been invited to "take a drink." The mob came into the home, chased the judges into the street, and threatened Ulibarri with a pistol. When the judge refused to turn over the ballot box and poll books, a Chaves supporter, Julian Duran, moved toward the house where they were kept, pulling out a pistol and pointing it squarely at Ulibarri's chest. One of the other men in the crowd caught Duran's arm, however, and the bullet missed Ulibarri. Although only one other shot was fired, a general riot "of stoning and clubbing" now erupted in the street and continued until sundown.

In the meantime, someone went to Ulibarri's house and told his wife he had been killed. She immediately went in search of him, leaving the door to the house open. While she was out (the story was apparently told to her only to get her out of the house), the ballot box was stolen. The witnesses never explained why the crowd had so strongly demanded an immediate accounting for the discrepancy between the poll books and vote count. It may have been the case that supporters of each candidate suspected the others of having stuffed the box. That would, for example, explain the apparent universal demand for an immediate and public accounting. The judges, for their part, might have been conscientiously protecting the integrity of the election as best they could. Ulibarri's decision to leave the ballot box in the custody of his wife, after he had publicly announced where it would be kept, suggests that he believed that no one in the community would violate the sanctity of his home. Whoever took the box, after presumably examining its contents and the implications for the candidate they favored, concluded that destroying the evidence was the best course of action. Since Chaves was well ahead in the count, acknowledging a ten-vote fraud by his supporters would still have been better than destroying the tickets. This suggests, along with Duran's violent demands for a public accounting, that supporters of the other candidate, Charles Clever, had taken the box and destroyed it, thereby eliminating at least a fifteen-vote Chaves margin at that precinct (if the fraud had been perpetrated by Chaves supporters) or thirty-five-vote edge (if the fraud had been staged by Clever partisans).

In the end, without a ballot box or poll books to evidence that an election had been held, no votes were ever officially received from Las Truchas.

Residency on the Frontier

Determining whether voters actually resided in the neighborhood of the most isolated polling places was difficult.[26] Most information came from those

---

[26] Mark Summers recites an instance in which a Mr. Purple became a member of the Nebraska territorial legislature by arranging for his own election from Burt County,

who regularly or irregularly traveled the main trails or, if they existed, roads. For example, Robert Kittle, who had recently transported "a load of corn and goods" to the Pawnee Indian Reservation, was asked whether Izard was "wholly an uninhabited county." Although Izard was a little to the north of what was probably his route to the reservation, he answered as best he could, "So far as my knowledge extends regarding that subject, it is so; and I never saw a settler of Izard county going to or returning from that county, or heard of one, and Fremont [where Kittle lived] would be a natural road for them to come and go." John M. Thayer, a farmer in Omaha who had actually passed through Izard in July 1859, similarly reported that the county "was a prairie country. I saw no sign of habitation through the whole extent of it. . . . I met with no person whatever."[27]

The most sparsely populated districts sometimes reported returns from precincts that, on later inspection, simply could not be found. Eliphus Rogers, a lawyer and farmer, investigated one such precinct, allegedly located in Calhoun County across the river from his home in Fremont. The official returns from this precinct had given twenty-eight votes to Estabrook, the Democratic candidate, and four votes to Daily, the Republican. Rogers first consulted the poll book from the county that, because Calhoun was unorganized, was in the possession of the Platte County clerk.[28] The poll book recorded that an election had been held at "the house of James L. Smith, in Calhoun precinct, Calhoun county; that William P. Glover, Mather F. Brown, and Eldred Scott were judges of said election, and Ralph Hawley and J. Ross were clerks." Rogers went searching for this precinct:

I crossed the Platte river at what is known as Shinn's ferry; proceeded down the old Indian trail towards Calhoun county; found the two voters [alluded to in previous testimony] about noon [they knew nothing about any election being held in the county]; traveled until night without finding any settlements. At night I came to a place of a former settlement, called Powhoco, and remained there during the night

> which, at the time, was almost entirely uninhabited. In Purple's words: "I harnessed up and took nine fellows with me, and we started for the woods, and when we thought we had got about far enough for Burt County, we unpacked our ballot box and held an election, canvassed the vote, and it was astonishing to observe how great was the unanimity at the first election ever held in Burt County. *Purple* had every vote! So Purple was duly elected, and here I am!" *The Plundering Generation*, p. 15.

[27] S.R. no. 1064: M.D. no. 12 (1859): pp. 11–12, 15–16. Although the 1860 census later reported no inhabitants in Izard County and although most testimony in the hearings indicated that no one lived there, the official returns gave the vote as 4 (Estabrook) to 3 (Daily) in Hammond Precinct and 17 (Estabrook) to 0 (Daily) in Beaver Creek Precinct. These returns were signed by John S. Willis, "clerk of the county of Izard" (an office that did not exist because the county was still unorganized) and John G. Valentine and Franklin Holt, "disinterested holders" (pp. 88–9).

[28] Because Izard and Calhoun Counties lacked organized administrations at the time of the election, the Platte County clerk was responsible for keeping their poll books and reporting their returns to the state. Ibid., p. 52. For the Calhoun County election results, see p. 88.

in a deserted house. There were several small houses about there without roof, floor, windows, or doors. Soon after daylight next morning I started again, and traveled till about three o'clock before finding any settlers or evidences of settlement....

At about that time, Rogers came upon a homestead comprised of "stables, a pigsty, hay and grain stacks.... The house was built of logs, about 4 by 18, I should think, all in one room.... I saw four or five children and a man who appeared to be a hired man." Rogers spent "an hour or two in conversation" with the "gentleman" who owned this small farm "with reference to the settlement which had been made at Powhoco and abandoned, and with reference to the number of people in Calhoun county." The gist of this conversation was that only seven adult men of voting age lived in the county: the first two Rogers had found on the "old Indian trail" and five who lived in the immediate vicinity of this man's home. None of them had heard of any election held in the county.

Evidently anticipating that someone might think that Powhoco might have been the missing Calhoun precinct, Rogers was asked "whether the vacant houses of which you speak at Powhoco had any appearance of having been recently occupied." He responded, "None had any such appearance except the one in which I stayed, which one had the appearance of having been recently occupied by campers." The Calhoun precinct, as far as he could determine, did not and had not ever existed.[29]

Phantom returns were evidently not rare in this Nebraska election. In investigating them, the general method was to begin, as Rogers had done, with physical inspection of the poll books in which the names of voters were recorded and the precinct was identified. Although difficult to detect in frontier districts, election fraud was still a crime. Legal liability compounded what were already the substantial political and material stakes embedded in the election outcomes. While Rogers had carried out a routine, although frustrating, investigation, not all queries were so uneventful. For example, James Coit quickly ran into trouble when he traveled to Niobrarah in order to inspect the poll books for L'Eau Qui Court county. Experience Estabrook had received all 121 votes cast in the Niobrarah Precinct, a return surprising both for its unanimity and number of voters. In his testimony, Coit provided

---

[29] Ibid., pp. 22–3. Later in the same hearing, James L. Hindman, who resided in Shinn's Ferry where Rogers had crossed the Platte, stated, "I believe that I am acquainted with all the settlers in [Calhoun County]. There is one settlement of two families in the northwestern part. There is another settlement, known as the Qauhoo, in the southeast part of the county; there are four families there. These are all the settlements.... There are but two voters in the northwest settlement, named Solomon Garfield and James Blair. In the Wauhoo settlement there are three voters, named Stambaugh, Totten, and John Auhey; besides a young man named Price, who, if twenty-one years of age, is also a voter" (pp. 75–6). Sometime after Rogers had examined the Calhoun County returns, the Platte County clerk reported that they had been stolen from his office (p. 80).

a particularly vivid description of Niobrarah that suggested why the number of voters reported in the return might have been suspect. To him, Niobrarah

appeared to be scarcely more than an Indian trading post. It contained a tavern, two or three vacant frame buildings, one of which was called Major Gregory's store-house, Major Gregory's office, the store which I have described, about four log-houses, one of them called the "dance house," and a building that appeared to be a broken down mill, and a blacksmith's shop near by. On the bluffs back of the place there was a building, and one just under the bluffs, which I understood were occupied by one West and one Starr.

Coit described the surrounding area, which otherwise could have provided the missing voters, as singularly uninhabited, with one exception:

[F]our miles this side of Niobrarah there is a very comfortable farm-house, with out-houses, fencing, and other improvements, occupied by Mr. D. B. Dodson and family. . . . Between that and the town of Niobrarah I do not remember any other improvements or habitations. Between Frankfort, which is the last place this side of Niobrarah on my way up, and Niobrarah, I passed only one dwelling house, occupied by a person named G. Collins. Back of Niobrarah, except in the valley of the Running Water, I saw no country that appeared suitable for agricultural purposes. Up the Running Water valley, about four miles, there was a vacant cabin.

When he first arrived in Niobrarah, he and William James, his traveling companion, stopped in

for a few moments at the tavern. . . . We [then] went to a small one-story frame building designated there as "the store." . . . The building was . . . divided into two rooms by a thin canvas partition. The room we first entered, fronting on the road, was occupied by a Mr. Westermond as an Indian trading store; the back room was used as a cooking and sleeping room, and contained the post office, the probate judge's office, and the county clerk's office. Robert M. Hagaman [who was at the store] being the county clerk and the postmaster, and [the witness] having a letter of introduction to Mr. Hagaman, went there to deliver it and to obtain from him, as the county clerk, a certified copy of the poll books of that precinct election. The two rooms I have just referred to are about the same size, each being about thirteen feet square.

Thus, Hagaman presided over a kitchen, a bed, the post office, the probate judge's office, and the county clerk's office, all of them located in a back room separated only by a sheet of canvas from a general store. After making the purpose of his visit clear, Coit and his traveling companion, along with the county clerk, then returned to the tavern in what was still early in the morning. Saying that he doubted whether he had the authority to comply with their request, Hagaman initially refused to provide a copy of the poll book. However, he relented after James offered to show him a copy of the statute requiring that poll books be open to public inspection and agreement was reached on the appropriate fees. The clerk read off the names in the poll book and Coit wrote them down. After comparing Coit's list with the original, Hagaman certified it as a true copy. So far things had gone smoothly, but they were soon to go very badly awry:

While looking about the place [and returning to the tavern for yet a third time]...while out of sight of our horse and buggy, which was hitched behind the office of one Major Gregory [federal agent for the Ponca Indians], our horse was removed from our buggy and secreted without our knowledge, and we were unable to find it.

After searching for the horse all day, James discovered that it was in Major Gregory's stable. Gregory admitted

that the horse was in his stable, but that Jimmy had the key, and that I could not get him unless I could find Jimmy. We found Jimmy in the evening and told him we wanted our horse. He replied that he would have to get a lantern; and I went with him to Major Gregory's office for that purpose. Major Gregory told him that his lantern was out of repair, and that he would have to get Westamond's. Jimmy told me to remain, and said that he would be back in a moment, and that was the last I saw of Jimmy.

Thus stranded in Niobrarah, the two men "were obliged to remain at the tavern over night." The tavern was evidently located in the lower part of the hotel, which occupied most of the large three-story frame building, "unfinished in the inside, not plastered...occupied by a widow woman who makes use of but a small portion of the house." The next morning they

resumed the search for our horse, and discovered that two wheels of our buggy had been removed. We spent the day in searching for the wheels and horse, endeavoring to get possession of them that we might return home, but without success. We had thus far been detained two days and one night. On the evening of the second day, at an early hour, several persons came to the tavern, of whom I remember one called Frank West and one called John H. Starr; they [West and Starr] asked Mr. James to see the copy of the poll-books, which they understood we had in our possession, stating, as a reason, that they were informed their names were on the list as having voted at the election, and that as they did not vote they would like to see if it was so. We thereupon produced the list, and they endeavored to snatch the same while I was reading the names, in which they did not succeed.

As James recalled, West "then swore that I never should leave the county with that list; at that time he had hold of me by the collar." Coit's account resumes:

After some boisterous conduct towards us, they left the tavern and went towards the store, threatening before they left that they would have the copy of the poll-lists which we had. Mr. James and myself, immediately after they left, held a consultation as to what we had better do under the circumstances, and it was concluded that one of us had better escape from the place immediately with our copy of the poll-books, while the other should remain at the tavern to look after our horse and buggy wheels which had been secreted.

James accordingly slipped out a side door to the hotel and set off on foot for Dodson's farmhouse (where they had spent the night before arriving in Niobrarah) and Coit retired:

I had been in bed over an hour, when I was aroused by noises outside of the tavern by persons demanding entrance into the tavern. They gained admittance, and were soon at my chamber door, calling for me to open the door and let them in, stating, in answer to my inquiry what they wanted, that they desired instant admission, and unless I opened the door they would burst it open. I told them that if they were after my copy of the poll-lists that I had not got it, that I would let them in as soon as I was dressed, which I did. They examined my clothing and the bed-clothing, and they, the sheriff of the county, whose name I do not at present remember, and the Hon. Judge James Tuffts, sitting democratic member of the legislature of Nebraska, requested me to go with them, and the other persons who were with them, about a dozen in number, and around, followed after us through the tavern, down stairs and out of doors. A few steps from the tavern the sheriff, who appeared to be spokesman for the gang, desired me to give them up immediately the copy of the poll-lists. I told them I had not got it, and that if I had, as I became legally possessed of it, I would not give it to them. The sheriff stated that they had come after it and would have it, peaceably if they could, forcibly if necessary. . . .

Niobrarah's leading citizens made the obvious deduction:

The gang, appearing satisfied that I had not the poll-lists, started in the direction of Mr. Dodson's, exclaiming "James has them!" "James has them!" About three hours afterward the gang came back to the tavern and to my chamber, and informed me that . . . the county was safe.

In the meantime, the posse had overtaken James and retrieved the copy of the poll book. As James recalled, he had started for Dodson's house

about 10 o'clock in the evening. Soon after arriving at Dodson's I went to bed. About half past one or two o'clock I was waked up by Mr. Dodson, who made the remark that those fellows were after me. At the time I awoke I could see a number of men at either of the two windows of my room, who immediately afterwards came in. James Tuffts [the member of the legislature from the district composed of the counties of Cedar, Dixon, and L'Eau Qui Court], who was one of the number who came into the room, said that they had come after a copy of the poll-list. Mr. Dodson advised them to let me alone. Tuffts replied that they "had walked four miles for that poll-list, and, by God, we were going to have it." I told Mr. Dodson that I was his guest, and wished to involve him and his family in no difficulty, but told him that I should like very much to keep the copy of the poll-list, but if he desired it that I would give it up. He said he thought I had better let them have it. I thereupon got off of my coat, which I was sitting upon at the time, and told them they could take it. They took the copy of the poll-list from my coat and immediately burned it up. Either Mr. Tuffts or Mr. Callahan, the sheriff of that county, said that the citizens of the Niobrarah precinct were all implicated in the frauds perpetrated at the last election, and that they were all alike interested in suppressing the evidences of the fraud. They said at the same time that they had no ill-will towards me, and that if I would drop the matter and say no more about it, that any thing that I might ask at the hands of the citizens of Niobrarah would be granted, and that if ever I was again a candidate for office that they would give me as many votes as were necessary to secure my election. At this time some one said they would give me six hundred if necessary.

Coit testified that the "next morning I found the wheels replaced on my buggy, and was told where to find my horse, and I immediately started for Mr. Dodson's." First, though, Coit attempted to get a second copy of the poll books from Hagaman, but the clerk "informed me they had been stolen, and he could get no clue to their whereabouts."[30]

Although there is much evidence of fraud on the Democratic side in this territorial election, the sparse settlement and changing nature of the frontier made estimations of "reasonable" voter turnout very difficult. For example, the absence of social landmarks, in the form of farmhouses, small settlements, and roads, often made it impossible for witnesses to state conclusively that they knew when they had crossed from one county into another (and there-fore knew how to identify the residents within them). This made fraud almost undetectable since no one could say that he had visited all the neighborhoods within a particular county. What was impossible for those traveling through these districts would have been equally impossible for judges of election; de-termining who among the men arriving at the polls was, in fact, a legitimate resident of the county often must have involved a leap of faith on the part of election officials, challengers, and even the voters themselves. Of course, the fraud at Niobrarah, had there been anyone who cared, would have been transparent; it was one thing to be unable to tell whether someone was an eligible resident, it was another thing entirely when the ostensible voters did not exist at all.

One of the most remote and desolate election districts in the United States had to be precinct No. 11 (otherwise named La Junta) in Mora County, New Mexico.[31] While the polling place was apparently chosen because it marked the geographical center of the precinct, no one lived within two and a half miles. The site itself contained no buildings, and in order to hold the election, a shed was built. Composed of four wooden posts with roof beams covered by timber and brush, this shed was otherwise open to the elements on all four sides. Several hours before the voting began, the election judges attached a tent that seemed to be open as well, directly exposing the judges to the crowd that gathered around the polls. The fact that the site was waterless might have partially explained the heavy consumption of liquor, although one witness stated there was "not as much [drinking] as usual on such occasions." Whatever might have been usual, there were, according to one of the election judges, "three demijohns of whiskey" under

[30] Ibid., pp. 27–30, 34–7.
[31] The following account draws upon testimony in S.R. no. 1350: M.D. no. 154 (1867): 68–73, 76–7, 101–3.

the table supporting the ballot box. This whisky was "freely" distributed by the Republican ticket distributor in an attempt to attract men to this isolated polling place. As the judge recalled, it "was understood generally [throughout the precinct] that Clever whiskey was at the polls" for those who voted the Republican ticket.

After the election opened, everything went smoothly for about three hours. Afterward, the polling place became fairly boisterous with many "quarrels and disputes," at least some of which were unrelated to the election. Of those disputes that were political, most were instigated by supporters of Charles Clever, the Republican candidate for territorial delegate. Between twenty to thirty of his partisans gathered at the polls during the day. Some of these men were hands employed by a rancher named William Kronig, an important Republican figure in the county; others came by mule wagon and horseback from Fort Union, a federal military post about five miles away. In addition, two wagon trains that happened to be passing through the area stopped about a third of a mile from the polls. Attracted to the polls by the free whisky, self-described "Kansas Boys" from the wagon trains intimidated Chaves supporters by saying that they "would whip . . . or punish them" if they tried to cast their votes. In one instance, a particularly assertive Democrat yelled out, "Hurrah for Chaves." The "Kansas boys" replied that anyone who backed Chaves was a "son of a bitch" and knocked him to the ground. Standing over him with their pistols drawn, the "Kansas boys" dared anyone to go near him (this was about ten "paces" from the polls, perhaps twenty feet). Finally, G. W. Gregg, justice of the peace for the La Junta Precinct, intervened and they freed their captive.

Trinidad Lopez, a challenger working for J. Francisco Chaves, reported that he was threatened by "Americans not known to me" because he objected to some of the Republican voters. Some of these non-Hispanic Republicans menaced him with a "mule whip." From the very first, most Chaves men were afraid to cast their tickets. As more and more men became intoxicated, Lopez himself feared for his safety and left the polls in the early afternoon.

While much of the rhetoric at this polling place seems to have indicated a rather strong ethnic division (between Hispanic Democrats and Anglo Republicans) over a hotly contested delegate seat, Lopez reported that he was personally far more interested in the county races being decided that day. In fact, Lopez had cut a deal with the Republican agent, John Mink, the bookkeeper on Kronig's ranch.[32] Lopez asked Mink to cut off the bottom of the Republican ticket (that part containing the county officers), promising if he did so that he (Lopez) would not challenge the vote of the man who cast the truncated ticket. Since there were apparently many illegal Republican

---

[32]   In addition to the Republican challenger, all of the judges of election and the election clerks both belonged to the Republican party and worked for Kronig. The one exception might have been Walter Fosdyke, whose experiences are related here.

voters at this precinct and Lopez had little hope of preventing them from casting tickets, the Democrat was in effect selling Chaves out, at least at this polling place, in return for a more or less honest count in the local races. When Mink agreed to the arrangement, he, in turn, indicated that he was more interested in the delegate race than in the local contests.

Mink, however, became "much intoxicated" by consuming some of the whisky he was offering to Republican voters. He then made several rather blatant attempts "to stuff ballots into the ballot-box," but on each occasion, Walter Fosdyke, one of the judges, "prevented him [and] ordered him to stand off." Whether Mink was in any condition to negotiate and to implement the arrangement that Lopez described is thus an open question.

In his testimony, Fosdyke described five or six wagonloads of men who came to the polls from Fort Union. These men appear to have been civilians employed at the fort by the quartermaster, and it was the quartermaster who provided the government wagons, teamsters, and mules that brought them to the polls. In the judge's own words:

Each wagon-load of men was brought up to the polls by the wagon-master, and these wagon-masters, in several instances, made threats if any of their men were challenged. One of these men in particular, when I challenged his men, asked: "Who is the son of a bitch that challenged my men's votes?" I deemed it my duty, as an officer of the election, to challenge such persons presenting themselves to vote as in appearance were too young. Others, who appeared to have the requisite years, I did not challenge, because I saw that the disposition on the part of the Clever men, who were in almost a unanimous majority, was to carry everything before them; and, although a supporter of Mr. Clever myself, I desired that the election should be honestly conducted, if possible; but I had no power to prevent the general course that affairs took. The principal part of the men who came down from the quartermaster's department were armed with pistols, and were capable of enforcing all demands.

Fosdyke believed most of the men from the fort to be underage and nonresidents, but since "they took the oath indiscriminately, and altogether without compunction," there was little he could do to prevent them from voting. He also described them as drunk and "very riotously" behaved. Mink asked them all, along with other men about the polls, to have more whisky.[33]

---

[33] Fosdyke was a Republican who, if he had been primarily motivated by partisan feeling, would probably have minimized the inebriated condition of the Republican challenger and the number of fraudulent votes cast for his party. Thus his account is more trustworthy than most accounts. However, he had no respect for his fellow Republican judges: "I do not regard them as intelligent; I do not think either can read or write, nor do I think they understood the principles upon which elections should be governed, judging from their conduct on the day of election, as no efforts were made by them to aid me in preventing illegal voting." He asserted that a hundred or so names had been added to the poll book and a corresponding number of Republican tickets stuffed in the ballot box after the votes had been counted. He also charged that the other judges, when they testified in the hearing, had committed perjury. Ibid., pp. 102–3.

It is likely that more than half of the votes tallied at the La Junta polling place were illegally cast (if this is a verb we can use for drunken men turning in tickets for a swig of whisky). But what is even more interesting is the structure of the polling place, with very large whisky bottles (almost the size of beer kegs) kept under the ballot box in an open air shed. The four identifiable groups of men at these polls probably did not know each other very well, if at all. It is likely, for example, that the "Kansas boys" did not recognize the quartermaster workers from the fort, Kronig's ranch hands, or the Chaves men. Although the quartermaster workers had a slightly greater chance of knowing the ranch hands or Chaves voters, they were probably both nonresidents and fairly isolated on the military reservation containing the fort. Although we do not know how big Kronig's ranch might have been, it does appear to have been a sizable operation and thus could have constituted a community almost as isolated as the fort. These groups all came together out in the middle, both literally and figuratively, of nowhere. In a sense they were all strangers to one another bound together only by drunken electoral rites "on the prairie." This was one of the ways in which frontier democracy played out in the mid-nineteenth century.

Establishing a County Seat

But it was particularly in sparsely settled regions that the political stakes, relative to the number of participants, could be very, very high. For example, in 1862, the citizens of a proposed Cole County in Dakota Territory were called on to decide the location of the new county seat. The stakes were high because the land around the new county seat would immediately become much more valuable when carved up into town lots. Those who held this land would thus profit from their victory, while the losers might find themselves occupying a ghost town. Three precincts had been established in the, at the time, unorganized county. Two were located at the competing alternatives for the county seat, Brule Creek and Elk Point. The third was at Big Sioux Point.

The electorate to be polled in this vote was very small. For instance, N. J. Wallace, an Elk Point resident who took a strong interest in the election, estimated that only twenty-six men could legally vote in the Brule Creek settlement. To this number he added ten soldiers who had resided in Brule Creek when they enlisted (thus making them legal voters) and the judge of election who hailed from Elk Point but could vote at Brule Creek. All told, there were no more thirty-seven men who could legally vote at Brule Creek; however, seventy-two votes had been returned.[34]

---

[34] In addition to deciding the location of the county seat, this election also presented candidates for the offices of territorial delegate, the territorial legislature, and county offices. S.R. no. 1199: M.D. no. 27 (1862): pp. 83–4.

Timothy Andrews, in whose house the election had been held at Brule Creek, had a ready explanation for the discrepancy between the number of eligible electors and the number of votes actually cast. He reported that men had voted at his house between midnight and dawn of the day of the election:

Candles were burning upon the table, where the voting was being done. . . . I was not [present]. I was, at the commencement, up stairs, in bed; heard a noise below stairs, and went down to see what it was about; found a number of persons in the room; saw three men sitting at a table, with a ballot-box in front of them. One man was writing. Dr. A. R. Phillips and Thaddeus Andrews, my son, were two of the persons seated at the table. They were acting as judges of the election then going on. Mr. Gore handed me a ticket as soon as I got into the room. I took the ticket, which was a Jayne ticket, handed it to Dr. Phillips, the judge, who put it in the box. Immediately after this, Mr. Gore stepped up to Dr. Phillips and said he voted this ticket (which he handed to Dr. Phillips) for another man, whose name he mentioned, but [I] don't remember it. He observed that the man was absent from the Territory, and he would vote for him. Dr. Phillips then placed the vote in the box.[35]

Among other things, Timothy Andrews was implicating his own son, who had served as one of the judges of election, in vote fraud.[36]

Corroborating this description of midnight voting in the Andrews home, Horatio Geddes, a carpenter, reported that these illegal proceedings allowed men who could not meet the residency requirement to vote; they would have been challenged during regular voting hours. However, he also reported one man who voted three times, twice under assumed names. Each of the tickets cast in the Andrews home "named Jayne for delegate to Congress, along with other candidates for other offices. The ticket also named Brule Creek for the county seat of Cole county."[37] Given that Governor Jayne had visited the settlement just prior to the election and that he would have influence over the canvassing of votes by the territorial election board, it appears likely that there was at least an implicit arrangement by which both his interests and the interests of Brule Creek residents had been joined.

When the polls formally opened at eight o'clock in the morning, Edward Lamoure, who served as clerk of election, was unaware that the ballot box had been stuffed. But he was suspicious:

I do not know positively [whether there already were tickets in the box when voting began], as the box was not opened, but my opinion was, when I picked the box up, that it was full of tickets. I noticed, after three or four ballots had been cast, they had to crowd them in, and shake the box to make room for any more. This was the first

---

35 Although Andrews had not been in the territory the required ninety days and was thus ineligible to vote, he cast a ticket on the advice of Governor William Jayne and Mr. Glaze, who had visited his house eight or ten days before the election. As Andrews put it, "upon his [the governor's] authority I did vote." Ibid., p. 84.

36 When Thaddeus Andrews later testified, he refused to answer the most incriminating questions posed to him. Ibid., pp. 109–10.

37 Ibid., pp. 90–1. Other witnesses gave similar accounts of the voting (pp. 92–7, 100–6).

[thing] that aroused my suspicion of fraud, as the box was sufficiently large to hold all the votes in the county. I should judge the box to be about six inches high, about eight inches wide, and twelve inches long.

At 1:30 in the afternoon, the three judges of election, one of whom was Thaddeus Andrews, asked Lamoure to enter into the poll book the names of men appearing on a list they handed him. As Lamoure put it, these were "persons that did not vote, but whose names they had on a piece of paper.... [The judges] told me that it was about time to put down the names they had got." As Lamoure later surmised, these names, when entered into the poll book, would legitimate the tickets that "were in the box before the opening of the polls." The clerk adamantly refused, telling one of the judges "most emphatically that I would not record the names of any voters who did not vote through the window, for this reason: if I was one of the canvassers of the county I would throw out every vote that did not come through the window." At that point, Lamoure resigned as clerk, refusing to participate any further in the election at Brule Creek.[38]

The Territory of Utah

In addition to polling places in anomic, sparsely populated regions and in settlements dominated by military forts and Indian reservations, frontier precincts also appeared in closed, isolated communities removed from the national mainstream. Precisely because the vast open spaces of the frontier protected deviant communities from outside interference, the West attracted ethnic and religious groups who wanted to live apart from other Americans. The largest of these communities settled what first became the territory and then the state of Utah. Because the Mormon Church, with the active consent of its members, utterly controlled territorial politics, Utah was in most respects a theocracy.

Mormon influence restructured the act of voting, turning an election into something almost surreal from the perspective of both modern and contemporary observers. One of the best accounts describes voting during the 1867

---

[38] Ibid., p. 87. Given the clandestine nature of the proceedings the previous evening, it was perhaps no surprise that the number of tickets exceeded the number of names in the poll book, even after the names in the book had been padded. After the polls formally closed, there were seventy-eight tickets in the ballot box and only seventy-two names in the poll book. In accordance with almost universal practice throughout the nation, the excess number of tickets were to be destroyed. However, while these tickets should have been chosen randomly, Thaddeus Andrews "commenced taking out of the ballot-box, which was open before him, the ballots, and destroyed six of them. While he was tearing up one ballot he was looking into the open box, where the ballots were in full view, before he drew out another ballot, and so until he had destroyed the said six ballots" (p. 108; also see pp. 108–9). The fraudulent return from the Brule Creek precinct appears on p. 107.

election for territorial delegate.[39] The Mormon candidate, William Hooper, received 15,068 votes in that election. The votes for his Gentile opponent, William McGrorty, totaled 105. Despite the huge disparity, McGrorty contested the election and hearings were held. One of the first of those to testify was Daniel McLaughlin, a native of New York temporarily living in "the city of Great Salt Lake." On February 4, the day of the election, McLaughlin visited the polls at the city hall, where he saw Bishop Wooley, a member of the Mormon heirarchy, acting as a judge of election. The polling place was set up very differently from the normal pattern in that Bishop Wooley sat behind the ballot box, which was placed on a table between him and men who wished to vote (at most polling places in the United States judges stood between the voter and the ballot box, in effect protecting it from the voters).

But the most interesting aspect of the election was the very different way in which tickets were accepted. If a man wished to vote for McGrorty, the Gentile candidate, he handed his ticket to Bishop Wooley, who then placed it in the ballot box. This conformed with normal practice throughout the United States. However, if a man wished to vote for Hooper, the Mormon candidate, he simply gave his name to the clerk who wrote it down in the poll book. Bishop Wooley would then pick up a Hooper ticket from a loose pile scattered on the table between him and the ballot box, write a number corresponding to the poll book entry, and deposit the ticket. Because Wooley in effect served both as election judge and ticket distributor for the Mormon-endorsed slate, the voter never touched his ticket. In addition to these secular roles, of course, Wooley also represented religious authority as embodied in the Mormon Church. Although McLaughlin spent a long time at the polls, he saw only three men, all of them Gentile voters, turn in tickets to Wooley. All the rest simply presented themselves to the bishop and his clerk. As McLaughlin put it:

The Mormon voters appeared to exercise none of the privileges of the elective franchise, except to make their appearance at the place of voting, pronounce their names, and then retire. They gave no ballots to the judge of election, nor signified any preference by voice for any candidate. The bishop did all the voting, so far as I saw....

Charles Biden, a Gentile originally from New York but now living in Salt Lake City, corroborated McLaughlin's description of the voting in most details. Biden added only that Bishop Wooley appeared to hold the Hooper tickets in his hands until he had seven or eight of them (apparently because he did not think it necessary to get up from his chair and immediately deposit each ticket as men voted). In some instances, men had thus left the polling

---

[39] The following is based on testimony in S.R. no. 1349: Contested Delegate Election in the Territory of Utah: M.D. no. 35, pp. 4, 10, 12, 14, 18–20. William McGrorty vs. William H. Hooper, election held on February 4, 1867.

place before "their" ticket had been deposited.[40] Biden also thought that many of the voters "appeared and spoke as foreigners," noting that they "were chiefly Scandinavians in appearance." Not surprisingly, perhaps, no voter was challenged at this voting place, and, in Biden's words, "[e]verybody voted that wanted to – that is, Bishop Wooley voted for them."[41]

Bishop Wooley did make one mistake, however, that revealed some of the assumptions on which he had organized the voting process. When Ederder Lewskey, a Gentile originally from New Orleans, gave his name to the clerk, Wooley immediately picked up a Hooper ticket and put it in the ballot box, apparently and incorrectly assuming that Lewskey was a member of the church. Lewskey protested and insisted that Wooley take his McGrorty ticket and deposit it in place of the Hooper ticket. Wooley, somewhat disingenuously, told Lewskey that he had already voted (note that Lewskey had said or done nothing that indicated he wanted to vote for Hooper). When Lewskey insisted that he be allowed to vote for McGrorty, Wooley took his ticket, opened and examined it, and told Lewskey that "such votes did not go at that table." Since Wooley could not have been afraid that McGrorty might win this election, his refusal to correct his mistake may have come from an unwillingness to open up the ballot box.

In any event, when a Mormon voter appeared and gave his name, the bishop told him that his vote was already in the box. That vote was apparently Lewskey's. If so, the bishop could now take Lewskey's ticket and deposit it in place of this Mormon voter without impairing the count. But the numbering still would have been incorrect (Lewskey had been assigned the number 111 and the ticket in the box with that number would have been for Hooper). So Lewskey continued to insist that Wooley take out the Hooper ticket with that number and replace it with his McGrorty ticket. As they continued to argue, more Mormon men appeared and gave their names to the clerk, and Wooley deposited tickets without asking for whom they wished to vote. Finally, Wooley consented to open the box and make the required substitution. From the way this all transpired, Wooley was probably very surprised to find someone who would so stubbornly refuse to recognize his authority to conduct the election in precisely the way he wanted to.

Probably because few Gentiles lived outside Salt Lake City, there were few reports of voting practices in the rest of the territory. One of these reports

---

[40] Although striving to be obedient, this process must still have seemed mysterious to first-time voters. George Miles, a Gentile originally from Ohio, thought he spotted "a boy not more than sixteen years of age walk up to the polls, give in his name, when the judge took up a ballot with Hooper's name on it and voted it. The boy then inquired if that was all they wanted of him, and the judge answered, yes." Ibid., p. 14.

[41] Both of these accounts were further corroborated by Captain James W. Stillman, an officer in a California volunteer infantry regiment and a native of South Carolina who had been living in Utah for four and a half years. Ibid., p. 13. For similar testimony, see pp. 16–18.

was given by John M. Smith, originally of Massachusetts, who happened to be in Coalville, Summit County. When the judge there asked him to vote, Smith said he was not a qualified voter at that polling place. The judge replied that that would not matter unless he were challenged. Although Smith still did not vote, he did stay and watch the election for a bit:

I saw quite a large number of votes polled – that is, if it can be called voting. Voters would come up to the polls, and be saluted by the judge or clerk with "Brother so-and-so, are you going to vote?" If answered in the affirmative, the clerk wrote out a ticket, gave it to the judge, who put it in the ballot-box. Numbers gave in the names of their friends up in the can[y]ons, or coal-pits, which were taken down by the clerk, and ballots cast for them by the judge. . . . The mode of voting appeared to be this: the voter gave his name, then walked off; the clerk wrote a ticket, gave it to the judge, and he voted it. This is the way I saw them do it at Coalville. The voting by proxy for those in the can[y]ons and coal-pits, and for those absent, seemed to be all right, and in accordance with their mode of voting. I expressed my surprise to the judge at the manner they conducted the election, and said I considered it a one-sided affair. He said "that was the way they done business; they only had a one-sided affair."

Proxy voting, in particular, appears to have been quite common and carried out with the consent of those absent from the polls. For example, James Jack, a Scot now living in Salt Lake City, asked some of his fellow countrymen where they had been on election day. They replied that they had been miles away, up in the canyons "after wood, or working in them. They said it [proxy voting] was all right, that their bishops had their names and voted for them, of course." When Jack asked them to file affidavits swearing that they had never been to the polls, they replied that "they would not consider their lives safe twenty-four hours" if they were to do so. "They stand in daily dread of the church leaders, obey their behest promptly, and ask no questions, and think to incur church displeasure is equivalent to losing their heads." But this high degree of social conformity might have originated in religious devotion, as opposed to individual intimidation. Either way, the church commanded obedience, selecting candidates for political office and then overseeing their election in a process that would have been the envy of many a totalitarian regime, let alone a highly organized American party. Nowhere in the nation was a man's vote as closely monitored as it was in Utah where Mormon bishops handled and marked the tickets for church members, all the while closely and apparently silently examining the men who approached the polls.[42] As William Rupp, a Gentile originally from Pennsylvania put it, "The unanimity with which the Mormon voters came up to the polls, gave their names, and then went away leaving the judges to cast ballots for them, without the voter seeing the name on the ticket, and

[42] According to the testimony, Mormon bishops acted as judges of election in American Fork, Battle Creek, Lehi, Provo City, Springville, Spanish Fork, Payson, and Summit, as well as precincts in Coalville and Salt Lake City.

in very many cases, without seeing the ballot cast, led me to believe that this was the Mormon mode of voting."[43]

CONCLUSION

As a sociological environment for the American polling place, the western frontier was incredibly diverse. Although polling places were usually small, a characteristic that in rural regions of the East promoted social consensus and deep, mutual familiarity between voters, many of the men at western polls did not know each other very well, if at all.[44] In this respect, many western polling places resembled large American cities where anonymity promoted stereotyping and, all too often, violence and intimidation. In sum, many frontier polling places combined characteristics of the rural and urban East in a way that promoted unique types of political behavior, including vigilante interventions in the electoral process and community-wide participation in what were illegal practices.

Western precincts were also strongly influenced by the heavy federal presence in many frontier communities. Federal officers, troops, and agents participated in elections as voters (many of them illegal), candidates or partisans of candidates, and sometimes violent intimidators of other voters. In the end, it seems to be an open question whether or not this federal presence, unmatched in almost all parts of the long-settled eastern portion of the nation, either enhanced or demoralized the polling place as a site of democratic practice. The evidence presented in the hearings certainly suggests a negative conclusion. But we return to this question in the next chapter where the polling place was transformed under the tremendous stress of civil war.

---

43   Ibid., p. 15.
44   Utah, however, exhibited a suffocating degree of mutual familiarity between Mormon leaders and voters, along with a coercive enforcement of religious conformity that could occur only in small communities. Not surprisingly for that reason, the social consensus constructed by Mormon authorities was weakest in the territory's largest center, Salt Lake City.

6

Loyalty Oaths, Troops, and
Elections during the Civil War

The American Civil War changed the way men voted. The most important change was the vast expansion of the role played by the federal government and its agents. This was the case everywhere except the eleven states of the Confederacy, which were, of course, out of the Union; although elections occurred in the South, there is very little information available on how they were conducted. In the North and in the border states, however, the Civil War imposed a new condition on voting: the legitimacy of an election now often depended on whether or not those loyal to the Union prevailed at the polls. This condition, in turn, justified the use of measures that had been almost unknown before the war. In the border states, for example, loyalty oaths were imposed as one of the requirements for determining voter eligibility. These oaths screened out those who had either actively supported the Confederate war effort or harbored southern sympathies without acting on them.[1] In the border states and some northern states as well, Union troops and loyal state militia also appeared at the polls. Their presence was ostensibly intended to maintain order and protect the polls from Confederate guerrillas. In practice, however, their influence was more commonly felt through their own informal tests of voter loyalty; those merely suspected of hostility to the Republican party were often physically ejected from the polling place, whether or not they were willing to swear the required loyalty oath.[2]

---

[1] For a review of these border state oaths, see Philip J. Avillo, Jr., "Ballots for the Faithful: The Oath and the Emergence of Slave State Republican Congressmen, 1861–1867," *Civil War History* 22 (June 1976): 164–74.

[2] Remarkably little evidence of guerrilla interference in the 1862 general election in Missouri turned up in the contested election hearings. There were, for example, no reports of guerillas breaking up or even appearing at Union polling places. However, a Confederate Captain, Joseph L. Hart, did steal depositions related to a contested election in a raid on the Clinton County courthouse in Plattsburg on May 21, 1863. Ser. Rec. (hereafter S.R.) no. 1199: Contested Congressional Election in the Sixth District of

In many areas, opposition to the Republican party marked men as disloyal to the Union cause because the Republican party was always the most fervent and often the only organization supporting the northern war effort. From the perspective of many of those attending the polls, to oppose the party was to oppose the war. The Republican party also controlled the federal government and, thus, most of the offices throughout the various departments and bureaus. When they carried out their duties as agents of the Union war effort, federal officials also acted as partisans loyal to the party to which they owed their positions.[3] This thorough conflation of party and national loyalty was augmented by the unchallenged role the party played as defender of national authority.

Opposition to the war in the northern free states tended to be strongest among those who had been born abroad. As long as they remained unnaturalized, they were exempt from the draft. However, they also could not vote. As they did before the war, the Democrats frequently, and with some success, encouraged aliens to vote, particularly in the larger cities. In response, Republicans rapidly adopted the draft as a counterthreat; if aliens appeared at the polls, Republicans contended that they were claiming to be American citizens. If they were American citizens, they should be in the army (Republicans seemed to be concerned less with illegal voting than with filling up the ranks on the front line). So Republicans, working through the central state machinery that they so thoroughly inhabited, stationed officials at the polls to check whether those who appeared to vote were on the enrollment lists and thus eligible for military service. When aliens presented themselves and their names were not found, they were added to the enrollment lists and subsequently vulnerable to the draft. Thus, military conscription became a means (albeit illegal) of discouraging Democratic sympathizers from participating in northern elections.[4]

The soldiers themselves became a vast reservoir of Republican and Union loyalists. Where the Republican party controlled the state government, arrangements were made through which Union soldiers could cast absentee ballots, either as individuals or in what were in effect temporary precincts

---

Missouri: Mis. Doc. (hereafter M.D.) no. 20, pp. 28–9. James H. Birch vs. Austin A. King, election held on November 4, 1862. On conditions in Missouri generally, see *American Annual Cyclopaedia for 1862* (New York: D. Appleton, 1872), pp. 589–95. For a brief discussion of intimidation of voters and election officials by Union troops in the border states during the Civil War, also see Glenn C. Altschuler and Stuart M. Blumin, *Rude Republic: Americans and Their Politics in the Nineteenth Century* (Princeton, N.J.: Princeton University Press, 2000), pp. 174–5.

[3] On the conflation of the Republican party and the American central state during and immediately after the Civil War, see Richard Franklin Bensel, *Yankee Leviathan: The Origins of Central State Authority in America, 1859–1877* (New York: Cambridge University Press, 1990), chapters 1, 3.

[4] Most of these voters were guilty only of evading the draft; they were qualified to vote.

created wherever they happened to be encamped.[5] Election returns from the front line overwhelmingly supported the Republican party; given the close identification of the party with the northern war effort and the fact that most Union soldiers were volunteers, some of this lopsidedness was to be expected. However, the election practices in and around these campsite precincts probably prejudiced the process to some extent. Soldiers cared passionately about the outcome of an election, knew exactly how their comrades voted, and carried guns (regularly using them to kill other men). In such a situation, it is not at all surprising that few votes cast in the army opposed the Republican party.

State Militia and Loyalty Oaths

Professional soldiers comprised but a very small fraction of the Union army, and almost none served in the state militia. The vast majority of the soldiers and officers who served in the Civil War had, in fact, never seen duty before. In the absence of experienced officers and trained enlisted men, discipline was notoriously lax, particularly in the state militia, which often seemed to be little more than informally organized vigilantes.[6] Under the best of circumstances, troops may not have understood the distinction between maintaining order at the polls and ensuring that those who were suspected of disloyalty lost the election. In any event, the distinction was fatally blurred by the fact that those suspected of disloyalty were the very men who also were suspected of attempting to disrupt the voting. Thus, excluding disloyal men from the polls was easily seen as the most effective way of conducting

---

[5] Soldiers from most Union (and Confederate states) could vote by absentee ballot. For a list, see Josiah Henry Benton, *Voting in the Field: A Forgotten Chapter of the Civil War* (Boston: privately printed, 1915), p. 4. For an analysis of Confederate legislation, see pp. 27–40, 107. In the Union, the Democratic party usually opposed voting in the field; as a result, most of the states that failed to provide for such voting had Democratic legislatures or governors (pp. 306–7). Also see Oscar O. Winther, "Soldier Voting in the Election of 1864," *New York History* 25 (October 1944): 440–58; Arnold Shankman, "Soldier Votes and Clement L. Vallandigham in the 1863 Ohio Gubernatorial Election," *Ohio History* 82 (Winter/Spring 1973): 88–104.

[6] In December 1861, Major General Henry W. Halleck, commander of Union forces in Missouri, described his troops as "no army, but rather a military rabble." Discipline did not improve as the war went on. Michael Fellman, *Inside War: The Guerrilla Conflict in Missouri during the American Civil War* (New York: Oxford University Press, 1989), pp. xv, xviii, 34, 81–2, 88, 169. Some of this disorganization was by design. Commanders simply did not want to know about and thus be obliged to control the conduct of their units; left to their own devices, soldiers and junior officers could persecute disloyal citizens in ways that could not be officially sanctioned. However, most of the lack of discipline appears to have been endemic to the way in which these troops were raised and motivated (pp. 55–6, 87–8, 93, 116–31, 171–2). A similar lack of discipline characterized the Confederate military command in Missouri (pp. 81, 97–112).

an orderly election. As most state militia and their officers saw the matter, their mission in guarding the polls necessarily conflated the two purposes.

This interpretation, however, overlooked the subtlety and uncertainty surrounding the notion of loyalty. Those who prepared militia enrollment lists in the border states ran up against this problem when trying to decide whether or not men were sufficiently loyal for service. One of those officers, Rufus Alexander, was the deputy enrolling officer in Randolph Township in St. Francois County in 1862 and made notes as to the "sentiments in regard to this rebellion" of the men he enrolled. He reported that he "would ask them what their sentiments were and sometimes we would have a lengthy conversation; I would conclude, from the scope of their conversation in what manner they should be enrolled, and I enrolled them accordingly." His notations strikingly illustrate the range and quality of political opinion in Civil War Missouri (see Table 6.1). Alexander recorded the names of seventy men who were between the ages of eighteen and forty-five and otherwise physically fit for militia duty. One of these men was an alien, and Alexander failed to provide a notation for another. Of the remaining sixty-eight, only three were classified as unambiguously "loyal." If suffrage eligibility had been restricted just to these men, the electorate would have shrunk by about 95 percent of antebellum levels.

Approximately a third of the men expressed sentiments that might be generally classified as "antebellum nostalgia." When asked to align themselves with either the federal government or the Confederacy, their response was to say that they preferred political arrangements as they stood before the war broke out. While their position must have frustrated both Union and Confederate recruiting officers, the more immediate question was whether they should be classified as "loyal" or "disloyal." If loyalty required support for the northern war effort, they failed the test. However, if disloyalty required support for the Confederacy, they failed that test as well. If they were allowed to vote, the electorate would have expanded to approximately 40 percent of antebellum levels. Another slightly larger group of men responded that they were in one way or another "neutral" between the two sides. If they were included in the electorate, a little over three-quarters of the antebellum electorate would have been eligible to vote. Nine men openly acknowledged that they leaned toward or sympathized with the South.[7] However, none of them admitted to active support for the Confederacy. If their political beliefs

---

[7] Not surprisingly, none of the men whose names appear on the enrollment lists indicated that they identified or sympathized with the North. Such sentiment, if it existed, was completely subsumed under the "loyalist" or "unconditional Union" headings. The flip side was that references to the Confederacy were also absent, apparently completely subsumed under the "southern" or "rebel" headings. Thus, state trumped region among loyalists, while region trumped state among southern sympathizers. This pattern was produced by the local institutionalization of Union goals in the form of federal and state authorities.

Table 6.1. *Notations Made by the Enrolling Officer for the Missouri State Militia: Randolph Township, St. Francois County, September 1862*

Number of men	Notation entered alongside their names by the enrolling officer
3	loyal
1	says he is loyal
2	Union
1	Union man
4	constitutional Union
4	constitutional
1	constitutional man
3	constitution as it is, and Union as it was
9	old constitution
1	Union non-combatant
1	non-committal
19	neutral
4	neutral southern man
2	loyal southern man (requested to be so enrolled)
3	southern man
1	southern
3	southern sympathizer
3	disloyal
1	returned southern soldier
1	prisoner of war on parole
1	southern soldier

Note and source: These notations were made by Rufus Alexander, the deputy enrolling officer in Randolph Township as he entered on the militia list the names of men between eighteen and forty-five years of age (males younger or older were exempt from service). For his testimony, see Ser. Rec. no. 1200: Contested Congressional Election in the Third District of Missouri: Mis. Doc. no. 43, pp. 71–72. James Lindsay vs. John G. Scott, election held on August 3, 1863. All the notations are verbatim. They have been reordered around common themes (e.g., the Constitution) and, more generally, along a spectrum running from rather robust Union sentiment (at the beginning of the list) to open defiance of the northern government (at the end). In addition to these notations, Alexander reported one man as an "Englishman." There was also another man for whom Alexander did not assign a comment. Including these two, there were seventy men on the enrollment list for Randolph Township.

and sentiments did not disqualify them for suffrage rights, the electorate would have expanded to about nine out of every ten antebellum voters. The remainder were either openly hostile to the Union or, in three cases, had actually joined Confederate units at some time.[8]

[8] It should be noted that those men who were currently serving in either the Union or Confederate armies would not have been interviewed by Alexander; all

In neighboring Perry Township, Armstrong O'Hare made out the militia list, enrolling "every man in the manner that he wanted to be."[9] Examined superficially, the men in Perry Township appear to have been somewhat more loyal than those in Randolph (see Table 6.2). For example, O'Hare considered almost half of the men unambiguously loyal to the Union. Another quarter were reported as describing themselves as loyal; however, their loyalty rested solely on their self-descriptions. Only six men, about 5 percent of the total, expressed neutral sentiments. Another nine sympathized with the South but did not admit to actively supporting the Confederacy. Thirteen more had taken some action in support of the rebels; twelve of the thirteen had, in fact, served in the southern army at some point. Compared with the return made from Randolph Township, the distribution is both far more favorable to the Union and far more polarized (with a higher percentage of men having fought for the Confederacy and a much lower percentage in the middle ranges of the political spectrum).

However, the Perry return may have been made under peculiar conditions that may account for much of the difference between the two townships. As O'Hare explained in his testimony, the "first time I enrolled [the township] the guerillas came and took my books from me, and I have not seen them since, and then I re-enrolled the township." It is not known why the guerrillas were interested in O'Hare's list. They could have wanted it in order to identify loyalists who, from their perspective, should have been punished. More likely, perhaps, was that these guerrillas wanted to destroy the information O'Hare had collected, thus denying it to Union authorities who would have used it for their own purposes. Since guerrillas generally operated in the same neighborhoods in which they lived, some of their names probably appeared on O'Hare's list. This raises the possibility that they were unhappy with how they had been described or had described themselves and thus stole the lists in order to eliminate the record. In any event, the reenrollment would have given every man an opportunity to revise the sentiments he reported to O'Hare. The internal evidence suggests that just such a recalculation of costs and benefits in fact took place, with many men now reporting loyalist beliefs that were suspect in O'Hare's opinion. Thus, compared with the Randolph list, the much larger number of self-described loyalists and the much smaller number of neutrals would have been explained by the "second-chance" opportunity given men in Perry Township.[10]

these calculations are thus restricted to the pool of men he was instructed to approach.

9   S.R. no. 1200: M.D. no. 43 (1863): p. 74. For other enrollment lists with similar notations, see pp. 83–4.

10   This possibility rests, at best, on informed speculation. For example, it is not known what, if any, new information on the consequences of being classified as "disloyal"

Table 6.2. *Notations Made by the Enrolling Officer for the Missouri State Militia: Perry Township, St. Francois County, September 1862*

Number of men	Notation entered alongside their names by the enrolling officer
2	in favor of putting down the rebellion
1	opposed to the rebellion
48	loyal
2	loyal man
1	loyal, has certificate of exemption
2	considers himself a loyal man
2	considers himself loyal
6	says he is loyal
6	he says he is loyal
9	he says he is a loyal man
2	says he is a loyal boy
1	constitutional Union man
2	neutral loyal
3	neutral
1	has taken oath on both sides, once by Jeff. Thompson and once by the United States
9	southern sympathizer
1	has been south, but never joined the rebel army
1	has been in the rebel army, and returned, and taken the oath
2	has been in the rebel army, returned and taken the oath of allegiance
1	has been in the rebel army, has returned and taken the oath of allegiance
1	been in the southern army, returned, and taken the oath of allegiance
1	been in the southern army, returned, and taken the oath
1	been in the rebel army, returned, and taken the oath of allegiance
1	been in the rebel army and taken the oath of allegiance
1	prisoner from the rebel army, taken the oath of allegiance
1	been in Price's army, taken prisoner, came back, and taken the oath of allegiance
1	returned prisoner, under bond to the United States
1	has been in the rebel army, under bond to the United States for disloyalty

Note and source: See note to Table 6.1. The notations in this table were made by Armstrong O'Hare, the deputy enrolling officer in Perry Township. For his testimony, see Ser. Rec. no. 1200: Mis. Doc. no. 43 (1863): pp. 73–4. In addition to these notations, O'Hare described two men as "he says he is a German man" and another as "not naturalized." Including these three, there were 113 men on the enrollment list for Randolph Township.

Although one of their formal responsibilities was to divide their lists into those who were "loyal" and those who were "disloyal," the deputy enrolling officers did not say in the hearing how they ultimately classified the men in Perry and Randolph Townships. However, William Williams, the enrolling officer for St. Francois Township in the same county, was asked to name those he did not consider loyal (see Appendix). Judging from his testimony, Williams was probably a little more strict in defining loyalty than most enrolling officers and he evidently considered many men disloyal despite their self-representations. Williams even categorized a man as disloyal who said "the rebellion should be put down." That being the case, it is likely that all those in the "antebellum nostalgia," neutral, and southern-leaning or -sympathizing dimensions of the political spectrum were classified as disloyal (not to mention those who were openly hostile to the Union).[11] In St. Francois Township, the total so classified came to a remarkable 267 men.

Although Williams was fairly confident that he could accurately gauge the political sentiments of the men he interviewed, loyalty was still a privately held sentiment; it was not something that was worn as a patch on a sleeve or marked indelibly on a forehead. When an enrolling officer noted the degree of loyalty of a man, he attempted to judge that man's political predilections. To the extent that the officer's own biases played a part in those judgments, the resulting notations would be inaccurate.

Another source of error would originate in the calculations of the men themselves. On the one hand, if they wished to evade militia service, they might have exaggerated their hostility or indifference to the Union war effort. On the other, they may have exaggerated their warmth toward the Union in order to avoid retribution by the authorities. Some of that retribution would have taken the form of discriminatory taxation and loss of suffrage rights; these would have been more or less administratively imposed with

would have led the guerrillas to wish to be reclassified. The important point is to suggest the kind of contingencies that influenced the ways in which men reported their otherwise privately held political sentiments. On the malleability of professed sympathies, see Fellman, *Inside War*, pp. 44–52.

[11] Of those classified as disloyal by Williams, at least eighteen voted in the congressional election held in August 1863. Four of these had claimed that they were loyal, a claim that Williams had dismissed when he finally categorized the men. Two more had described constitutional sentiments that fall under the antebellum nostalgia heading. Two were neutral, and seven sympathized with the South. At the far end of the political spectrum were three voters who had been described as "disloyal," "rebel under parole," and "has been arrested, taken the oath, and been released at the Pilot Knob" in the militia enrollment. S.R. no. 1200: M.D. no. 43 (1863): pp. 79–82, 88. On the political beliefs of Missourians, particularly the strength of what is called here "antebellum nostalgia" and neutrality sentiment, see Fellman, *Inside War*, pp. 5, 8–9, 51.

calculable consequences and limits. More serious would have been the vulnerability to irregular abuse by the militia. The latter risk would have been both more difficult to calculate and had no limits; many noncombatant men were murdered for their political beliefs in Civil War Missouri. Operating in the other direction but with much less force was the possibility of retribution by Confederate regulars or guerrillas. All these risks certainly affected how men responded to an enrolling officer's questions, although the extent of their influence cannot be known. However, the contextual evidence presented in the hearings suggests that enrolling officers honestly attempted to summarize what men told them.[12]

In setting their requirements for voting, Union authorities in the border states attempted to detect privately held sentiments by imposing "loyalty oaths." These oaths, in part, addressed the past behavior of the oath taker. However, other passages in these oaths identified attitudes toward governments and institutions that were ambiguously contentious.[13] For example, was a man loyal to the Union *if* the Union was understood as being that set of institutions and constitutional understandings that had characterized the antebellum political order? This was, in fact, the way most northern Democrats understood loyalty; their almost universal campaign slogan during and immediately after the war was "The Constitution as It Is; the Union as It Was."[14]

Northern nationalists rejected this interpretation because they regarded the antebellum Union as an anachronism that would have fatally hampered the war effort. In this, they were undoubtedly correct. But their own

---

[12]   The best source for political and military conditions in Missouri is Fellman's *Inside War*.

[13]   To the extent that these tests of loyalty attempted to identify a state of mind, they imposed almost impossible tasks on judges of election. Even those most willing to impute sentiments to their neighbors had to admit there were men they simply could not classify. For example, when James Moore, election judge at Belleview Township, Washington County, was asked to identify those voters who "are considered rebels and southern sympathizers," he confidently went through the poll book picking out disloyal men until he reached "Thomas Deurin, ballot No. 42, (Union when sober, rebel when drunk)." Presumably, Deurin could swear the oath only before he had a drink. S.R. no. 1200: M.D. no. 43 (1863): p. 52. On the ambiguities associated with the definition of loyalty, with reference to the attitudes and beliefs of Iowa Democrats, see Hubert H. Wubben, *Civil War Iowa and the Copperhead Movement* (Ames: Iowa State University Press, 1980), pp. 223–5.

[14]   Dr. Hamilton Smith, a resident of Savannah, Missouri, testified that, in his opinion, "a large mass of those who are reputed as rebel sympathizers are loyal, and for the Constitution as it is and the Union as it was." Despite their loyalty, however, Smith agreed that "democrats and conservative men in this section [are] very often denominated as rebel sympathizers." Smith himself voted for the Republican candidate for Congress in the election at issue. S.R. no. 1198: Contested Congressional Election in the Seventh District of Missouri: M.D. no. 13, p. 78. John P. Bruce vs. Benjamin F. Loan, election held on November 4, 1862.

interpretation of loyalty was equally problematic. The primary difficulty was that they interpreted loyalty as a complete, unwavering devotion to the Union cause, a cause that the Republican party and northern nationalists were making up as the war progressed.[15] Thus stripped of its ideational foundations in a stable constitutional order, the Union appeared to many men to have become a partisan fetish. Seen from that perspective, "preservation of the Union" seemed to mean only "preservation of the Republican party."

In a very real sense, both positions were correct. Republican appeals to "save the Union," for instance, rested on a (substantially reworked) recollection of antebellum conditions that was, in fact, vacuous. Nonetheless, Republicans wrapped themselves in this memory in order to pose as defenders of the "Union of their forbearers"; such a strategy cloaked what, in reality, were very different political projects and ambitions, projects and ambitions that could not even have been imagined before the war broke out. On the other hand, nationalists were undoubtedly correct that adherence to the antebellum political order, as understood by those who opposed Republican designs, would have fatally hamstrung the northern war effort. In sum, the antebellum political order was a dying horse because, no matter which view was adopted, it would not survive the war. Many Democrats preferred to ride that horse precisely because the war against the South would thus be lost. Although they described it differently, many Republicans preferred to ride the same horse because they needed a nationalist ideology in which to clothe their war measures. In between the two positions, there were some men who thought the war could be fought and won within the ambit of the antebellum political order. But they were very few and they were certainly wrong.

For all these reasons, loyalty to the Union, understood as patriotic attachment to a political order that had existed when these men had grown to adulthood, could not have been an enforceable condition on suffrage during the Civil War.[16] Consider, for example, the following exchange

---

[15] For example, William Williams, the enrollment officer for St. Francois County, was asked his opinion of someone who called "himself a constitutional Union man." The officer replied, "I would call him a copperhead – in other words, a man who is in favor of the independence of the south, of destroying our government, and opposes all the measures of the present administration." He was then asked whether, in order to be considered loyal, a man must "advocate and indorse all the measures of the present administration." He responded that such a man "must indorse all that is necessary to put down the rebellion." When asked whether such a man can "differ with the President and his cabinet as to what is necessary to put down the rebellion, and yet be loyal," he answered, "I think not." S.R. no. 1200: M.D. no. 43 (1863): pp. 82–3. Also see Fellman, *Inside War*, p. 52.

[16] This would have been a different matter altogether had material support for the Confederate cause been involved, but few men who presented themselves at Union polls could be shown to have provided such support. If they had, they would already be in prison.

between counsel for an Unconditional Union candidate for Congress (allied with the Republican party) and a man who had supported his opponent:

Question: "You will please state whether or not you applauded the capture of Fort Sumter in the spring of 1861?"
Answer: "I don't think I did, sir."
Question: "You will please state whether or not you did not condemn the tearing down of the confederate flag hoisted in the city of St. Joseph, Missouri, in the summer of 1861."
Answer: "I did not either approve or disapprove of it."[17]

Most of those who served in the state government and militia during the war would have disfranchised a man if he had answered either question in the affirmative. That being so, there was little or no reason that would-be voters would honestly respond to such questions. In practice, because the Republican party controlled the border state and national governments, loyalty to the Union became almost completely identified with support for the northern war effort and, through that identification, with the Republican party. And this is the way that federal troops and state militia came to see the matter. Because of the conflation of party and nation, there was only one loyalist, and thus acceptable, outcome in an election: Republican victory.[18] Democrats could vote only in numbers that did not threaten that outcome. Given the hopelessness of their chances and their often brutal treatment, it is a small wonder that they went to the polls at all.

The Seventh Congressional District of Missouri

Missouri, where guerrilla warfare afflicted most of the state, was particularly hostile to fair competition between the major political parties. In this and

---

[17] S.R. no. 1198: M.D. no. 13 (1862): p. 43. Later in this hearing another witness, Dr. A. Lamme, was asked "whether or not you did, in the summer or fall of 1861, at the time the United States flag was erected over the post office building, in the city of St. Joseph, Missouri, by federal soldiers, propose and give three groans for the man who put up said flag on said building." He responded, "I did; and also opposed putting up the secesh flag a few days previous, and used my endeavors to prevent it; that the erection of flags, as I believed, from either party, had a tendency to increase the excitement then prevailing." Lamme also said that the St. Joseph city council had previously passed an ordinance prohibiting the raising of flags, whether they be Union or Confederate (p. 47). In May 1861, a mob had previously destroyed a Union flag that had been raised over this same building; that flag had been raised by a postmaster newly appointed by Lincoln. At about the same time, Confederate flags were raised at various points in the city. *Daily News' History of Buchanan County* (St. Joseph, Mo.: St. Joseph Publishing, 1898), pp. 203–4.
[18] This conflation of Republican victory and loyalty to the Union was made all the easier in elections where many of the candidates were also enrolled in the state militia. See, for example, S.R. no. 1198: M.D. no. 13 (1862): pp. 17, 75.

the following sections, we examine a few of the narratives describing the conduct of elections during the Civil War, beginning with the Seventh Congressional District. Located on the eastern bank of the Missouri River on the border with what was then the Territory of Kansas, St. Joseph was both a frontier city and the largest population center in the district. Founded just two decades earlier, the 1860 census recorded 8,932 people, and the city grew rapidly during the Civil War. St. Joseph was the most important point of departure for the emigration routes to Oregon and California, supplying settlers with wagons, teams, and other equipment.[19] Buchanan County, of which St. Joseph was the seat, contained another 14,929 people; just over 8 percent of the county population was enslaved. Although estimates are hazardous at best, the city and county contained hundreds, if not thousands, of southern sympathizers during the war. In his own testimony, the deputy sheriff estimated that between 300 and 500 men had joined General Sterling Price's Confederate army in the early months of the war.[20]

As was the case throughout northwestern Missouri, the state militia in St. Joseph was not only Republican, it was disproportionately German as well.[21] When Democrats recalled their experiences in and around the polls, they often used the terms "German" and "Republican" interchangeably. Edward Knapp, for example, had visited a number of precincts in St. Joseph on election day:

I was at the Allen House, the market-house, the court-house, and at the precinct near the Harness House, in the upper ward.... At the Allen House, in the first ward, I saw an old man, John Cowie, seventy-five years of age, a lawful voter for forty years, and a peaceable, quiet man, went up to the polls, presented his vote to the judges; the judges commenced calling off his vote, and a member of the enrolled militia, a German, with his uniform on, stepped up and took Mr. Cowie by the back of the neck or coat and jerked him over on to the floor, and the first place struck was his head and shoulders, and the blood gushed from his nose from the fall. Mr. Cowie was then voting what was then called here the democratic ticket. At the market-house, in the second ward, I saw there a number of persons prevented from voting by the enrolled militia. I saw a lieutenant in Captain Mast's company take the ticket out of

---

[19] St. Joseph's population was estimated at 15,000 in 1865. At that time, it was reported to have contained "10 churches, 1 synagogue, 2 banks, 5 other banking offices, 3 savings banks, 12 wholesale stores, about 120 retail stores, several steam mills, 1 iron foundry, 1 large woollen factory, several manufactories of carriages and wagons, and 3 large pork houses." *Lippincott's Pronouncing Gazetteer of the World* (Philadelphia: J. B. Lippincott, 1866), p. 1658.

[20] S.R. no. 1198: M.D. no. 13 (1862): p. 27.

[21] Germans joined the first Union regiments raised in Missouri in far greater numbers than any other group and were considered the most loyal element in the state. For that reason, southern sympathizers often abused them and their families, abuse that naturally invited retaliation from the militia units in which Germans served. Fellman, *Inside War*, pp. 39–40, 89–90, 158. For a description of the loyalist and Republican sentiments of German residents in St. Joseph, see S.R. no. 1198: M.D. no. 13 (1862): p. 22.

a voter's hand, and then tell him to leave, he could not vote there. He remarked that Union men could not vote in New Orleans, and secessionists can't vote here. This lieutenant was a German. There was a number of militia present, and some of them had their guns, with bayonets on them. It was a one-sided affair – that if a man voted the republican ticket there was no objection made; but they would not permit them to vote the democratic ticket.[22]

The state militia's behavior at the polls was often, as at the Allen House Precinct, unpredictable. In some instances, they would abruptly resort to violence, even in situations where physical force was clearly unnecessary to accomplish their purpose. In others, they would merely stand aside and let men vote.[23]

Residing about two miles east of the city, twenty-seven-year-old Orton Loomis had come into town to vote at about 9 o'clock in the morning.

On the corner of market square I saw Mr. Maxwell, of the firm of Maxwell & Warfield; he said to me that they were going to take possession of the polls, and that no secessionist should vote. He had the uniform of the enrolled militia on. I heard then in a short time a noise at the market-house precinct, and went up there with Scott and others. When I got there, where the voting was going on up stairs, I saw said Maxwell standing at the door with others of the enrolled militia. He, Maxwell, was telling an old man, by the name of Axell, that he could not vote there. He, Axell, was a milkman. I passed in by those to where they were voting. I intended to vote for John P. Bruce; I stood there two or three minutes, and Philip Arnold, a member of the enrolled militia, came to me and tole me that I could not vote there, and told me to leave.

When Loomis did not immediately leave, several of the militia "took hold of me and I went out much sooner than I came in." Philip Arnold, the militiaman mentioned in this account, accused Loomis of belonging to John Boyd's rebel band, which operated in the neighborhood. Arnold went on to say, as recalled by the witness, that men who "did not vote the unconditional Union ticket were called rebels." Thrown out of this precinct, Loomis went in search of another:

When I got down stairs a good many said I had better go up to the court-house, as they were going there to vote.... When I arrived at the court-house precinct, the judges had adjourned for dinner; waited until they returned and opened the polls, then, in company with eight or nine voters, was sworn to vote. I offered my vote; there was a guard of five or six stationed around the polls with muskets in their

---

22 S.R. no. 1198: M.D. no. 13 (1862): p. 6.
23 To some extent this unpredictability originated in a "deep split at the top of the Union command between those urging punishment [of suspected southern sympathizers] and those stressing reconciliation, the 'hards' and 'the softs.' No sustained policy could come from such deeply divided leaders: they passed down conflicting and rapidly changing policies." In addition, a few militia units were composed of men who more or less openly sympathized with the southern cause. Fellman, *Inside War*, pp. xviii, 53–4.

hands; at that time another squad of from twelve to sixteen armed Dutch [Germans] of the enrolled militia came around the polls, drove back the other guard, caught me by the coat collar and pulled me out. I then staid about the door a little while and left; previous to my leaving they drove the other voters back from the polls, as they had done me, and stood around the table themselves. I then left to hunt another place to vote; as I was leaving I saw voters jumping out of the windows, apparently alarmed. I then went to Nunning's Brewery precinct to vote; they said I could vote there if I was not enrolled under order No. 24. I remarked that I did not know whether I was or not; they examined their list, did not find my name and I voted. Directly after I had voted a Dutchman came up there and told the judges that if they did not take my name off the books that he or they would tear them up.[24]

In many instances, members of the state militia recognized the men who approached the polls as neighbors and fellow citizens.[25] Maxwell and Arnold, for example, personally knew Loomis. If they had been in civilian clothing and this had been an election before the war broke out, they might have simply challenged his right to vote, leaving it up to the judges of election to decide whether or not he was eligible. But, in uniform and backed by other militiamen with bayonets, they viewed themselves as empowered to intervene directly; the men they abused, on the other hand, viewed them as little more than pretentious thugs.[26]

At the time of the election in St. Joseph, Samuel Ensworth was the Buchanan County sheriff and thus responsible for superintending the election in the city and surrounding area. He was also a candidate for reelection on a ticket opposed to the Unconditional Union party. As he noted in his testimony, the conduct of the militia at the polls led him to abandon his

[24] S.R. no. 1198: M.D. no. 13 (1862): pp. 10–11.
[25] James Bradley, a second lieutenant who had commanded a squad of men at the Germantown Precinct in Henry County, explained how he knew the political attitudes of men approaching the polls: "J. Robert Bradley was with Price at the Lexington fight. I know Henry Bradley to be a very noisy secesh, and has taken the oath twice before going into the militia. I have heard Mr. Majors talk secesh, and I know from his talk that he is a secesh. The same of Mr. Davis that I said about Mr. Majors." S.R. no. 1199: Contested Congressional Election in the Fifth District of Missouri: M.D. no. 16, p. 229. Thomas L. Price vs. Joseph W. McClurg, election held on November 4, 1862.
[26] In Stewartsville, attorney George Rose discovered that "two members of the enrolled militia were posted, with sabres and pistols, apparently guarding the door [to the house were the election was held]; they were acquaintances of mine, to wit: Samuel Chenowith and Robert Ellis. So soon as they saw me coming to the door, they remarked, there comes one of the 'Bruce men,' and said to me that I could not vote . . . I commenced reasoning with them; and insisting upon my right to vote, I told them they were acting out of their sphere of duty; they replied, that it was no use to talk about it – I could not vote; not that they had any objection to me; that they knew how I was going to vote, and that was enough. I found it was useless to persist, as I was unwilling to force a passage through a guard who had sabres and pistols." S.R. no. 1198: M.D. no. 13 (1862): p. 136. For a similar account, see p. 116.

candidacy on election day; he himself did not vote and urged others, for their own safety, not to attempt to do so:

I was . . . at three different precincts of voting. I was two or three times at the Allen Hotel. The votes were taken in a room with two doors, and the members of the militia guarded each door with bayonets crossed, and to get the privilege to go to the polls I had to ask the permission of the judges, although it was my duty to attend at the election and superintend the same. I did not then see any other interference. I was at the polls at the market-house, which was after the disturbance commenced. I started up the stairs. At the head of the stairs was a person in the uniform of the militia. The old man Langston came up the opposite stairs; Langston had a ticket in his hand; and the person in uniform asked him to see his ticket; Langston handed him his ticket; he took the ticket and tore it up, and drove Langston down. There was considerable commotion around the market-house. I went into the room where votes were taken, and the place of voting was surrounded by a crowd of excited persons, and some seemed afraid to present their votes, and so stated to me; but persons who favored the election of the [Unconditional Union] nominees had no fears nor seemed to dread any danger from offering to vote. In the excited crowd, and those that intimidated the persons from voting, were Union-clothed soldiers. I was not at the court-house until after the voting there was discontinued. But when I was at the court-house the place seemed to be under the control of a set of persons who belonged to the militia with their arms.

After taking his lunch, the sheriff concluded that the voting had been irretrievably tainted by interference by the militia and did not thereafter "look after the election." Although he could not say with confidence who those who had been barred from voting would have supported, he did "not think that the nominees of the unconditional Union ticket were deprived of many votes."[27]

As Loomis had already testified, men had jumped out of the windows at the courthouse precinct. Cyrus Kemp was the clerk of election at that precinct and said that the "election proceeded pretty quietly until about one o'clock," when "a band of enrolled militia men entered the court house." The militia "instantly crowded around the table, shoving the voters back by force. I don't know whether they call it violence or not. Several Dutchmen [Germans] halloing 'Out!' 'Out!' [T]he voters then became alarmed, and did not want to be insulted, and left the room." About half an hour later, the polls were

again opened, and new judges appointed by the bystanders, under the direction of the sheriff. The election then proceeded quietly for about one-half an hour. There was a great crowd around the table at that time of persons who had been sworn before voting. Just at this time, another company of the enrolled militia, armed, about twenty in number, came into the room, and closed around the table, and forced the voters back, and scattered them in all directions. Some of them jumped out of the windows.

---

[27] Ibid., pp. 12–13. Ensworth, not surprisingly, was defeated in this election.

The judges also immediately left the table, and I could not conceal the poll-book in time to prevent the militiamen from destroying it, by tearing it to pieces. The militia men seized my poll-book while I was yet sitting at the table, and tore it into strips, and threw it on the floor. They had muskets in their hands. The election was then broken up for the second time, and the polls were not any more re-opened at the court-house.

About a hundred men had cast their votes when the poll book was destroyed.[28] Since this part of Missouri held oral elections in which men announced their choices to the judges, the only record of their votes was in the poll book, and, thus, the votes were lost when the militia ripped it to shreds.[29]

This was but one of several incidents in which the militia disrupted the polls at the court house.[30] S. S. McGibbon, "a dealer in boots and shoes" who belonged to one of the rare militia squads in which the rank and file favored Bruce, had monitored the courthouse precinct earlier in the day:

At eleven o'clock, or about that time, I went on guard at the court-house with some eight or ten others, and everything went on quietly until about 12 o'clock. About that time a squad of Germans came up and said that we had to leave there; that they were going to take charge of the polls themselves. We formed in line and told them that they could not interfere with either the judges or the election while we were there. They were without arms, and after a good deal of parleying they went off. In the mean time an order came up from some person in town that we should leave

---

[28] In addition to the votes that had been cast, between 50 and 100 men were inside the polling place, most of them waiting to vote. Ibid., pp. 16–17, 21, 23. The other clerk at this precinct estimated that 90 percent of those who had voted had voted for Bruce, the congressional candidate whom the militia opposed (pp. 38, 42).

[29] In March 1863, the state legislature abolished oral voting and required that all subsequent elections be conducted by ballot. A. F. Denny, *General Statutes of the State of Missouri* (Jefferson City, Mo.: Emory S. Foster, 1866), p. 61. In the following August, however, the congressional elections were conducted both orally and by ballot because election officials at the individual precincts were still uncertain as to the mode of proceeding. For example, Josephus Moore, an election judge at the Benton Township polls in Wayne County, reported, "We had tickets, but we voted openly, and wrote the name of the voter on the ticket.... We left [the tickets] on the bench where we voted; the most of them were torn up." Since the tickets were numbered and often had the voter's name written on them, it was still very easy to tell who had voted for particular candidates. S.R. no. 1200: M.D. no. 43 (1863): pp. 31, 44, 61.

[30] The militia also closed down the markethouse polling place for about half an hour, but the clerks were able to save the poll books by concealing them under their coats. John Scott, a farmer and a practicing lawyer, recalled that the soldiers "were there in considerable numbers.... If [a man] insisted on voting the ticket called the Union Ticket, on which the name of John P. Bruce appeared for Congress, he was forcibly ejected from the room by the soldiers, and in some instances I saw them kicked down the stairs and while there I saw some fifteen or twenty armed soldiers approach with bayonets fixed. They cleared the ante-room, and marched into the room where the polls were opened and drove the voters out." S.R. no. 1198: M.D. no. 13 (1862): pp. 38–40.

the polls, which we refused to do. General Hall being present we appealed to him, and he told us to remain at the post. We did so until our time expired, which was about one o'clock. . . . I saw a number leaving who did not vote, for when the squad of militia [which was replacing McGibbon's detail] were loading their muskets and forming in line, the people became alarmed, and scattered in all directions.[31]

This account is particularly noteworthy in that the two militia squads, divided by ethnicity and partisan allegiance, may have been ready to fight for control of the polling place. If so, only the fact that the "Germans" were unarmed appears to have prevented violence. Yet when the time came for the troops to be rotated, McGibbon's squad gave up their place without a protest.

On June 10, 1862, the Missouri legislature had passed a loyalty oath that had to be taken before a man could cast his vote:

I, ____, do solemnly swear (or affirm, as the case may be) that I will support, protect, and defend the Constitution of the United States and the Constitution of the State of Missouri against all enemies and opposers, whether domestic or foreign; that I will bear true faith, loyalty, and allegiance to the United States, and will not, directly or indirectly, give aid and comfort or countenance to the enemies or opposers thereof, or of the provisional government of the State of Missouri, any ordinance, law, or resolution of any State convention or legislature, or any order or organization, secret or otherwise, to the contrary notwithstanding; and that I do this with a full and honest determination, pledge, and purpose, faithfully to keep and perform the same, without any mental reservation or evasion whatever. And I do further solemnly swear (or affirm) that I have not, since the 17th day of December, A.D. 1861, wilfully taken up arms or levied war against the United States or against the provisional government of the State of Missouri: so help me God.

With the exception that a man might have fought for the South prior to December 17, 1861, this oath appears to be ironclad, certainly with respect to loyalty to the Union cause after that date.[32]

Several months later, on August 4, 1862, the headquarters of the Missouri State militia issued General Orders No. 24, which read, in part:

All disloyal men, and those who have at any time sympathized with the rebellion, are required to report at the nearest military post, or other enrolling station, be enrolled, surrender their arms, and return to their homes or ordinary places of business, where they will be permitted to remain so long as they shall continue quietly attending to their ordinary and legitimate business, and in no way give aid or comfort to the enemy. Disloyal persons, or sympathizers with the rebellion, will not be organized into companies, nor required, nor permitted to do duty in the Missouri militia. . . .[33]

---

[31] Ibid., pp. 45–6.
[32] Ibid., pp. 57–8.
[33] Ibid., p. 62. The men encompassed in this order were named by the enrolling officers as they made out the militia lists for each township. Several of these lists were described above in this chapter.

Under this order, lists were accordingly made of those who had "at any time sympathized" or given "aid or comfort" to the southern cause. By including in these categories actions and thoughts that occurred before December 17, 1861, it was possible that men could both honestly swear the voting oath and yet be encompassed within the order. The state militia, apparently without any higher authority than their own predilection, took it upon themselves to prevent those enrolled under General Order No. 24 from voting, whether or not such men would swear the oath of allegiance.[34] Lists of those enrolled under the order were accordingly copied and circulated by the militia; polling places in which officials refused to disfranchise men who were enrolled under the order were often broken up.

The militia had evidently planned for some time to prohibit "order 24" men from voting. Sheriff Ensworth, for example, had heard threats "that persons enrolled under order No. 24 and secessionists would not be permitted to vote." In the days preceding the election, James Matney, the acting deputy sheriff, was also aware of such threats, adding that several men had told him they would not go to the polls for that reason. Matney thought that the "class of voters" who had been most intimidated

"were those who were opposed to emancipation and abolitionism in the State of Missouri, and are generally called democrats and old line whigs, who preferred to act with the democratic party [and were opposed] to the emancipation or abolition party.

On the day of the election, many lower and middle-ranking officers ordered the arrest and imprisonment of all "order 24" men. One of those taken up early in the morning was "a young man ... reading in [Sheriff Ensworth's] office." On seeing him "marching off to the guard-house," the sheriff asked why he was being arrested and was told that all "order 24" men who tried to vote were to be imprisoned. The men in the guardhouse were released when this order was countermanded later in the day.[35] The laxity of election judges at the courthouse precinct in enforcing this illegal order apparently sparked the destruction of the poll books and the closing down of the polling place. However, the judges appeared to have made some effort to detect "order 24" men even at that precinct. Attorney James Ringo, for example, went to the courthouse intending to vote at about

[34] For example, this appears to have been the practice at the Maryville polling place in Nodaway County. Ibid., p. 41. The experience in St. Joseph, for which much more extensive information exists, is treated in the text. Because they wished to prohibit those on the "order 24" list from voting, Missouri Republicans were especially eager to conflate membership on the list with disloyalty as defined in the oath mandated by the legislature. See, for example, S.R. no. 1199: M.D. no. 20 (1862): pp. 19–20.

[35] The young man was apparently "reading" the law (i.e., studying in preparation for a legal career). S.R. no. 1198: M.D. no. 13 (1862): p. 13; also see p. 24.

ten o'clock in the morning. After he had given the judges his name, one of them began to examine a printed list

of persons who had enrolled under order No. 24. I told him he need not look on that list, for my name was not there; that I did not enrol under that order. Well, I was sworn [under the loyalty oath], and gave in my ticket. After I voted, a Dutch [German] sergeant came to me, that he had orders to arrest every man that came there to vote, that did not have soldier's clothes on, and took me to the guard-house. I told the guard if there were such orders out, they did not come from proper authorities. I told the sergeant that I desired to go by Gen. Hall's office to see him. Henry M. Vories went up into Gen. Hall's office and brought him down. He inquired of the guard by what authority he arrested me. The guard then said, he had orders to arrest every man that was enrolled under orders No. 24, from Capt. Hat, officer of the day. Gen. Hall asked me if I was enrolled under orders No. 24. I told him I was not. He told the guard to take me to the guard-house, and release me when I got there. I was put into the guard-house. I saw several men there, citizens, who informed me that they were also arrested for attempting to vote. Mr. Ensworth, the sheriff, also went with me to the guard-house, and induced Capt. Hat to release me and the others, stating to Capt. Hat that it was an outrage on the elective franchise. After some little squabbling and a fuss, we were released.

While Ringo was in the guard house, "a difficulty got up between R. F. Maxwell, one of the militia, and one of the prisoners, and Maxwell attempted to stick a bayonet in him."[36] In other words, a militiaman who was little more than a civilian dressed up in a uniform had attempted to bayonet an unarmed neighbor who had been imprisoned in the guardhouse because he had legally attempted to vote.[37] Actions such as this tainted the atmosphere of every polling place in St. Joseph.[38] Ringo, for example, had voted for Loan, the Unconditional Union candidate but, "after I saw the way his friends acted I was sorry I ever had any intention of voting for him, and if I had had the thing to have done over again I should have voted for John P. Bruce."[39]

Militiamen apparently attended the polls whether or not they were on duty. Because of their lack of discipline, it was difficult for civilians to tell

---

[36] It is unclear whether this was the same Maxwell, "of the firm Maxwell and Warfield," who had warned Loomis that the militia were going to take possession of the polls.

[37] Although he had sworn the loyalty oath, John Abell was still imprisoned in the guard-house and, along with eight others, had "received a great deal of abuse from a parcel of Germans who were on guard there." Abell may have been singled out because he was the brother-in-law of "General M. Jeff. Thompson, of the confederate army." Ibid., pp. 44–5.

[38] On his release from the guardhouse, Abell (mentioned in the preceding note) "picked up one of the ["order 24"] lists of those who were to be arrested if they attempted to vote.... It was soon rumored around that I had the list of those who were to be arrested for voting, and persons were calling nearly all day to see if their names were on the list; and if they were they did not attempt to vote, saying that they did not wish to be interrupted [by an incarceration]." Ibid., p. 44.

[39] Ibid., pp. 34–5.

whether they were in service and, therefore, might be acting under orders.⁴⁰ In the rural areas of the Seventh Congressional District, conditions were as bad or even worse than they were in St. Joseph. In the small town of Savannah, for example, Joseph Nickel, a farmer, testified that he had gone to the polls at about eleven o'clock in the morning. When he arrived, he saw a great deal of pushing and shoving as "an organization around the polls" tried to prevent "certain men" from voting:

I frequently heard the cry, "Union men to the polls, and rebels to their holes," or "tories to their holes," or "secessionists to their holes." Many of those attempting to vote were held back, kept back, or thrown back, with considerable violence both of words and gestures. . . . I did not see any arms. I am satisfied that many would have been hurt if they had further attempted to vote after having been once checked. . . . [The crowd] was boisterous, and appeared to be dangerous.

This intimidation was directed at those believed to be southern sympathizers whether or not they appeared on the "order 24" lists.

Nickel also gave an extraordinarily detailed description of the political landscape in which he also summarized how Republicans distinguished between loyalists and others:

Since the November election in 1860, I think perhaps some four or five hundred men have left the county of Andrew, a part of whom are reported to have joined the rebel army, and a part of whom have joined the federal army, and a part of whom have joined the State forces, and still another part of whom have removed from the county with their families. Of those who are reported to have joined the rebel army, I think a large majority of them have returned to the county; of those who joined the federal army, I think perhaps half have returned; and of those who joined the State forces, comparatively few have returned. Of those who left the county with their families, their places mostly have been filled by others moving into this county from other counties and States. The most of those who moved into this county, referred to above, came here in the fall of 1861. . . . The men [who would have voted for Bruce in a fair election] consist partly of men who uniformly call themselves democrats, and many of whom have been arrested and imprisoned by the military authorities at some time since 1860; partly of men who had at one time been in the State or confederate army, and some of whom are now under military bonds; and partly of those who are said to be enrolled under order number twenty-four. Of the last, there were but few at Savannah, comparatively. All three of the above classes are, by the republican party, called rebels and rebel sympathizers.⁴¹

⁴⁰ Ibid., p. 87. When Dr. Hamilton Smith saw Democratic voters physically barred from the voting window in Savannah, he asked the commanding officer "to maintain order; [Lieutenant Colonel] Nash stated that if called upon by the civil authorities he would do so, if he could, but doubted whether he would be able to maintain law and order on that day." Smith, a Republican, also reported that the crowd around the voting window in Savannah was composed of "mostly enrolled militia" (pp. 76–8).
⁴¹ Ibid., p. 91. Nickel also reported that he had heard of similar interference in the rural precincts of Fillmore, Whitesville, and Amazonia in the county.

Unlike St. Joseph, Savannah was small enough that most men who approached the voting window were probably known to those attending the polls; printed lists were thus not necessary for the identification of those who might be less than ardent supporters of the Union war effort. Jacob Hittibidal, for example, testified that he was prevented from voting by men who "were favorable to Benj. F. Loan. One reason for my thinking so is that there was a young man by the name of Miller, whom I have known ever since he was a child, and he said to me, on the day of the election, at the time I was trying to vote, 'Uncle Jake, we do not want any democrats to vote.' "[42]

Chillicothe held just under a thousand people, and the sole precinct in the town was located in the county courthouse. Before the polls opened, Dr. Hughes, editor of the *Chillicothe Constitution*, went around "putting up posters" warning that "no disloyal person should vote." One of the judges of election, Thomas Bryan, described Hughes as "a radical abolitionist." Observing these and other preparations, John Garr, the other election judge and a plough manufacturer, "expected to have some disturbance" as they opened up the polls:

I saw the military going to Spring Hill, in Jackson township, in this county, and I saw a poster near the gate, at the entrance in the court-house yard, and one in the court-house, where the polls were opened; they were large, printed poster[s], with the words on each one: Special Order! No disloyal person shall be allowed to vote. We had received but few votes, when Dr. A. S. Hughes came in, and told us that no disloyal person should be allowed to vote there; the first vote he objected to was John Garr, junior [this was the son of one of the election judges], because he had stated, if he could not vote the ticket he wanted to, he would vote for Black Bill; this objection was overruled, and he voted; Hughes objected to two or three more, on the ground that they were disloyal, but they were allowed to vote.

Like Savannah, Chillicothe was small enough that Hughes could personally identify men who, in his opinion, should be prevented from voting. Up to this point, all Hughes could do was challenge the eligibility of men who appeared at the polls; he had no more authority than any other private citizen would have had in that role. And the judges were able and willing to reject his challenges, as they did when they allowed Garr's son to vote.[43]

But this ended when, in Bryan's words, "Lieutenant Colonel Jacobson, of the Missouri 27th regiment, marched into the court-house, where the voting was going on, with some twenty or thirty armed soldiers." After Jacobson peremptorily announced that he would not allow any "disloyal" man to vote at that precinct, Bryan

read to him General Willard P. Hall's order – that the judges of election were to be the sole judges of the qualification of voters, and the military was not to interfere.

[42]   Ibid., pp. 85, 88–9.
[43]   Ibid., pp. 103, 105, 107. "Black Bill" may have been William C. Quantrill, leader of one of the most notorious Confederate guerrilla bands then operating in Missouri.

Lieutenant Colonel Jacobson then said he disregarded the order of General Hall, and I said I would report him. Lieutenant Colonel Jacobson then said to Dr. Hughes, who was standing close by: "Any man you will point out as an illegal voter I will take him out of the house." Afterward the judges swore several men, and out of that number Hughes first pointed out James Hutchinson, and said he was feeding bushwhackers; and James Hutchinson was the first one of that lot that offered his ticket to vote, which I took. Lieutenant Colonel Jacobson ordered his men to take Hutchinson out of the house, which they did; then there seemed to be a good deal of confusion in the house. Mr. Berry, one of the judges, said we could not go on with the election until order was restored. During the interruption Dr. Hughes made a motion that they organize the election over and elect new judges, and then proceed with the election, and no one sanctioned it. During the time we were waiting for order to be restored the telegraphic operator brought in a despatch to Lieutenant Colonel Jacobson, which, I understood, was from Governor Gamble. Lieutenant Colonel Jacobson then remarked to the judges, that then they might have it their own way, and took his soldiers and left.

After Jacobson and his men left, Hutchinson voted.

John Garr described the incident the same way, adding only one or two details. When Jacobson had ordered the judges not to receive Hutchinson's vote, for example, Garr testified that he had "told him we would go by the law of the State convention, Gov. Gamble's orders, and Gen. Hall's instructions, and to the letter of the law as we understood it." It was at that point that Jacobson brought soldiers into the polling place and physically removed Hutchinson. However, Garr also recalled that "Captain R. S. Moore, of the enrolled militia, ordered Lieutenant Colonel Jacobson to halt; said Jacobson pushed Moore aside, and said, I will overpower you; Captain Moore replied, I surrender." Moore's intervention, while in keeping with the orders that had been issued to them by their commanding officer, General Willard Hall, came close to insubordination.[44] At that point, Garr went to a Colonel Shanklin, who would have outranked Jacobson and appears to have been in Chillicothe at this time. Garr asked Shanklin "to send a despatch to the governor, which he sent, and received for answer that the said twenty-seventh regiment must leave the court-house and go to their quarters, which they did."

Jacob Myers, the clerk of election, recalled the incident in much the same way, adding only that Colonel Shanklin had "requested the judges to hold on" while he telegraphed the governor. In the meantime, Myers, in what seems to have been the habitual response by clerks when the polls were occupied by troops, "folded up my poll-book and put it in my pocket." When Jacobson read the governor's message and said that he would leave the polling place, Myers reported that "Dr. Hughes became insulted, and left with them."[45]

44   Hall was both a general and the lieutenant governor of the state.
45   Ibid., pp. 102–3. For corroborating accounts from Hutchinson, Garr, and Myers, see pp. 101–2, 105–6, 108. Hutchinson testified that, in addition to the thirty or so men

This incident was remarkable in several respects. For one thing, Hughes, the Republican newspaper editor, and Jacobson probably coordinated their occupation of the polls. Hughes appeared at the courthouse early in the morning to put up his warning posters and was at the polls when Jacobson arrived. Jacobson immediately identified him as the person whose instructions the troops would follow when preventing disloyal men from voting. While this coincidence suggests prior planning on their part, they also apparently abandoned any pretense of formality; when Hughes charged Hutchinson with "feeding bushwhackers," this charge was sufficient for Jacobson despite Hutchinson's denial and the absence of any other corroborating information.[46] Regular procedure would have been to have sworn in Hutchinson, which evidently was done, and then to have received his vote. If, on later evidence, he had been shown to have aided the enemy, he could have been prosecuted for perjury. Hughes and Jacobson simply abandoned this process and rendered their own peremptory judgment. Finally, and most interestingly, the evidence revealed dissension within the militia itself. Although in different ways, Captain Moore and Colonel Shanklin both opposed Jacobson's occupation of the polls.[47] The blending of party, loyalty, and military power was well under way in 1862 Missouri, but the conflation of these elements was not yet complete.[48]

Elections throughout Missouri were more or less tainted by military intervention; however, the situation seems to have been generally worse in those areas where Union sentiment was already strong. For example, the

that accompanied Jacobson, there were "about one hundred [more] on the outside of the north side of the court-house square" (p. 101). Although he appeared moderate when compared with Jacobson, Shanklin actually belonged to the "hard" wing of the Missouri militia. Several years later, for example, Shanklin described guerrillas as "not only enemies of our country, but of Christianity and civilization, and even of our race, and the only remedy for the disease is to kill them." Fellman, *Inside War*, p. 113.

46 "Bushwhackers" was a colloquial term for irregular guerrillas. As a verb it later appeared in the 1865 revision of the Missouri Constitution, where "marauding commonly known as 'bushwhacking'" was one of many activities or sentiments related to the war that disqualified men from voting. Denny, *General Statutes of the State of Missouri*, p. 24.

47 Colonel Shanklin similarly intervened in the election being held in Utica, a small community in the same county. As in Chillicothe, a printed poster had appeared announcing: "No disloyal man shall vote." Early in the day a detachment of soldiers, also belonging to the Twenty-seventh Missouri Regiment, arrived under the command of a Major Howe, who announced that "he was sent there to arrest all men who had been enrolled as disloyal and voted." When the judges of election refused to open the polls on those terms, a Captain Reed "sent a despatch to Colonel Shanklin, at Chillicothe, to know what was to be done, and word was sent back to proceed with the election, that Major Howe with his soldiers were ordered to return to Chillicothe." S.R. no. 1198: M.D. no. 13 (1862): pp. 104–5.

48 The militia seem to have occupied precincts throughout the Seventh Congressional District. Ibid., pp. 116–18, 132–3, 135.

Seventh Congressional District, in the northwest corner of the state, was one of the most loyal regions of Missouri. When the election was contested, depositions could be taken in only a few of the rural counties. In the others, it was feared that mobs would break up the hearings. One of these counties was Nodaway, where attorney Washington Jones reported that testimony could not have been taken "unless it had been done privately." Attorney Silas Puryear reported the same situation in Atchison County, where Bruce had engaged him to take depositions:

I heard on several occasions that said Bruce would not be allowed to take depositions in said case, that if he came for that purpose he would be mobbed. These threats I understood were by A. B. Durfree, esq. I also heard threats of mobbing any one who would act as his counsel. Notwithstanding, I spoke to Jacob Hughes and William Sparks, the two justices of the peace, who promised to attend and take the depositions, but the day before the day for taking said depositions Sparks informed me he would not act; that the militia would not permit the taking; that when witnesses came they would be spattered with rotten eggs. I then went to see Judge Needles, who promised to attend, if well enough. On my return to Rockport I was informed there was a notice posted up requiring me to leave the county, on pain of being hung if found in the county next day. After reflecting on all the circumstances and threats, I was convinced that the depositions could not be taken, and that to attempt to do so would result in the witnesses being abused, and perhaps endanger their lives. The witnesses were mostly old men and the best men in the county, and I thought it best not to endanger nor expose them to insult, when nothing could be accomplished by so doing.[49]

One of the most interesting aspects of this and other Missouri elections during this period is the way in which government authority and vigilante-like activity combined in support of the Union cause. A striking example of this combination occurred in another 1862 congressional election, held in the Sixth District straddling the Missouri River on the western border of the state. Slavery was more deeply entrenched in this region than in the northwest corner of Missouri, and sympathy for the Confederacy was correspondingly greater. Union loyalists thus faced a more difficult task, and, probably in response, militia activity in support of the Republican candidate began very early in the campaign.

The Sixth Congressional District of Missouri

In what turned out to be the most important event of the congressional campaign in this district, Judge James Birch addressed a rally in Carrollton on October 6, 1862, about a month before the election. Lying about eight miles north of the Missouri River, Carrollton was the county seat of Carroll

---

[49]　Ibid., pp. 37, 117.

County and held about 700 people. As the following account describes, Judge Birch never finished his speech:

His audience, with a few exceptions, was composed of rebels; and, of course, he made a first-rate secession speech. When about half through, Captain Wakefield Stanley, commanding the post at this place, deeming his speech calculated to fan afresh the flames of rebellion and bushwhacking in this section, ordered him to stop his secession speech; and further, gave him orders to make no more speeches in Carroll county. All loyal men, and even some secessionists, who are disgusted with guerilla warfare, approved of Captain Stanley's course. Birch, fearing he was in danger (and perhaps he was) from the insulted militia, immediately left the county. On the next day the citizens of Carrollton and vicinity held an indignation meeting.

William Sinnard, esq., was called to the chair, and George Pattison appointed secretary. A committee was appointed to draught resolutions denouncing the course of Judge Birch. The following gentlemen composed said committee: Samuel Winfrey, Samuel Turner, O. J. Kirby, James Minnis, Levi Shin, James O'Gorman, and Lieutenant David Utt. While the committee retired, the secretary addressed the meeting, showing that the labors of the militia will all be in vain in their attempts to restore peace, if men like Birch fan afresh the now expiring flames of rebellion, by exciting young men with the absurd belief that the present war is for the purpose of freeing the slaves. Old men, who knew Judge Birch's former political course, could not be deceived, as they knew him to be as vacillating as the vane on the court-house steeple. Mr. P[attison] rebutted the position of Judge Birch, by quoting from the letter of General Jackson to A. J. Crawford; also the remarks of Senator Johnson of Tennessee, and the course pursued by certain southern senators. He advised those secessionists who make such a bug-a-boo of *nigger equality* to give their children a higher order of *moral* and *intellectual* education; then there would be no danger of their ever sinking to an equality with negroes, or falling below the standard that God and their country require.[50]

In short, the crowd that had assembled to hear Judge Birch, the Democratic candidate for Congress, was broken up by Union loyalists.[51] The next day

---

[50] This description of events during and immediately after the speech first appeared in the *Missouri Republican* and was reprinted in S.R. no. 1199: M.D. no. 20 (1862): p. 13. The texts of numerous resolutions adopted by the meeting were also reprinted.

[51] Even though candidates for office often took diametrically opposed positions with respect to prosecution of the war, party lines were still extremely confused in Missouri and the other border states. For that reason, formal party labels are difficult to assign to either James Birch or his opponent in the congressional race, Austin King, despite their alignment at the national level with the Democrats and the Republicans, respectively. In this and other races in the border states described in this chapter, the candidates and their supporters are described generally as "Democrats" and "Republicans" or "Unionists." However, these labels often overemphasize the importance of formal party organizations in these races; far more important, in many instances, was the general division between candidacies backed by the military and state authorities and rivals who opposed, often fiercely, the Union war effort. For the party designations under which border state candidates for Congress actually ran, see Michael J. Dubin, *United States Congressional Elections, 1788–1997: The Official Results* (Jefferson, N.C.: McFarland, 1998). Birch and King are, for example, described as

these Union loyalists called a public meeting to demonstrate popular support for their intervention. The men who organized this public meeting can be identified from other testimony. For example, William Sinnard, the man who assumed the chair of this public meeting, was one of the members of the "board of military assessors" that levied taxes for the support of the local units of the state militia. Samuel Winfrey and Levi Shin, who served on the committee that drafted the resolutions for the meeting, were the other two members of this assessing board. James Minnis, also named as a member of the drafting committee, was the provost marshal for Carroll County. Another member, O. J. Kirby, was the adjutant of the regiment of state militia raised and serving in that county. Lieutenant David Utt was an officer in that regiment. James O'Gorman was a private in one of the regiment's companies. Samuel Turner was the Carroll county sheriff. George Pattison, who served as secretary for the meeting, was the Republican candidate for the state legislature. In one way or another, every member of the group that prevented Birch from finishing his speech was either a Republican politician, officeholder, or associated with the state militia. As one witness put it, "[in] some manner or other they all belonged to the military police of the county."[52]

When compared with Democratic rhetoric in other northern states, Judge Birch's speech appears to have been quite ordinary. One Union loyalist believed that he could best demonstrate the speech's treasonous content by describing the reaction of the crowd:

secessionists . . . were much pleased with his [Birch's] bitter denunciation of the abolitionists of the north, and his bitter denunciation of the September emancipation proclamation of President Lincoln, and his declaration that he would not, if elected to Congress, vote either men or money for the purpose of carrying said proclamation into effect, and continuing the war upon that policy. They were also pleased with the idea advocated by him of holding out the Crittenden compromise principles to the people of the south; ceasing hostilities until they could have time to reflect and return to the Union; and that if such terms of peace were not accepted, that some arrangement had better be made by which the north and the south might part in peace, than to further prosecute this unfraternal war, under the present policy of the administration.[53]

In suppressing this speech as a treasonous act, the militia in Carrollton were condemning a great majority of the northern Democratic party, along with almost all effective opposition to Republican war policies. In the immediate vicinity of that small town, "the proceedings of that [loyalist] meeting had

"Peace Democrat" and "Democrat," respectively (p. 194). Once in Congress, King was labeled a "Unionist." Kenneth C. Martis, *Historical Atlas of Political Parties in the United States Congress, 1789–1989* (New York: Macmillan, 1989), p. 116.

[52] S.R. no. 1199: M.D. no. 20 (1862): p. 16.

[53] Ibid., p. 45. This description of Birch's speech was repeated almost verbatim by another witness (pp. 48–9).

the crowning effect they were intended to have, in deterring the friends of Judge Birch from making any further effort in his behalf, and of keeping them from the polls on the day of the election."[54]

The Republican candidate for Congress, Austin King, a former governor, delivered a speech in Russellville that conflated an act of voting for Judge Birch and disloyalty as defined by "order 24." As described by one witness, King denounced Birch

as being as grand a traitor as Jeff. Davis ever was, or worse, if possible; and he declared in continuation, that any man who voted for him (Birch) ought to be placed upon the disloyal list. At that point of his speech, Lieutenant (or Adjutant) Hemry, who was upon the stand with him, in full uniform, and who was also recognized as an assisting enrolling officer, rose from his seat waved his hat over his head and proclaimed aloud, "Yes, governor, and I *will* place, or see to it that every man is placed upon the disloyal list who does vote for him," or words to that effect.[55]

The intimidating effect of this public display of cooperation between the Republican party and the state militia was reinforced by individual threats of imprisonment.[56]

Aside from imprisonment, there were material reasons to avoid the militia's displeasure. Perhaps the most important consequence of being placed on the "order 24" list, for example, was vulnerability to discriminatory impressment of forage and livestock. Lieutenant Colonel Thomas Swearingen, who commanded a militia detachment during the months preceding the election, succinctly described how his unit was supported:

My orders from my superiors were to subsist my command . . . from several weeks before the election until several weeks after the election, by levies of such articles of provisions and forage as we needed, upon those who were enrolled as sympathizers or regarded as sympathizers, and to cause them, as a general thing, to deliver such

[54] Ibid., p. 16.

[55] Ibid., p. 17. For contrary descriptions of King's speech, see pp. 43, 46. King later came to oppose the Republican party. William E. Parrish, *Missouri under Radical Rule, 1865–1870* (Columbia: University of Missouri Press, 1965), p. 43.

[56] For example, when one Democrat approached the polls, he was told by one of the election judges "that if I voted for Birch I would be put in prison before sundown." He then cast his vote for a minor, third party candidate. In another instance that occurred about two weeks before the election, "Lieutenant Colonel William A. Wilson, in command of the militia of Saline county, put up at the 'Sedalia House,' of which I [the testifying witness] am clerk. The conversation turning upon the subject of the congressional election then pending in the sixth congressional district, Colonel Wilson publicly declared his intention to arrest any man in Saline county who voted for Judge Birch as a traitor, and *punish* him as a traitor." S.R. no. 1199: M.D. no. 20 (1862): pp. 13–14. Threats such as these were not idle in Saline County. By the time of the election, several men had already been murdered by the state militia and several more were killed during the remainder of the war. For even-handed, detailed accounts of atrocities on both sides in Saline county, see anon., *History of Saline County, Missouri* (St. Louis: Missouri Historical Company, 1881), pp. 317–23.

articles as corn, hay, beef, wheat, bacon, potatoes, wood, &c., at our quarters or camps, wherever they might be. These articles, of course, were not paid for, being simply levied, according to my best discretion, upon such sympathizers, and in such quantities as I thought equitable and proper, under the general order by which I was governed. It was also within my orders to press horses and equipments from those who were regarded as sympathizers, in order to mount such portion of my command as had not suitable horses of their own, and this was done accordingly, with the understanding that the stock would be returned, if living, when we were done with them.[57]

If the militia, for any reason, "regarded" a farmer as a southern sympathizer, his livestock and crops could be impressed without compensation. When the militia equated a vote for Judge Birch with disloyalty, the penalty for casting such a vote was probable destitution.[58] The consequence of this conflation of loyalty, support for the Republican party, and susceptibility to impressment was that, as one witness described, the election was "the most 'quiet and orderly' I ever witnessed, but it was emphatically the quiet of despotism upon the side which had all the arms of the county in their hands, and of submission upon the side which had been wholly disarmed...."[59]

The Fifth Congressional District of Missouri

Each county in Missouri had a board of assessors that was empowered to levy taxes for the support of "widows whose husbands had been killed, and men who had been wounded by the guerillas, and...those whose property had been stolen or destroyed by them," as described by Daniel Bliss, a farmer and member of the assessment board in Miller County.[60] Bliss stated that the

[57] S.R. no. 1199: M.D. no. 20 (1862): p. 32. For a description of the "disloyal" list and the susceptibility of men on it to taxation for the support of the militia, see p. 27. There were 631 men on the "order 24" list in Clay and Clinton Counties alone, and even in those counties, the list was said to be incomplete. Because "order 24" assessments were levied under martial law, there could be no appeal from the decisions of local boards. *American Annual Cyclopaedia for 1862*, p. 590. Instituted as a statewide policy on June 23, 1862, abuses in application were so counterproductive that Union authorities abandoned discriminatory tax assessments in January 1863. Fellman, *Inside War*, pp. 94–5.

[58] For example, a witness from Richmond, Ray County, stated that the "people were impressed with the opinion that the military authorities...could exercise almost any power they pleased, discriminating in their assessments and other oppressions [whether] in favor of those who voted with them in the election, or against those [who] voted against them; and the public ear was continually filled with such denunciations as that Birch was a traitor, and that all who voted for him would be treated as traitors; that their stock would be pressed, and the militia subsisted upon them." S.R. no. 1199: M.D. no. 20 (1862): p. 37.

[59] The witness was describing the conditions in Plattsburg, Clinton County, on the day of the election. Ibid., p. 26.

[60] S.R. no. 1199: M.D. no. 16 (1862): p. 255; also see p. 275.

board identified southern sympathizers by "their daily walk and conversation," in addition to "the roll on which persons had enrolled as sympathizers before Mr. Bass, provost marshal."[61] In this county, men were notified that they had been placed on the assessment list by the posting of a public proclamation. Thomas Scott, a farmer and one of the board members who served with Bliss, described this process when he contended that Edmund Riggs had to have known that he had been assessed

for the following reasons... he and Owen Riggs, his brother, live only four or five miles apart, and Owen Riggs comes to Tuscumbia either by or near Edmund Riggs's house. When the board made the assessment for their district they had a notice put up at West's mill, in the Riggs settlement, with all the names of those assessed, and Owen Riggs came to my house to see what proof he would have to make to get off.[62]

Because Owen Riggs had appealed his assessment, Scott believed he had seen the posted proclamation and surmised that, even if Edmund Riggs had not seen the proclamation himself, his brother must had told him about it.[63]

Miller County was in the Fifth Congressional District of Missouri, a district that ran from Jefferson City, the state capital, in the center of the state, to the western border with Kansas. Like the Sixth, which lay just to the north, this district contained many communities in which southern sympathy ran high and more than a few in which guerrilla bands and more formally organized Confederate units were active. In several counties, some or most of the normal polling places in outlying districts were closed on election day because they were said to be vulnerable to Confederate or guerrilla raids. It should be noted, however, that many of the precincts that the military

[61] This roll was probably the "order 24" list. The average assessment levied on "southern sympathizers" was 5 percent of the valuation of their property. Ibid., p. 255. Thomas Flood, a farmer and voter in Miller County, reported that about two weeks after the election the assessment board "came about to collect the tax levied upon the rebels....I asked them why they assessed me with thirty dollars, saying that I had always supported the Constitution and laws. Daniel Bliss asked me if I did not vote for Thomas Price. I told him I did. He said that was enough to tax me, if nothing else" (p. 110).

[62] The proclamation was posted by several members of the state militia who had been detailed to the assessment board. After ten days, the proclamations were taken down. Ibid., pp. 267–8.

[63] Since Edmund Riggs lived about five miles from West's mill, it was not unlikely that he would never have seen the proclamation personally. The question was important because of the possibility that he would have been intimidated at the polls by a threat of assessment; if he already knew that he had been assessed as disloyal, no more harm could have come from that direction if he voted for Thomas Price, the Democratic candidate for Congress. He would have thus voted anyway. These assessments were often difficult for poor men to satisfy; the clerk of the Miller County court, for example, reported that Edmund Riggs had sent his "boy...to borrow money...to pay the assessment a few days after the election." Ibid., p. 266. In earlier testimony, Riggs had claimed that he feared that if he voted for Price, he "would be put down as secesh, and taxed as such," and he had not voted for that reason (p. 117).

considered unsafe were those in which southern sympathy ran fairly high; from the perspective of Union authorities, closing the polls in those precincts discouraged voting by those who opposed the war effort under cover, as it were, of maintaining security. As elsewhere in Missouri, there is little actual evidence of Confederate interference with the election and, indeed, little reason for southern-leaning men to have interfered; they would have carried the election in precisely those precincts that the militia closed down.[64]

As elsewhere in Missouri, the militia sometimes used physical intimidation as a means of discouraging southern-leaning men from voting. However, most loyalists in this district chose an alternative strategy, threatening men with enrollment in the militia if they appeared at the polls and swore the oath enacted by the state legislature.[65] Although their logic was faulty, the militia contended that a man who took the legislature's oath thereby gave conclusive evidence of his loyalty and, for that reason, made himself susceptible to militia service.[66] Thus "order 24" men, who were usually physically prevented from voting in the Seventh Congressional District, were discouraged by the threat of enrollment in the Fifth.[67]

These threats were often made prior to the election. For example, Lawrence Lee, a resident of Clark's Fork Township in Cooper County, reported that he had been in the provost's office in Booneville, the county

[64]   For accounts of the operation of guerrilla bands and Confederate units in this district, see ibid., pp. 24–5, 30, 35, 45–7, 192, 198, 201, 208, 210, 213, 218, 224. In one county, the poll books were taken by "rebel guerillas" as they were being delivered to one of the polling places (pp. 207, 217–18). In St. Clair County, there was only one precinct (in Oreola, the county seat) because there "was imminent danger of being interrupted by rebel guerilla bands that then invested that county" (p. 310). Five of the ten precincts in Johnson county were not open for the same reason (p. 325). In Bates County, only one precinct was open "in consequence of the principal portion of the county being overrun with rebel guerillas, under the command of Quantrell and others" (p. 326). In Henry County, three of the seven precincts were not open because "it was not considered safe, on account of the condition of the country, to open the polls. The clerk could get no one to carry the poll-books to any one of those precincts." (p. 329). For numerous descriptions and general analysis of guerrilla activity, see Fellman, *Inside War*.

[65]   For descriptions of intimidation by the militia in Cole, Cooper, Henry, Miller, Moniteau, and Pettis Counties, see S.R. no. 1199: M.D. no. 16 (1862): pp. 8, 18, 88–90, 101–5, 114–17, 127, 129, 146–7, 156, 158, 163–4. At the polls in Jamestown, Moniteau County, a militia captain stood at the table where votes were received, personally interrogating and threatening voters. On at least one occasion, he ordered the arrest of a voter immediately after he had deposited his ticket (pp. 148–9).

[66]   See the earlier discussion comparing the legislature's oath with regulations for preparation of "order 24" lists; it was possible for a man to swear the oath and still qualify for exemption from militia service under the order. However, from the militia's perspective, this errant conflation of the oath with service eligibility was nonetheless attractive because it discouraged voters who were unsympathetic to the Union cause.

[67]   For examples of such threats and evidence that they discouraged men holding ambivalent Union loyalties from voting, see ibid., pp. 7–15, 17–20, 23, 25, 140, 149, 192.

seat, several days prior to election day. While there, Colonel Reavis, the commanding officer of the militia regiment that had been raised in Cooper County, asked Lee

Whether we were going to vote out there [in Clark's Fork]. I told him some of us were, and some were not. He said those who were able-bodied men and subject to military duty would be put in the militia if they voted. At that time Colonel Pope stepped in and said it was our disloyalty that kept us out of the militia, and if we took the oath and voted it would establish our loyalty, and he could not do otherwise than put us in the militia. He said he did not say so to prevent me from voting or to intimidate me, but it was his duty to do so.[68]

Colonel Pope, the commanding officer of the Fifty-second Regiment of the state militia then garrisoning Cooper County, was speaking with his tongue firmly in cheek. As commander, he openly campaigned for Joseph McClurg, distributing among his troops "political circulars" supporting the Republican candidate. Every soldier in his command must have known the election outcome that his colonel desired. On election day he dispatched these troops to all the precincts in the county (Black Water, Clark's Fork, Clear Creek, Kelly, Lebanon, Moniteau, Palestine, Pilot Grove, and Saline). In addition to patrolling the polls, Pope used his troops, along with cooperating private civilians and election officials, to identify voters who had been exempted from militia service, sometimes inspecting the poll-books for that purpose. In one township, he even ordered the arrest of men who voted with the ostensible intention of forcibly enrolling them.[69]

Union troops had good reason to suspect the loyalty of many of the voters who appeared at the polls; the ambivalence of many voters toward the Union

---

68 Lee was in the provost's office because he needed a pass from the provost in order to travel to another county. Because he had been enrolled on the "order 24" list, Lee was exempt from militia service. When asked whether he had "ever acted as a guide to a guerilla band passing through" Cooper County, Lee responded that he had been "called up one night about 11 o'clock, and made to go with a band of men who called themselves confederate soldiers." Ibid., pp. 23–4. Colonel Reavis later described Price voters as "[r]ebels and rebel sympathizers and copperhead democracy." By copperhead democracy, he meant "the class of Union men styling themselves democrats and affiliate with secessionists" (p. 202).

69 Ibid., pp. 185–6. At Clark's Fork on the day of the election, Lawrence Lee and several of his friends were "talking of voting" near the polling place when "Captain Mahan stepped up and told us to come up and vote. Said he had just received a letter from St. Louis urging him for recruits, and he would like to have us to fill up old regiments" (p. 25). On martial law in the county, see pp. 22–3, 27, 35. The entire state of Missouri was formally under martial law, but the extent to which military rule actually displaced civilian governments varied from place to place. In communities where military rule more or less replaced civilian institutions, "provost marshals were often the only available agents of the law." Their authority was often absolute. One provost marshal, for example, contended that a man who appealed one of his orders to a civilian court should be arrested for treason. The appeal apparently failed when his attorneys abandoned the case. Fellman, *Inside War*, pp. 33, 41, 42–3.

cause was plainly evident even in the hearings.[70] One witness, when asked whether he was a "loyal man or a southern sympathizer," responded that he considered himself "a law-abiding, constitutional man." When asked to explain what a "constitutional man" was, he answered a "loyal man to his country." But this description later fell to the ground when the same witness was asked whether he had "furnish[ed] provision, or in any other way give[n] aid and comfort to a guerilla band, or, as they call themselves, confederate soldiers, at Camp Harness." He refused to answer. Later, when the question was repeated, he again refused, adding, "I don't admit that I gave aid and comfort to the rebels at Camp Harness, or anywhere else." William Newberry, who had voted for Thomas Price at the Palestine Precinct in Cooper County, had been arrested by the militia several days after the election. In the hearing, Newberry was asked whether he was a "loyal citizen." He said, "I can't say whether I am or not." He was then asked whether he had ever been "at any time in arms against the authority of the United States government." To this he responded, "I do not wish to answer this question." He did, however, recall that when the military had "asked my politics" he had "replied that I was south."[71]

By all accounts, the militia strongly influenced the voting in Calhoun, Henry County. At a public meeting the night before the election attended largely by soldiers, the provost marshal, Captain Murphy, made a speech in which he said

> that he wanted [his men] to stand shoulder to shoulder at the ballot-box, like they had at Lone Jack, and he was perfectly satisfied they would cast no votes for secesh. The remark was made in the house, that men would be marked who voted the secesh ticket.[72]

The next day, the militia voted early and were almost finished before the citizens began voting. Some of the soldiers positioned themselves, with their weapons, around the polling place. One witness reported that these "soldiers were drinking some, and generally boisterous." Another recalled that he had

---

[70] Many of the judges of election were also suspect, even if they never expressed any reservation with respect to the Union cause. For example, Randolph Lane, who had served as election judge in Iron County, was asked how many of his sons were serving in the Confederate army. He answered, "If they are alive, I have got three in the rebel army." S.R. no. 1200: M.D. no. 43 (1863): p. 19. A number of other judges were asked the same question; in several cases, they answered: "None that I know of." See, for example, p. 20.

[71] S.R. no. 1199: M.D. no. 16 (1862): pp. 30, 32; also see pp. 33, 144.

[72] Ibid., pp. 88–9. A small battle had occurred at Lone Jack roughly three months before this meeting. Federal troops had been ambushed and defeated by Confederate raiders (one of whom was Quantrill), but the southerners had later been driven off by Union reinforcements arriving from Kansas. E. B. Long with Barbara Long, *The Civil War Day-by-Day: An Almanac 1861–1865* (New York: Da Capo, 1971), p. 251; *American Annual Cyclopaedia for 1862*, p. 594.

"heard one soldier say no secesh should vote there. He [this soldier] was standing close to the window where they were voting, on the outside of the house. He observed, not to say anything to them – to shoot them down as fast as they go in." This may have been the same soldier who so impressed Mortimor Hukill. Hukill testified that between ten and eleven o'clock in the morning, a

soldier came on the platform at the door where the crowd was, at the house where they were voting; he had a large revolver in his hand; he was swinging it around in the crowd, and swearing if there was any secessionist there he intended to kill him if he showed himself, and said he was going to vote; he drove the crowd pretty much all from the platform....[73]

One of the officers told this soldier "to put his pistol up" and called for Captain Murphy. This was about eleven o'clock:

Captain Murphy and a lieutenant went across from headquarters; by the time he got within ten steps of the door, he commenced swearing that there were bushwhackers voting there; by God, he intended to break it up; he called to the judges that he wanted a copy of the poll-books before they were taken away from there; and, by God, if they did not suit him he would tear them up....[74]

This appears to have been the same incident in which, as Peyton Parks recounted, Captain Murphy

made the remark that the damned bushwacks were coming there and voting right under the noses of his men, who had been fighting the battles of their country, and, damn them they should not do it; he further said he intended to have their names, and forage off of them all winter.[75]

[73] The platform before the voting window on which the soldier displayed his revolver was fifteen feet long by eight feet wide, somewhat larger than usual. It could thus have easily accommodate a number of men. As for the gun, Hukill described it as "one of those large self-cocking revolvers, and he [the soldier] was as liable to shoot one as another was the reason why I went away, and I suppose others were like myself....He [the soldier] was in liquor." S.R. no. 1199: M.D. no. 16 (1862): pp. 89, 101–3.

[74] Ibid., p. 102. For a corroborating account of this incident, see pp. 104–5. After the polls had closed in Calhoun, the clerk of the election "delivered a copy of the poll-book to Captain Murphy; he [the captain] then observed that he had been informed that the people at Belmont [another precinct in the county] were all voting for Price and Allen, and that he had detailed sixteen men to go up and take the poll-books in. He then exhibited them, swearing that he had taken the damned thing prisoner." The clerk also reported that "the next day when he [the captain] got sober, he convened the judges and the clerks and had them make the certificates, and then he returned the poll-books" (pp. 163, 165).

[75] Ibid., pp. 89–90, 94. For corroborating reports of threats that the militia in Cooper County would impress the property of those voting for Price, see pp. 97, 110, 117, 123. In Liberty Township, Cole County, a witness reported that the "common talk in my township was, that Thomas L. Price was a secessionist, and that any man voting for him would be considered a secessionist also; and if they did vote for him the soldiers would take all the flour, bacon, and all that belonged to them, from them"

Another man, Mark Finks, overheard Murphy say that he had "thought that this election was to decide the war in Missouri; instead of that, it would prolong the war if they suffered every person to vote, and it should not be." At this point Finks left the polls and headed for home; however, he stopped for a moment to discuss the situation with friends on the village square. While there, he was told that his son, Fisher Finks, had been arrested by the militia and was in the guardhouse. The father "hunted up Captain Murphy. . . . When I found him, I asked him what they had Fisher in the guard-house for? He said he did not know they had him there; he said he would hunt up his orderly" and find out. Some time later Mark Finks again saw Murphy: "[I] told him my son wanted to know whether they were going to let him out in time to go home; if not, he wanted me to take his horse home. He [Captain Murphy] told me he could not attend to him before morning; that I could take the horse home." Fisher was released later that evening. What is remarkable, of course, is the informality with which martial law was carried out in such small communities; Fisher could be arrested, imprisoned without charges, and later released without any explanation whatsoever, all the while his father is personally discussing both the arrest and the consequent minor domestic inconvenience it caused with the commanding officer.[76]

About noon, after the election officials returned from lunch at a nearby tavern, Captain Murphy came back to the polls. He asked James Caldwell, the clerk of election,

how the election was going between Price and McClurg; I answered, Price is running ahead. He exclaimed, "I will be damned if I don't put a stop to it." He then enjoined upon me to clear out the election room. I did so, and invited him in. He undertook to make a speech; he went on and accused the judges and clerks for letting them vote for Price, and condemned it. Then we stated to him that we were all proceeding according [to] law. He then turned to me and remarked, "I enjoin it on you to give me a list of all those names who voted for Price and Allen," and remarked he had a use for all such men; that he expected to call on them in a few days; he also wanted

---

(p. 145). Samuel Fisher, who resided in Blackwater Township, Pettis County, recalled that he was afraid the soldiers "would do me some private injury, burn my house or my barn" (p. 131).

[76] Three men were arrested at this polling place that day: James Byar, Fisher Finks, and George Walker. A neighbor, William Jennings, a carriage and wagon maker in Calhoun, later accused Mark Finks of being a "secessionist," stating, "I have taken pretty good notice of the company he keeps; I have generally noticed that he has associated with secessionists. The time the rebels were starting to Lexington, from Calhoun, Captain Finks was there; his son James Finks was in the crowd, also other neighbors; when he, Mark Finks, shook hands with a secesh officer, on leaving, he remarked, 'I wish you well; I wish you great success.'" Ibid., pp. 94, 104–5, 239. For other reports of arrests or threats of imprisonment in the Fifth Congressional District, see pp. 86–94, 141, 143–4, 147, 156, 160, 317–18.

their places of residence; he wanted to know where to find such men. That was said in a very threatening manner.[77]

Murphy also said, "[W]e ought to be very particular and not let bushwhackers vote; that he had understood there had been bushwhackers voted in the fore part of the day." At that point, George Squires, one of the judges of election,

> observed to Captain Murphy it was impossible for us to tell whether men had been in the brush or not. We would administer the oath to them; that was all we could do. We could not tell whether they had been in the brush or not, they could [have been]. I then observed to Captain Murphy, if we had to be the judges where men had been, or what they had been doing, it was not worth while to record any more votes. He then observed, he wished to impress it upon our minds, if we knew of any, not to allow any of them to vote.[78]

After this incident, which took place in the election room with all the doors and windows closed up, the militia more aggressively policed the polls. There were threats made that the militia would forage off Price voters after the election and, at one point, Caldwell was told "to get out of the way, in order that they [the soldiers] might shoot those who had just been sworn, while in the act of voting." Very few men cast tickets for Price in the afternoon; one man even returned to the polls in order to switch his vote from Price to McClurg after he had been told by one of the local Union men that he had voted the "secesh" ticket.[79]

What transpired at the polls in Calhoun on November 4, 1862, lay somewhere between organized state repression of suffrage rights and spontaneous intimidation of friends and neighbors.[80] The federal and state authorities certainly empowered the militia to patrol the polls and maintain order. But they also, at least formally, enjoined the troops to allow voters "without

---

[77]   Ibid., p. 163. Most precincts apparently recessed for lunch, at which time militia officers sometimes addressed the voters. For example, at the Blue Spring meetinghouse in Miller County, Lieutenant Babcock, a preacher and militia officer, publicly accused the Democratic candidate for Congress of disloyalty (p. 110). At Big Lick Precinct in Cooper County, a militia captain, again during the break for lunch, publicly stated that "any man who voted for T. L. Price would be forced in the militia within ten days" (p. 149).

[78]   Ibid., p. 88.

[79]   Because of these threats, Caldwell and one of the other judges did not vote. They would have voted for Price. Ibid., p. 163.

[80]   Much of Missouri was the site of guerrilla operations in which members of the militia and their families were often targets. For that reason, personal revenge was often a more powerful motive for the persecution of southern sympathizers than an abstract loyalty to the Union. In describing the Union garrison in Warsaw, Missouri, for example, Lieutenant Colonel T. A. Switzer stated, "Many of the soldiers are in the neighborhood of their homes, and all have private wrongs to avenge, and it is plain to see the effect." Fellman, *Inside War*, pp. 62–3; also see p. 185.

molestation of any kind, to cast their votes as they please."[81] Just how well this injunction was expected to control the actions of the militia is an open question.[82]

Repression was often, in fact, a spontaneous reaction of loyal men who happened to be newly clothed with government authority. Given almost unlimited power over their friends and neighbors, many of whom were at least ambivalent toward northern prosecution of the Civil War, these men conflated suffrage rights and a loyalist victory: Men could legitimately vote if and only if they supported the Union cause. Those who did not support the cause were traitors who could be thrown out of the polling place, arrested, and "foraged upon" at will. This conflation was not quite complete; in many places men could still, at their own risk, vote for Democratic candidates.

The practical outcome was that the militia guaranteed a loyalist victory at the polls. This outcome, however, was not the result of a close calculation of just how much democracy could be allowed in Missouri without losing control of the state. Instead, much of the intimidation had the same kind of quality that civilians had practiced before the war (e.g., the widespread use of alcohol, as well as verbal and physical intimidation). What was different was that one of the parties was now armed, both with weapons and with the authority of the state. Unused to this new role, the party-as-militia improvised rough and ready procedures as they

[81] For a copy of General Order No. 45 (October 23, 1862), which regulated militia conduct at the polls, see S.R. no. 1199: M.D. no. 16 (1862): p. 183. For a copy of the implementing order, issued by Colonel Pope for Cooper county, see p. 195. On the "brutality" of Union occupation of Missouri, see Fellman, *Inside War*, pp. 10–11, 29–38, 43, 56, 73–4, 87.

[82] Union authorities were certainly capable of systematic repression. For example, when Sample Orr, the register of lands of the State of Missouri, delivered a speech in Jefferson City that the authorities considered disloyal, he was arrested by the order of General Loan (who, incidentally, was also a Republican congressional candidate in another district; p. 318). In addition to Orr's arrest, the acting provost marshal general of Missouri prohibited the editor of the *Jefferson City Examiner* from reporting on or reprinting Orr's speech "in the next or any other issue of your paper." For a copy of the order, see p. 168. On occasion, the military would shut down a newspaper altogether. In 1863, while he was provost marshal in Ironton, for example, Carroll Peck "received an order to stop the circulation of (*The Crisis*) and some other disloyal papers." S.R. no. 1200: M.D. no. 43 (1863): p. 39. This censorship appears to have been under a general order issued on January 9, 1862, which required "all publishers of newspapers in Missouri [outside of St. Louis] to furnish him [the provost marshal general] a copy of each issue for inspection, under penalty of having their papers suppressed." *American Annual Cyclopaedia for 1862*, p. 590. On suppression of newspapers that opposed Republican direction of the northern war effort, particularly in the border states, see Mark E. Neely, Jr., *The Union Divided: Party Conflict in the Civil War North* (Cambridge, Mass.: Harvard University Press, 2002), pp. 89–117. As Neely points out, Lincoln himself appears to have ordered the suppression of opposition papers in Kentucky and Missouri (pp. 91–2).

went along.[83] Some of these, like the soldier pirouetting with a cocked revolver before the voting window in Calhoun, were not likely to become enshrined in militia regulations. However, other actions, such as foraging off political dissenters, were much more easily turned into at least informal practices with consequent firm expectations as to the probable consequences of voting. Either way, the state, in both its federal and its local incarnations, had come to the polls in Missouri.

Kentucky

In Kentucky, elections were conducted much as they were in Missouri. The major difference was in the slightly greater formality with which the militia directed the proceedings.[84] For example, the 1863 general election was conducted under martial law, which had been declared by Major General Burnside three days before the election was held on August 3. As the last paragraph specifies, martial law was to be imposed only in the election proceedings:

General Orders   Headquarters Department of the Ohio
    No. 120   Cincinnati, Ohio, July 31, 1863.

Whereas the State of Kentucky is invaded by a rebel force, with the avowed intention of overawing the judges of election, of intimidating the loyal voters, keeping them from the polls, and forcing the election of disloyal candidates at the election on the 3d of August; and whereas the military power of the government is the only force that can defeat this attempt, the State of Kentucky is hereby declared under martial law, and all military officers are commanded to aid the constituted authorities of the State in support of the laws and the purity of suffrage, as defined in the late proclamation of his excellency Governor Robinson.

As it is not the intention of the commanding general to interfere with the proper expression of public opinion, all discretion in the conduct of the election will be, as usual, in the hands of the legally appointed judges at the polls, who will be held strictly responsible that no disloyal person be allowed to vote, and to this end the military power is ordered to give them its utmost support.

---

[83] Some of these improvisations must have been quite effective. On the morning of the election, for example, a Price supporter attending the polls at Linn Township in Moniteau County gave some of the tickets he was distributing to the officers and men of a militia company. "I saw no more of the tickets until a short time afterwards the company marched down to the front of the place of voting, with the tickets sticking on their bayonets; the company remained in front of the polls until they had all voted. During the time they were standing there I saw some of them take the tickets off, tear them up and stamp them." S.R. no. 1199: M.D. no. 16 (1862): p. 151.

[84] Unlike Missouri, volunteer units of the U.S. Army patrolled many of the polling places in Kentucky. The fact that these units were often composed of out-of-state men who did not have a personal stake in the election outcome, combined with tighter discipline under federal officers, made military behavior at the polls less irregular and arbitrary than was the case in Missouri.

The civil authority, civil courts, and business, will not be suspended by this order. It is for the purpose only of protecting, if necessary, the rights of loyal citizens and the freedom of election.

By command of Major General Burnside.

Lewis Richmond
Assistant Adjutant General.

The primary effect of the order was to empower the militia to exclude men whom they or the election judges considered to be disloyal. In some cases, the militia prohibited men from serving as election judges as well.[85] Despite the opening paragraph of this order, there is no evidence in the hearings of Confederate interference with the voting.[86]

Burnside's order appears to have been issued in support of another proclamation issued by Brigadier General Shackleford on the previous day, July 30:

Headquarters 1st Brigade, 2d Division, 23d Army Corps,
Russellville, Ky., July 30, 1863.
General Order,
No. 23.

In order that the proclamation of the governor and the laws of the State of Kentucky may be observed and enforced, post commandants and officers of this command will see that the following regulations are strictly complied with at the approaching State election:

None but loyal citizens will act as officers of the election.

No one will be allowed to offer himself as a candidate for office, or be voted for at said election, who is not in all things loyal to the State and federal government, and in favor of a vigorous prosecution of the war for the suppression of the rebellion.

---

[85]   T. S. Knight had been appointed sheriff of the election (a position equivalent to a judge of election in other states) at the Walnut Bottom precinct in Henderson County. He testified that a detachment of the Sixty-fifth Regiment of Indiana volunteers under the command of a Captain Childs arrived just after the polls had opened in the morning. Childs, he stated, "showed me an order from General Shackleford, and asked me if I was loyal. I replied affirmatively, but pointing to a paragraph in the said order having reference to the vigorous prosecution of the war, dissenting from it, saying I was for peace. The captain then said I could not serve as an officer of the election, as he knew where my sympathies were; the voting was then suspended." Childs demanded that the clerk give him the poll book, which was done under protest. Once in possession of the poll book, the troops apparently closed down the polling place. S.R. no. 1200: Contested Congressional Election in the Second District of Kentucky: M.D. no. 36, p. 32. John H. McHenry, Jr., vs. George H. Yeaman, election held on August 3, 1863.

[86]   Ibid., p. 68. After the election, a Louisville judge addressed a public memorial to President Lincoln in which he complained: "On August 1st, Colonel Mundy, commanding at Louisville, issued his proclamation, with generous assurances to the citizens that their election should be protected against the interference of raiders, of whom no man had the slightest fear, but giving no promise against his own soldiers, as to whom at least one half of the voters stood in the greatest apprehension." *American Annual Cyclopaedia for 1863* (New York: D. Appleton, 1864), p. 563. For a succinct summary of political conditions in Kentucky in 1863, including related military orders and actions, see pp. 562–70.

The judges of election will allow no one to vote at said election unless he is known to them to be an undoubtedly loyal citizen, or unless he shall first take the oath required by the laws of the State of Kentucky.

No disloyal man will offer himself as a candidate, or attempt to vote, except for treasonable purposes; and all such efforts will be summarily suppressed by the military authorities.

All necessary protection will be supplied and guaranteed at the polls to Union men by all the military force within this command.

By order of
>> J. M. Shackelford
>> Brigadier General, Commanding.
>> J. E. Huffman,
>> > Assistant Adjutant General.

In what appears to be a postcript to the order, Shackleford dictated an oath that was to be sworn by all voters:

Oath to be taken at the election.

I do solemnly swear that I have not been in the service of the so-called Confederate States, in either a civil or military capacity, or in the service of the so-called provisional government of Kentucky; that I have not given any aid, assistance or comfort to any person in arms against the United States; and that I have, in all things, demeaned myself as a loyal citizen since the beginning of the present rebellion: so help me God.[87]

This oath was to be sworn in addition to one previously enacted by the Kentucky legislature. The main difference between the two oaths was that the word "voluntary" appeared before "aid and assistance" in the legislature's version. The omission of that word meant that the military oath could not be sworn by men whose property or services had been involuntarily impressed by Confederate forces. Because southern troops had been active in much of Kentucky, forcibly requisitioning supplies and other aid, this omission disqualified many voters who could have taken the legislative oath.[88] In

---

[87] S.R. no. 1200: M.D. no. 36 (1863): pp. 56–7.
[88] For example, John S. McCormack reported that, a short time after he had sworn the military oath and voted in Henderson County, "the adjutant of the 65th regiment Indiana volunteers, under command of Colonel Foster, came and informed me that I was wanted at headquarters. I was kept there a few minutes, and then taken to the court-house, where we met Colonel Foster, who asked me if Johnson's men had not eaten at my house last summer. I answered yes; they had impressed their breakfast of my wife during my absence from the house. He then ordered me into the military prison, where I was detained about 23 or 24 hours." In effect, McCormack was arrested because his wife had involuntarily fed breakfast to Confederate soldiers. Ibid., p. 36. McCormack's situation was not uncommon. In fact, Michael Fellman reports that when Missouri guerrillas confronted isolated farm families, the "most frequent demand [they made] was for food." *Inside War*, p. 26.

practice, the military oath made the legislative oath redundant since any one who could swear to the first could obviously swear to the second.[89]

In the Second Congressional District, two candidates stood for election in 1863: George Yeaman and John McHenry. Yeaman was sponsored by the Union party and was aligned with the Republicans. At the time of the election, he was a member of the lower house of the Kentucky legislature. McHenry was Yeaman's Democratic opponent. While McHenry had previously served the Union cause as commanding colonel of the Seventeenth Kentucky Cavalry, there was some dispute as to his fidelity to the northern war effort. At Vanover's Precinct in Daviess County, for example, one of the judges of election reported that all but one of the soldiers voted for Yeaman and that they heaped a "good deal of abuse" on McHenry. As the judges continued to take votes, imposing the military oath, Colonel McHenry

asked leave to address the crowd for a few minutes, which was granted him, and we suspended taking votes for this purpose. Colonel McHenry then denied that he was a rebel, saying that he was about the first to raise the national flag, and to call for volunteers in Green River country, and his regiment was about the first to fire a gun in battle, when Marion Iglehart, of the 3d Kentucky cavalry, said he was a damned liar.[90]

In general, the military considered McHenry's loyalty to the Union cause as less than complete but allowed his candidacy to stand. However, at many precincts, only men who supported McHenry were asked to swear the oath.[91]

As in Missouri, troops patrolled the polls and actively participated in the proceedings. However, some of the detachments belonged to the Union army and were composed of men from outside the state.[92] For that reason, there were more instances in which the troops did not personally know the men approaching the polls, thus compelling the military to rely more heavily on oaths and the reports of local loyalists when excluding men from voting.[93] In

[89]   S.R. no. 1200: M.D. no. 36 (1863): p. 69.
[90]   Ibid., p. 14. Most of these troopers belonged to the Third Kentucky Cavalry and thus had not served under McHenry.
[91]   The military did order that the name of the Democratic candidate for governor, Charles Wickliffe, be stricken from the poll books. Since Kentucky used oral voting in elections, this meant that votes for Wickliffe were simply not recorded by the clerks of election. Ibid., pp. 9, 11, 18, 20, 32–3. Despite the fact that voters in many precincts across the state could not support him, Wickliffe still received about 20 percent of the total votes.
[92]   In the city of Henderson, for example, the Sixty-fifth Regiment of Indiana volunteers policed the polls. Ibid., pp. 32–4.
[93]   At other polling places where the troops were from Kentucky, soldiers sometimes acted on their own initiative and knowledge of the community. For example, George Ashby, a farmer who voted in Ohio County, reported, "When I first came to the polls in the morning, William C. Morton, a soldier of the 26th Kentucky volunteers, (Colonel Maxwell,) was challenging the votes of all persons whom he supposed would not vote the Union Ticket. . . . They only administered the oath to such persons as the soldiers

some cases, the military imposed informal oaths that set out much more rigorous conceptions of "loyalty." One of the election judges at the Curdsville Precinct in Daviess County, for example, reported that the military required voters to take the oath, "You do solemnly swear that you will support the Constitution of the United States, the present administration, and the enforcement of its laws, the constitution of Kentucky and the enforcement of its laws." This oath clearly made opposition to the Lincoln administration's policies tantamount to disloyalty. And as R. H. Fenwick, one of those who appeared at the Curdsville polls reported, this interpretation was plainly spelled out to potential voters. In his testimony, Fenwick complained, "I did not vote at the last election because Colonel Spray, judge of election, said in my hearing that no man was allowed to vote unless he would support the administration, and give the last man and the last dollar in support of the prosecution of this war.... Fifteen or twenty of us saw Colonel Foster's order, and were willing to take the oath therein required; but Spray said we could not vote unless we would also take an oath to give the last man and the last dollar in support of the administration."[94]

In Hartford, a town of about 500 people and the seat of Ohio county, copies of the military orders under which the troops were operating were posted on "the bar-room door of the hotel . . . the house where the vote was taken," and other places. These notices intimidated many men who otherwise would have presented themselves at the polls.[95] For those who did appear before election officials, the reception was no less intimidating. At "lower town precinct No. 1" in Owenborough, one of the loyalist judges testified that election officials administered the military oath only to those who were strangers to them and to "men that I believed to be disloyal, and were identified with the party engaged in war against the existence of the national government; and by this I mean not only men under arms, but such as were, in purpose, aim, and object, opposed to the Union." While this judge considered a refusal to take the oath to be conclusive evidence of disloyalty, he also was willing to exclude those who swore the oath if "a knowledge of their [the voters'] antecedents" demonstrated a lack of commitment to the Union cause.[96]

---

challenged. I do not think that the officers of the election challenged any votes." Ibid., p. 41; also see pp. 43–4.

[94] J. H. Hodgkins, one of the election judges, confirmed that some of the election officials serving with him "were opposed to allowing any persons to vote unless they were in favor of a vigorous prosecution of the war." Ibid., pp. 11, 13.

[95] Ibid., pp. 45, 47.

[96] Ibid., p. 10. This judge reported that men supporting the two congressional candidates divided rather cleanly between loyalists and disloyalists: "There were no southern rights votes cast for Yeaman that I know of . . . [while] I am inclined to think that there was a majority of disloyal voters [among those who supported McHenry], though some loyal men voted for him." The judge also reported that there were "ten or twelve [soldiers] armed with muskets and fixed bayonets. The guns were loaded in

A man who had witnessed the voting at Ellis's Precinct in Ohio County reported that one of the election judges there publicly stated "two or three times during the day, while the voting was going on, that he was astonished to see any man take the [military] oath required there, for any man who was required to take it, and did take it, their property would be taken from them and they would be sent across the lines."[97] Any man required to take the oath by the election judges was thereby branded as disloyal to the Union cause. Suspicion of disloyalty, in turn, triggered military impressment of a man's property and imprisonment or transportation beyond Union lines.[98] Men were, in fact, often arrested in and around the polls for voting; although the official charge was disloyalty, these men had invariably supported candidates to whom the military was opposed.[99]

As in Missouri, the property of men who were suspected of disloyalty was impressed for military use, often without compensation.[100] In many cases impressment was probably in retaliation for voting for or otherwise

our presence. I think they were about ten or twelve feet from the window through which we received the votes" (p. 11).

[97] Ibid., p. 50.

[98] Robert G. Rouse, Jr., who monitored the polls in Henderson, testified that a man named S. B. Vance "was at the polls talking to the judges about voting. He was willing to take the oath prescribed by the legislature of Kentucky. They (the judges) wanted him to take an oath that was said to be a military oath, which he was not willing to do, when Colonel Foster [of the Sixty-fifth Regiment of Indiana volunteers] asked the judges if Mr. Vance had voted; they answered that he had not. He then told Mr. Vance that he could vote if he chose to do so; but if he did, that he would arrest him. Mr. Vance made no reply, but immediately left the court-house." Ibid., p. 34. Parentheses in the original. This account was corroborated by R. T. Glass, who quoted Foster as saying, "Mr. Vance, you can vote if you desire; I shall not prohibit you from voting, but I warn you, if you do vote, I will arrest you and put you in the military prison. You have been disloyal to the government for a long time. You have no right to vote, and you ought not to ask the privilege" (pp. 35–6). One of the election judges at Vanover's precinct in Daviess County similarly reported that some men "refused to be sworn in order to vote . . . because they said they were afraid to vote for McHenry, fearing that they would be arrested and their property confiscated" (p. 14).

[99] Lazarus Powell, the senator from Kentucky, attended the polls in his hometown of Henderson where he personally saw "several persons . . . arrested as soon as they voted the democratic ticket, and taken to Colonel John W. Foster's headquarters. . . . Those arrests caused the democrats to cease voting; very few democrats attempted to vote after the arresting commenced." Ibid., pp. 33–4. At one polling place in Ohio County, a man was arrested simply for refusing to take the military oath. For other reports of arrests, see pp. 35–6, 41, 43–4.

[100] This was the publicly proclaimed policy of the Union military. For example, Henry McHenry, brother of the Democratic congressional candidate, reported that he had seen "posted up at Rochester [Butler county] and Skylesville, and at several places, the order of General Boyle, the substance of which was that horses and slaves of those men who were for 'no more men and no more money,' and their *aiders* and *supporters*, would be first pressed by the military if they needed horses or slaves. This order had a very great effect on the public." Ibid., p. 48.

supporting candidates to whom the military was opposed. For example, John O'Bryan, who had voted at the Knottsville Precinct in Daviess County, testified:

[a] lieutenant in Captain Cummings's company came to my house about ten days after the election in the night, with nine other soldiers and fifteen horses, and asked to stay all night. I permitted them to stay, and fed them and their horses. The lieutenant said he intended to take two of my horses for public service. I replied, I suppose you will pay me for them. He said no; and I asked him why, and he said because you are a rebel. I told him I had always been a Union man, and said to him, if all my Union neighbors except one, and all the home guards, did not say I was a Union man, he might take all my horses and all I had, and me with them. He replied, I am not going to give you that chance. He said, you voted for McHenry, who, he said, was a rebel, and said in the morning he would take one of my horses any how. I should have stated above that in the conversation with the lieutenant I told him McHenry had been in the Union army, and I considered him, therefore, the best sort of a Union man. He took one of my horses away, for which I have a receipt signed by Captain Cummings. It was stated at Knottsville that the horses of all those who voted for McHenry would be taken from them, and I know that a number of persons would not vote on this account.[101]

W. S. Brittain, who had attended the polls at Owenboro, in Daviess County, approached Captain Cummings several days after the election. Brittain told Cummings that "he had my horse. He asked me what my politics were; I told him I was as good a Union man as he was. He then asked me who I voted for at the late election; I told him that I wanted to vote for Wickliffe, and did vote for McHenry. He then said that I was the kind of man he wanted to get horses from."[102]

Elijah Hocker, a resident of Hartford in Ohio County, had a similar experience. On the Saturday following the election he was attending a quarterly meeting of the Methodist church at Goshen meetinghouse about three miles from Hartford:

During the progress of the meeting, observing an unusual excitement out doors, I inquired the reason, and was told some soldiers were then pressing horses. I went out, and a lieutenant of the 3d Kentucky cavalry, as I understood, pointing to a horse, asked me whose it was. I told him it was mine. He asked me what was my politics. I told him I was a Union man (and I have always been loyal, and do still regard myself as a Union man, and am so regarded.) He asked me how I voted. I answered for Miller, McHenry, and Wickliffe. He then ordered some soldier to take the saddle off, and said he would take my horse; and he did take it, and gave me a receipt signed Captain John P. Cummings, and valued at $130. I have not received anything for my horse except that receipt.

[101] Ibid., p. 12. In his testimony, O'Bryan protested, "I am a loyal man, and have been so regarded [by my neighbors], and I am still loyal yet."
[102] Ibid., p. 16. Brittain added that this "was the only horse I had. He was a valuable family horse, but not fit for a cavalry horse."

It was unlikely Hocker ever received compensation for his horse; as another witness who corroborated his account noted, Hocker's receipt "was marked 'rebel' across the face of it."[103]

While many of the polling places in Kentucky were desperately contested by Union loyalists backed by the military and ambivalent or covertly disloyal citizens, others were more relaxed. For example, H. P. Taylor, a doctor in Hartford, reported:

> Colonel Shanks, William J. Lewis, and myself were sitting in front of the bank late in the evening after the votes were all about polled; Shanks was rather crowing over us as to the result of the election, he being a warm supporter of Yeaman, Lewis and myself friends of Colonel McHenry. After a little while our conversation turned upon the military interference; I alluded to Sergeant Paul's challenging Smith Stevens's vote, and thereby causing others not to vote who would have voted for Colonel McHenry. Colonel Shanks immediately spoke up and said that he was sorry to see Paul challenge Stevens's vote, and that he told Paul not to do so any more. Paul remarked that he had his orders from Colonel Maxwell, and that was to challenge any man's vote he considered disloyal; and then Shanks told him to never mind, that he would make it all right with Colonel Maxwell; he then said that Paul was satisfied, and did not challenge any more votes.[104]

But as evident in even this account, the mere presence of troops at the polls heavily compromised the democratic quality of the proceedings.

In many democracies, there are two issues that are placed beyond the reach of elections. One is the foundation principles of the democratic system; many citizens believe that parties, candidates, and voters that oppose a democratic system can rightfully be excluded from the process. The other is national sovereignty; secession, being tantamount to treason from the perspective of those opposing the breakup of a nation, is equally illegitimate. In Missouri, Kentucky, the other border states, and throughout much of the North, citizens willingly abandoned, if only temporarily, their democratic principles in order to assure that loyalist candidates would prevail at the polls.[105] Although firsthand reports of elections in Maryland during the Civil War are unavailable, military intervention was probably at least as extensive as it was in Kentucky and Missouri. In the 1863 elections, for example, General Robert Schenck issued an order imposing an oath of allegiance on all

---

[103] Ibid., pp. 42–3. For a separate incident in which horses were taken from those who were suspected of supporting McHenry and the receipts marked "disloyal," see p. 50.

[104] Ibid., pp. 40.

[105] In an exchange that neatly framed the dilemma posed by secessionist principles in a democracy, William Newberry of Cooper County, Missouri, was asked whether "men who have taken up arms against the government should be permitted to vote for those who are to control the government." He answered, "I think if they have to live under the government, they should have the right to choose." S.R. no. 1199: M.D. no. 16 (1862): p. 32. In Missouri and elsewhere along the border, men who were ambivalent toward or supported southern secession were sometimes free "to choose" but only so long as they were not free to win.

Table 6.3. *Party Strength in the U.S. House of Representatives at the Opening of the Thirty-eighth Congress in December, 1863*

Party identification	Number of members	Percent total
Republicans	85	46.2
Independent Republicans	2	1.1
Unconditional Unionists	16	8.7
Unionists	9	4.9
Democrats	72	39.1

Source: For the party identities of members of the House of Representatives, see Kenneth C. Martis, *The Historical Atlas of Political Parties in the United States Congress, 1789–1989* (New York: Macmillan, 1989), p. 117.

Maryland voters. Provost marshals and Union military officers were commanded to police the polls and enforce the oath's application by judges of election.[106]

Military intervention at the polls may very well have made a difference in the outcome of the war. In the Thirty-eighth Congress (1863–5), for example, "Unconditional Unionists," all of them elected from border states in which the military had played a major role in the conduct of the election, gave the Republicans a working majority in the U.S. House of Representatives (see Table 6.3). Without the support of the Unconditional Unionists, the Republicans would have fallen short of a majority by five votes when the Thirty-eighth Congress convened.[107] If more conservative "Unionists" had served in place of these men, the Democrats would probably have organized

---

[106] Noting the absence of a state law authorizing either military intervention at the polls or an oath of allegiance, Governor August Bradford protested Schenck's order. There is no doubt that military intervention in the election strongly aided administration candidates. In his annual message to the legislature in January 1864, for example, the governor reported that the "'Government ticket' . . . was . . . designated by its color; it was a yellow ticket, and armed with that, a voter could safely run the gauntlet of the sabres and carbines that guarded the entrance to the polls. . . . In one district, as appears by certificate from the Judge, the military officer took his stand at the polls before they were opened, declaring that none but 'the yellow ticket' should be voted, and excluded all others throughout the day." For the correspondence associated with Schenck's order and conduct of the election, see Benton, *Voting in the Field*, pp. 230–4; *American Annual Cyclopaedia for 1863*, pp. 618–24.

[107] Fourteen of the sixteen Unconditional Unionists voted for the Republican candidate for speaker, Schuyler Colfax of Indiana. The other two abstained. In addition, one Unionist also supported Colfax, along with both Independent Republicans and all of the Republicans. Without the backing of the fifteen Unconditional Unionist and Unionist members, Colfax would have fallen six votes short of a majority. For a recapitulation of the vote, see *Journal of the House of Representatives of the United*

the House and the Union war effort would have been seriously compromised.[108] Whether the Union could have won the Civil War if "southern sympathizers" had been allowed to participate on an equal footing with loyalists in northern elections is thus an open question. What is not open to question is the fact that many loyalists believed that democratic principles had to be violated in order for the Union to survive.

Federal Troops in Garrisons

Because they were serving outside their home states when elections were held, most federal troops needed special legislation permitting them to vote. Northern states controlled by the Republican party usually enacted the necessary laws and allowed soldiers to vote, either individually by mail or in groups by setting up temporary precincts in the field. Democratic states were much more reluctant. When permitted to do so, federal troops primarily voted in two very different contexts: in temporary encampments within the seceded states of the South and in permanent garrisons in the North. When they voted in the field, they were usually located in southern territory where no local elections were being held. If they voted while in more or less permanent garrisons, they were usually posted in Union-held territory where local elections were sometimes conducted. In this second case, which is considered in this section, troops were usually garrisoned in or around a major city that provided supplies for the troops. Unlike troops stationed in military forts on the frontier, the men stationed at these posts could not overwhelm local electorates if they fraudulently participated in a local election. But these Civil War garrisons nonetheless contained hundreds or thousands of adult men who could make a difference in the outcome.[109]

States for the First Session of the Thirty-eighth Congress (Washington: Government Printing Office, 1863), pp. 9–11.

[108]   As Edgar Robinson noted, the Republicans won a minority of the vote and a minority of members of the House from the free states. Only by "a silent and drastic process" was "the election of a sufficient number of Republican members to provide a majority in the House . . . secured in the border states, – Missouri, Kentucky, Maryland." *The Evolution of American Political Parties: a Sketch of Party Development* (New York: Harcourt, Brace, 1924), p. 161. For the party breakdown in the House, see Kenneth C. Martis, *The Historical Atlas of Political Parties in the United States Congress, 1789–1989* (New York: Macmillan, 1989), pp. 117, 408–9. On party support for the northern war effort in the House, see Bensel, *Yankee Leviathan*, chapter 3.

[109]   Military hospitals were also usually located in large cities and held large numbers of soldiers who might participate in elections. In the Twenty-second Ward in Philadelphia, for example, the town hall doubled both as an election precinct and as a military hospital. Convalescent soldiers were allowed to vote in the October 1862 election even though they could not meet the residency requirement (one year in Pennsylvania and the last ten days in the election district). When the inspectors of election divided over accepting these votes, the election judges broke the deadlock "in favor of receiving the [convalescent] soldiers' votes . . . after that we received all

One of the most blatant instances in which northern garrisons fraudulently influenced an election occurred in St. Louis, Missouri, in the fall of 1862. Benton barracks was located on the fringe of the city and held "paroled" federal prisoners.[110] These paroled troops had been captured by the Confederate army, returned to Union lines on parole, and were now awaiting "exchange" with similarly captured rebel soldiers. In the meantime, they were held at Benton barracks much as if they would have been held in a military prison if the South had kept them. Before the Union stopped exchanging prisoners in 1864, exchanges were made by making notations on lists of those who had been captured by either side, one Union for one Confederate soldier. In the meantime, they were held by their respective governments in a kind of limbo.[111]

At the time of the congressional election in November 1862, Robert Nickles was one of those held at the barracks and commanded company F of the Fourth Battalion of paroled men. About a hundred men were assigned to this unit, almost all of them from Wisconsin. Including this company, Nickles testified that there were between 1,400 and 1,500 paroled troops held at Benton Barracks. Because St. Louis was in the western theater, almost all of these troops had homes in the Mississippi and Missouri valleys. All but a handful had been recruited from the states of Illinois, Wisconsin, Missouri, Iowa, Kansas, and Arkansas, along with the Nebraska Territory. Nickles could not remember any men who hailed from St. Louis and, thus, might have been legal voters in the congressional election.

On election day, these paroled men were taken to the polls in droves and induced, apparently with little effort, to vote for the Republican candidate Francis Blair.[112] Nickles reported the fraud in detail:

There were wagons employed in taking paroled prisoners from said barracks to the polls on [election] day; I have no idea of the number, but I think some six or

---

such votes, noting on the tally-list the word 'soldier,' as they voted." S.R. no. 1199: Contested Congressional Election in the Fifth District of Pennsylvania: M.D. no. 17, pp. 38–9, 51–3. Charles W. Carrigan vs. M. Russell Thayer, election held on October 14, 1862. For the tally lists containing their names and commentary that soldiers from Pennsylvania might have legitimately claimed residency on the grounds of having been in the hospital (and therefore the district) for the ten days prior to the election, see pp. 94–9. All of these soldiers evidently voted Republican (pp. 95–6).

[110] Benton Barracks had been originally constructed in September 1861 as a "boot camp" for federal recruits. Robert B. Roberts, *Encyclopedia of Historic Forts: The Military, Pioneer, and Trading Posts of the United States* (New York: Macmillan, 1988), p. 454.

[111] In 1862, the Union and Confederate armies were still releasing almost all prisoners they captured. These prisoners were "paroled" with the condition that they not again take up arms until they had been exchanged for prisoners captured by the opposite side. Once exchanged, they could again become combatants. James M. McPherson, *Battle Cry of Freedom* (New York: Ballantine, 1988), pp. 791–2.

[112] For a description of irregularities in an earlier congressional election involving Blair, see Chapter 4.

eight...they were wagons employed by the government; I don't know the name of the man under whose charge they were, but he was at that time wagon-master of Benton barracks, under Captain Constable; they were thus employed from some time in the forenoon until dark, until late in the afternoon; the number of paroled prisoners thus taken, which I saw, was between 200 and 300; the wagons would take a load, go off, return and take another load. I asked several of the men where they were going. They answered, "to vote for Frank Blair," and as they left the barracks they shouted "Hurrah for Frank Blair."...Some of the drivers mentioned that their horses were very tired, and the men who appeared to have charge of them, collecting them, answered, "Never mind that; if fresh ones were required they could be got," or words to that effect.

Although he could not identify the home states of all the men in these wagons, he did know that at least some of them were from Illinois and Minnesota.

On the same day, while walking toward nearby Jefferson Barracks, a second federal installation, Nickles and a friend met another caravan of wagons on a bridge over a little stream. These soldiers were also going to St. Louis in order to vote.

They were in five or six wagons, and some on foot. They were altogether, including both those in the wagons and those on foot, some[where] over a hundred; might have been two hundred for all I know; I did not count them. The wagons in which they were were government wagons. I asked them where they were from, and they said they were from the barracks. I asked them where they were going, and they stated they were going to St. Louis to vote.... The gentleman that was with me said, "Hurrah for Knox." The answer came from the wagon – one wagon, "To hell with Knox; we vote for Frank Blair."... The wagons were in company of each other. The men on foot were around and behind the wagons, with some stragglers now and then.... I noticed the letters on their caps. According to those, they were from Illinois and Ohio; they were all the States that I remember.

Nickles recalled that the men who denounced Knox "sat behind the wagon on the reach, and appeared to be half tight." In concluding his account, he stated that he had no particular reason to follow this election closely because he knew neither of the candidates but, even so, could not fail to see "how the thing was working."[113]

Serving as adjutant of the Fourth Battalion of paroled men, George Meyer was also at Benton Barracks on election day. He, too, saw

paroled prisoners leaving the barracks in wagons.... I counted twelve different ones. They were quartermaster's wagons in charge of government teamsters. The most of the men I saw leaving thus were paroled prisoners and a part of the 35th regiment Missouri volunteer infantry.... The paroled prisoners I saw leave were not from the

---

[113] Nickels identified himself as "a know-nothing, right straight through." When asked whether he was "not also an abolitionist," he answered, "Not that I have heard of." S.R. no. 1198: Contested Congressional Election in the First District of Missouri: M.D. no. 15, pp. 15–18. Samuel Knox vs. Francis P. Blair, Jr., election held on November 4, 1862.

county of St. Louis. . . . At the time of their return they said they had voted for Frank Blair, and hurrahed for Frank Blair. I heard some of the men say they had voted twice. The inducement, they stated, was lager beer and drink. Most of them when they returned were intoxicated. . . . I have heard them brag about it several times since, that some of them had voted for Frank Blair twice, and some for General Loan and Frank Blair. . . . The wagons commenced running early in the morning, and were running at three o'clock in the afternoon, when I left the barracks to go to town. I have seen as many as from 12 to 15 men in one wagon; they were standing up, and some sitting on the edge of the box. . . . Some of them [the wagons] I saw return twice, and some three times.[114]

In addition to these wagons filled with paroled prisoners, soldiers were also taken to the polls in smaller groups.

The polls of the Fifth Ward were located in the courthouse, in the basement office of William Cozzens, the surveyor for St. Louis County. As he monitored the election there, Cozzens saw "squads of three or four" soldiers delivered to the polls by "a person who was driving a two-horse buggy." Because "they generally voted closed tickets," Cozzens could not tell for whom they voted. His suspicions aroused, he discovered that these soldiers lived in Phelps and Crawford Counties, which, although they were in Missouri, lay outside the St. Louis Congressional District. At that point, after more than a dozen soldiers had cast their votes, Cozzens objected "to the judges about receiving any more of these votes," and all the votes subsequently cast by soldiers were thrown out. After their votes were refused, the man in the buggy, who said that he was supporting Blair, "swore by God they should vote." Cozzens asked one of his subordinates to follow the buggy and was later told that the soldiers were taken to the Sixth Ward polls where at least some of their votes were accepted.[115]

Another witness, the publisher of the *Missouri Democrat*, identified the man in the buggy as George Deagle, manager of the Varieties theater. According to a third witness Deagle was also captain of a company of soldiers to which most "of his [theater] employes belonged . . . some [of the soldiers] came from the St. Louis theatre, some from the Bowery theatre, and some merchants and business men in the city." However, the men whom Deagle took to the courthouse polls in his carriage did not belong to his military company.[116]

---

[114]   Meyer added, "I have only a feeling for the right, and I don't want to see any underhanded game, as the transaction showed at Benton barracks on the day of the election. . . . I am a democrat. . . . No, sir, nor ever was [an abolitionist]." Ibid., pp. 19–22.

[115]   Ibid., pp. 36–7.

[116]   This last witness was Leslie May, who was a "gymnast and acrobat" who had performed at the Melodeon the previous evening. In an attempt to besmirch the reputation of the contestant (Samuel Knox), May was asked whether the Melodeon had been the site of "a whore dance . . . last night." May replied, "I don't know, sir; I left as soon as the show was out. There was a masquerade there, or it was called a

The problem in this instance was similar to the more general difficulty in determining whether men were legal residents at urban polling places. However, there were several things that aggravated this difficulty. One of these was the scale and visibility of fraud. Approximately 70 percent of all men in the Union army were of voting age.[117] Whether in camp or in barracks, they were easily collected and taken to the polls in large numbers. In addition, these men were under the command of Union officers who usually strongly supported the northern war effort. In this St. Louis election, for example, the complicity of these officers was clearly required for their men to be gathered together and transported to the polls in government wagons. If these officers had wanted to stop the fraud, all they had to do was order that all out-of-state soldiers remain in their barracks on election day. This could have been easily accomplished because, unlike judges of election, the army had accurate records identifying just who was and who was not a resident of Missouri.

When this election was held, Missouri was also under martial law, and federal troops and state militia more or less routinely arrested those who opposed the administration, particularly in and about polling places. For that reason, judges of election would have run at least some risk of arrest if they had challenged the large masses of soldiers who appeared before them. In this and other ways, the election baptized federal intervention in local political affairs. This intervention was covered with a veneer of patriotism within which the strong administration loyalties of most soldiers were identified with the survival of the Union; the military simply pursued in the political arena the same goals for which it fought in battle. In this respect, when out-of-state soldiers illegally voted in St. Louis, they constituted a kind of loyalist fifth column.[118] As such,

---

masquerade on the bills." Counsel persisted, "Was [the masquerade] not understood to be a whore dance, or a dance at which that class of females alone are known to attend?" May responded, "I do not know; I do not meddle with those things." A masquerade ball would have provided a convenient venue for prostitution, a booming business in wartime St. Louis. The testimony implied that the Melodeon was owned by Knox. Ibid., pp. 47, 95–7.

[117]   Benton, *Voting in the Field*, p. 311.

[118]   They also constituted such a fifth column when they voted legally. In the 1864 election, for example, Lincoln urged General William Tecumseh Sherman to furlough Indiana men in his army so that they could go home and vote in that state's election: "The State election of Indiana occurs on the 11th of October and the loss of it, to the friends of the government, will go far toward losing the whole Union cause. The bad effect upon the November election and especially the giving the State government to those who will oppose the war in every possible way, are too much to risk, if it can possibly be avoided. . . . Indiana is the only important State voting in October whose soldiers cannot vote in the field. Anything that you can safely do to let these soldiers or any part of them go home and vote at the State election will be greatly in point. They need not remain for the Presidential election, but may return to you at once. This is in no sense an order." Ibid., pp. 291–2. The point was not lost on the Democrats.

their participation transformed polling places into celebrations of nationalist power.

Voting in the Field

When they were not pulling garrison duty, soldiers were usually encamped in the field away from major cities and often deep in enemy territory. Although they could not illegally participate in local elections (because local elections were simply not held in occupied Confederate territory), voting in the camps often exhibited other irregularities. For one thing, many of the officers and men who conducted the elections were unfamiliar with election law and improvised the proceedings.[119] Even if they did know how an election should be conducted, circumstances beyond their control often precluded conformity with state regulations. Sometimes, for example, men were under marching orders when the election was conducted and the voting was consequently held as an intermission in the unit's movement. Military discipline also carried over into the conduct of elections, giving a unit's officers the ability to strongly influence the proceedings. Since most of the voting was done by companies, apparently because their recruitment most closely corresponded with the jurisdictions of precincts in the home communities, captains and lieutenants were in a good position to sway the votes of the men under their command.[120] Finally, the actual casting of tickets was usually public, with soldiers depositing their votes in hats, tin cups, and cigar boxes under the

When the New York legislature was considering a bill to allow soldiers to vote in the field, John Van Buren, a member of the assembly and son of the former president, sought to amend the title to read: "An Act to Transfer the Elective Franchise from the Qualified Voters of this State to the Commander-in-chief of the Army and Navy of the United States" (p. 135).

[119] Most state laws attempted to erect a precinct in army encampments in which soldiers could cast their tickets en masse. The remainder provided for proxy voting in which a surrogate would cast a ticket authorized by a soldier in his home precinct. Ibid., p. 15. For descriptions of poll books from soldiers in the field and the text of election laws regulating the votes of soldiers, see S.R. no. 1270: Contested Congressional Election in the Thirteenth District of Ohio: M.D. no. 8. Charles Follett vs. Columbus Delano, election held on October 11, 1864; S.R. no. 1270: Contested Congressional Election in the Twenty-first District of Pennsylvania: M.D. no. 9, Pts. 1–3. Smith Fuller vs. John L. Dawson, election held on October 11, 1864; S.R. no. 1270: Contested Congressional Election in the Fifth District of Michigan: M.D. no. 10. August C. Baldwin vs. Rowland E. Trowbridge, election held on November 8, 1864.

[120] For example, John Loyd wrote home that he "had several fall-outs with some of the boys in the army and with an officer about politics; they insisted on him voting the republican ticket." Loyd was described as an "ultra democrat." S.R. no. 1271: Contested Congressional Election in the Sixteenth District of Pennsylvania: M.D. no. 117, p. 140. William H. Koontz vs. A. H. Coffroth, election held on October 11, 1864.

watchful eye of their commanding officers.[121] Everything considered, military camps ranked among the less democratic polling places in American history.[122]

Henry Kraut, a major on General Fremont's staff and a resident of St. Louis, described one such election in the field. On November 4, 1862, the day of the election, Kraut was in Bowling Green, Kentucky, with the Second and Fifteenth Regiments of the Missouri volunteer infantry and a company of the First Missouri artillery. He reported that most of these men were German, forming a brigade under Colonel Schaefer's command. Both Schaefer and most of the men in these units were from St. Louis. A few days before the election, Schaefer had told Kraut that "General [Francis P.] Blair promised him a brigadier general's commission; and if that would arrive before the election, he [Schaefer] would do his best to get General Blair elected; and if not, he would tell his officers not to vote at all." Several months before, Blair had resigned his St. Louis congressional seat in order to become a colonel in the Union army. He was, at the time of the election, serving on General William Tecumseh Sherman's staff while campaigning for election to the next Congress, running once again in the St. Louis district he had previously held.[123]

Kraut had traveled to Bowling Green as an agent of the "central committee of the anti-corruption party." The treasurer of that committee had paid his expenses, which came to about a hundred dollars, in order that their "anti-corruption" or Democratic tickets might be carried to the soldiers in the camps. Kraut also carried the poll books in which the votes were to be recorded; these he handed over to the adjutants of the regiments to be passed

---

[121]   Noting that 78 percent of all Union soldiers voted for Lincoln in 1864, a rate much higher than the 53 percent recorded by civilians, McPherson concludes that the difference could be ascribed to peer pressure and experiences in uniform (which tended to convert those who had been Democrats into Republicans). To these factors should be added self-selection into Union ranks; those opposed to the war would have tried, often successfully, to avoid service in the army. James M. McPherson, *For Cause and Comrades: Why Men Fought in the Civil War* (New York: Oxford University Press, 1997), pp. 176–7. For an exhaustive record of election returns from soldiers, see Benton, *Voting in the Field*, pp. 22–3, 51–2, 66, 77–9, 89, 101, 107, 117, 127, 131, 203, 217, 246, 249.

[122]   Although official election returns from the Confederacy are scarce, the same pattern appears to have held in the South. For example, in the 1864 race for governor in North Carolina, the "soldiers voted almost unanimously" for Zebulon Vance, who supported the Confederate war effort, over William Holden, the peace candidate. Among North Carolina soldiers recuperating in hospitals in Richmond, Virginia, Vance received 867 votes to Holden's 25. *American Annual Cyclopaedia of 1864* (New York: D. Appleton, 1872), p. 589. On the paucity of surviving records of voting by Confederate soldiers, see Benton, *Voting in the Field*, p. 28.

[123]   S.R. no. 1198: M.D. no. 15 (1863): pp. 47–8. Colonel Schaefer could not be called on to confirm this conversation because he had been killed in the battle of Murfreesboro in early January 1863.

on to the captains of the companies. Kraut reported that a majority of the men in these units, although divided in their political sentiments, probably favored Samuel Knox, Blair's opponent:

I explained to soldiers who were round the sutler's tent that I came to give them their rights, and take their votes. They asked me, several of them, what kind of ticket I had; I told them, then, what kind of ticket I had, and the greatest part of them were pleased.... More than a hundred [men were around the sutler's tent]; the exact number I cannot state, but not as many as two hundred at a time. They went to and fro during the whole forenoon of Sunday.... I cannot tell how many times [he discussed the ticket with soldiers]; it may be ten or twelve times that I was asked what kind of ticket I had.... There was some electioneering doing in camp, besides that, that I saw.

However, Schaefer's adjutant, either on his own initiative or on Schaefer's instructions, "on the night from the 3d to the 4th of November...altered all the names from Knox to Blair on the Knox tickets, in my presence."[124]

This incident is interesting as an example of the mutually contaminating influence of politics and military discipline. Blair's sojourn in the army conferred on him a political currency, in the form of military promotions, which he could then use to encourage favorable political activity in the camps. This influence then trickled down through Schaefer because he commanded units that had been recruited from the city of St. Louis where Blair was standing as a congressional candidate. It can be surmised (but not conclusively demonstrated) that the adjutant, a man named Dietz, was similarly susceptible to influence from Schaefer. Although he held a contrary political allegiance, Kraut was also a military officer. In that capacity, he even attempted to intervene in military operations by going to General Rosecrans's headquarters in order to request that these units not break camp so that the voting could take place on the day appointed for the election.[125] As the ostensible voters, the enlisted men appeared to have been little more than pawns in these machinations.

Military discipline usually made elections held in the field more orderly than those in civilian communities. For example, when Company H of the 208th Regiment of Pennsylvania volunteers voted near the front lines south

---

[124] These Missouri soldiers evidently voted viva voce (orally); the tickets altered by Schaefer's adjutant were to be used as prompts by the men when they declared their votes. For a description and commentary on the Missouri law authorizing soldiers' votes (which required a loyalty oath by men serving in the Union army), see Benton, *Voting in the Field*, pp. 43–4.

[125] He failed when he was not granted an audience with Rosecrans. As a result, these Missouri units voted a day early because they were to break camp the next day. S.R. no. 1198: M.D. no. 15 (1862): pp. 47–8, 49, 52–3. Rosecrans apparently was opposed to electioneering in the camps because the soldiers, in Lincoln's words, "will get drunk and make disturbance." In the 1864 election, Lincoln had to order him to allow Missouri soldiers under his command to vote. Benton, *Voting in the Field*, p. 45.

of Richmond, Sergeant Joseph Long, one of the judges of election, testified that all the proprieties had been observed, including the administration of oaths, the "production of [poll] tax receipts, and other satisfactory evidence of a right to vote." The polls were open from early in the morning, between eight and nine, until seven o'clock at night. Lieutenant William Eicholtz made the lid for the ballot box.[126]

At Soldiers' Rest, in Washington, D.C., Private Josiah Anderson, a new recruit, served as clerk of election. He testified that the unit had just arrived in Washington that day. In the late hours of the afternoon, just as the sun was going down, a colonel from another unit drew the men "up in line" and handed out tickets "to suit" them. Anderson reported that the colonel provided "tickets to suit all parties." Even so, some of the men already had tickets, probably mailed from home. In the absence of a ballot box, the tickets were deposited in a hat.[127] Just before the voting, the men asked one another whether anyone had previously served as an election official and selected those who had to oversee the voting. One of the soldiers testified that the men were asked for tax receipts and certificates of assessment, but, although required by law, this kind of close inspection of credentials seems a little unlikely. In any case, none of the men were sworn as to their eligibility to participate, and it is probable that a few did not meet suffrage qualifications.[128]

Company G of the 105th Regiment of Pennsylvania volunteers was stationed about two miles from City Point, Virginia, on the day of the election. This would have been about thirty miles southeast of Richmond, the Confederate capital. The polls kept regular hours, opening at seven in the morning and closing at eight in the evening. The officers of election were sworn in the regular manner, but some of them were unable to oversee the entire proceedings. For example, George Clymans and James Smith, two of the three election judges, had been on picket duty the night before and went to bed before the returns were made out. When he was still awake, Sergeant Clymans

---

[126] S.R. no. 1271: M.D. no. 117 (1864): pp. 26–7. As a condition on suffrage, Pennsylvania law imposed a tax of ten cents, to be paid in the township, in lieu of all other taxes that might be owed by a soldier. *American Annual Cyclopaedia of 1864*, p. 649. The law under which these soldiers voted specified the organization of polling places by company at the quarters of the commanding officer and also provided for proxy voting if men did not belong to a Pennsylvania unit at the time of election. Benton, *Voting in the Field*, pp. 201–3.

[127] S.R. no. 1271: M.D. no. 117 (1864): pp. 27–8. The men of Company C of the 202nd Regiment of Pennsylvania volunteers also deposited their tickets in a hat. This was at White Plains, Virginia, on what must have been the extreme left of the Union lines around Richmond and Petersburg. Because the men were on picket duty in the morning, the polls were opened in the afternoon, closing at sundown (pp. 80–2).

[128] Ibid., pp. 30–1. Barton Cooper, the other clerk, said the election was hurried because he and the other men voting there "were on our way to the front" (p. 29; also see p. 30). These men were apparently new recruits who had not yet been assigned as replacements to companies in the field (p. 31).

had filled in for James Kendall, who had been selected as clerk of election, because Kendall became ill and had to leave the polls. The soldiers were asked to swear as to their suffrage eligibility, and most of the other normal requirements were met in one way or another.[129]

The election held by Companies B and G of the 138th Regiment of Pennsylvania volunteers was conducted at Front Royal in the Shenandoah Valley, not far from Confederate lines. The voting was a little hurried because they had received marching orders and were preparing to break camp. Most of what is known from this election comes from Second Lieutenant George Mullen in Company G, who served as one of the judges of election:

It was our belief that the election must be held by commissioned officers, the same as at the election held by us when at the Relay House, in Maryland, in 1862; that was our impression, and the papers had come on just before the election, perhaps the day before. I was the only commissioned officer with company G at that time. . . . The election in the two companies was held jointly, in order to have enough commissioned officers to hold the election; the officers consulted together and concluded that was the best way. . . . The election was held, so far as I could judge, with as much care as elections at home. The proof of qualifications of voters was required; we required proof of payment of taxes, and some votes were rejected because the men had not certificates to prove the payment of taxes.[130]

The tickets were deposited in a cigar box.

When company officers oversaw an election in the field, their political leanings sometimes affected how the men in their command voted.[131] This

[129] The only major deficiency was that the election judges who had been on picket duty failed to sign the return that was sent back to Pennsylvania. Ibid., pp. 49–52. Anticipating that conditions in the field would impair the conduct of elections in military camps, the Pennsylvania legislature had provided that "No mere informality in the manner of carrying out or executing any of the provisions of this act [enabling soldiers to vote outside the state] shall invalidate any election held under the same, or authorize the return thereof to be rejected or set aside." When the returns sent to Menallen Township in Adams County were in fact thrown out, the minority among the judges of election at that precinct filed a written protest in which they set out a reasonable interpretation of this exemption: "The intention of the legislature, in our judgment, as expressed in this section, is very clear. Contemplating the probability that in many of the camps the provisions of the law might be imperfectly understood, or the returns be defectively certified, the law forbids the return judges from rejecting returns on account of mere informality in the manner of carrying out or executing the provisions of the act, and expressly reserves to the courts and bodies having jurisdiction the duty of determining the legality of elections held or of votes cast" (p. 62).

[130] Ibid., pp. 68–9. Although many Democrats served as officers, some of them quite high-ranking, the vast majority appear to have been or to have become Republicans. Almost all army officers commanding Iowa units, for example, were Republicans. The party even levied these officers and their staffs for campaign contributions. Wubben, *Civil War Iowa*, pp. 172–3.

[131] For an example of deference to superior officers in the holding of elections, see S.R. no. 1271: M.D. no. 117 (1864): pp. 87–9.

influence was openly acknowledged when Company I, of the 210th Regiment of Pennsylvania volunteers, voted on the front lines facing Petersburg, Virginia. The company's first lieutenant, Charles Sefton, "declined acting as an officer of the election, of the reason that I feared that, being an officer, some of the men might think I would interfere with their voting, and therefore I advised that the privates should hold the election. The election was held by privates." However, the polls were set up at the "officer's quarters," and Sefton was present throughout the voting, as he explained, "to keep order."[132] In his own words: "I stood by looking at them taking in tickets; I cannot say I saw every man vote whose name is on the list; I may have been called to the rear, and some may have voted in my absence; but I made it my business to be in my quarters most of the time." In practice, it probably made little difference to the men whether or not the lieutenant formally served as one of the election officials. The tickets were deposited "in the ordinary tin cups which the soldiers have for their coffee; they had no lids to them." Each county from which the soldiers in this unit had been recruited was given a cup so that the vote could be separately returned. Most of the formalities were apparently observed; for example, men were sworn as to their suffrage eligibility. The polls opened in the morning and were closed late in the afternoon. This was somewhat shorter than would have been the case at home but probably long enough for all the soldiers to vote given that they were all in camp.[133]

Although soldiers usually voted in units, they could also vote as individuals. However, they still needed to involve a commanding officer in the process. One recruit from Berlin, Pennsylvania, could not vote because a commanding officer was not available:

I was at City Point, in Virginia, on the day of the election in October, 1864. . . . There were more than ten voters at City Point from [Somerset] county – some sixty or seventy Pennsylvania soldiers. I wished to vote at that election. . . . I can't say that

---

132   Pennsylvania law required that soldiers vote by company at polls erected at the captain's quarters (or at the quarters of another officer if the captain was unavailable). However, military officers were not required to oversee the election. *American Annual Cyclopaedia of 1864*, pp. 649–50. Because the captain was on picket duty, Sefton was the company's ranking officer when the election was held. Ibid., p. 75.

133   Ibid., pp. 75–6. Although some of these receipts and certificates were sent on by friends and neighbors, most were probably provided by the party organizations in the home communities. Given that most soldiers either belonged to or sympathized with the Republican party, Republican partisans had a particularly strong interest in providing probable supporters with the documents they needed to vote. For example, for the 1864 election, the chairman of the Republican committee in Somerset County, Pennsylvania, personally "paid the taxes for two hundred and fifty soldiers of this county of Somerset, as near as I can say. . . . The taxes I paid [between sixty and seventy dollars in total] were upon the presentation of the certificate of assessment by the assessor of the different townships. I then forwarded the certificate and tax receipt to the respective soldiers in the army" (pp. 116–17; also see pp. 140, 191).

there was an election held there; nor had I an opportunity to vote. There was no commissioned officer there to indorse my vote, that I could send it home. . . . I paid my taxes and took a ticket along with me when I went into the army. We were confined in a certain space, and could not go in or out without being accompanied with a guard. We were recruits there, and had to wait until they sent us to our regiment.

His account was corroborated by a number of other soldiers who had been at City Point that day. All had paid their taxes and had tickets, usually brought with them when they entered the army.[134]

Polling places erected in army camps at or near the front lines were one of the most unusual voting venues in American history. While Democrats worried that military discipline combined with the Republican predilections of officers produced coercion and fraud when soldiers voted in the field, their concerns were probably overstated. However, the sociology of these polling places almost certainly created a context in which peer pressure played a more important role in voting decisions than at almost any other time or place in the American experience.[135] Men died on the field of battle every day; these were the comrades, neighbors, and friends of those who voted in the camps. To vote against aggressive prosecution of the war must have seemed, within the collegiality of the camps, a most singularly hostile commentary on their sacrifice.[136] In addition, when these soldiers again faced the enemy, they would depend on their comrades for mutual protection. A man who voted a Democratic ticket must have appeared suspect to his messmates who, with reason, might have wondered whether someone who opposed the war would

[134] Ibid., pp. 141–3. Even when properly endorsed, the votes cast by individual soldiers could run into technical problems when received at home. Elias Cunningham, for example, testified, "[T]here were two ballots sent to me from company A, 10th regiment Pennsylvania reserve corps [for the October 1864 election]. . . . I presented them to the Somerset township board of election officers [because the solders were both] residents of Somerset township." However, he himself was a not resident of the township and the tickets were, for that reason, rejected (p. 143).

[135] The most comparable case would probably be rural southern communities during Reconstruction, in which peer pressure on whites to support the overthrow of Republican regimes was extremely intense and, at times, backed with deadly force. One of the major differences between the two contexts was that abstention was far less visible in these southern communities than it would have been in the close, confined quarters of a military camp.

[136] When the Democrats took control of the Illinois legislature in 1863, fifty-five infantry and four calvary regiments from the state adopted resolutions protesting their pacifist-leaning policies. Many of these declarations promised armed support for the Republican governor in putting down the legislature if "treason [should] rear its monstrous form at home . . . we will only wait for the first base act of treason, to turn back and crush" it. Despite the incendiary quality of these resolutions, only ten of "the thousands of soldiers assembled by their officers" dared oppose their adoption. Neely, *The Union Divided*, pp. 42–5.

nonetheless stand firm when the bullets began to fly. Given the social context of the camps, the pressure to vote Republican must have been intense.[137]

The Draft

In the early years of the war, peer pressure may have been less important in the voting of soldiers because volunteers filled the ranks of the Union Army; men who opposed the war consequently did not have to serve. However, when McClellan's peninsular campaign stalled during the summer of 1862, northern men became increasingly reluctant to volunteer. In response, on July 17, Congress passed the Militia Act under which the states were compelled to restructure and upgrade their militias, and on August 4, President Lincoln ordered a draft of 300,000 men for nine-month service in the Union Army, to be drawn from these militias. Although this draft was not implemented, the states did prepare lists of eligible men who could be conscripted in order to fulfill state quotas when and if the draft were ordered. As Secretary of War Edward Stanton interpreted the Militia Act, all unnaturalized men were exempt. However, if those who had taken out their first papers, thus announcing their intention to become citizens, subsequently voted in an election, they would lose their draft exemption.

Because many states permitted aliens who had taken out their first papers to vote, this interpretation of the law created a potentially interesting situation at the polls.[138] Aliens who had taken out only their first papers usually declared themselves exempt from the draft when enrollment officers made their rounds. They thus did not appear on the enrollment lists of potential draftees. However, if they appeared at the polls, the mere act of voting would make them eligible for the draft. The list of names that were logged in the poll books could thus be cross-checked against the enrollment rolls in order to detect those aliens who had earlier declared themselves exempt from the draft and subsequently voted.

In other states where both first and second papers were required, it was possible for an alien to take out his second papers after enrollment for the draft was completed. For such a man, the act of voting would reveal his (new) eligibility for the draft. However, in this case, the act of voting did not constitute one of the criteria for determining his draft eligibility; he had already become eligible when he took out his second papers. Voting merely

---

[137] In practice, of course, distinguishing between intense peer pressure and overt intimidation would have been almost impossible. However, some scholars have nonetheless concluded that the returns reported from the field were, in at least some cases, suspect. On the likelihood of at least some coercion and fraud, redounding to the benefit of the Republican party, see Joel H. Silbery, *A Respectable Minority: The Democratic Party in the Civil War Era, 1860–1868* (New York: W. W. Norton, 1977), pp. 160–1; Wubben, *Civil War Iowa*, pp. 87–9, 142–3, 210.

[138] For more on first and second papers, in relation to naturalization, see Chapter 4.

revealed that he was now a citizen and thus should appear on the enrollment lists. Either way, the point was not lost on Republican partisans who controlled most of the administrative machinery for conscription: Polling places and poll books could be monitored in order to detect immigrants who should be but were not on the draft rolls. By advertising that fact, immigrants who were, in effect, evading the draft would be discouraged from voting. Since most of them opposed the war and were strongly inclined toward the Democratic party, monitoring the polls in this way could only help the Republicans.[139]

Pennsylvania was one of those states requiring both first and second papers for voting.[140] The state was also one of those in which immigrant opposition to the war was particularly strong.[141] Republicans exploited the situation by publicly connecting the act of voting to compulsory service in the Union army. In the October 1862 election in Philadelphia, for example, Republican party agents posted notices warning aliens that they would, in voting, make themselves susceptible to the draft:

Notice is hereby given that the
U.S. DEPUTY MARSHALS

Will attend at each election poll to enrol the names of all citizens that present themselves to vote, who have been omitted from the enrolment, in order that such may be made

LIABLE TO THE DRAFT
By order of the marshal of the United States.

At one of polling places in the city, such posters appeared on the schoolhouse where the voting took place, the wall of a nearby building, and several nearby trees. A witness attending the polls testified that he "heard [voters] speak about [the posters] there, and say this was put up to catch those men who

---

[139] Eugene C. Murdock, *One Million Men: The Civil War Draft in the North* (Madison: State Historical Society of Wisconsin, 1971), pp. 6, 308. For Stanton's interpretation, see *Official Records of the Union and Confederate Armies*, series III, vol. II (Washington: Government Printing Office, 1899), p. 369.

[140] Frederick C. Brightly, *A Digest of the Laws of Pennsylvania, 1700–1872*, vol. 1 (Philadelphia: Kay and Brother, 1873), p. 548.

[141] Because of intense hostility to both the war and conscription, Pennsylvania experienced difficulty in preparing lists of eligible draft-age men in the coal districts and among immigrants. Schuylkill and Lebanon Counties, in the anthracite region of the state, were particularly violent centers of opposition. Murdock, *One Million Men*, pp. 6, 308. For a detailed account of draft resistance in the anthracite regions of Pennsylvania, see Grace Palladino, *Another Civil War: Labor, Capital, and the State in the Anthracite Regions of Pennsylvania, 1840–1868* (Urbana: University of Illinois Press, 1990), pp. 3–8, 12–13, 95–117, 135–6, 143–62, 169–70. For a detailed account of the military occupation of one county for the purpose of suppressing resistance to the draft, see John G. Freeze, *A History of Columbia County* (Bloomsburg, Penn.: Elwell & Bittenbender, 1883), pp. 392–513.

had gotten out their naturalization papers after they had been served with the militia notice, so they [draft officials] could get their names."[142]

At another precinct in the Twenty-second Ward, a Republican named Samuel Eastburn monitored the polls with "a piece of linen pinned on his coat, with United States deputy marshal printed on it." When immigrants presented themselves, he would check their names in a book he had with him and then tell them whether they appeared on the draft rolls. Whether he actually had such a list was disputed. One witness, a bar owner, testified that on one of these occasions "there was a man going to vote, when he [Eastburn] told him that his name was not on his list as being liable to the draft; on being requested to show his book, he would not do it." However, Eastburn's primary purpose was to intimidate immigrant voters, not to perfect the conscription lists, and in that he seems to have been successful.[143]

Intimidation was even more effective when the Republican monitoring the precinct was also the government official in charge of making up the draft rolls. At Eastburn's precinct, for example, Samuel Ishem combined both roles. As a Republican, he kept the "window-book" of voter names for the Republican party; as a U.S. deputy marshal, he posed as the official responsible for enrolling men for the draft. As he stood at the window, he "wore a badge marked 'U.S. Deputy Marshal,' printed in conspicuous letters. He wore it all the time he was on the ground."[144] At the Third Division,

---

[142]   These notices appeared in the Twenty-second Ward. S.R. no. 1199: M.D. no. 17 (1862): pp. 65, 184. A poster was displayed in a voting window at another precinct in the same ward (p. 34). In the Third Congressional District, a similar announcement was nailed on "the window-shutter at the side of the window where they were polling the vote" at one of the Philadelphia precincts. S.R. no. 1199: Contested Congressional Election in the Third District of Pennsylvania: M.D. no. 26, p. 48. John Kline vs. Leonard Myers, election held on October 14, 1862.

[143]   S.R. no. 1199: M.D. no. 17 (1862): pp. 33–5, 40, 100. For a description of similar instances at other precincts in Philadelphia, see S.R. no. 1199: M.D. no. 26 (1862): pp. 21, 48. At one of them, a Democratic deputy sheriff reported that a U.S. deputy marshal was also present and "when German citizens were offering their votes . . . [h]e would get out his book and say: I haven't you enrolled as militia, I believe, and I put you down now and make a soldier of you. . . . He would always look at the heading of the ticket. If he found it was the democratic ticket he would most generally speak of the enrolment; but if it was the heading of the republican ticket he would say nothing about it; and several times I have said to him, here comes a republican; he would say, I don't want him – we have him – or something to joke it off" (pp. 46–7).

[144]   S.R. no. 1199: M.D. no. 17 (1862): p. 40. At another precinct, Benjamin Shallcross, one of the inspectors of election receiving tickets, had also served as an enrollment officer for the draft. In that capacity he had prepared a list of aliens who were draft-exempt. However, because he did not want to compromise his role as an election official, he gave that list to one of his Republican colleagues who monitored the polls outside the voting window. Shallcross testified that it "was understood if any men presented themselves there to vote, who had sworn they were not citizens, to enrol them as citizens" (pp. 87, 89). At the Fourth Division polls in the Twenty-second Ward, an

Twenty-second Ward, another Republican, James Waterhouse, had also enrolled men for the draft, going "from house to house" throughout the
precinct. On election day, he conspicuously monitored the polls for the entire time they were open. Although the enrollment had been completed, men
assumed that Waterhouse was still acting as a draft official as he stood alongside the voting window. Because he had previously visited every residence in
the neighborhood, Waterhouse did not need an identifying badge in order
for immigrants to recognize him in his double role as Republican partisan
and conscription agent.[145]

Immigrants were often unable to speak or read English and thus unable
to read the English-language newspapers or communicate with most native-
born citizens. This isolation left them somewhat vulnerable to manipulation
and abuse, their vulnerability varying with the social and political context.
In the case of this Philadelphia election, in which military conscription (a
novel innovation in American life in any case) and intense partisan feelings
came together at the polling place, most immigrants may have been fearful of
voting the "wrong way" in the presence of a Republican enrollment official
even if they already appeared on conscription lists. They could have easily
imagined, for example, that casting a Democratic ticket would demonstrate
infidelity to the Union war effort, an infidelity that would make them somehow more vulnerable to the draft when and if it came. While the Republicans
could and did claim that their purpose was solely to detect men who were
evading the draft, the Democrats could counter that the conflation of parti-
sanship and conscription had an unavoidable and significant impact on the
turnout rate of legitimate foreign-born voters. At some precincts at least, the
Democrats had the better argument.

Immigrant fear of Union authorities ran rampant in many northern cities,
so much so that foreign-born residents viewed federal officials with suspicion.
In 1864, for example, a close race developed in the Eighth Congressional
District in New York City between William Dodge, the Republican candidate, and James Brooks, the Democrat. After losing, Dodge contested the
election and hired a man to verify the residences of Democratic voters. This
investigator, an Union veteran, wore an old army uniform as he went door
to door in immigrant neighborhoods; his investigation failed to locate many
of the men who had cast Democratic votes. The attorney for the Democratic
candidate implied that the Dodge investigator intentionally discouraged

election inspector who had previously enrolled men in the draft actively challenged
"all those men that he thought voted against his side, and made them show their
papers and tax receipts.... Johnson [in this double role] acted as window inspector,
took the tickets and put them in the boxes, all day" (p. 66). At a precinct in Bucks
County, A. S. Cadwallader, who had previously served "as the deputy United States
marshal for making the enrolment for the purpose of the draft" in Bucks County,
also acted as an election official (pp. 173–4).
[145] Ibid., pp. 36–7.

those residing in the homes of voters from acknowledging their presence because, as was apparently well known at the time, foreign-born families would deny the presence of an adult male in the home when confronted with someone in a military uniform. Thus, the investigator's failure to locate immigrant voters was purely an artifact of a misapprehension on the part of their families that he was somehow connected with the draft.[146]

Once the draft had been made, an election could provide the authorities with an opportunity to apprehend evaders. When men appeared at the polls, their names could be checked against a list of those who had been drafted but failed to report to the military. In Bedford County, Pennsylvania, troops monitored the voting for that purpose. For example, at the Southampton Township precinct, a voter stated that there

were soldiers at the polls from a few minutes after they were opened until after they were closed. They said they were there for the purpose of taking any conscript that came there to vote from the township. There was a right smart company of soldiers there, ten or a dozen.

The troops stationed at this and other polls in the county apparently did not apprehend anybody; as this voter testified, the draft evaders "saw the soldiers there, and knew that they would be taken up." That being the case, draft evaders simply avoided the polls on election day.[147]

Richard McMullin was one of those deterred from voting. In a deposition filed in support of the Democratic contestant, he reported that he had been arrested several days before the election for draft evasion but that he had escaped from the soldiers who held him. He also stated that, at that time, he had "sent his papers down by the deputy provost marshal, who thought

---

[146] When the Republicans asserted that their investigator had carefully explained, as he made his rounds, that he had no connection to the draft, the Brooks attorney posed a hypothetical scenario to one of the managers of the Dodge campaign: "If Patrick O'Reilly was an able-bodied man, twenty five years old, and a stranger in a military cap and vest should come and ask his wife if Patrick O'Reilly lived at that place, do you think that the wife of Patrick O'Reilly would be apt to tell him truly whether her husband lived there or not?" To which the leader reluctantly admitted, "Well, assuming that a draft was on, I should say very likely he would not be very apt to find Patrick." S.R. no. 1269: Contested Congressional Election in the Eighth District of New York: M.D. no. 7, Pt. 2, pp. 41, 43, 69–71, 74–5, 119–21. William E. Dodge vs. James Brooks, election held on November 8, 1864. This election occurred a little more than a year after the New York City draft riot. In what still ranks as one of the most serious civil disturbances in American history, Irish immigrants took to the streets, violently attacking blacks and the homes of the wealthy over the course of three days.

[147] S.R. no. 1271: M.D. no. 117 (1864): p. 184; also see pp. 184–5 for corroborating testimony. At the Bedford Township polls, Jacob Crouse, the deputy provost marshal, "stood the greater part of the day on the platform" before the voting window. He "carried a revolver" and said that he had the authority to arrest those who had not reported to the draft. Soldiers were also present and apparently available as support if Crouse had needed them (p. 188).

that he could fix by me paying him a little." This may have been a bribe but probably involved the hiring of a substitute to serve in his place. On the day of the election, McMullin was told that there were soldiers at the polls whose "business there was to arrest all deserters." He stayed away from home that day and never came within six miles of the polling place. On the Friday following the election, he reported to the conscription officers in the town of Somerset and "was discharged" from the draft. As was the case with all men who were deterred from voting, McMullin would have voted for the Democratic candidate had he been given the opportunity.[148]

With rugged mountain tops, thickly wooded hillsides, and steeply walled river valleys, Bedford County was almost a perfect landscape for draft evasion. In a deposition, Peter Miller reported that he had been drafted on August 25, 1863. Having "managed to escape the officers" for over a year, he reported the he had been "across between the top of the mountain and the foot of the mountain" on election day. Wherever that may have been, he did not go anywhere near the polls in Napier Township because he was afraid of arrest. Another draft evader who would have voted at the same polls was similarly deterred by "the fellows with the blue clothes on....I was around at home on the day of the election; about my father's house, shoemaking, a little sneakingly...was trying to keep out of the way; that [was] my game." He added that when "the soldiers caught me at last," they "treated me first-rate." John Oldham, also a resident of Napier Township, testified that he and another draft evader "had a little tent where we laid together; to tell the plain truth, it was about a quarter of a mile from my house, in the woods." He slept there on the night of the election. Like the others, he did not vote because, "according to military law, I was a deserter" and he feared arrest. Although all these men made their affiliation with the Democratic party quite clear, Oldham was particularly emphatic: "I have always voted the democratic ticket, and always will....If Jeff. Davis should get upon the democratic ticket I would vote for him....If Thaddeus Stevens should get upon the democratic ticket I would vote for him."[149]

There was only one report of violence at the polls in Bedford County. That was at St. Clair Township, where A. J. Crisman, a draft evader, reported that

---

[148] McMullin also said that his home had been searched by soldiers several times, once on the day of the election. Ibid., pp. 185–6. For statements by other men who were similarly deterred from voting, see pp. 186–7. To understand how such testimony might have helped the Democratic candidate in his contest, it must be remembered just how divisive the draft was in the northern states. Most Democrats simply believed that conscription was unconstitutional and therefore illegal. If so and if men were deterred from voting because they refused to submit to the draft, then the election was illegitimate, at least to the extent to which the votes of these men might have changed the outcome.

[149] Thaddeus Stevens was a Republican representative from Pennsylvania who had a (deserved) reputation as one of the most fire-breathing loyalists in the Union Congress. Oldham was probably illiterate; he signed his testimony with his mark rather than a signature. Ibid., pp. 189–90.

he and others had been prevented from voting:

There were soldiers at the polls to take up deserters.... There were fourteen of us [draft evaders] in the crowd, all voters ... we started down to the polls [about three o'clock in the afternoon] and were within a 100 yards of the polls [when] we saw the soldiers [a sergeant and six enlisted men] without their guns; we saw them go off the election ground, back on to Trent's porch, where they had their arms stacked; they got their guns and were coming towards us, and we were coming towards them; some of our men [who were] democratic leaders came to us and told us that we had better go away; some of us or some of the soldiers would be killed. At that time the soldiers were within 60, 70, maybe 80 yards of us; we went off; they halted us, but we didn't halt; we went on; there were three shots discharged. We didn't get to vote. There was a man killed that night, I heard.... I didn't see the man killed; I saw him lying a corpse; I didn't go to the funeral; the same cause that kept me from the polls kept me from the funeral; I was afraid of being arrested.

Crisman and the men with him spent the day of the election skulking about the polls, "sometimes in the woods, and sometimes in the field."[150]

The most theoretically interesting aspect of draft enforcement efforts at the polls was the relationship between the draft as policy implementation and the election as policy choice. As in almost all parts of the North, the war was the most important issue in Pennsylvania. And the draft was one of the most controversial policies associated with the war. In that sense, the draft was an issue to be decided by the election, not a policy to be implemented by using the polls to detect draft evaders. In practice, however, enforcement of the draft at the polls had the (intended) effect of reducing opposition to the draft as policy choice. Because almost no one who evaded the draft supported the policy, draft resisters almost universally backed the Democrats as the party most likely to repeal conscription. When these men were discouraged from voting by enforcement efforts at the polls, the Republican candidates were that much more likely to win, particularly in closely contested districts, and their victories made legislative support for the draft that much stronger.[151] From this perspective, enforcement of the draft at the polls clearly enhanced

150 Ibid., pp. 190–1. During the 1864 elections, federal troops were similarly stationed at or near the polling places in Beaver, Benton, Briarcreek, Centre, Fishingcreek, Hemlock, Jackson, Mount Pleasant, Orange, and Sugarloaf Townships of Columbia County. Freeze, *History of Columbia County*, p. 404.

151 In November 1863, the Pennsylvania State Supreme Court had issued a preliminary injunction against enforcement of the federal Conscription Act of 1863 on the grounds that the latter was unconstitutional. Although this injunction was dissolved only a month later (after an election had replaced one of the judges), the publicity attending these proceedings may have led some men to believe that the draft would not be enforced in the October 1864 elections. If that were the case, they would have been surprised, when they arrived at the polls, to see Republican agents link their eligibility as voters to their susceptibility to conscription. For a brief synopsis of Pennsylvania court proceedings over conscription, see Harold M. Hyman, *A More Perfect Union: The Impact of the Civil War and Reconstruction on the Constitution* (Boston: Houghton Mifflin, 1975), pp. 221–3.

political support for the policy. For all these reasons, it is probably a good thing that policy implementation has rarely been connected to suffrage rights; northern conscription during the Civil War may have been the strongest such instance in American history.[152]

CONCLUSION

The American ballot box changed dramatically during the Civil War. The most visible transformation was the insertion of federal agents into the polling place. Appearing as soldiers, provost marshals, and draft officials, these agents took up positions on both sides of the voting window. At times they confiscated and destroyed poll books recording the votes of, from their perspective, disloyal men. At other times, they simply threw such men out of the polling place. Sometimes they threatened voters with the confiscation of their property or conscription into the army or militia. On occasion, they would actually shoot at these men in order to keep them from the polls. Most but not all of these interventions took place in the border states, states in which many men, rather futilely, attempted to remain neutral or openly sided with the Confederacy.[153] In all these ways, Union troops guaranteed what the Republicans considered to be the only "democratic" outcome – victory for candidates who loyally supported the northern war effort.[154]

[152] The closest parallel was probably an Idaho law that barred from voting anyone who had ever associated with an organization that advocated plural marriage. In application, this law banned from the polls voters who had ever belonged to the Mormon Church. Unless older voters could have anticipated the passage of such a law (unlikely at best), this prohibition rested on ascriptive characteristics, characteristics involving past behavior that people could not change. New voters who reached adulthood after the restriction was passed and wished to support plural marriage would have had to isolate themselves from the Mormon Church until they could, acting collectively, change this suffrage restriction. The intent, of course, was to guarantee election majorities for laws prescribing monogamous marriage. The net effect was to remove the choice between plural and monogamous marriage from democratic control. For the text of this Idaho statute, see *Appleton's Annual Cyclopaedia of 1891* (New York: D. Appleton, 1892), p. 361. For a history of the exclusion of Mormons from the franchise, see Edwin Brown Firmage and Richard Collin Mangrum, *Zion in the Courts: A Legal History of the Church of Jesus Christ of Latter-Day Saints, 1830–1900* (Urbana: University of Illinois Press, 1988), pp. 233–5. Some of the loyalty oaths described above in this chapter similarly rested on behavior that had occurred before the oath was adopted. These, too, were intended to guarantee election majorities for loyalist policies and thus removed a broader but less definite range of policies from democratic control.

[153] If these states had been occupied by southern armies, Confederate agents would probably have intervened in elections in much the same way. However, the South had little experience with the occupation of hostile territory (East Tennessee is an exception).

[154] For an alternative description of democratic practice during the Civil War, see Neely, *The Union Divided*. Neely, for example, says that "the two-party system had nothing in particular to do with the war effort" and that party competition "was a matter of business as usual" (p. 34).

APPENDIX: NOTES ATTACHED TO THE MILITIA
ENROLLMENT IN ST. FRANCOIS TOWNSHIP, ST. FRANCOIS
COUNTY, MISSOURI, IN 1862

The following notations were made by William B. Williams, the deputy enrolling officer in St. Francois Township as he entered on the militia list the names of men between eighteen and forty-five years of age (males younger or older were exempt from service). Williams queried each man "as to their sentiments upon the subject of the rebellion" and then made a brief notation "written as they [each man] desired them." Only men whom Williams did not consider loyal (and thus could not serve in the militia) are included here, since Williams was asked in his testimony to omit loyalists. As can be seen, Williams ignored many of the self-descriptions when he classified men, thus producing the large number of men who claimed to be "loyal" but were put down as "disloyal". For his testimony, see Ser. Rec. no. 1200: Contested Congressional Election in the Third District of Missouri: Mis. Doc. no. 43, pp. 79–82. James Lindsay vs. John G. Scott, election held on August 3, 1863. All the notations are verbatim. They have been reordered around common themes (e.g., personal claims of loyalty) and, more generally, along a spectrum running from rather robust Union sentiment (at the beginning of the list) to open defiance of the northern government (at the end). In addition to these notations, Williams reported one man as having been "discharged for disability" and another as "not naturalized in full." There were also two men on the enrollment list for whom Williams did not assign comments. Including these four, there were 267 men on the enrolment list for St. Francois Township whom Williams considered disloyal.

Number of men	Notation
1	says the rebellion should be put down
1	has enlisted in the United States service, and has a certificate of exemption from the same
2	is now in service as a railroad guard
1	he says he is a loyal man, and his property is subject to the call of the government
2	loyal as far as can be ascertained
1	I claim to be loyal
1	claims to be loyal
3	claims to be a loyal man
5	claims to be a loyal citizen
1	claims to be a loyal citizen – with the south, I think
1	he thinks he is a loyal citizen
2	he says he is a loyal citizen

Number of men	Notation
9	he says he is loyal
1	he says he expects to be loyal
3	he says he is a loyal man
1	says he is loyal
2	says he is a loyal man
1	says he considers himself a loyal man
1	he says he considers himself a loyal man
1	he says he considers himself loyal
1	he considers himself a loyal man
1	he considers himself loyal
1	considers himself loyal
1	has sworn allegiance to the United States and the provisional government of this State
1	has taken the oath of allegiance
1	I consider myself a loyal man, and have taken the oath
1	he says he has taken the oath, and considers himself a loyal man
1	has taken the oath, and considers himself loyal
1	has taken the oath
3	taken the oath, and says he has not violated it
1	taken the oath, gave bond, and says he has not violated the same
1	has taken the oath, and is under bond, and claims he has not violated the same
2	under oath and bond – says he has not violated the same
1	says he has taken the oath of office as justice of the peace, and complied with all other requirements of the government
1	taken the oath of loyalty, and wishes to comply with the oath
1	he claims to be a law-abiding man
1	for the old Constitution, and no other way
1	for the old laws and Constitution
1	in favor of old Constitution
2	is in favor of the old Constitution
2	he is in favor of the old Constitution
1	in favor of the Union as it was
1	for the like it used to be
1	is for the Constitution as it always has been
2	a constitutional man
1	constitutional man, unconditionally
1	says he is a constitutional man, unconditionally
1	says he is a constitutional man – unconditional man – unconditionally
2	he says he is a constitutional Union man
2	he says every State has equal rights
1	claims to be a constitutional man, with southern sympathies

(cont.)

Number of men	Notation
1	he is for southern rights under the Constitution
1	constitutional southern man
1	he says he is and ever has been a Union man
2	says he is a Union man
1	calls himself a Union man
1	says he wishes to remain neutral, and considers himself a loyal man
1	is not disposed to take either side, but considers himself a loyal man
1	says he is neutral
2	neutral
1	a neutral man, in favor of a compromise
1	sworn on both sides
2	has taken the oath on both sides
1	has taken the oath on both sides, and intends to remain neutral on both sides, if he can
1	wishes a compromise
1	wants a compromise
1	he is for a compromise
1	he considers himself a loyal man, and is for a compromise
1	he considers himself a loyal man, and in favor of a compromise
1	considers himself a loyal man, and is in favor of a compromise
1	I want them to stop it
3	won't fight on either side
1	refuses to go into the militia
1	refuses to serve in the militia
1	refuses to be sworn into the militia
1	non-combatant
1	he says he wishes to stay at home, and not take part on either side
1	indifferent
2	opposed to coercion
2	peace
1	wants peace
1	is for peace
1	is for peace, and is a southern sympathizer
1	a little south, as far as the grocery
2	southern sympathizer, slightly
33	southern sympathizer
26	a southern sympathizer
2	is a southern sympathizer
1	southern sympathizer, under bond
1	sympathies with the south
1	a southern man in feeling, has taken the oath on both sides
9	southern in feeling
1	southern man in feelings
1	feelings south

Number of men	Notation
1	feelings with the south
1	he says he is with the south
1	his interest lies in the south
1	his interest in the south
1	southern principles
6	southern
1	says he is southern
1	says he is a southern man
1	he says he is a southern man
1	he is a southern man
1	is a southern man
25	a southern man
5	southern man
1	a southern man under oath
1	southern man under oath and bond
1	a southern man clear through
1	southern man, dead out
1	with the South
2	is for the south
1	a southern man, and has been sworn on both sides
1	has taken the oath on both sides, and expects to live and die a southern man
1	has complied with the law requiring security for good behavior
1	he says he is not loyal
1	disloyal
1	a disloyal man
1	started south, but returned, and now promises to be loyal
1	started and was wounded
1	has been arrested, taken the oath, and been released at the Pilot Knob
1	has been arrested, taken the oath, and was discharged
1	surrendered a prisoner, and has taken the oath of allegiance
1	says he has been in the southern army, and has taken the oath on both sides
1	has been in the southern army, taken prisoner, and taken the oath of allegiance to the United States
1	a rebel under oath for good behavior
1	rebel under parole
1	a prisoner on parole
1	paroled prisoner, under bond to the federal government

7

Conclusion

Scholars have celebrated American democracy from many different perspectives. Some have seen democratic practices as a social ritual through which communal identity is learned and reinforced.[1] This identity, in turn, underpins the social cohesion and understandings that allow any society to function as a political community. Others have valued democracy more for what it requires than for what it does. They have viewed freedom of speech, freedom of religion, and freedom of assembly – all of them products of democracy – as the most important ends served by a democratic system. From this perspective, democracy becomes an ideology that entails freedom as a consequence. And it is the consequence, not the process itself, that justifies democracy. From yet a third perspective, members of the pluralist school have seen democracy as the best defense against public chaos and disorder. The way they see it, democratic institutions almost magically adjust government policy to the popular will – much as the hidden hand of the market matches economic production to consumer demand. Finally, there are those who take a more jaundiced view. These scholars cite the pathologies associated with popular government, among them tyrannical majorities, simplistic election slogans, and the social inefficiencies thus induced in public policy. For them, the only things worse than democracy are the alternatives.

Not surprisingly, perhaps, nineteenth-century American democracy can be viewed from all of these perspectives. As communal identity, for example, suffrage eligibility marked the boundaries and shaped the content of what it meant to be an American during the global flowering of the nation-state.[2]

---

[1] For a discussion of the powerful symbols and rituals associated with the material setting and paraphernalia of the polling place, see Jean H. Baker, *Affairs of Party: The Political Culture of Northern Democrats in the Mid-Nineteenth Century* (Ithaca, N.Y.: Cornell University Press, 1983), pp. 262–3, 267, 271, 276–9, 279–81.

[2] In her interpretation of voting practices in New York City, for example, Mary Ryan describes elections as "the stormy centers of democratic and participatory civil society."

The core of that identity was the northern, rural, native-born, white, Protestant male. Facing almost no barriers at the polls, such males voted at rates higher than any other group in American history. Others faced formal barriers or social discrimination of one kind or another. Southern and border state whites, for example, were often disabled on grounds of suspect loyalty. Blacks, both North and South, were thought to be mentally and culturally deficient. Western Mormons were viewed as immoral heretics (although they turned the tables in Utah). Urban immigrants were incompletely assimilated, thus possessing flawed understandings of American institutions and ideals. It did not help that many of them were Catholic. When these groups claimed suffrage rights – and they all did – the polls became charged with passion and, all too often, violence, fraud, and intimidation.[3] There were, of course, material reasons for this passion. Public policy did affect the life chances of the typical citizen, particularly in those situations and communities where this struggle over American identity was most intense. However, participation in the election ritual underpinned a social legitimacy and standing in the community that went above and beyond mere access to the material resources of politics. Nineteenth-century America was a place where the right to make a living was something that had to be defended through both individual and social competition. Although dressed in masculine identity and display, the act of voting nonetheless marked those who were worthy contenders in that competition.

There were two remarkable silences or, perhaps better phrased, consensual understandings at the polls. On the one hand, wealth, in and of itself,

She then goes on to say, "We have come to take this particular kind of civic engagement for granted – its demagoguery, inflated rhetoric, venal motivation, vote tampering, and simple silliness. . . . By a combination of organization and competition, challenge to established authority, and legitimation of opposition, political parties installed democratic representatives in positions of state power. These partisan battles – a kind of routine civic warfare – also defended and gradually expanded the rights of citizens." She later extends this interpretation into the 1840s and 1850s. "Civil Society as Democratic Practice: North American Cities during the Nineteenth Century," *Journal of Interdisciplinary History* 29 (1999): 573–4.

3   Because of the scarcity of firsthand accounts and the tendency to accept physical roughhousing as normal, we will never be able to determine just how violent polling places were in the mid-nineteenth century. However, when conditions at the polls were noteworthy for other reasons, both violence and fraud were often incidentally recorded as well. For example, the polling place in Springfield, Illinois, in November 1860 became noteworthy because Abraham Lincoln turned in his ticket at that precinct. Incidentally, the newspaper account records that a Republican lawyer caned a Democratic editor after the Republicans had distributed hundreds of "imitation" Democratic tickets carrying Republican names. Kate Kelly, *Election Day: An American Holiday, an American History* (New York: Facts on File, 1991), pp. 112–13. Somewhat similarly, George Templeton Strong casually noted in his diary that several men had been killed in the First Ward as he described otherwise placid conditions at the New York City polls during the 1856 presidential election. Reprinted in Robert J. Dinkin, *Election Day: A Documentary History* (Westport, Conn.: Greenwood Press, 2002), p. 82.

was neither a formal qualification nor a social prerequisite for voting. There was, of course, rampant discrimination between groups and individuals in and around the polling place, and much of that discrimination targeted those who happened (often happened, in some cases) to be poor. But poverty was incidental to the racial, cultural, religious, and nationalist distinctions that primarily motivated men as they contested the right to participate. If anything, it is likely that the very wealthy sometimes stayed away from the polls, leaving the defense of their material interests to others who became their willing agents.[4] If they belonged to the right groups, the social standing of the wealthy was secure without demonstrating that standing through voting. And if they belonged to the wrong groups, wealth would not prevent physical intimidation at the polls. With little to gain and much to lose, very wealthy men probably found better uses of their time. The second consensual understanding involved women. As an ideal, all women were too virtuous (and too fragile) for the rough and tumble of the voting window. But they were good only if they remained above the political fray. If women stepped down from their pedestals and defended the right of their men to vote, they were dragged through the mire of public slander and innuendo in ways that defy modern comprehension.[5]

In all these respects, communal identity was first constructed and then learned and reinforced at the polls in the middle of the nineteenth century. But the social rituals and practices involved in the construction of that identity were of a kind that we might not want to celebrate, at least not without serious qualification. The most deep-seated problem might lie not with the social rituals of nineteenth-century democracy but, instead, with the notion of communal identity. Such an identity inevitably implies the exclusion of those that do not belong. As this communal identity has weakened, as has been arguably the case over the last century or so, two seemingly contradictory things appear to have followed. First, the barriers to suffrage rights have been lowered as voting eligibility is expanded and made easier to evidence. Entrained with this broadening of suffrage eligibility has been the reduction of social discrimination at the polls; crowds of citizens no longer mass around the polling place in ways that intimidate the members of ostensible out-groups. Second, turnout rates have declined as participation in the

---

[4] This inverse relationship between wealth and voting participation was probably limited to the very wealthy residing in communities where the polling place was very contentious. In such situations, the probability of social embarrassment by men whom the elite would have regarded as their inferiors would have been unacceptably high. In communities where wealth distinctions were comparatively narrow and the polls less intimidating, there was probably a positive correlation between wealth and voting turnout. See, for example, Paul Bourke and Donald DeBats, *Washington County: Politics and Community in Antebellum America* (Baltimore: Johns Hopkins University Press, 1995), pp. 237–41.

[5] See, for example, the testimony concerning Nancy Massongal and Katharine Hill in Chapter 3.

social ritual of voting becomes increasingly irrelevant to the social standing of individuals.[6] This increasing irrelevance follows, in part, from the fact that there is no longer anyone at the polls to watch citizens vote; the crowds are gone, leaving behind only very small numbers of gentle-spirited people to mark down names as voters quietly, almost surreptitiously, trickle in to the polls. Voting no longer involves an assertion of rights or identity; even if it did, there would be almost no one left to witness that assertion.

Modernization theorists might argue that democratic practice in the nineteenth century represented a necessary stage in the development of the modern American nation. They might contend that the nation needed a core conception of an American citizen both as a model and as a constituting agent. As a model, the northern, rural, native-born, white, Protestant male enshrined in suffrage law and social practice gave other groups in American society something to emulate and, thus, reduced conflict that might have otherwise arisen had all contending values and identities had an equal claim on social legitimacy. As a constituting agent, the American nation-state was undoubtedly strengthened by the unswerving and unmitigated loyalty of this group; without its support in the last half of the nineteenth century, the United States would not exist today.[7] But that time is long past, and the social rituals of democracy no longer affirm or reinforce a communal identity for most members of American society.

As for whether democracy is responsible for its products (e.g., freedom of speech) or vice versa, the evidence presented here is more or less beside the point. The polling place in the late nineteenth century was usually not a forum for public debate or consultation. Speech, for example, was frequently suppressed, as was the right to assembly. Religion and race were often badges that attracted intolerance and abuse. From the broadest perspective, the social practices surrounding the voting window were simply not oriented toward a public exploration of the issues contested at the polls. Policy disputes usually surfaced at the polls – if they surfaced at all – as claims that either legitimated or undercut the right to vote (e.g., that only Union loyalists could cast tickets during the Civil War). And like everything else in and around the polling place, a man's position on those issues was assigned by other men in the crowd. Irish Catholics in antebellum St. Louis *were* proslavery Democrats in much the same way that they were

---

[6] Party agents, of course, facilitated participation in this social ritual in many ways. For a discussion of practices in and around the polling place that encouraged voter turnout, see Glenn C. Altschuler and Stuart M. Blumin, *Rude Republic: Americans and Their Politics in the Nineteenth Century* (Princeton, N.J.: Princeton University Press, 2000), pp. 70–82.

[7] As the bedrock foundation of the Republican party, members of this group were primarily responsible for the suppression of southern separatism during the Civil War. Richard Franklin Bensel, *Yankee Leviathan: The Origins of Central State Authority in America, 1859–1877* (New York: Cambridge University Press, 1990), chapter 1.

Irish and Catholic; if they were not proslavery Democrats, they were, first and foremost, disloyal to their ethnic and religious community. While free-soil Democrats welcomed the defection of Irish renegades, the hostility of their fellow countrymen was much more intense and apparently persuasive. As a result, most free-soil, Irish Catholics apparently either swallowed hard and voted the proslavery regular Democratic ticket (putting ethnic and religious solidarity above the slavery issue) or abstained from voting (thus avoiding the conflicting claims of their ethnic comrades and their own preferences on the slavery issue).[8]

The sheer physicality of voting underscores the presumption that men's opinions on policy issues were fixed by their ethnic and cultural identities, along with previously acquired loyalties to party organizations. Because their opinions were fixed, winning elections became a matter of raising the practical barriers for opponents and lowering them for friends. Men placed their bodies in the path of opponents attempting to approach the voting window. They shoved, poked, threatened, grabbed, and sometimes stabbed or shot those they saw as politically damned. But, whatever they did, men at the polls rarely engaged in an open and free debate of the issues that divided them.[9] In sum, the social practices associated with the act of voting in the last half of the nineteenth century probably weakened those freedoms commonly associated with democracy, rather than vice versa. This, of course, presents a quite startling paradox; although popular voting is the quintessential characteristic of a democratic political system, the polling place, in nineteenth-century America, was often one of the less democratic sites in the nation.

[8] With the evidence immediately at hand, we can do no more than suggest how the material environment of the polling place enhanced the ethno-cultural flavor of mass democracy in the United States. However, we might still venture to speculate that ethno-cultural influence in American politics was (1) partially an outgrowth of the fact that the common voter's understanding of the elite policy demands and alignments was often seriously deficient or altogether lacking, (2) abetted by the immediate politics of the polling place, as party agents facilitated or obstructed the act of voting (using visual and auditory evidence of ethnicity, race, and religion as a basis for projecting partisan affiliation), and (3) largely limited, in terms of policy impact, to the politics of the polling place (in that legislative policy making was driven, for the most part, by material interests in the local and national political economy).

[9] Although policy issues rarely seem to have entered into the otherwise extensive negotiations between party agents and voters (or any other conversation in the immediate vicinity of the polling place), such issues were almost endlessly discussed in stump speeches and newspapers during the campaigns preceding the elections. What is quite remarkable is that the men listening to these speeches and reading these newspapers did not attempt to communicate to other men at the polls what they heard or read. For detailed, policy-centered narratives of party campaigns that place newspapers, party conventions, and personal correspondence among party leaders at the center of political competition, see Michael Fitzgibbon Holt, *Forging a Majority: The Formation of the Republican Party in Pittsburgh, 1848–1860* (New Haven, Conn.: Yale University Press, 1969).

Despite these undemocratic aspects, mid-nineteenth-century elections may have still induced political stability by matching government policy to changing policy attitudes in the society at large. There are, however, at least three reasons to be skeptical of this conclusion. First, voting in this period was not a neutral register of mass political opinion. By controlling the polls in one way or another, political gangs, federal troops, and ethnic mobs filtered the opinions that could be registered at the voting window. These groups were thus more heavily weighted in the official election returns than those whose participation was precluded by their intervention. Whether or not this distortion of mass public opinion, as registered in the election returns, enhanced national political stability is at least an open question.

Second, mass political opinion with respect to most policy issues was both remarkably uninformed and indifferent.[10] Only rarely were policy issues articulated in the noisy clamor that otherwise intensely colored the social environment in and around the polls. This presents another paradox. On the one hand, state and national party organizations openly declared their positions on numerous public policies in extremely detailed and strongly worded platforms. Contests over what was included or not included in these platforms frequently produced splits at party conventions as the losers bolted, either running their own candidates or fusing with one of the opposing parties.[11] Policy positions clearly mattered to party organizations and their activists. On the other hand, political discourse in and around the polls was remarkably silent with respect to these very issues.[12] Somewhere between party conventions and the streets and squares abutting the voting window, policy issues became subsumed into the ascriptive characteristics of the voting public.[13] From the perspective of Union loyalists, Irish Catholics in Civil

[10] On voter indifference to issues, even during the Civil War, see Altschuler and Blumin, *Rude Republic*, p. 177.

[11] For a review of party splits and the content of platforms in the last quarter of the nineteenth century, see Richard Franklin Bensel, *The Political Economy of American Industrialization, 1877–1900* (New York: Cambridge University Press, 2000), chapter 3. For a narrower sampling in the years just before the Civil War, see William E. Gienapp, *The Origins of the Republican Party, 1852–1856* (New York: Oxford University Press, 1987).

[12] Very, very few of the thousands of men interrogated in the contested election hearings volunteered evidence that indicated that they were strongly committed with respect to the policy issues implicated in elections. When directly questioned on the policy stances of the parties, most men could do little more than follow the lead of the questioner. This was particularly true of men of below average intelligence who were asked to demonstrate their capacity to comprehend the act of voting (see Chapter 3).

[13] How voters understood the relevance of party platforms to their individual life circumstances was often embedded in street-level competition among races, ethnic groups, and/or religious communities. For example, when James Wagoner of Zanesville, Ohio, was asked to describe the "difference between the principles" of the Democratic and Republican parties, he replied, "Well, I suppose one party goes for the niggers, and the other for the Union. If you don't get out of a nigger's way they will knock you off the

War Philadelphia or New York City became southern sympathizers at best or treasonous aliens at worst. But it was their ethnic and religious identities, not their attitudes toward the war, that colored speech and behavior in and around the polls.

The third reason to be skeptical is that the United States was not a particularly stable political system in the middle of the nineteenth century. None of the major European nations, for example, fought a civil war that even remotely approached the ferocity of the conflict that rocked the North American continent. Perhaps the best case that can be made is that, given the existence of manhood suffrage and democratic institutions in the United States by 1850, abandoning popular voting would have been even more destabilizing. Even so, as actual practice, elections were probably not a stabilizing factor in the operation of the American polity. They were peaceful and facilitating precisely where they were unnecessary to stability (e.g., much of the rural Northeast and Midwest, where the vast majority of the electorate was white, Protestant, and native-born) and were destabilizing precisely where conflict over the very basis of the American political system was at stake (e.g., along the border between North and South and in the larger cities).

Thus, the social rituals of the nineteenth-century polling place constructed a core nationalist identity that excluded many Americans from the inner circle of citizenship. In addition, the social practices associated with that polling place shaped what was sometimes the least democratic site in all of American politics. And elections, as both social ritual and social practice, were not a particularly stabilizing factor with respect to the preservation of the American nation. If only by way of excluding the alternatives, the last of the four perspectives on democracy may, in fact, be the most viable justification for nineteenth-century democracy – that it was not particularly appealing until compared with the alternatives.[14] This conclusion, maintained here

> sidewalk. They take up a white man quicker than they would a nigger." When asked whether he thought "that the Union party is in favor of giving the negroes the right to vote," Wagoner replied, "They would, if they wouldn't be afeared of being called butternuts." Since "butternuts" was a slang term for southern sympathizers who were almost always Democrats, Wagoner had this connection wrong. When asked what he did for a living, Wagoner answered in a way that underscored his proletarian roots: "I haven't got any trade at all; I play the fiddle once in awhile; that's all the trade I've got; when I get into trouble I can play it out." Ser. Rec. no. 1313: Contested Congressional Election in the Thirteenth District of Ohio: Mis. Doc. no. 38, Pt. 2, p. 653. Columbus Delano vs. George W. Morgan, election held on October 9, 1866.

14 Mark Summers offered an even more benign evaluation of mid-nineteenth-century election practice. After citing the many laws that subsequently limited fraud and other abuses in elections, he contended that these reforms "did not just purify the voting process. They stultified it, actively discouraged the poorer sort from voting at all, strengthened the dominance over office that the two major parties held, and weakened the democratic basis for government generally." Put another way, although measures

only as a possibility, rests on a realist perspective on political development. A modernization theorist, for example, might view the tensions associated with national integration and industrialization as too strong for most mature political democracies to overcome. Yet that same theorist might also conclude that some semblance of democratic practice during periods when these tensions most strongly challenge a polity vastly increases the chances that the ultimately modern nation will be democratic in reality, as well as theory.[15] Everything considered, a pragmatic muddling through the tangle of sectional, racial, ethnic, and class conflicts besetting the period might have been the best one should have expected of nineteenth-century American practice.[16]

IMPLICATIONS FOR UNDERSTANDING AMERICAN POLITICAL DEVELOPMENT

From that perspective, analysis of practices in and around the mid-nineteenth-century polling place squarely addresses what might be considered the most central theoretical problem in the study of American political development: the very wide interpretive gulf between, on the one hand, political economic analysis of national policy decisions and, on the other, much more cultural explorations of voting participation by individual citizens.[17]

such as registration and the Australian ballot reduced the incidence of illegal voting, they also undermined the sociological conditions in and around the polling place that encouraged popular participation in the first place. *The Plundering Generation: Corruption and the Crisis of the Union, 1849–1861* (New York: Oxford University Press, 1987), p. 67.

[15] This is one way, for example, of reading Barrington Moore's *The Social Origins of Dictatorship and Democracy: Lord and Peasant in the Making of the Modern World* (Boston: Beacon, 1967).

[16] For an interpretation of political corruption and violence as endemic characteristics of a rapidly modernizing society, an interpretation that views corruption as a facilitating accommodation to stresses engendered by rapid social change, see Samuel P. Huntington, *Political Order in Changing Societies* (New Haven, Conn.: Yale University Press, 1968), pp. 59–64. From Huntington's perspective, the political incorporation of men into American democratic practice, regardless of the terms and arrangements under which that incorporation was accomplished, was a remarkable achievement.

[17] Noting the dominant role of economic disputes in legislative halls and their decreasing visibility in electoral politics, Robert Wiebe described this chasm as "a division of politics into two spheres that usually had no relation with each other." Remarking on election practices, he went on to say that upper-class Americans constructed their decisions as deliberating individual citizens, while the "more deeply a campaign penetrated into the lower class . . . the less distinct the act of voting became and the more broadly social it grew." The latter made the trip to the polls "a holiday gathering, a boisterous march, perhaps some singing and fighting along the way." *The Opening of American Society: From the Adoption of the Constitution to the Eve of Disunion* (New York: Alfred A. Knopf, 1984), p. 351. Although he referred to a slightly earlier period in which national policy decisions were less prominent

Bridging this chasm requires a closer examination of the party agents who manned the polls. As challengers, ticket distributors, judges of election, and recording clerks, they ran the machinery of democracy, manipulating the returns where they could, manhandling their opponents where they must. Again and again in their testimony, they describe themselves as professionals, experienced in the customs, traditions, and techniques of party competition in and around the polling place. This competition was extremely intense; some men died and many more were injured while voting. Nonetheless, party agents described their work, including the shenanigans of the opposition, rather dispassionately. They would have done the same thing if they, and not the enemy, had had the opportunity.

Given the extremely important mediating role of party agents in producing election results, we should reconceive our understanding of the tabular columns of votes that have been inherited from the past. These resturns should be seen as a concatenation of (1) the solicitations and machinations of party agents in and about the polling place, (2) the socio-economic world in which the voting took place, and, only last, (3) the individual decisions by self-reflecting citizens. Even setting aside fraud and corruption, what we would now consider "improper influence" was endemic to nineteenth-century American democracy. Although such practices were viewed as more or less irrepressible, they were not random occurrences. For party agents to practice the higher (or lower) arts of their craft, they needed a sympathetic and conducive socio-economic environment. Thus, even returns tainted by fraud and corruption present a pattern to be analyzed, a pattern just as important to the rotation of office and political power as that produced by "free and honest" elections.[18] Put another way, mid-nineteenth-century

than they later became, the division he described became even more pronounced in subsequent decades. For an earlier call for "a framework which will link top-level national policies and grass-roots political behavior," see Samuel P. Hays, "Political Parties and the Community-Society Continuum," in William Nisbet Chambers and Walter Dean Burnham, eds., *The American Party System: Stages of Political Development* (New York: Oxford University Press, 1967), p. 153. For a recent and perceptive discussion of the theoretical problem posed by the disjunction between public policy and voting behavior, see Samuel DeCanio's unpublished manuscript, "Ethnocultural and Economic Determinants of Nineteenth Century Voting Behavior: An Individual Level Analysis of the Indiana Electorate, 1870–74."

[18] Conventional interpretations of election returns implicitly assume that political preferences are formed before people go to the polls; these preferences are simply translated into officially recognized votes when people mark ballots or turn levers at the precinct. Seen from this perspective, each individual act of voting is more or less independent of every other act. For example, if someone chooses not to go to the polls, this decision means only one vote less for one of the candidates and their party. If that person does turn out, their presence means only one additional vote. In the mid-nineteenth century, however, many men formed their voting preferences in and around the polling place. In addition, many men were attracted to the polls by the social spectacle that could be found there, including petty bribery and free alcohol. From this angle, the

voting returns should be studied as ritualized competition between party agents in which the ceremonies of democracy merely provided a context for struggle. Very real, material interests were at stake in this competition, and the tangible instruments of political power were the prize. But any notion that the returns manufactured by this struggle exactly or even roughly corresponded to a "free will of a mass democracy" radically idealizes reality.[19]

Party platforms mobilized parties as organizations of interests and ideational zealots. Along with more mundane considerations such as patronage, platform declarations placed party agents on the field. Once there, these agents practiced their craft, mobilizing the lumpen proletariat of a nation within the accustomed norms of a contentious democracy. The American polling place was thus a kind of sorcerer's workshop in which the minions of opposing parties turned money into whisky and whisky into votes. This alchemy transformed the great political economic interests of the nation, commanded by those with money, into the prevailing currency of the democratic masses. Whisky, it seems, bought as many, and perhaps far more, votes than the planks in party platforms.

roles played by party agents introduced a radical inequality among participants at the polling place; if a party agent chose not to go to the polls, the voting decisions of many men could be affected (i.e., by being lost to the opposition party). If a party agent went over to the opposition, the effect on voting decisions at that precinct would have been even greater. For similar reasons, the preferences of brothers of imbecilic men, when they "voted" their brothers, were weighted twice as much as those who came to the polls alone. In sum, preferences were formed at the polls by men who, for one reason or another, were suspended in a network of social, familial, and political ties and obligations. For that reason, the returns produced by these men should be seen as the product of these networks (i.e., lumpy agglomerations of patron-client and leader-follower relations). They should not be viewed as the mere enumeration of separate decisions by autonomous individuals.

[19] As Peter Argersinger has noted, how we characterize the activity of these party agents carries extremely important implications for scholarly interpretation. Extensive fraud and corruption, for example, undermine the utility of election returns as accurate records of sincere, individual expressions of partisan and policy sentiment. "New Perspectives on Election Fraud in the Gilded Age," *Political Science Quarterly* 100 (Winter 1985–6): 669–87. Also see Howard W. Allen and Kay Warren Allen, "Vote Fraud and Data Validity," in Jerome M. Clubb, William H. Flanigan, and Nancy H. Zingale, eds., *Analyzing Electoral History: A Guide to the Study of American Voting Behavior* (Beverly Hills: Sage, 1981), pp. 153–93. The latter in effect redefine petty bribery and gifts of alcohol as mere incentives offered to potential voters to participate in an election. In so doing, they maintain that these incentives did not and were not intended to change the voting preferences of the men to whom they were offered. In addition to straining the credulity of the reader, their interpretation rules out the possibility that men sometimes, if not often, participated in elections without caring which party won (or being able to identify the parties and the policy decisions at stake). The votes of such men were the product of activity by party agents, regardless of whether that activity is termed "bribery."

The economic and social elites in the United States negotiated pacts with the great political parties. Those pacts were publicly crafted in platforms containing, by way of separate planks on a wide variety of policies, coherent visions of political economic development. As such, these platforms motivated upper- and middle-class men both to go to the polls and to fund the organizational efforts of the competing political parties. In turn, the party agents who actually mobilized the great mass of the American electorate used elite wealth to entice support for their candidates. Using ethnicity and religion as identifying markers of party identity, these same party agents contested the polling place, challenging votes for some men and facilitating suffrage for others. Almost as an ecological by-product, their practice strengthened ethno-cultural divisions in American politics. These divisions were certainly real but they were nonetheless but a sideshow in the actual business of legislatures and congresses. The vast majority of party agents fully realized and appreciated this disjunction, but political education of the masses was not their task or obligation.

In these professional roles, party agents necessarily confronted a world very different from that inhabited by upper-class elites and middle-class men.[20] At the ground level of American politics, party agents were compelled to appeal to the ideational understandings of the common man, a common man who rarely understood or cared about the great economic policies and debates that dominated legislative halls and congressional chambers. There was thus an independent, almost autonomous sociology to the American polling place in the mid-nineteenth century. Viewed from above,

---

[20] In his analysis of antebellum Michigan politics, Ronald Formisano contended that elites "played the most important role in creating parties [and] manipulated the institutional environment [e.g., electoral law] with ease, but their relative lack of control over the social arena meant that many consequences of their actions would be unintended." This was, in part, because "conflict among subcultures pervaded the sociopolitical milieu in which organizers worked to build parties," and elites were just not in a position to calculate the ideational and emotional impact of their strategies. *The Birth of Mass Political Parties, Michigan, 1827–1861* (Princeton, N.J.: Princeton University Press, 1971), p. 13. From my perspective, Formisano's interpretation slights the role of petty party agents in several ways. First, the connection between voters (as party followers) and elites (as both policy demanders and party leaders) was mediated by these agents who, particularly in and around the polls, framed the act of voting for the common voter. These agents were to some extent motivated by the kinds of policy positions taken by elites (again, as both policy demanders and party leaders), but they were also, in much more mundane and personal terms, rewarded by money payments, social recognition, and patronage appointments. In turn, these agents understood both the ways in which the common voter perceived (if at all) policy alignments at the upper levels of government and how to couch the policy positions of their party in colloquial ideologies (as "world views" of personal relevance to the common voter).

it constituted an underworld of small-time intrigue, petty scandal, and parochial gossip. But when seen from below, the American polling place was a rich brew of community norms, traditions, customs, and contestation – a place where popular culture met and was transformed by great political economic forces and interests. And unlike the often funereal placidity of contemporary polling places, it was exciting.

Index

CPSIA information can be obtained
at www.ICGtesting.com
Printed in the USA
LVHW031952230221
679754LV00006B/665